WITH THE HUNTED

Selected Writings

SYLVIA TOWNSEND WARNER

ed. Peter Tolhurst

BLACK DOG
BOOKS

ACKNOWLEDEGMENTS

My thanks to the following for help and advice in compiling this selection of Warner's non-fiction; Judith Bond at the Sylvia Townsend Warner/Valentine Ackland Archive, Caroline Davison, Mary Jacobs, Ray Russell and Judith Stinton. My thanks also to the Sylvia Townsend Warner Society for a most generous grant towards the cost of producing *With The Hunted*.

This selection was only possible with the agreement of Tanya Stobbs of the Sylvia Townsend Warner estate. The photograph of Warner on the front cover is courtesy of the Dorset County Museum and Morine Krissdottir in particular.

Peter Tolhurst

First published in England 2012, Black Dog Books,
104 Trinity Street, Norwich, Norfolk, NR2 2BJ,
www.blackdogbooks.co.uk

Text © the estate of Sylvia Townsend Warner,
Introduction & Editorial © Peter Tolhurst

A CIP record of this book is available from the British Library.

ISBN 978-0-9565672-3-9

Printed in Great Britain by HSW Print, South Wales

CONTENTS

LIFE LINES

LITERARY CONCERNS

For
Mary Jacobs
Warner scholar and friend

INTRODUCTION

Sylvia Townsend Warner was one of the most accomplished writers of the last century and yet, despite the success of her first novel, *Lolly Willowes* (1926), she was largely ignored during her lifetime. With seven novels, four volumes of poetry, 150 short stories for the *New Yorker* and a biography of T. H. White to her name this neglect is hard to explain but according to her biographer Claire Harman 'Being a woman and a lesbian and a Communist certainly didn't endear Warner to the establishment or to the literary canon-mongers ...'

The death in 1969 of her lifelong partner, the poet Valentine Ackland, cast a long shadow over Warner's remaining years. She chose to stay on in the Dorset home they had shared since 1937 where, she confided, 'at least I am in the reality of my loss,' and where the daily routine of correspondence, her diary and arranging Valentine's work for publication helped assuage her grief. Warner had turned from novel writing years before – her last, *The Flint Anchor*, was published in 1954 – but her short stories had long been a regular feature of the *New Yorker* and, she found, they still 'demanded to be written'.

Beside the river at Frome Vauchurch, having 'grown tired of the human heart', she turned again to the supernatural that had brought success fifty years earlier with *Lolly Willowes*, the tale of a maiden aunt liberated by a witch's coven in the Chiltern beech woods. The Elfin stories that resulted from this late burst of creativity contained some of her finest writing according to William Maxwell, her editor at the *New Yorker*, and 'an eerie authenticity that suggests first-hand knowledge'. These satires on the human condition brought to a close Warner's literary career but she lived just long enough to enjoy the success which came with their publication as *Kingdoms of Elphin* in 1977. The collection triggered a revival of interest in Warner's work just months before her death in May of the following year, aged 83, with paperback editions by the feminist press of her early novels – *Lolly Willowes, Mr Fortune's Maggot* (1927) and *The*

True Heart (1929). This revival has since gathered pace with new collections of poems and stories, editions of her letters, a selection from the diaries and an award-winning biography by Claire Harman in 1989. The extent of Warner's achievement can now be fully appreciated.

Friends were often struck by the brilliance of Warner's conversation; the novelist David Garnett recalled a trip to the Essex marshes in 1922 when 'Sylvia gave an extraordinary display of verbal fireworks. Ideas, epigrams and paradoxes...poured from her mouth as though she were delirious.' William Maxwell too was captivated when Warner travelled to New York in 1929. 'Her voice had a slightly husky, intimate quality. Her conversation was so enchanting it made my head swim. I didn't want to let her out of my sight. Ever.'

Something of this conversational style is evident in the hundreds of letters which have survived. Warner valued friendships highly and corresponded over many years with those she rarely saw. When Maxwell offered to edit a selection, she readily agreed, although she did not live to see the result – *Selected Letters* was not published until 1982. Warner and Ackland wrote to each other at least once a day when apart and sometimes when together, and in her last years Warner busied herself arranging these for publication, entrusting the task to her joint executor Susanna Pinney. The result, *I'll Stand By You* (1998), is an intimate and moving portrait of their love, the agonies of Ackland's affair with the American Elizabeth Wade White and her return to Catholicism. Mutual admiration is at the heart of lengthy correspondences with David Garnett, edited by his son Richard in 1994, and with William Maxwell as the title of their letters, published as *The Element of Lavishness* (2001), suggests. Written with a spontaneity, wit and precise observation, Warner's letters are always entertaining and some of her best illuminate a wide range of interests – in music, travel, French literature and her involvement in the Spanish Civil War – as well as the little dramas of life at Frome Vauchurch. Setting aside Maxwell's obvious affection for her, his remark that Warner's letters make Virginia Woolf's 'very poor reading' rings true and the comparison persists with her diaries.

Apart from some gaps in the 1930s and '40s Warner's diaries, begun in 1927, run to some forty notebooks. As their editor Claire Harman argues, while Woolf's are equally voluminous and often read like conversations with herself, Warner is rarely self-analytical, recording for her own pleasure the quiet observations of daily life where 'nothing is beyond the reach of her extraordinary descriptive powers'. Warner was more protective of her diaries than her letters, considering them 'too sad' for publication. In 1970, in the immediate aftermath of Ackland's death, Warner writes with two voices, one more conventional, the other a deep undercurrent of almost unbearable grief, and the remaining years are a continuing narrative of loss and resignation. With plans for *I'll Stand By You* Warner's estate agreed to an edition of the diaries, published in 1994, which provides a more balanced picture of Warner's life in her own words, and from which, according to Harman, she emerges as one of the 20th century's great diarists.

The source of Warner's formidable imaginative powers may lie in her upbringing. Like many women of her generation, including Woolf, she had no formal education or, as she pointed out 'I wasn't educated, I was very lucky', her luck being that she was uniquely placed to benefit from the best private education without the constraints of school or the exam system. Her father was a housemaster at Harrow and Warner, having been removed from kindergarten for mimicking the teacher, was educated at home, especially by her father to whom she was devoted. George Townsend Warner was, by all accounts, a brilliant teacher of history and his only child, who had the run of his library, soon acquired a voracious appetite for reading. Sylvia could so easily have become an historian too, and most of her novels are, in a sense, 'historical' although she was always anxious to avoid the 'arthritis of antiquarianism'. This she achieved most noticeably in her favourite novel, *The Corner That Held Them* (1948), about life in the medieval nunnery of Oby, 'the epitome of humdrum'. By setting out to write a novel 'on the purest Marxian principles' Warner manages to subvert the notion of an historical novel by evoking the life of Oby in all its impecunious detail, both materially and spiritually, with no plot and no central character.

Warner had also been a pupil of the music master at Harrow, Percy Buck. She learnt both composition and the history of music and with Buck's help – they had already begun a lengthy 'undemanding' affair – she obtained a post on the editorial board of the Tudor Church Music project which ran from 1917 for ten years, and to as many volumes. The salary from this Carnegie Trust-funded venture, together with her allowance, enabled Warner to move to London and a flat in Bayswater. Here she entertained a group of bright young Old Harrovians, among them a charming young sculptor, Stephen ('Tommy') Tomlin, who in 1922 introduced her to the reclusive Dorset writer T.F. Powys. Warner, much taken with Theodore and Violet Powys, resolved to rent a cottage in the village where she met another Londoner attracted by the hermit of Chaldon Herring; the tall, handsome Valentine Ackland. The memorable events of that year continued when Warner decided on a whim to visit the Essex marshes. She stayed for a month reading and exploring the austere beauty of the Dengie peninsular when, one day, '...socketted in the universe and passionately quiescent', she discovered 'that it was possible to write poetry'.

In an attempt to get Powys into print Stephen Tomlin sent Warner off with a bundle of stories to see David Garnett in his Taviton Street bookshop. The meeting proved fortuitous; Garnett liked the stories and, in turn, showed them to Charles Prentice at Chatto and Windus. He, too, was impressed and they were published as *The Left Leg* in May 1923. Later that year, having read her poems, Garnett arranged for a nervous Miss Warner to see Prentice. The meeting resulted in *The Espalier* (1925), and a lifetime association with the London publishing house. The collection attracted some favourable notices and a few influential admirers – Housman, Quiller-Couch, and even Virginia Woolf declared (at least in her diary) 'indeed she has some merit'. Warner's early verse (*Time Importuned* followed in 1928) drew comparisons with Hardy although the churchyard themes and mordant wit of both the poems and the short stories owed more to the influence of her mentor T.F. Powys and the Chaldon landscape.

By now Warner was able to write in her diary 'My fingers drop myrrh. I really am writing a poem a day.' With this growing confidence and a growing realisation that the English pastoral was 'a grim and melancholy thing' she produced *Opus 7* in 1931. This long 'truthful pastoral in the jog-trot English couplet' about a village drunk called Rebecca Random owes much to Crabbe. It is set in Love Green, the title of Warner's essay the following year, a place of poverty, cruelty and drunkeness that is clearly Chaldon. Motivated by the love for Valentine Ackland that blossomed in that same village, Warner tried to persuade Chatto to accept a selection of Ackland's own verse. Charles Prentice was less enthusiastic but found himself pressured by Warner, now an established literary figure, into accepting the idea of a joint selection, in effect an experiment in non-attribution. This was a mistake. When *Whether a Dove or Seagull* (1934), dedicated to an embarrassed Robert Frost, came out on both sides of the Atlantic, critics were confused and generally unimpressed – it proved to be 'more of a dead duck' according to Claire Harman.

The repercussions were considerable. Although Warner continued to write poems, both personal and political, for her own pleasure – several inspired by the Spanish Civil War were printed in *Left Review* and elsewhere – she never offered another collection for publication. *Boxwood* (1957), in which she 'illustrated in verse' the woodcuts by her Dorset friend Reynolds Stone, and *King Duffus and Other Poems,* printed privately in 1968, were the only others to appear in her lifetime. She preferred rather to be 'a posthumous poet', an ambition fulfilled four years after her death when *Collected Poems* included the large number of new poems Warner had left ready for publication. Her reputation has been enhanced still further since the release in 2008 of a substantially revised and enlarged edition – *New Collected Poems* – edited by Harman.

Warner's decision in 1934 to retire from poetry, at least in public, certainly contributed to her neglect. She never managed to repeat the initial success of *Lolly Willowes* which had been the first Book of the Month Club choice in America, where she remained more of a literary celebrity. In 1928 she made her first trip to the States as guest editor on the *New York Herald Tribune.* Her duties were not onerous – four articles during her stay when she was caught up in a round of glittering social engagements. Among the literati were the writers Joy and Marchette Chute, the novelist Anne Parrish and the poets Nancy Cunard and Louis Untermeyer; friends she saw again on her visit in 1939 to deliver a paper on 'The Historical Novel' to a writers' congress, and with whom she corresponded long after. On this occasion she met and immediately liked the young composer Paul Nordoff who had written an opera based on *Mr Fortune's Maggot.* His friendship helped Warner cope with the affair that had just flared up between Valentine and Elizabeth Wade White. By now Warner was also an established favourite with readers of the *New Yorker,* having submitted one of her Dorset stories some years earlier at the suggestion of Untermeyer's wife, Jean. The result was a long association with the periodical that published around 150 of

Warner's stories over a fifty year period. The work provided a regular source of income and an increasing outlet for her creativity.

Warner and Ackland joined the Communist Party in 1935 and, exercised by events in Spain, pledged their support for the Republican cause and travelled to Barcelona the following year to join a Red Cross unit. Their spell of active service lasted just three weeks but during that time Warner declared herself passionately in favour of Spain, its people and its culture. They were back in the country in June 1937 among *los intelectuales* attending the 2nd International Congress of Writers in Defence of Culture. Also among the delegates was Stephen Spender and it soon became apparent that he and Warner were temperamentally unsuited. Warner, 'the communist lady writer', was later ridiculed in his autobiography *World Within World* (1951) while she found him 'an irritating idealist, always hatching a wounded feeling'. Wendy Mulford's conclusion, in her study of the Warner-Ackland relationship, *This Narrow Place* (1988), that Warner remained little more than a footnote in left wing politics, puts her spat with Spender in context. More contentious is Valentine Cunningham's dismissal of Warner as a 'mediocre poet' in *British Writers of the Thirties,* (also 1988), during the period dominated by the Auden clique of which Spender was a leading figure.

Throughout the 1940s Warner produced a series of amusing pieces which, like her wartime stories, *The Museum of Cheats* (1947), were aimed largely at a domestic readership. Articles on social etiquette or Victorian advice manuals were readily accepted by women's magazines. Even here, what Mary Jacobs calls 'her unsentimental commitment to the cause of the dispossessed' shines through 'like a line of steel'. In 'Soldiers, Weeding Women and Linnets' Warner celebrates those minor characters – Byron's charwoman 'of unbelievable ugliness' and Gilbert White's garden helper – who step briefly from the pages of other literary diarists, a theme revisited at length in 'A Class Distinction', a touching portrait of love between a Victorian gentleman and his kitchen maid, that emerges from the diary of Arthur Joseph Munby.

Of the many periodicals that carried Warner's work her loyalty to *The Countryman* is perhaps most instructive. It was through her experience of factory conditions that she found 'the pen could be used as a sword' and went on to acquire what Maxwell regarded as 'a hatred of the assumptions of privilege. Her heart was with the hunted, always'. Impressed by Robertson Scott's pioneering articles on rural life in *The Nation* and concerned for the lot of farm labourers, Warner decided in 1924 to rent a cottage from the Robertson Scotts in the Cotswold village of Idbury. While she was finishing *Lolly Willowes* her philanthropic landlords set about reviving village life and soon after launched *The Countryman* as a radical voice for change in the countryside. In addition to the poems and several autobiographical pieces in the 1930s, Warner's contributions included 'Recommendations to Starvation', a scathing attack on the nutritional advice put out by the BMA. Her plea for the modernisation of Spanish agriculture – 'Soldiers and Sickles' – was among a flurry of articles prompted by the Spanish Civil War that include some of her finest reportage. Anxious to promote the Republican cause Warner placed her work in periodicals, political and literary, on both sides of the Atlantic.

Soon after the end of World War II and with one novel left to write Warner tried her hand at non-fiction with a charming introduction to *The Portrait of a Tortoise* (1946), her selection of extracts from Gilbert White's journal and letters. She seemed to have enjoyed the experience and followed it with *Somerset* (1949), her guide to the county, but as she explained 'since I am constitutionally incapable of resembling a guide, an err-and-stray-book would be nearer my measure'. The result is a sensual delight; given full rein to follow her inclination Warner's contribution is by far the most personal and entertaining volume in the Vision of England series. From her short spell on the *Herald Tribune* it was clear that Warner could produce literary criticism of the first order and it was no surprise when, in 1952, she was asked by the British Council to write a monograph on the life and work of Jane Austen, the author with whom she is most often compared. The research gave her ideas for a more ambitious work on the novels, *The Six-fold Screen,* but sadly she only found time to write the introduction to a limited edition of *Northanger Abbey* in 1971.

Since the days of her French governess at home in Harrow Warner had been fluent in the language, so when Chatto wanted a translation of Proust's recently published *Contre Sainte-Beuve* she found the task hugely enjoyable. On publication in 1958 *By Way of Sainte-Beuve* was a critical success and 'a new achievement in English prose' according to Proust's biographer George Painter. Although Chatto's plans for Warner to follow this with a new translation of *A la recherche du temps perdu* were thwarted by legal wrangles, she did complete an English version of Jean-René Huguenin's novel *La Côte Sauvage (A Place of Shipwreck)* in 1963.

What we have of Warner's life comes straight from the letters, the diaries and a few short pieces in *The Countryman*. Of these 'The Way By Which I Have Come' is most revealing; a chronology of her younger self that takes the reader from Harrow to Chaldon via the Essex marshes, and a year (1933) in Norfolk at Frankfort Manor, before alighting once more in Dorset on the banks of the Frome. This much we are told – but when asked if she would write an autobiography Warner replied 'No, because I am too imaginative.' It was this same tendency that undermined *Animae Effigies*, her attempt to conjure up a life of Theodore Powys, a very private man who confessed to doing very little. In the process we learn as much about Warner and about Powysland where, by her own admission, the author lingers too long. What remains of this 'rather Tristram Shandyan' portrait is a fanciful and affectionate, but not always accurate, picture. Convinced that her friend did not really approve, Warner had, by 1930, abandoned the project but was soon perfecting the biographical sketch with portraits of radical activists – Rosa Luxemburg, Josephine Butler and Countess Markievicz – for *Woman Today*. By now Warner seemed capable of tackling almost anything, as she proved some years later with her most challenging commission, a life of T.H. White. Calling on all the research skills honed during her time as a musical scholar, Warner worked her way though boxes of personal material for the next two years to produce in 1967 the much admired life of the 'friend I never managed to have'.

Although Stephen Tomlin and David Garnett provided a ready entrée into the world of Bloomsbury bohemia and although Virginia Woolf had met the young 'poetess' shortly after the publication of *The Espalier*, Warner seemed indifferent to the allure of this metropolitan elite. For Tomlin, best remembered for his bust of Woolf, the attraction proved fatal, while Warner chose to leave London for Dorset and a more retiring life with Valentine Ackland among the circle of family and friends gathered about Theodore Powys. She never craved attention, cared not one jot for the fickle nature of literary fashions and, long before the age of festivals and book awards, slipped quietly in and out of the limelight. Latterly in Frome Vauchurch there were welcome interruptions with visits to

Reynolds and Janet Stone over the hill at Litton Cheney where she was more at ease in the company of artists and musicians. Here she met John Piper, John Nash, Benjamin Britten and Peter Pears and afterwards conducted largely epistolary friendships with the Finzis, Ursula Vaughan Williams and with Pears who arranged a celebration in her honour at the Aldeburgh Festival in 1977.

In the light of her prolonged 'inattention' Warner was genuinely surprised at the recognition she received 'in extreme old age' and would probably have greeted her continuing success with a mixture of amusement and quiet satisfaction. Alone beside the waters of the Frome she remained to the end beyond the literary mainstream, still 'socketted in the universe and passionately quiescent', still 'amass[ing] a solid fury' at the injustices of the world and still producing 'her blend of unpredictable imaginative flights with a wit as tangy as quince.'

EDITORIAL

I first became aware of the large number of essays, articles and reviews lodged in the Warner/Ackland archive at the Dorset County Museum while editing the journal of the Sylvia Townsend Warner Society. The majority, written to order, are filed alongside typed manuscripts that had never made it into print. By far the earliest piece, attributed to 'A Lady Worker', is 'Behind the Firing Line', an account of Warner's time in a munitions factory for *Blackwood's Magazine* in February 1916. Lauded by the literary press for *Lolly Willowes*, Warner made her mark in *Time and Tide* the following year (1927) as an equally engaging and original contributor. The pieces, which ran from Blake and Beethoven to 'Horrid Females' and 'On Choosing a Country Residence', set the pattern for much of her later journalism. It was, however, her incisive reviews two years later in the *New York Herald Tribune* that established Warner as a literary critic of some distinction, a role resumed much later for a domestic audience with a brief spell in *Britain Today* in the early 1950s and a final stint on the *Spectator* in the late '60s.

While this selection contains most of Warner's non-fiction it is clear from her own list of submissions that a few pieces were never accepted and others have been lost. 'An Island in Norfolk', written in 1935 for serialisation in *News Chronicle* shortly after Warner and Ackland's stay at Frankfort Manor, was never used. A similar fate appears to have befallen 'Churches Remembered' sent to the *New Yorker* in 1964, where William Maxwell may have decided that the inclusion of 'Bathrooms Remembered' was sufficient revelation for one year. A more obvious victim was Warner's feature 'Defoe's Tour' for the BBC in 1939 which, she noted, was 'commissioned, not broadcast, nor paid for, nor returned because of war.' Rather more frustrating was the discovery that Warner's exhilarating account of her visit to the Essex marshes breaks off in mid-sentence on page four of her typed manuscript.

I was anxious to include those longer pieces – the essay on Jane Austen, the introduction to *The Portrait of a Tortoise* and an edited version of Warner's *Animae Effigies* – not just for their intrinsic value but because they are otherwise unlikely to be republished. Conversely, other essays proved too long or too specialised for this selection. Warner's appreciation of Edmund Fellowes, her colleague on the Tudor Church Music project, is here, but not her contributions to the *Musical Times* ('Madrigalists and Lutenists' 1922) or to *Music and Letters* on editing and musical theory ('Doubting Castle' 1924) – her early career as musicologist and composer is only now being fully investigated. For reasons of length I have also omitted the transcript of a lecture on French literature given, at Leonard Woolf's invitation, to the Lewes Literary Society in 1960, shortly after the success of Warner's translation of Proust.

The substantial body of work that constitutes *With The Hunted* will, I hope, give fresh impetus to the re-evaluation of this remarkable writer.

Peter Tolhurst

STARTING OUT

THE WAY BY WHICH I HAVE COME
(The Countryman, July, 1939)

I was born at Harrow[1] in Middlesex. Now Harrow is part of London. As I first remember it, there were meadows of a heavy clay (that had once grown good corn), massive hawthorn hedges, and a few slouching farmhouses.

But the agricultural aspect I best remember was the tramps. They came for the hay-harvest, and when they went away they left their cast-off belongings – broken boots, old billycans – in the ditches. I used to look covetously at these, and long to take them home, and my nurse would say to the other nurses that I was a child with low tastes.

In spite of these remnants, our life was so much a town life that, when holidays came, we 'went to the country'. My grandfather had a country living on the Surrey-Sussex border[2]. There I was the usual happy and innocent little townee. Meadows meant buttercups and white violets, the village meant going to tea with kindly parishioners who had a great many flies in their parlours. One more realistic experience was being taken to drink milk 'from the cow'. The milking shed was filthy, so was the animal. I swallowed a mugful under protest, and was instantly sick.

Long afterwards my grandmother told me that not till she went to this village – she was an elderly woman then – did she realise that iniquities she had thought of as rare vestigial occurrences in crime-sheets persisted and were taken as a matter of course among these cottage homes of England. One punctual church-goer lived in open incest with his daughter. Rape and brutality accompanied the course of true love, children had the upbringing of little hell-fiends. Worst of all was the indifference of public opinion and the ignorant hopeless animal resignation of the victims.

I doubt if it is possible for a 'nicely brought up' child to get more than a superficial feeling of the country. The country was a place where the pleasure of picking flowers and running barefoot was chequered with thoughts of bulls and adders, where mothers and aunts painted in watercolours, where one was taken in wagonettes, with a clattering picnic-basket, to see the beauties of the district. I remember a holiday in Wales, when it rained incessantly, and all the beauties – it seemed – were wet too, either lakes or waterfalls.

Certainly I did not begin to get my teeth into the country until I was about eleven years old, when we began going every summer to the Ettrick valley in Selkirkshire[3]. Now I was old enough to ramble alone; I knew the Border ballads and legends, so I had company out of the past if I wanted it; and, as we went year after year to the same place, I made friends with the present too, and saw how it linked on to the other.

> *It fell about the Lammas-tide*
> *When the muir men win their hay.*

I had known these lines, and felt their melancholy music. But they came home to me one raining August when the small dark pokes of rushy hay went floating down the flooded valley, and the farmer stood watching them go by with never a word.

Sheep-farming, though, was the dominant industry. I had been told a shepherd knew every sheep in his flock by sight, and I spent much time in staring at one sheep after another and trying to memorise their physiognomies. I began to think it was possible; then it occurred to me that shepherds do not always identify sheep full-face. I learned, too, that the natural gait of sheep is about two miles an hour, and that to drive them faster is to overdrive them. To this day, though I have been for so long 'forth of the kingdom of Scotland', I feel scornful when I see English flocks being jostled along the road, limping and sweltered, and I recall the Jemmy Grieves and the Watty Hoggs, keeping up hour after hour their skilled dawdle as they drove the year's lambs to their southern wintering.

If when the war of 1914-1918 came there had been a demand for shepherdesses I think I would have volunteered for such work. As it was, I turned to man and metal. At first I worked for Belgian refugees; then I joined up on a scheme for doing supplementary work on munition-making[4]. The plan was that women of the leisured class should have a rapid training and then work at the week-ends in order to relieve the regular hands; and the leaflet of information about the spell of preliminary training said, 'Low-heeled shoes are advisable, and evening dress is not necessary'. I now see that this was a 'dilution' scheme, devised to avoid the payment of overtime rates to the regular workers. I am ashamed of an ignorance that made me a blackleg: on the other hand I am glad to have worked, even for a little time, in a factory. The conditions were bad, there was an incessant shortage of essential small tools, there was no canteen, and the sanitation was an outrage.

My father encouraged me to write an article about my experiences, and I did so. It was youthfully precious, but lively, and a magazine paid me sixteen guineas for it, an interesting comparison with the six shillings odd (if I got the shilling bonus) for an eight-hour shift. Then a daily paper asked me for a short 'middle', emphasising the bad conditions. The ms. was acknowledged in a letter that remarked that, since the object of the article was to better the lot of the munition workers, they felt sure they need not offer me payment. I replied that it would not better the condition of any workers to write commissioned articles for nothing. They saw the force of this, and paid.

One's first earnings are delicious, more so if one has grown up a member of a class and sex presumedly subsidised but unpayable. Even better was the discovery that the pen could be used as a sword.

But my pen was soon inditing of a very different matter. In 1917 the Carnegie U.K. Trust, bound under their charter to benefit music, guaranteed the preparation and publication of a corpus of fifteenth and sixteenth century English church music[5]. By what I can only look on as an inspired perversity, this was the musical epoch I had chosen to study. I was admitted to the editorial committee, with a salary, and went to live in London[6], where I was immediately absorbed by the fascinating discipline of living alone.

For five years I was a complete cockney. If I went into the country it was to disport myself, or to visit.

Then, one hot August morning, I bought an ordnance map of the Essex marshes. I liked maps. I liked place-names, and the picture-making technique of map-reading. Now I thought that I might like marshes. I chose a place on the Blackwater estuary[7] where the map said 'Inn', made out a bridle-path route from Southminster station, packed a knapsack and went off for a week-end. As far as the route was concerned the map was infallible; but there was no inn. I saw a small farm-house, and asked there where I could find lodging for the night. The woman of the house suggested I should stay there, since there were no lodgings. I stayed for a month, replenishing my wardrobe and my library by letters to drapers and booksellers. All day I walked over the marshes, or sat on the sea-wall listening to the grasshoppers, absorbed in the discovery that it was possible to write poetry; and every evening I talked to Mrs. May, or rather Mrs. May talked to me. She was an admirable talker, with the usual country-long memory for local stories and local characters. And she had the less usual gift of being able to talk clearly and illuminatingly about agriculture and the problems of the small farmer.

Some six years later I used my memories of this stay in the Essex marshes[8] in a country story called *The True Heart*[9]. At the time I wrote it I was thinking a good deal about the technique of narrative and as an experiment I retold in this novel, and in the terms of late nineteenth-century rural England, the legend of Eros and Psyche. I supposed that most readers would recognise the story, but few did, though I had reproduced it closely, and named my characters to recall, either by sense or sound, their originals. Venus was Mrs. Seaborn, the wife of a clergyman (as a divinity she had to be placed among the gentry), and I received a highly reproachful letter from the wife of another clergyman, saying that Mrs. Seaborn was completely unrepresentative.

I went back to London from Essex thinking about the country. That winter I read the Hammonds' *Village Labourer, Piers Plowman,* and Cobbett's *Rural Rides,* and thought on. I read also, in manuscript, a novel called *Mr. Tasker's Gods,* by one T. F. Powys[10]. In the spring I went to Dorset, where I met the writer, and read more of his work - in manuscript then. I was much impressed by it, and, further, I believed in it. Cobbett and the Hammonds and Mrs. May and Crabbe and my grandmother, and a series of articles called 'England's Green and Pleasant Land', which had come out in the *Nation*, were a cloud of witnesses towards the likelihood that the English Pastoral was a grim and melancholy thing.

That summer[11], also in the *Nation*, I read an advertisement of a cottage to let, with 'privacy and electricity'. I liked the idea of such a conjunction. What I found when I arrived to take possession I liked even better. For the cottage was at Idbury and its lessors were John and Elspet Robertson Scott[12].

We met, so to speak, round the same cauldron. John and Elspet had also been thinking – for a long time – about the country. It seems incredible now; but, for all that, it is true that when they first went to the Cotswolds it was with intentions of a peaceful retirement, a well-earned rest. The honesty of their hearts set them off again on the most dragon-tracking, Jerusalem-building years of their lives.

They had been thinking about the country, there and in Essex; and they had already got down to doing. I had never before met reformers with such a well-adjusted equation of lack of illusion and fullness of hope. Idbury was then a melancholy little hamlet, full of picturesque cottages that had gone bad; and houses that have gone bad weigh heavily on those who live in them. But it takes more than new roofs – J. was having a dozen cottages built – to make a new man. Culture and social intercourse enter after the sweeping and garnishing[13]. John and Elspet had got the use of the church school on Sunday afternoons. On the Sunday before my arrival Edith Evans had read about the death of Socrates to a village audience; before Edith Evans a skilled man had shown, on a week-night, how to re-upholster worn-out chairs; and before the upholsterer there had been May Muckle's string quartet. 'They didn't care so very much for the upholsterer', said Elspet, 'but they loved Socrates and the music.'

Some years after came a letter from John saying that he was convinced that, whether people would like it or no, there needed to be a magazine that would treat of the country not only as a place to grow corn and rear cattle in, and hunt and shoot in, but as a place where people lived. Though I am proud to be one of the original subscribers to *The Countryman*, I am prouder to be, so to speak, one of the original subscribers to Idbury; and I still praise as superlatively tonic that early vintage of *The Countryman* when the editor and his immediate circle wrote almost the whole of it.

It was towards the end of this decade that I bethought me that it was about time to try to do for this date what Crabbe had done for his: write a truthful pastoral in the jog-trot English couplet. And I wrote a narrative poem called *Opus 7* about a comfortless old woman in a village who turned a random flower-patch into a commercial success in order to buy drink to warm her old bones. I wrote it in London, but by the time it was published[14] I was a cockney no more. As casually as I had gone to Essex I began to live in Dorset.

17

A publisher's cheque and a small freehold cottage in a place I knew well happened to coincide. 'This small and undesirable residence', said a surveyor's report. It seemed desirable enough to me; for it had a plain face, a slated foof with the long salt-box slope, good for gathering water, and no claims to be picturesque[15]. By now I was exceedingly wary of that falsification of values which puts week-enders into sunbonnets and causes genuine regrets at any proposal to pull down a vermin-ridden, sixteenth century nuisance and build a sound dwelling in its place. But still I proposed to be a week-ender, though unsunbonneted.

> *Bind me about, ye gadding vines*
> *And, courteous briars, nail me through.*

It was couch grass, I think, that did me that service. The garden had gone back, for the cottage had stood empty some time. We set ourselves to clean it, Valentine Ackland[16] and I. A good deal of couch grass remained. So did we.

For three years. Then we went to Norfolk and lived in a very beautiful house, the colour of a ripened pear in the sun, and much too large for us[17]. It was so much too large that we had to employ labour. This was a mistake. If you arrive to a large house, and have a servant, though you live hard and poor and sell your surplus potatoes to the fish and chip shop (we did – it is important to grade them the right size) you become gentry, and are mistrusted. Equally, if you sell your surplus potatoes to the fish and chip shop and live hard and poor, though you live in a large house and have a servant, you are eccentric, and disliked by people with visiting cards. So we lived in a sort of Mahomet's coffin, mistrusted by the earthy and scorned by the heavenly. We decided to come down to ground.

Meanwhile the freehold cottage with its redeemed garden was let to a labourer and his wife. A confident tenant is better than any bailiff, and mine watches over the freehold salt-box like a lynx. If anything needs doing he tells me, and I do it. And if he can possibly help in the doing, he helps. But I do not flatter myself that such a relationship would be possible if I had a great many cottages and a great many tenants. A bishop should be the husband of one wife.

Another pleasant thing about the let is that it establishes, in a village of tied cottages, one farm-worker whose tenure of his home need not depend on the tenure of his job. I need not repeat that the system of tied cottages is bad for the agricultural worker. What is not said so often is that it is bad for the farmer too. A rental of 3s a week is £7 16s 0d. If 16s a year goes back on repairs it is a wonder. A farmer may have a dozen tied cottages; allowing lavishly for rates and repairs and insurance and income-tax if the cottages are his own, this means that he gets £72 per annum by something which has nothing whatever to do with farming; and this sort of bonus pauperises any man's pride in his profession.

I do not believe in becoming fast-rooted. I am ready, I hope I am able, to move anywhere and remain myself. But I acknowledge certain modifications which have come to me from living in the country. One is my attitude towards this same matter of grubbing up couch grass, the responsibility towards one's half-acre or whatever it may be of tillable ground. When I began my warfare with weeds I wanted to grow herbs and flowers. After a year or so I discovered that it was harder, and more interesting, to grow vegetables. Latterly I have realised that what I most deeply care for is the ground itself, and that a plot of earth, clean, and well dug, and raked fine, and in good heart, is the deepest gratification that gardening affords me.

A rather similar process has taken place in my appreciation of my neighbours. At first it was the flowers I enjoyed: the wisdom, the good friendships, the traditions, the racy speech, the idiomatic quality of the English country worker – or the other flowers, the *fleurs du mal*, the twists and patiently-wrought vices that develop under thatch, the violent dramas that explode among green pastures. Then my interest turned to the pursuit of more serious cabbages: the average amount of unpaid overtime filched from the labourer (he knows it right enough, but daren't speak); the average weekly mileage covered by the labourer's wife who fetches all her water from the well and carries all her slops to the ditch; the average yearly increase of thistles in the neglected pasture that once grew such fine crops of barley; the relative attendance at church and at inn; the average consumption of cheap and bulking starch foods, and the consequent spending on aperients; the amount of repairs done to cottages and the amount that should be done; the cost of milk to the combine and to the town consumer; the relative value of this same milk put into children and into umbrella handles; the average number of sleepers per bedroom and of rats per sleeper, and the speculation whether insufficient sleep is not quite as serious a defect in country hygiene as bad housing, impure water, and monotonous diet; this, and bluebooks, the admirable bluebooks of the Ministry of Agriculture, calm and painstaking chronicles of a tragedy that looks neater in print than it does in being.

I still grow flowers and I still grow vegetables. I still appreciate the goings-on of my neighbours, and I still amass a solid fury at the conditions they have to endure. But meanwhile, between these people and these facts, I have realised that the essential thing in gardens is the soil, and that the soil from which these people grow, the conditions which deform their lives, are more than Britain and the decay of British agriculture. One must look farther. I am glad to think that many of them do look farther, and have come to know that the defeat of those peasants in Spain, defending their olive and orange co-operatives, is their loss, and that the new tractors swinging over the U.S.S.R. collective farms are their gain. To put things right, that have so long and so intricately been going wrong, may be a long job, must be a wide-span job. But I believe that these people I know, and their fellows in other countries, other continents, can do it, and I trust they will. For unless they put their skilled hard hands to it, we can whistle for a remedy.

MEMORIES OF LAUREL LODGE, MOTH HALL
AND FINESHADE PRIORY
(*New York Evening Post*, 1927)

No one has seen English gentry life at its finest who has not visited in the best dolls' houses. These stately homes are fast vanishing from the land. Modern conditions are against them. Hygienic nurses accuse them of collecting dust, and there is no room for them in flats. While I yet remember I will set down these few recollections. Grandchildren, unfortunately, I have none, but perhaps I may interest my contemporaries.

20

Laurel Lodge was a moderately sized residence situated in the County of Surrey. It was built of red brick, I suppose in the seventies, but faithfulness to an earlier tradition gave to its façade a trim, semi-Georgian appearance. This façade swung open upon a hinge, the doorstep depending over space, while the outer world as seen through the windows, each of which was supplied with a pair of valenciennes curtains looped back with blue paper bows, slid rapidly sideways. And within, gracefully disposed in their proper stations, were Captain and Mrs Seymour, their family and dependents.

Mrs Seymour, dressed in blue moiré, her still luxuriant hair surmounted with a small lace platter, reclined on the drawing-room sofa, close to the bird cage, her work-table beside her. The canary sang, Louisa and Mabel practised their duet, seated on mushroom-shaped music stools before the upright piano, while mademoiselle counted aloud. 'Un, deux, trois; Un, deux, trois. Non, Louisa, c'est un bémol. Un, deux, trois. Mabel, ma chère enfant, voilà encore une fois que tu as raté ce trait de la main gauche.'

Mademoiselle counted, the canary sang, the gasolier seemed to revolve in sympathy as Mabel and Louisa beat their impartial way through the Grand Rondo. They were not musical, but it did not matter, since they were both coming out at the hunt ball, and with such small waists they would soon marry. Meanwhile Captain Seymour and Willy were partaking of a late shooting lunch in the bottom, right-hand corner – a delicious lunch of pink and white, high-shouldered ham, an open tart and a dessert of peaches. Captain Seymour and Willy were the only adult males of the family. But in the nursery were Alice, Edith and Beatrice, un, deux, trois, besides the baby, who, if he could be taken out of his bathtub and dressed, would probably turn out to be a boy, while in the kitchen, rallying with cook in pink print and Mary in black alpaca, were two splendid footmen.

Laurel Lodge was a simple, countrified establishment, with quite a short drive and a greenhouse, but not a hot-house. It belonged to the world of Miss Younge's novel, *The Heir of Redelyffe*. Fineshade Priory[18] belonged to an earlier and more grandiose epoch. Its literary parallel was Disraeli's *Coningsby*. Of Elizabeth's gift to the second earl nothing remained but the name; Fineshade Priory was a neo-gothic building, and at a guess I should say its architect was Wyatt. You will have some idea of the splendour of its proportions when I tell you that the battlemented front opened in two halves, for no single set of hinges could support its undivided weight. As Fineshade Priory was situated in County Kildare these everlasting doors were apt to be swollen with damp and did not open without a slight struggle. When they yielded a peculiar smell gushed forth – a smell so romantically rich and mildewy that it seemed to be the authentic odour of aristocracy, thus cloistered and reserved from the common air within these walls.

Yellow satin upholstered the saloon, mirrors flashed from every wall, and marble-topped tables were as plentiful as in an A. B. C. restaurant. As for the housekeeper, she was so stately that when I first met her I mistook her for the lady of the house. The apartment that I admired most, however, was the kitchen. There, on the dresser, which occupied the whole of one wall, was displayed a porcelain dinner service, perfect down to the last gold sprig on the sauce-boat; and spread out on the kitchen table were the dishes for a complete banquet. A salmon and a lobster (such a lobster!), a haunch of venison, a turkey, a pair of golden chickens, a raised pie, an arched and glistening tongue, various Byzantine creams and jellies, a plum-pudding, a pineapple and a noble Stilton. Ah, there are no such melting and Barmecide banquets as those eaten in dolls' houses!

If I were put to it I think I could draw up a tolerable inventory of the contents of Laurel Lodge and Fineshade Priory, for in both these mansions I was on a footing of intimacy. Moth Hall I visited only once. We drove thither, not in a car – it was before the time of cars, – but in an open Victoria, a vehicle of elegant scooping curves. As we bowled along the Hertfordshire lanes my mother told me that we were going to visit two very old ladies who would show me a doll's house as old as they. And she impressed on me that I must be attentive, for never again might I have the opportunity of seeing such a doll's house nor old ladies who had lived so long before I was born.

It was autumn; robins were singing, separate palms of the chestnut leaves detached themselves and twirled to the ground, and even before we arrived haze was gathering and the perspective of the lanes led to dusk. The Victoria turned in by a white gate and we drove under the shadow of conifers to a rather ugly house. Inside the house it seemed to be almost dark. I could scarcely see the old ladies, and the tea table with its white cloth and faintly shining cups and saucers was like a pool in a wood reflecting the evening sky. The two old ladies were very courteous to me. They spoke in sweet treble voices and their voices were so much alike that I could not tell which of them was speaking. After tea we went to look at the doll's house.

In order that I should see it properly one of the old ladies lit a small taper and held it inside the doll's house rooms. They looked very real thus waveringly illuminated and I seemed to be exploring a real house by candle light. I suppose there were inhabitants but I cannot remember them. I can only remember the shadows following the taper from room to room. Then the door was closed and the doll's house left in darkness. And then I suppose we said goodbye and drove home again.

A drive in the dark is an adventure to a small child, but I do not remember anything of this one. Perhaps the hood of the Victoria had been put up or perhaps I fell asleep. Indeed for all my mother's injunctions I do not seem to have recollected very much about the old ladies and their doll's house. Yet I know that I shall remember the expedition all my life long for it was the first time that I was aware of what I have since learned to call atmosphere, the first time that I surpassed the child-sharp broken consciousness of detail and perceived an experience as a whole.

THE NIGHT SHIFT
(From 'Behind The Firing' Line, by a Lady Worker, *Blackwood's Magazine*, February, 1916)

About 7 p.m. the church next door used to ring a small bell for intercession service, and then I, working on the nightshift knew that it was time to bestir myself, and to begin my dishevelled day[19]. Never have I heard such a despondent bell. 'Dingle' – it said – 'I don't expect any one to come; Dingle – they never do; Dingle – I'm only ringing from a sense of duty; Dingle – and because the verger is pulling my tail.' Gloomily inspecting my bruises under the meagre gas-light, and wondering how much of them was dirt and would wash off, I used to execrate that bell.

There is little 'food for the young soul, Mr Carlyle,' to be found in lodgings. Violet, bringing me coffee and cold pork told me that she had been to the cinema. (Violet was the landlady's daughter: the other lodgers called her Virelet, but her mother pronounced the name, saving your gentility, to rhyme with harlot.) Needless to mention, the working man was good and his employer was bad: he doth ravish the poor unfailingly at all the cinemas here. Sitting in that bleak parlour, eyeing a large black fireplace like a mausoleum and eyed, suspiciously, by Violet's late Uncle Albert, as 'taken' in the prime of manhood and mouse-coloured whiskers, I used to long for the hour when I might start work: for then adventure began.

Indeed, it began for me as soon as I went out into the dark street and saw the search-light switching restlessly over the sky, like a sick head on a pillow. The workers on the previous shift would be leaving the factory as I went in, their feet stumbling over the cobbles and their voices straggling on the air as they went by: one of them, perhaps, would call out to me with some chaff on the eight hours' work that I must do before morning. The factory yard was like a rubbish-heap seen in a nightmare, with all the old tins grown to the size of boilers. They lolled about on the bruised earth, with one rusty side stove in, opening vast, foolish mouths: their shadows, like the shadows of monsters, lay across the heaps of cinders and of steel-filings. Hooters cried over the waste place with the voices of fiends. Small stertorous trains trotted about in the darkness, like good housewives going to market on the Last Day: and once a crane descended on me, silently, with the deadly certainty of the Devil who had got me at last.

Through the open doors of the workshop came noise and light and warmth: it looked gay as a ballroom. Once inside it, the place wrapped me round like a familiar garment. Up in the roof the big driving-belts slid over the rollers: I thought of them going on, shift after shift, day after day, like a waterfall sliding over the top of a crag. Shell-cases, 4.5's and 18-pounders, were piled high against the walls and stacked on every spare foot of floor, with numbers and hieroglyphics chalked on their grey sides and sleek faces. 'Scrap' was written coldly and briefly on some of them. 'Why,' I had said, entering for the first time, 'this place looks like a petrified grocer's.' All the driving belts in motion dazzle the eyes like a mist, and looking across row after row of machines, the other side of the shop seemed a mile away. Last of all one notices the workers, inconspicuous, inconsiderable – mere human beings among these infallible Titans of iron and belting.

I walked off to my own particular Titan, and cleaned her face slightly: then I began work. My luck was out; I had picked a hard shell. The steel came off it in wicked-looking blue shreds, the hot surface smoked with an evil smell, and little red sparks jumped out at me. The jar was so strong throughout the groaning machine that, holding the lever which forces the knife against the revolving shell, my hands felt like sand vehemently shaken in an hour-glass. My neighbour, standing about three feet from me, shouted her sympathy and her good advice: by listening attentively I could make out what she said.

Toujours gai, our 'street' during the first hour of the shift is a mixture of pandemonium, of that impassioned moment with the gong in the Domestic Symphony and of the close of a wet day in Solomon's nurseries. The shift before has left the place in a tangle, – all shifts do, except one's own. The foreman rushes up and down like a 50 h.p. wasp; the viewer, she too lifts up her voice: people maraud about for tools, and stumble over the precarious erections of shells left in the gangway; these, thereon, settle down on everybody's feet with a prolonged and hideous yell. In short, as a Scotch coachman remarked to me after we had passed two waggonettes in the same half-mile of lonely road – 'It's a pairfect Peecadeely.' Even after the first turmoil has been tidied away, there is always some extraneous uproar in the shop, apart from the normal wasp-like hum of the driving-belts and the clatter of machinery. A deal of hammering goes on: a lathe slips and screams – there is no sound more blood-curdling than that of a machine in pain – and Boy Scouts throw shells into wheelbarrows with a merry noise. 'Let your conversation be Eh? Eh?' should be the apostolic injunction to machine-hands.

At 1 a.m. a bell rings for the half-hour interval. All cast down their tools and hurry out. All, that is, except the earnest and injudicious beginners: and they soon learn other ways.

Most of the workgirls are still young enough to look coltish; as they ran through the shop, dodging between the machines and curvetting over stray shells with awkward and exaggerated leaps, they nuzzled each other with the unthinking affection of animals let loose.

Fortunately the night was fine, and I could stay out of doors. The workgirls had one wooden shed to sit and eat in, and the lady-workers (they are called the Miaows, by the way, among the regular hands) took up another one. I never noticed any difference in the smell. Sitting in the cool dark one resumed one's personality; I remembered my friends, and felt as thankful as a mother that they were all safely abed at last, even the tardiest of them.

Between 1.30 and 4.30 I went on working, and wound up my watch. I used to save it for these three interminable hours, and made the winding of it as ritual as I well could, although it was only a Low Church keyless one. Such an action should be a solemn thing. Those who on Sunday mornings wind up the clock in the hall are, all unknowingly, priests who, with an antique ceremony, testify to the imposed order of the universe. Whoever winds a clock sacrifices to Phoebus Apollo, Lord of the Sun and the Intelligence, and abjures thereby the dark heresies of chaos. By doing it carefully, one turn at a time between the shells, I could, with luck, make that watch last for half an hour.

Sometimes at an unwonted breath of air I would look round to see a burlesque engine and two or three laden trucks go clanking down the central gangway, or an old dray-horse, such a beast as Albrecht Dürer would have drawn, standing sedate and unconcerned among the tumult of machinery, while shells were thrown into the cart behind him – each descending with the clatter of a brazen fiend.

Then there was the man with the watering-pot. A true bhishtie, one of the ignoble army that sweeps up filings, carries shells, and does the chores of the factory, he shuffled down each row, giving an exiguous sprinkle to our wooden platforms. The spout of his 'instrument of aspersion', as Martha Brown the celebrated stylist would call it, lacked its rose: instead it was stuck full of twigs, this being a primitive method of spraying the water. Looking at that watering-pot and again at the lop-eared spanner that I had secured by diligent free-booting, and remembering the large fortune that my employers were making, I applauded the humble-mindedness with which they retained these decayed friends of the family, I pictured a Director walking through our shop. 'Ah, yes' he would say, gazing fondly at the aforesaid spanner, 'my dear father cut his teeth on this. The rose? No – I can't recollect ever having seen it.'

And after the man with the watering-pot, there was Thirst. He evoked it: it was always lurking in one's throat. The air of the shop is feverishly dry, so dry that it feels harsh in the nostrils. It cannot well be anything else, seeing that it is full of microscopic steel-dust and the smoke from hard shells, I thought of all the different drinks I knew: from the chill, slender trickle that wears itself a stony channel among the hillside grasses, to the complex 'bosom-caresser' – the kind with flushed strawberries winking at the brim. I remembered beer, the manly; and barley-water, the inoffensively nasty; and the lemonade that I made as a child (I give the recipe for this delicious but unappreciated drink: dissolve one acid-drop in a tumbler filled at the garden tap). While I was thus musing the bell rang for the second interval – one of seven minutes – but it was a long while in ringing. I cannot conscientiously recommend thirst as a method of passing the time. . . .

Still grousing, and still good-tempered, they troop in again, jostling each other in the narrow doorway. I suppose men would grumble more effectively. The workgirl, being (after all) a woman, is different. She will accept with the easy philosophy of oblivion heavy work and poor wages: and rail untiringly at five square inches of speckled looking-glass. 'If these girls went on strike,' I thought, 'it would be about that looking-glass: public opinion would overawe them into saying that it was for better pay: then they wouldn't know their case, and so they'd lose it.' Remembering that dirty and inadequate dressing-room, with its bad smell, the wet clothes tumbled together, the drinking-water in the unappetising tap over the stone sink, I wondered if, apart from philanthropy, the experiment of giving these girls a clean room, airy and well lighted, with lots of shiny mirrors, would not be justified by the better work that they would do. And I believe that such an experiment would be so justified.

All at once I noticed a new reflection in the polished steel that had revolved before me all night, and looking at the skylight overhead I saw that it was painted with the lovely blue of twilight seen from a lighted room. Past the windows flashed little lights: they looked like the People of the Hills, that fly home lest the first ray of the sun should clip the wings from their shoulders. That undelightful guest that lodges, unbidden, within me, chose

27

this moment to remark that the trams begin to run at five o'clock.

Enchantment, alas! was turned off with the electric light. I looked at the other workers, and seeing how tired they were, resembling with their dirty white faces and their dirty blue overalls the personages of some leprous old fresco, I began to feel tired myself, and to stretch myself to find out where the aches had come. And they were many. Such fatigue did away with past and future. It seemed as if I had done nothing all my life long but take up shells, mark them, pare them in a machine, and, one being finished, begin another. All round me were other women doing the same work: no doubt, I thought, but that we had been at it from the beginning of the world; the worst evil that could befall us a hard shell, and an easy one our greatest good fortune, we should go on like this for ever, our only emotion an inarticulate regret when the finished shells piled beside each machine should be taken away from us to be viewed and to be stacked up somewhere else in gaunt pyramids, whence other workers in their turn would take shells and mark them and pare them in a machine, and so pass them on – a hundred and sixty processes, didn't some liar tell me? –

'Eartburn' – explained my friend the largest mechanic, taking away his hand – 'comes of pouring cold tea on a hot stomach.' If I was tired, here was some one more tired than I. Bone-weary, working the long hours of necessity, living in the vitiated air of the shop, where the noise eats them like a secret poison, the mechanics go to and fro, tending the machines that have as many ailments as a hypochondriac, and as many whims as a hysteric. Priests of a new rite, they stand before a thousand clattering altars. Unswerving from the most exacting of standards, they set the knives which must be true to a hair's-breadth, and rigid as steel and muscle can clinch them: and going from one machine to another, always watching, always setting to rights, they flirt with all the workgirls – flirtations that are algebraic in their detachment and universality. It is said – I know not with what truth – that the Miaows took counsel together as to the terms that they would be on with these men: and in the end they agreed to treat them with 'distant politeness.'

When at last the third bell rang that released us I found myself regretting my fatigue as one might regret a treachery.

Going back through the mean streets, I in my turn met the workers who were coming in on the next shift, and I pitied them with a vast and saturnine pity, as my predecessors had pitied me. The streets were beginning to wake up. Dogs barked, shutters were taken down, the milkman and the paper boy cried their wares, and the fish-shop unfolded slowly to the sun, like some unlovely flower. Sea-going voices sounded from the wharves, and the pink and tawny sails were moving up the river.

THE ESSEX MARSHES
(*Sylvia Townsend Warner Society Journal*, 2007)

It was in July, 1922, a hot day, I was wearing a cotton dress, and some domestic need took me to Whiteley's cheap section, which was then in the old Westbourne Grove part of the shop, through the golden passage. There was a table which displayed cheap books and stationery, and I always looked at it, though as a rule the cheap books were Reading for Lent, or such-like. This time there were maps. I bought a map of Essex, because I had never been there. It was a Bartholomew map, inch to the mile, coloured for elevation. The blue creeks, the wide expanses of green for marsh, the extraordinary Essex place names – Wick, Old Shrill, High Easter, Willingale Spain and Willingale Doe, High Laver and Little Laver and Shellow Bowells, all delighted me. So on Bank Holiday I went to Fenchurch Street station, and got on a Southend train: meaning, I think, to combine a traditional Bank Holiday custom and a discovery of Essex. I can remember nothing of the journey except my surprise at seeing so many diamonds; almost all the people in my compartment were wearing diamond rings. I can remember nothing of Southend, either, except that I decided to stay in the train till it reached Shoeburyness. At Shoeburyness I found a bus going to Great Wakering. I had not brought my map, but I had read it enough to know that Great Wakering was in a green section with blue creeks. Thence I walked on along a dusty white road with dusty dark elms standing beside it, and turned off along a track into what I knew must be a marsh. So I walked on, and came to a creek, and beyond the creek was a low green shore. I stood there for a long time, watching the slow pushing water, and an old white horse grazing on the further shore. I followed the creek, foolishly supposing that there would be some way across. It curled either way, and I began to realise that the low green shore was an island. And this again was marvellous to me, and I stood for another long time, staring, and letting my mind drift with the tidal water.

By this time I was pretty much lost, but I judged by the sun, and began to walk over the mainland marsh. Judging by the sun showed me a very large thundercloud coming from the east. It overhauled me, it covered the sun, the marsh instantly darkened into an alarming flatness. If lightning were to strike the tallest object, then lightning would strike me. The storm broke very suddenly, with a slash of lightning and a spatter of violent rain, and I took to my heels, frightened, like an animal. Then I heard a man's voice calling to me, laughing, rough, and friendly. It came from one of a group of farm-workers, who had taken shelter in a cattle-shed. I sheltered with them, we watched the lightning stabbing at the marsh. It was a considerable storm. In the intervals of the thunder the man who had called me in talked to me, and after the storm had cleared he said I must go with him to his wife, who would dry me.

So I went with him to a small brick cottage, one in a group, and his wife was short and kind with a loud voice, and there was a daughter too, and I think the daughter's young man, and a very loud canary in a cage in the window. The woman took me into a bedroom, and stripped off my drenched clothes, and dressed me in clothes of the daughters, rough home-washed clothes; and while mine were hung to drip in the back-kitchen I had tea with them. The tea was strong, there was a nosegay of violent coloured flowers on the table, the canary sang all the time, there was a great deal to eat, I was very happy. Finally I put on my outer clothes, but retained Maggie's blue woollen bloomers because the woman of the house would not let me, for my health's sake, go home in my own wet cotton drawers. They put me on the road to Gt Wakering, and I went home. I think they were called Judd. The man was a builder's assistant, not a farm-worker; he had been patching up the shed when he saw me.

I decided that the next time I went to Essex I would spend a night and see more. This time I went to Southminster, partly because it was the last station on a line (as Shoeburyness had been) and also because it was in the middle of a promising bare green section of the map, with a track walk to the name of Stansgate on the Blackwater estuary.

The track walk took me northwards out of Southminster over a low ridge; and into a valley, and up a second ridge; and from the second ridge I looked out over the Blackwater marsh, deeply coloured, dotted with trees, elms in clumps or sprinkled willows. I walked on till the lane ended in a few houses and a sort of small jetty running into the Blackwater. I sat down there, and stared about me, and saw with rapture the sail of a boat moving behind some trees, and seeming to move across the land. After some time I began to look about for an inn, and then to enquire for it. There was no inn. Consulting my map, I saw there was no inn on the map, either. I had been divinely misled.

I was resolved not to go back. If need be, I would sleep out. But a boy who had been looking at me now came nearer, and agreed with me that there was no inn; and then added that perhaps Mrs May would let me stay for the night. Mrs May, he said, at Drinkwaters. I had passed Drinkwaters, he said, half a mile back along the road, it stood off to the right. About six in the evening I walked back, careless from contentment, and saw the track running straight across two small meadows to a small straight up and down brick house with some farm-buildings beside it. There was a tall thin woman moving about among rows of scarlet runners, I went up to her, and asked if she were Mrs May, and if she could give me a bed for a night. She looked me up and down, carefully, but without haste or fluster, and said I might stay, adding that as it happened her sister who had been staying with her had gone that same day, and that she had not put the room back yet.

She spoke kindly, yet I am sure she did not take me in from kindness only. It was partly interest, and partly liking. We liked at first sight: it is quite as definite a process as love at first sight. She showed me the bedroom. It was small, with a double bed, and a large washstand with a very large white basin and ewer and chamberpot; large and round as moons. The floor was covered with deliciously cold smooth oil-cloth. It was clean, solemn, and unusually austere for a cottage room. There was a sitting-room downstairs, into which I was put for my supper. It had darkish green walls, and a large centre table, and more delicious oil-cloth, and solid dark mahogany furniture. My supper was bread and cheese, and some of the runner beans she had been picking, and a choice of tea or

31

herb-beer. I chose the herb-beer. Mrs May had made it. It was served in a heavy cut-glass tumbler, and tasted of no particular herb, but was solid, and cool, and extremely refreshing, and seemed of a piece with the darkish green walls and dark mahogany furniture. After supper I sat on alone in a sort of solemn rapture till Mrs May asked me if I would like the lamp, and I said I would prefer to go to bed.

When I woke in the morning and remembered that I had spent the night in the middle of an Essex marsh I jumped out of bed to look out of the window. I could see nothing but an intense blue sky, and a thick white mist, a mushroom mist, from which the thatched roof of the barn and some low tree-tops emerged. This melting veil over my new landscape pleased me more than any clear sight could do. I watched it thin, and become stained with the appearance of a barn, and some sheds, and the bean-vines in the garden, and some apple trees, and the green of the marsh beyond. Going downstairs I found Mrs May, and at once asked her if I could spend another night at Drinkwaters.

A whole day in the marsh, and another evening in the green-walled room and another night in the dusky bedroom with the moony glimmer of the wash-stand china was before me. I took my map, and set out northward for the estuary. I took my book, too, an Inselverlag Pandora edition of Villon's *Testament*, also bought at Whiteley's cheap counter; and coming to the Blackwater I sat down in a nest of tall grass, and began to read.

The nest of tall grass gave onto a little bank of shingle, the ripples clinked over it, the sun shone. I knew that mysterious sensation of being where I wanted to be and as I wanted to be, socketted in the universe, and passionately quiescent. But beyond any other sense, my sense of smell substantiated my pleasure. Refreshed all night by the mist, and now penetrated by the warmth of the sun, the marsh was exhaling its particular smell, pure, fertile, sweet with vegetation, and yet slightly salt; a smell . . .

I COOK ON OIL

(from 'Concerning Authors' Cottages', *The Countryman Book,* 1948)

'I have a country cottage,' may mean the possession of anything from a bungalow to a small manor house, from a semi-detached villa to a reed-thatched, old-oaked architect's fancy, plumbed within and half-timbered without. My cottage[20] has four rooms, and would let, unfurnished, at the usual local rental of 2s. to 2s. 6d. a week. It is neither picturesque nor convenient. But it is freehold, and stands in a small garden, and its price was £90 only.

When I bought it its water-supply consisted of a water-butt and an understanding that the tenant might fetch water from a well farther up the road. Fortunately, its back kitchen, being a lean-to, had a roof sufficiently lofty to allow of a small tank being fitted indoors, collecting the rain water off the slate roof.

To this I added a small sink, draining into a sump in the garden; and while heaven permits (and in this convenient climate heaven generally does) this allows me a water supply for kitchen purposes. Only those who have had to carry water into the house and out again can appreciate the beatitude of a tap and a run-away.

I have, when I choose, constant hot water also, for the lofty back kitchen had a copper in it. There is a general idea that a copper is useful only on washing day or for boiling Christmas puddings. This is a great mistake. A copper is most valuable in solving two great problems of village living: how to have enough hot water, and how to dispose of rubbish. To work well, it must be kindled like a fire; with sticks, cinders, and enough coal to raise the water almost to boiling point. After this, and fifteen to twenty minutes should be long enough, it can be fed with the surprising quantity of papery rubbish which accumulates in any present-day household; and with a little more attention, and a few handfuls of cinders, the water will remain hot all day. A copper will burn almost anything, it will even calcine tins; but it is a waste to feed it with vegetable rubbish, which can be rendered into garden manure.

Like most village people I cook on oil, with a twelve-gallon oil-drum replenished by the monthly van. As the copper is one mainstay, the stock-pot is another. With a stock-pot I can snap my fingers at tinned soups and meat extracts. At its richest, it gives me a consommé; at its most exhausted, the basis of a mulligatawny. And in its way it is as useful as the copper at engulfing fragments. But, people say, a stock-pot, unless constantly reboiled, is apt to go sour. It will, if, when taken from the fire, the lid is left on and the steam allowed to drip back; it may, if vegetables are put with the bones and meat trimmings. But it is not necessary to add vegetables; a bouquet of herbs will give it an aroma, and if vegetable stock be needed, it is far better made of vegetables alone.

After buying her stock-pot (and let it be of stout aluminium, not the traditional iron tank so unwieldy and slow to boil) the cottage cook will be well advised to stock a herb-bed, the nearer the kitchen door the better. It should contain at least a dozen herbs: sage, green and purple, mint, marjoram, tansy, chives, parsley, thyme, common and lemon-scented, tarragon, hyssop, basil, savory, southernwood, rosemary and balm. Nasturtium leaves and seeds are admirable in their season, fennel is liked by many, and there may be a use for rue, though I must say I have not found it. Having grown these herbs, and they will all grow as obligingly as weeds, she must study their flavours, learn to compound them, and learn, above all, not to use too many of them at once. Such combinations as chives and nasturtiums, tansy and balm, thyme and southernwood, are as exquisite as the usual mess of mixed herbs is dreary.

From the kitchen door it should be easy to keep an eye on the garden to avoid that wasteful tragedy, the too-well-matured vegetable. A broad bean kept till its green jerkin has turned to a fawn spongebag is a broad bean misunderstood. Bullet-like peas, long, tough, hairy runner beans, harvest-festival marrows – those who live in towns or placate a gardener must put up with these; but the cottage cook, if she grows her own vegetables, need not submit to such odious longevities. She must pounce on the innocents; nature will always see to it that there are enough sexagenarians.

ON BANKS
(unpublished ms, Warner/Ackland Archive, Dorset County Museum)

Banks delight me, they are always so scrupulously clean. When I was a child I used to visit our bank once a week with my mother. After she had cashed a cheque we went round the town paying the tradesmen, and at the butcher's or the fishmonger's I would recall how deliciously the bank smelled of furniture polish. And on Sundays when I was taken to church I continued to prefer our bank, it was not cluttered up with pews and seemed more truly devotional.

Presently I had an account of my own, and when I went to live in London I still kept it at our old bank from natural piety. Quite soon I received a letter from the manager saying that my account was overdrawn and that I would oblige them by looking into this. Whatever the sum was, I hadn't got it. Whatever the sum was that I hadn't got, it didn't seem to me in keeping with the dignity of so much quiet furniture polish to make such a fuss about it. So I went by the Metropolitan Railway to find out what they were up to.

The bank was just as usual, clean and calm, and the manager in his boudoir was clean and calm too, there was nothing in his demeanour to indicate that his heart had changed for the worse. I laid his letter before him and waited for it to sink in. After a few moments of my reproachful silence he asked if I had brought the money with me. 'Why should I bring it?' I asked. 'If that were all I would have sent you my cheque for it.'

He started, and began to smooth the top of his head as if it were a horse and might rear. Then he said that I had an overdraft. I said I gathered so much from his letter but could not understand why it should bother him so.

He said that the bank could not allow overdrafts, even for a short time – and that I had been overdrawn for some weeks. I pointed out that for a much longer time I had been underdrawn, and surely he could take the thick with the thin?

He repeated dully that overdrafts could not be allowed.

I saw that this was getting obsessional. Quitting the subject of overdrafts I asked him what he thought people went to banks for, instead of going to post offices or keeping their money in teapots. Partly, of course, the nice clean ink and the furniture polish, but essentially because of the feeling of repose. He said nothing.

Repose, I continued, was impossible without confidence. It had never occurred to me not to trust his bank and I was painfully surprised to find that they did not feel the same about me. It was not as if I were a stranger. Had I not known him for years, did I not remember him in the days of the gold currency, when he – a clerk then and no manager – used to weigh out sovereigns in little brass scales so carefully. Was all this, I asked, to be blotted out by a mere overdraft?

He rearranged his hair and said that the bank would make an exception about my overdraft, but that it mustn't go on too long.

I thanked him, and after a while I also paid off the overdraft. But this experience cost me my first illusions, I realised that all is not gold that glitters, and that a great deal of the other-worldly serenity which inhibits banks is not inherent in the banking system but due to the fact that banks employ so many and such efficient charwomen. If bankers had to clean up themselves after hours and if they trafficked, say, in herrings instead of in debits and credits, I doubt if they would seem any more supernatural than fishmongers.

Fortunately their circumstances allow them to have as many charwomen as they wish, so it continues to be a pleasure to any cleanly orderly person to go to a bank. Indeed, I wonder that more people do not go to banks in order to sit there quietly and free of charge for a well-warmed hour or so, just as people in rural America go and sit at their grocers. Perhaps because as a nation we have no talent for public sitting. Perhaps because our banks have so few chairs.

A bank I used in New York City[21] was much better fitted for the social sedentary life. It, too, was extremely clean; but it had none of the aloofness of an English bank, it was as cordial as a Corner House and decorated as lavishly, with a free use of marble and gilding in the Venetian manner, which made me think of the Romantic Age of banking when clients deposited goblets or drew out a few ingots.

Another striking feature of this bank was that many of its officials instead of being caged up behind bars, as at the Credits Lyonnais, or invisible from the waist down, as in English banks where counters prevail, sat at handsome writing-tables all ready to be talked to. On each table was a little framed card displaying the name of the table's gentleman. This, like the photograph of the driver in New York taxis, is a step towards cordiality which might well be introduced into English banks now that we are engaged in beguiling foreign tourists; though I do not see how it can be done compatibly with counters, for the clerks might have to move about and confusion would result if they forgot to carry their identifications with them, and one could not ask them to wear their names round their necks, it would impair the dignity which a bank should always preserve.

On first entering this bank I spent some time walking round, studying the seated gentlemen and their names and musing which of them looked the likeliest to appreciate handling a cheque from the *New Yorker* – for that was what I was there for. Then one of them answered his desk telephone and began a conversation with a lady called Babs. Here, thought I, unobtrusively eavesdropping, was my man. There seemed to be any amount of mutual confidence and esteem between him and Babs, and when their talk drifted on to a party they had both been to the night before it was clear to me that he was certainly the kind of man to read the *New Yorker*[22]. I did not want to give myself over to some austere person who read nothing but *The Atlantic Monthly*.

So I sat down at his table and introduced myself, and never regretted it, for Mr Elphinstone was the soul of cordiality and gave me a great deal of useful advice about theatres and restaurants. Babs, too, though I never met her, became a very real person to me, for they were constantly in consultation over the telephone, fixing up transfers and luncheons and what not. But one fell day I walked in and found the writing table with a new name on it, and a new gentleman to correspond with the name.

It was as though I had exchanged summer for winter, Warren Gamaliel Harding for Calvin Coolidge. Good heavens, I thought, suppose that, by some mischance poor Babs . . . ? Meanwhile he was asking to see my passport.

Simpering guiltily I said I would go at once to fetch it, and fled.

I was free of course to try one of the other gentlemen at one of the other tables. There were dozens of them. But to transfer myself under Calvin Coolidge's very nose (and after all I thought, striving even in my flight to be fair-minded, it takes all sorts to make a bank: possibly he is an

Isolationist and disapproves of the *New Yorker* encouraging aliens, possibly he dislikes fiction and only reads the works of professional bankers and True Life Stories, possibly he is cold to all varieties of literature and only breathes for bird-fancying, possibly, even, he has just been put into telephonic communication with Babs) to transfer myself under Calvin Coolidge's very nose to Another might seemed rather marked, for it was no fault of his that he and I were never made for mutual esteem.

So I betook myself to another bank, further up town. It was only moderately marbled and only moderately esteemed me. But it did all right.

Long after this my editor asked me what I did about my cheques. Cashed them, said I. But this, he assured me, was unheard of, he had known strangers in New York wander for weeks from one bank to the next, begging them to believe that the cheques they carried were honestly come by, and be everywhere sternly and incredulously rejected. I said that banks were like bees – another type of thriftful saving; it was just a matter of knowing how to handle them.

BATHROOMS REMEMBERED
(the *New Yorker*, January 11th, 1964)

An aunt of mine had a haunted linen closet. The door would be found half opened, and inside a lady with a little shawl over her head would be peacefully examining the shelves – a natural rendezvous with its mortal coil for any spirit with a domestic turn of mind, I think. Yet I have never heard of a haunted bathroom. This strikes me as very odd, since in no apartment is one more securely, expandedly, unaffectedly oneself. If I have to haunt at all, I shall hope to haunt a bathroom and there continue to expand.

The first bathroom that made a distinct impression on me was at my grandfather's rectory in Surrey[23]. Three things combined to make it memorable: the soap, the outlook over the churchyard, my dauntless courage in exposing my toe. The bath had a very powerful runaway, and it was my custom to stand with my right big toe over the hole, feeling the water deliciously swirling past it and waiting for the moment when with a final resounding gurgle the last of the bath water was sucked away and my toe sharply jerked downward, no longer a toe I could call my own but a thing imperilled, at the mercy of forces far beyond its control and poised above a mysterious pit.

I must have had my baths at very odd times – to fit in with the claims of my elders, I suppose – for I remember one occasion when, standing with my toe above the pit, I watched from the bathroom window another, equally abrupt descent – a coffin being lowered into a grave. But in fact weddings made more impression on me, because of seeing how the village brides were dressed. There was a fawn-coloured tailor-made bride trimmed with pink who still remains with me as an apprehension of elegance – most children have bad taste; mine was excruciating. As for the soap, it was a ravishing lettuce green, and called White Rose and Cucumber – an intimation of poetry. I expect it was supplied by the Army and Navy – a store my grandmother thought well of. My father chose to buy soap from Italy. It came assorted in crates from a place called Pontelagoscuro – a romantic name, though not, I believe, a romantic place – and was a soul-stirring experience to unpack, for some of the cakes were purple, others bottle green, some even navy blue. Hard as Parmesan, it kept its scent down to the last wafer. Except for the Italian soaps, I mainly remember the family bathroom as a place where I did a great deal of reading, occasionally rousing to turn on more hot water, occasionally roused by my mother banging on the door with invidious comments on whatever author was engaging my attention at the time. 'Still soaking in Zola? No wonder you fall asleep.' My mother disapproved of me reading in the bath. It was bad for the books. So when I set up in London with a job and a bathroom of my own, I furnished it with a bookcase.

But I never got much reading done there. It lacked repose. There was a gas water heater of a kind called a geyser – after something volcanic in Iceland. Roaring, rattling, spitting out blue flames, on winter mornings my geyser fully bore out that attribution, and at no time of year could I trust it, since when it was functioning it threatened to explode and when it was quiescent it leaked. If for a time I managed to forget about the geyser and settled down to do some reading, my peace of mind would be rent by a sudden uneasiness as to whether I had brought along my latchkey. In this imperfectly adapted flat a common landing and a short flight of stairs separated my bathroom from the rest, so that if while remembering to slam my front door I forgot to bring my latchkey, I had to get out of the passage window, traverse a wall above a glass skylight by clinging to a drainpipe, and squirm in at my bedroom window – a feasible route, but so smutty that I then had to have another bath.

After a while I gave way to a bourgeois craving to be self-contained, and moved. The new flat[24] pandered to every bourgeois gene in my being; not only was it self-contained, it was positively genteel, in a residential terrace instead of a shopping street, and looking down on a small back garden with several trees and a fine assortment of hardy weeds. The agent who showed me over it seemed rather reserved about its bathroom, giving me his words that it was structurally sound, and otherwise preferring to dwell on a marble mantelpiece and what a bargain I should get in the fittings. But it was the bathroom that caught my fancy. It had glass walls and a glass roof – lid, perhaps, would be a truer term, considering its dimensions; it clung to the outside of the back wall like a snail, and was entered by a French window. It was, in fact, one of those small conservatories that embellished Victorian back drawing rooms, with a pony-sized bath in it. I liked it so much that I consented to the outrageous price for the fittings (two lugubrious curtain poles and a piece of dirty carpet), and felt myself a match for Semiramis. Semiramis might have thought it rather small, and if it had fallen off while I was in it I might well have been killed. But the agent said it was structurally sound, and I had no reason to disbelieve him. (I could see for myself that the mantelpiece was marble to the core.) The decency arabesques on the glass walls were the worse for wear, and a scrupulously modest person might have judged them insufficient, but I was not obsessed by modesty, and at that time there really wasn't enough of me to make a fuss about. Besides, there would be steam; and in summer trees.

The trees were sycamores, as thick-tressed as if they had been transplanted from the Greek Anthology. On summer evenings I bathed with the windows open, watching cats and sparrows, looking into those gently moving recesses of green; while at all seasons the garden beneath exhaled breathings of lilies and violets whenever a surge of bath water went down the overflow. It was a most amiable bathroom – trustworthy, too, for it never fell off. If I should have to haunt, I daresay it would be the one I should choose, if the house had not afterward been destroyed in an air raid.

The same air raid damaged the house further down the terrace in which, my lease having run out, I set up with my newly married cousin and his wife. By this time I was over thirty, and beginning to feel rather frail, so I chose to inhabit the lower half rather than be forever carrying groceries upstairs. This gave me a magnificent Victorian kitchen and two period coal cellars. One of these I converted to a bathroom. I had it painted rose colour to wipe out its past, I trimmed it with the rosiest-posiest chintz I could find, I lavished rose-geranium soaps and essences on it, and in summer I bought it tight bunches of Anne Boleyn pinks from the flower seller at the corner of the street. But it never became a successful bathroom. It always had an oddly cavernous smell, black beetles roamed there, and coal dust seeped through its rosy walls. Looking back on it with a maturer judgement of conversions, I think I was too total with my Ethiop. It would probably have settled down better if I had respected its prejudices and made a trifling acknowledgement of its former way of life; I could have kept some coal in it, for instance.

Then in a whisk I went off to live in the country, in a cottage[25] so small that it barely afforded foothold for a collapsible rubber bath. In this I reflected on the adjacency of cleanliness to godliness – a truth I had not realised before – until my charwoman came down from London on a visit, bringing her little girl, and was glad to see I had a copper, Miss. The copper in its sturdy brick casing took up one corner of the kitchen and looked like an altar dedicated to some minor Molloch. Coppers, I knew, were used for boiling a family wash, or Dickensian plum puddings. I had not had the imagination to see my altar to Molloch as a potential Baden-Baden. My charwoman was too polite to intimate that I needed a good wash. Instead, she said that young Ivy could do with one, if I had no objection. And while the copper was being got ready for young Ivy, she taught me the method and its niceties. In filling the copper, you have to allow for displacement if you don't want a splosh all over the place; and as the water must heat gradual – otherwise it will go off as soon as you're in it – the fire underneath has to be kept in bounds. There is a right moment to throw in the soap, there is a right moment to draw away the fire. When you judge that the metal has cooled while the water is still hot, you lift off the lid. A gush of steam arises, you plunge your arm through the suds, test the heat, and, if all is as it should be, mount on a chair and step in. Then, moving discreetly, you sit down, your toes drawn in, your knees drawn up, your arms embracing your shins, in the posture of ancient British pit burials. And if you have estimated your displacement rightly, the suds and the steam will do the rest.

One would think that such a very small and inoffensive dwelling might have been left to end its days in peace, but here, too, was to be no haunting place for me. One May night in 1944, the young woman who was my tenant woke with such an acute premonition of danger that she got the household up and out of the cottage before they had time to be reasonable. They were standing in the lane, in the gentle moonlight, and one of them was saying, 'Listen! Isn't that –' when the single, irrational bomb was loosed. When they recovered their senses, the air was choking with dust and they were netted like fish in the branches of an uprooted tree.

So many of the houses I have lived in have afterward come to violent ends that I wonder my friends still invite me under their roofs. For there is yet another: it died by the act of God, and a wave was its winding sheet.

It stood on the north coast of Norfolk[26] – a coast always under menace from the sea. I remember a man's pointing to a long-shore fishing boat and telling me that precisely beneath it there had been a bridge over a stream, and that his grandfather as a boy had seen waggons loaded with corn driven over it. Further out, there was a submerged market town, larger than the market town inland, and the bells in its church tower could be heard ringing in a ground swell. The usual Ys legend, in fact, only distinguished by an insistence that all this was pretty recent, was almost still something being talked about. The house was called the Folly, and it had a legend, too. It had been built by a lady in the market town (the visible one), who had loved a sea captain. Every night, she drove out to it along the causeway over the sea marsh to a light in a beaconing lamp in its window. After her day, it was used by coastguards, and it was they, so I was told, who put the battlements on its roof. When the coastguards moved to a new station further along the coast, the Folly was abandoned, and stood empty till a family from London bought it as a holiday house and put in two bathrooms.

The lady of the lamp, the battlements, the two bathrooms, the schoolteacher on the roof – they were known far and wide; they were part of the story, part of the legend. And we, by renting the Folly for the winter, excited local interest much as though we were the first page of another chapter. Even if we did not prove so notable as the schoolteacher – also a winter tenant, who, when the house was cut off by a series of high tides flooding the marsh, was seen walking on the roof and believed to be signalling, though as it was impossible to get to her no one could learn what she meant, till the flood withdrew and she explained to enquiring visitors that she had been admiring the spectacle – even if we did not prove so notable as she, we were at least notable in going there at all that time of year.

'You aren't afraid of the old waves, then?' shouted the man who was delivering coal. Waiting for a pause between one wave and another, I said we hadn't been afraid so far. He stared at me as if I were something a long way out to sea.

It was a two-storey house, stockily built and looking assertively bolt upright on its little hillock, a residue of rabbity turf and crouched gorse bushes on the eroded beach. On either side of the hillock the pebble ridge stretched featurelessly away. In front the beach sloped sharply downward; at low tide it was quite difficult to clamber up its subsiding lower terraces. Behind was a wide stretch of sea marsh, and a causeway connecting us with the real land, where people lived and vegetables grew and where we went for supplies of drinking water. On a calm day, we could hear the sounds of real land – a cock crowing, a car hooting; for the rest, we heard nothing but wind and sea and sometimes snatches of conversation from passing boats. I was several times terrified during that winter; never, I think, frightened. The boom and explosion of the waves breaking along the wide stretch of beach, the snarl of the pebbles dragged back and forth, was so compulsive, so hallucinating, that by dint of always being aware of it I scarcely noticed it. It was only when the sea broke its own spell, perhaps by some exceptionally ringing rattle of spray against the windowpanes, perhaps by one of those silences that presage a wave much larger than the others, that I was tossed into terror. It was a stormy winter. We grew accustomed to being shouted down by waves, we grew accustomed to being flayed by winds. It soon seemed natural to me that if I wanted to empty the trash basket into the rubbish pit I should cross the hillock on all fours. It was much harder to grow accustomed to the indoor inclemencies: to an unheated kitchen that faced east; to the boldness of famishing rats; to oil lamps that flared and candles that guttered; to so much being poised on the edge of going wrong, like the petrol engine that raised or didn't raise the water supply from a brackish well; to the taste of coffee made with semi-salt water; to having to fetch whatever one needed from inland, often from quite a long way inland, and in a gale, and finding the fire out when one got back. Yet, in the main, we were intensely happy; the game dealer in the market town sold the best pheasants I have ever cooked, and we had two bathrooms. At the end of a day of vicissitudes it was a queer Elysium to lie soaking in that brackish water, listening to the assault of the waves and to the steadily screeching wind, and to reflect that the water one lay in (for even the pools on the marsh were whipped into waves by the force of the gale) was the one unvexed surface for miles.

It seemed that the end of such a house must have been laid with its foundations. Sooner or later, it was agreed, the sea would get the Folly; and because its isolation and its battlements gave it a particular air of bulldog panache, it was assumed that the close of the story would be dramatic. There was this much drama. When the people on the real land had struggled out of their share in the general calamity – the tidal inundation of 1953 that swept along the east coast, up the Thames estuary, on over Holland, everywhere drowning and destroying – and found time to look seaward beyond the sea at their doors, the Folly appeared to be still there. They saw what they had always seen – the landward aspect of the house. But the tide, tugging away the northern slope of the hillock, had brought down half the structure. The solid-seeming house was a shell.

That autumn we went to look at it. The marsh was marsh again, the causeway passable; but where it formerly ran out in the fishermen's path down to the beach a mass of heaped-up pebbles blocked it, and we had to clamber over this to get to the house. The door was gone, the windows were gone. Part of the stairway remained. One of the baths had come to rest across the stair foot. What was left of the front of the house stood leaning above its downfall, with the unsupported floor of the upper room dangling like a crazy shelf. Light poured in from above and was reflected upward from the water below. The sea was so still that one would have thought it motionless if the light reflected from it had not danced on the rent walls and the dangling ceiling. Another winter would finish it.

I choose to hope that my current bathroom – which, with a few interims such as the Folly, has been my bathroom for over twenty years – will peacefully survive me[27]. It is a trifle too small – but it holds everything I want it to hold, including Burton's *Anatomy of Melancholy*, which I intend to finish in time, and then I shall probably go on to Lemprière's Classical Dictionary; it faces west, and ideally a bathroom should face east – but I can see herons fly past the window and listen to moorhens squabbling like the church workers they so closely resemble; it is quite undistinguished – but happy is the bathroom that has no history. Having said that I immediately recollect that it contains a particle of history – a minute gem, but authentic. During the war, we had two American soldiers billeted on us. They were young Irishmen, of gigantic strength, and between them, they intimated that it was a joint effort – they broke off the knob of the basin cold-water tap. There was a kind of Ombudsman with the detachment, and to him I went, and represented that it was inconvenient to have no means, short of a spanner, of turning cold water on and off. At first he inclined to the view that in times of war one must accept trifling inconveniences. I put it home to him that everyone knew that the U.S.A. forces had brought enormous stores with them, and were self-supporting as no army had ever been, and complete with every amenity except washing machines and mothers. Touched in his pride, he said it should be seen to. Seen to it was. A tap was supplied and fixed, a gem of history was incorporated. On one side of the washbasin is the original tap, lettered 'HOT' in black capitals on a white enamel ground. On the other is the replacement – a plain, soldierly affair, stamped with a capital 'H.'

To me, of course, the distinction is perfectly clear.

45

NOTES

1   Dame Armstrong House, Harrow School, where Warner's father, George Townsend Warner, was an assistant master

2   Alford, where Warner's paternal grandfather, also George Townsend Warner, had taken the living in 1895

3   Warner's maternal grandmother, Flora Warner (née Moir), was from Edinburgh. See p.368

4   Vickers munitions factory in Erith, south London, where Warner took lodgings See p.23

5   The Tudor Church Music Project which ran from 1917 to 1928

6   Initially a flat at 125 Queen's Road, Bayswater

7   Drinkwater St. Laurence in July 1922. See p.29

8   Warner went back later in the year and lodged with Mrs May for a month

9   Warner's third novel, 1929

10 Dorset novelist and brother of J. C. Powys and Llewelyn Powys. He was discovered by Stephen Tomlin and Warner while living in Chaldon Herring

11 1924

12 The Robertson Scotts lived at Idbury Manor where they began publishing *The Countryman*

13 For a full account see 'Robertson Scott and *The Countryman*' by Neil Philip, *Sylvia Townsend Warner Society Journal*, 2008

14 1931

15 Miss Green's, opposite The Sailor's Return, Chaldon Herring. Purchased in June 1930

16 Poet and friend of T. F. Powys. Warner and Ackland met through Powys, became lovers and lived together in Dorset until Ackland's death in 1969

17 Frankfort Manor, Sloley, May 1933-Sept. 1934

18 Based on Moore Abbey, Co. Kildare, home of Warner's great aunt Anne Ponsonby Moore. Warner stayed here with her parents in the summer of 1900

19 See Note 4

20 Miss Green's, Chaldon Herring

21 As guest critic of the *New York Herald Tribune* Warner wrote four articles during her seven week stay in 1929 and became a great success in New York literary circles

22 From 1936 until her death in 1978 Warner wrote over 150 short stories for the *New Yorker*

23 Alford Rectory

24 113 Inverness Terrace, London

25 Miss Green's, Chaldon Herring

26 Great Eye Folly, Salthouse, rented by Warner and Ackland in the winter of 1950-51

27 The house at Frome Vauchurch, Maiden Newton, Dorset. Warner and Ackland moved there in 1937 and later bought the place that was to be home for the rest of their lives

FRIENDS AND FAMILIARS

T.F. POWYS AND CHALDON HERRING

(Extracts from Warner's accounts of Theodore Powys[1]
in the *Powys Review* No. 5, 1979; No. 7, 1980; and
Recollections of the Powys Brothers, ed. Belinda Humfrey, 1980)

In September 1921, Stephen Tomlin[2] had come to London from the lodgings he had taken in the village of Chaldon Herring in Dorset, to pack his sculptures and a second-best suit in a large crate and to buy provisions for the winter. At the close of a conversation about soap and candles he remarked:

'There is a most remarkable man living just beyond the village. He is a sort of hermit, and he has a very fine head. He reads Dostoyevsky.'

I had known so many of Tommy's swans – indeed I had been one myself—that I was not much impressed.

'What does Dostoyevsky do?'

'I believe he writes.'

A little while after this Tommy wrote to me from Chaldon asking that I send a play I had just written, as Mr. Powys would like to read it.

I sent it with the greater readiness because I had just read the *Soliloquies of a Hermit* [3], and was very curious to know more of this strange character who mended his fence with string and wrote in a manner which reminded me a little of primitive Greek sculpture by the way in which the slow violence of its thought was expressed in a gentle and rather uncouth decorativeness, but which was quite unreminiscent of any living writer. . . .

In March 1922 I went down to Chaldon to see Tommy. From Bournemouth I travelled by a slow train, and when we drew up at the stations I heard the wind blowing. Just before I got to Wool a few long spikes of rain crossed the window-pane. Immediately after an early tea Tommy took me for a walk. We followed the track along the top of the Five Maries ridge[4], and pointing to the opposite hillside Tommy told me of Nelly Trim[5], a dairy maid who, it was said, would yield herself to any wanderer who chanced to come to her lonely dwelling. Towering wreaths

49

of mist were following each other along the valley, and I thought how glad the cold traveller would be of a warm woman. We walked as far as the Weymouth road, and there we turned east again and came back over the downs with the wind behind us to West Chaldon, a farm lying close under the shoulder of High Chaldon, which is a high grassy hill, isolated among the encompassing and interlocking downs. It was now raining hard, and quite dark. We walked along a road which had gates crossing it. After the third gate we passed a rickyard, and on the hillside, close to the road but set askew to it, I saw a black box-like shape.

'That is the Powys's house[6]. We will go in for a little. Theo knows you are coming, and he will want to see you.'

Tommy had previously seen fit to impart a little admonishment and instruction as to how I should behave on meeting Theo, and now, remembering this, I began to feel wet and blind. It was Violet[7] who came to open the door, Violet who I loved at first sight; and while she was helping me off with my coat Theo came and stood in the parlour doorway, and I heard for the first time that soft deferring voice.

'Is this Sylvia? Tommy, how very kind of you to bring her so soon. But I hope it will not harm her, bringing her out in the rain. Her hands are rather cold. Perhaps you should have let her rest a little longer after her journey. It would be terrible if you made her tired on her first evening. She might not come here again.'

Violet made tea. The room was hot; it had a good deal of furniture in it, and a bright lamp stood on a large table in the middle of the room. My head swam and I felt a little like a cat that has been let out of a hamper but knows it has come to a good home. I talked to Violet and looked, sometimes at Theo, sometimes at the overmantel.

They were neither of them in the least what I had expected; indeed, I had not expected the overmantel at all, and to this day I have never really assimilated it, for it has tiers of small shelves and on these are numbers of objects which have but one quality in common – the quality of not being easily impressed upon the mind. . . .

In the first moment of meeting Theodore Powys I forgot all my preconceived notions about him. In speaking of Theo it is natural to use the words of the Bible, and the phrase that comes to my mind when I try to recall my first impression of him is 'in the fullness of his presence'.

Most people have personalities that sit with them in the corner of the room or else, like balloons on a string, float from one member of the company to another, and are twitched back at the end of a conversation. But to enter a room where Theo sits is to enter into his presence, and when I go for walks with him at night he fills the darkness like a soft wind, and the strength of the hills seems to be his also. . . . I know that I must have expected him to look like something hagiological – a hermit or a prophet consumed with the fire of God's word, because the first thing that struck me about him was that his beauty was of a pagan and classical kind, and that instead of a hermit or a prophet I was looking at a rather weather-beaten Zeus. . . .

That night the wind changed, and in the morning patches of rigid snow lay under the hedges, and the turf was crisp with hoarfrost. We walked over Chaldon Down, and went down the cliff to a shingle beach by a chain – an exploit which nothing would induce me to repeat. The sun blazed on the chalk cliffs, we were out of the wind, and after the vividly-pale immobile landscape of the downs the sea appeared astonishingly deep-coloured and supple. I paddled, and lost an earring. . . .

On Tuesday I was to leave Chaldon, walking over the downs to East Lulworth, where I was to join Bea[8] for the rest of my holiday; but when I went to take farewell of Theo and Violet they begged me to bring her and myself over for the day, and knowing how much pleasure it would give them to meet someone as beautiful and charming as Bea I promised to do so. While I had been at Chaldon the weather had been rough and wintry, but when Bea and I had passed the farm called Slight's and began to descend into the green valley which has an ash-tree growing in it we saw that the hazels were putting out their lambs-tails; the old wallflower stock by Theo's doorstep was in bloom and the warm sun fetched wafts of scent from it. Theo was in the parlour, writing, but he came out and sat down on the doorstep between us, while Tommy and Hew Anderson[9] lay at our feet, pulling up handfuls of grass which the winter had loosened. We were going up the valley to show Bea Rat's Barn, to hope for a sight of the white owl who lived there, and to prospect my improbable plan of living in the deserted cottage – Rat's House – which was attached to the farm building. Theo very much approved of this plan, and did all that he could to encourage me in it, telling me that though it had stood empty for many years the people in the village still recounted what a good baking oven it possessed, and that there was actually a tap with water laid on from Lulworth, so that should I chance to feel out of the world I need only turn on my tap to feel myself once more linked to civilisation. True, it was a mile or more from the road but Violet would gladly take in my parcels, and as for coal I could wheel it up the field path in a second perambulator. . . .

. . . on Midsummer Eve I suddenly decided to go to Chaldon to see what it was looking like, and I know that when I arrived the tale of my sufferings was hot on my lips. It was looking very beautiful. I walked out from Wool through the dusk. Long wisps of cloud stayed still in the sky, and in Farmer Child's meadows the hay lay in swathes. That night as I looked out of my bedroom window in Mrs Baggs's cottage – Mrs Baggs who on my previous visit had given me a lemonade bottle filled with hot water in my bed, such was the kindness of her heart and her knowledge of the world – I saw a white poaching cat run by like a white moth; and I felt that she was not more at home in that moony landscape than I. . . .

As the Gothic cathedral is the expression in stone of the mysticism of the middle ages, as the cobb cottages in Chaldon village are the expression in mud of the domesticity of the peasant, so Theo's house is the expression in brick of the respectability of the later Victorian middle-classes. The Gothic cathedral is like the largest possible cage woven in stone osiers by the logic of the schoolmen to contain that queer bird, God. The cobb cottages are like swallow's nests with copper in them. But Theo's house belongs to the type of architecture which is neither theoretical or practical. It is necessitarian. Compared to it Crabbe would seem like Shelley. By this I do not mean that it lacks ornament or amenity. On the contrary, it has a bow-window, and the blank side that faces the road is trimmed with a stripe of pale buff ornamental bricks. But these are purely necessitarian in spirit for it is necessary for the parlour to exhibit some mark of class-consciousness and it is also necessary for blank surfaces to be trimmed. For a long time I chose to believe that it had been built by a stationmaster as a private residence for his retiring age, and I daresay this notion was strengthened by the fact that it is built of the same very hard red bricks that signal boxes are built of, but now I have come to disassociate it with

52

any human desires, and to think of it as having been dropped from above like some rectangular meteorite upon the slope of the green down.

This arbitrary look it has is emphasised by the fact that it is not tethered to the ground by any scheme of gardening. In the *Soliloquies* Theo represents himself as a modest Dioclesian, walking among large but mild cabbages, and repairing his fence with string. At one time I believe he tilled his half-acre very diligently, and certainly he grew onions, for Violet tells how he planted them under the weeping ash 'to give it something to weep for'. But though Theo is strongly built he is not strong; and gardening is fatiguing work, and in the neighbourhood of rabbits, disheartening. Moreover the desire to write became more insistent, and the hand that has once learnt to hold a pen to some purpose soon loses its knack for any other tool. So the cabbages, being cut, were left to burn themselves out in seventy-branched candle-sticks of flowering shoots, the weeping ash but wept over a memory, and soon only the greenness and the unusually vegetable look of the grass told that the soil it grew in had once been laboured by the spade.

But there are always compensations in this world which is so nicely balanced in space. As Theo himself pointed out when, feeling that as a host he should make conversation, he remarked to a young London barrister: 'This has been a bad year for thistles, but a good year for nettles'. Similarly as it lapsed from being a good garden for vegetables, so in exact ratio did Theo's half-acre become a good garden for fowls. Free to scratch and ramble where they list, a dozen hens, various in breed but alike in happy confidence, together with a pair of India runner ducks who were won in a raffle at the Winfrith bazaar, wander amongst the undergrowth of what, if I were lowland Scots, I should call Theo's hen-park. At one time this troop was augmented by some blue rabbits, and the latest recruit is a gosling called Tommy, because a little girl in the village said to Violet: 'I am sure that your goose is a tom-goose.' Besides these there are of course the cats, a rather fluctuating tribe whose head-quarters is the coach-house. But I do not see much of the cats, for on my visits to Theo I am accompanied by a chow who holds the same views about cats that large-hearted country gentlemen hold about foxes: that they enjoy being chased.

Other features in this garden are a bush of sweet briar, three poll apple-trees that look not unlike birds-nests, a hand pump whose air of being a widower may have aroused compassionate feelings in the lilac-bush and the elder-bush that every year push their green petticoats more closely around his leg, and a bleached and ricketty bench where on the first fine mornings of the year Theo likes to sit sunning himself, at the same time keeping a wary look-out for queen wasps. But in my haste to describe the garden I have omitted to enter it . . . I have said no word of the white gate.

In order to approach the white gate properly I must walk the reader up the lane from the village.

The village of Chaldon Herring[10], as it is properly called in the Ordnance map though the postal name is East Chaldon, lies at the western end of a stretch of water meadows. The road from Winfrith skirts these water-meadows, and though there is a short cut across two hay-fields belonging to Farmer Child, it is best on a visit of ceremonious inspection to keep to the Winfrith road and enter the village by the approach of state which leads one directly to the village green and the post-office. Should the time be early afternoon the Royal Mail may be observed waiting courteously at the corner of the green. When I first visited Chaldon the Royal Mail functioned in a very nondescript manner by means of a push bicycle; two or three years ago this was ennobled into a motor bicycle with a large scarlet box attached to one side of it; but now His Majesty's Government appears in the form of a van, nothing less, and this crescendo of magnificence I attribute entirely to Theo's correspondence with his publishers.

Crossing the Winfrith road is a lesser road, which to the south soon turns into a track over the downs, in winter a muddy and in summer a dusty one. The poor estate of this bit of road is probably due to the fact that it passes Billy Lucas's cottage, for no road could listen to Billy Lucas's[11] language without losing its self-respect. North of the green however, this road plucks up heart, and having been comforted on the right hand by the Methodist chapel and on the left by the Inn, is given a new name like other redeemed creatures, and under the title of the Drove climbs the Five Maries and goes down into the Dorchester road.

The sign-board of the Inn bears the inscription: The Sailors Return. It was here that Mr William Target lived with his Tulip[12], though, I am sorry to say, since his day the liquor is by no means what it was, indeed on two occasions I have gone there to buy a bottle of Old London Gin and found no gin at all of any description . . . a sad blow on a dark winter's night when one has got to pass the churchyard. It will be seen that the name of the Inn as given by the sign-board is susceptible of two interpretations. The reading chosen by David Garnett, who supplies a possessive comma, has no doubt much probability to commend it. It is also supported by parallel instances; The Peter's Finger, The King's Head, The Cyclist's Rest. Nevertheless I should feel myself lacking in open-mindedness if I omitted to point out that the name of the Chaldon Inn can equally well be read as an exclamation: The Sailors Return! . . . I consider it inherently more probable that the name of an inn should commemorate or invoke the return of several sailors rather than of one sailor who might not even be a two-legged one. Moreover, in dealing with any manuscript text, it is essential to consider it by the light of paleography. The signboard of The Sailors Return is no less a manuscript because it happens to be written in painting; but the use of this medium may, in no ordinary sense, be called a determining factor in the choice between a possessive or an exclamatory interpretation. It is the common experience of those who have had anything to do with paint that the supply is never quite equal to the demand. . . . Which then, is the more likely hypothesis: that, the paint running out, a penultimate comma or a final mark of exclamation should be lacking? To my mind, and I have been considering this problem on and off for years, the evidence is overwhelmingly in favour of the exclamatory reading. Not that I bear Professor Garnett, F.R.Z.S. any enmity for preferring the other reading. I am sure that he did not adopt it without proper deliberation. No. I could have wished that is all.

But perhaps I have lingered overlong at the Inn. We have yet to pass the Churchyard, and to any mind tempered to country delights and in a fit frame to be led up to Theo's gate, a Churchyard is as good a spot as the other to dawdle in, and to learn something of one's neighbours. Besides, at the hour that I have in mind the Inn is closed.

Leaving the green the Winfrith road turns a little to the left, and begins to go uphill into a darkness of trees. It narrows, too, like Hamilton Place, and like Hamilton Place its natural sombreness receives a deeper tinge, a moral tinge, cast by the dwelling-places of the select and splendid. For here are the everlasting habitations of Mr Child and Mr Todd, farmers of Chaldon. . . . Mr Todd's gate is of iron, and usually shut. A low retaining wall prevents the Churchyard earth from tumbling into Mr Todd's garden, but any misanthropical bones that did chance to burrow their way there would find Mr Todd's garden infinitely more congenial. No beam of a living sun could elude the dark pressure of Mr Todd's trees to mock them with warmth and spangles, no weed growing in shriven mould is of so charnel a green, is of so despairing a profusion as Mr Todd's hemlock, and though the voices of children might still be heard admiring the nosegays in the memorial jam-pots or calling I spy among the headstones, the bones need fear nothing, for no children play in Mr Todd's garden. The bones need not even dread the advent of a monkey, for solitary as an old black eunuch with rheumatism among the dank growth of alder and sycamore stands an inexpressibly melancholy monkey-puzzler.

At this point the road becomes extremely dark, and here, one on either hand are the Vicarage and the Churchyard, like Sin and Death. Sin is far the worse of the two. Sin is large and gaunt, it is built of pale bricks, it is roofed with sad slate, it has lean Gothic-gables and hungry windows, on its forehead is a birthmark like the brand of Cain, and inside it is full of pitchpine and destruction. The people who live too long in it go mad. Sin is ghastly at all times and seasons; as a bulk in the darkness, as a pallor by moonlight at which time its birthmark shows most and shows most terribly, as a shadow behind a shifting curtain of rain on a winter day, as a pale cheat on a summer afternoon, as a hollow trap in the spring sunlight. Theo believes, and I think he is right, that Sin is the habitation of a Demon, or as some say, an Elemental.

It would be difficult to walk with any courage past Sin if one were not able to turn one's eyes toward what stands over against it with the reflection that Death came into the World to save sinners. Death lies high above the road, which here runs along the side of a slope, and is approached by a flight of wide stone steps. These steps are worn into dipping curves so that it is a pleasure to go up and down them. They are worn, not by the tread of the coffin-bearers, nor the due feet of the clergymen, nor the Sunday soles of Mrs Todd and Mrs Child, but by the feet of children; for they lead, not only to Death, but also to the village school, a dejected, religious-looking building whose drains are said to be out of order. Death is entered by a squeaky gate: officially entered, that is, for there is no reason why one should not leap in over the wall, as I suppose suicides do. It is very grassy, and the grass is very green because there are trees all around it, except at the north-east corner, where one can look out and see how Mr Todd's turnips are getting on. From this corner too one can look across Death into a narrow view of the road leading up to the Five Maries; and as I still love the world, and also as I am extremely fond of cow-parsley, which is allowed to grow here in great peace and beauty since it covers only the graves of suicides and babies, this is the resting-place I choose out for myself when Theo and I walk round Death playing at the game of disposing of our remains. From this corner too, I shall have a fine prospect of the Resurrection, when I hope to satisfy my curiosity about a number of people who are as yet but names to me. But to choose the site for a house is not more ticklish work than choosing the site for a grave, and much as I like the north-east corner I am sensible that there are several things to be said against it. The weightiest of these objections is, that, unless he should take a mind to stroll round the corner and look at the turnips, I shall not see the Resurrection of the Reverend Joseph Cope[13].

For this, as for so many other things, the Church may be held to blame; not, however, in this case the whole estate of the Church militant here upon earth but the small stone building with a squat tower which is its outward and visible sign to the parish of Chaldon Herring.

I make no apology for not having mentioned the Church before in this account of Death. I am only following the local use, a use pefectly consistent with the country frame of mind. To the villagers of Chaldon Herring, and to any normal villagers, the Church is a building in the Churchyard. In winter, if it be nicely heated, it is a place where one may sit warm without the trouble of tending the fire. At Easter it is a place that smells of damp moss and primroses, a copse where a modest girl can sit beside her young man without any danger of her new dress getting rumpled or stained green, and where ants will not crawl up her legs. In the season of harvest it is a place where a farmer that is a churchwarden can contemplate in a mystical way not possible out-of-doors the colour of his wheat or the fulness of his roots. To the labouring man the Church is a place where he can wear his Sunday trousers and where his wife must leave off talking. To the married woman it is a place where her children are not likely to cry. To the aged it is a place where they can feel at home because they have been there so many times before. To children it is a place where the clergyman's boots may squeak, where a bird may perch on the collecting box or where Theo may turn over two pages at once. It is all things to all men, a table where all may feed according to their desires, the house of a God who provides crumbs for the sparrow and blood for the eagle and grass for the lamb and lamb for the nursery dinner. To Mrs Vesper it is a place where the robe of the woman of Samaria in the stained glass window is the colour of tinned salmon, and to Mr Samways the sexton it is a tomb, larger than any altar tomb in Death, but not so permanent. . . .

After passing Sin and Death the mounting road leaves the trees behind. The air seems to grow lighter and more living; along the grass bank columbines grow under the brambles, and on the right hand, only a very rickety fence divides the road from a green field sloping down to the stream whose higher reaches so much resemble Venice. Here we can look up the valley, observing how beautiful the contours of High Chaldon are, seen thus close; or one can look back at the village, the roofs in a loose flock, like sheep feeding, under the wavy line of the Five Maries. It is just here, walking up from the village with Theo in a November dusk, and perhaps carrying the afternoon milk, that I am apt to remember the sea, little more than a mile away, but hidden behind the tall downs. And it will suddenly become very real to me: I shall hear the slow speech of the waves locked in a winter calm; a reserved, whispering voice; as though I had come to the edge of the cliff, I shall feel the authentic stab of surprise, almost of terror, with which one realises, as though one were perceiving the true stature of an enemy, how far up the sky is the line of the sea. But mixed in my mind with thoughts of the sea, and with thoughts of Theo's house, waiting just round the corner, is a last backward glance of affection for the Reverend Joseph Cope. Now is the moment – for I don't suppose that I shall mention him again – to reveal my key reason for cherishing his memory as I do. If Mr Cope had not lived at Chaldon Herring Theo might not be here at all: he certainly would not be in his present residence. For Theo's house was built at Mr Cope's command[14], some say for a curate; others, for a gardener; on this nice point I cannot pretend to an opinion. Perhaps it is a little grand for a curate, but equally one might advance that it is too grand for a gardener. Thomas Hardy's brother[15], who was the architect, placed in the centre of the north wall a terra-cotta plaque representing pomegranates in bas-relief, and this might be intended as an incentive to a gardener, reminding him to be a profitable labourer in his master's strawberry beds. Pomegranates, though, are a religious variety of fruit, and equally applicable to a curate. They are also the symbol of fertility; but I don't think we need linger over this aspect of pomegranates, for I am confident that Thomas Hardy's brother intended no insinuations of this sort – one has only to look at the house as a whole to realise that here we have the expression of a mind unbending to mystical innuendo. Indeed I think we should be very guarded in attaching any significance beyond what is purely structural to these pomegranates. The north wall is a blank wall, but as the house is set sideways to the road, it is also in a sense a facade, and to an architect, mentally stepping a little back from his creation, it might naturally occur that such a wall needed trimming, needed something to collect and steady the eye; and then he would add the pomegranates, very possibly a stock pattern.

Whether the house was intended for curate or gardener neither curate or gardener possessed it. Indeed I believe I am right in saying that neither curate or gardener has ever spent a night under its roof. Mr Cope died while the house was yet a-building and for some time it stood unfinished and abandoned, like Baalbec, or the Hyde Park Hotel, and became an habitation for foxes, which are very plentiful on Chaldon Down, and a dumping-ground for Mr Tod's sacks of kainite. Lovers would climb in by the window on foggy afternoons, and the school children would dare each other to go up and knock on the door, braving the ghost, the melancholy ghost who lives in all empty houses. Theo and Violet, might walk by too – for at this time Theo had come to Chaldon Herring and met Violet – shaking their heads over such a waste of good bricks and mortar. Perhaps Violet may have had her eye on it even then, at any rate I expect she allowed her fancy to walk in and inspect the pantry shelves and the copper, for no young woman worth her salt who is going to get married can pass any empty house without picturing how the clock would look on the mantelpiece. She may even have given her fancy leave to speak, and then Theo would observe discreetly that new houses are sometimes apt to be a little damp.

Any such dampness was avoided by the simple expedient of not being the first tenant. Theo's warming-pan was a retired rate-collector from

Dorchester, and when this good gentleman had fulfilled his office and taken his rheumatism to Swanage, Theo bought the lease and moved in.

Theo knows this countryside like an old dog fox. Of all the field gates he has opened for me I have never known him err as to which end had the fastening. Every gap in a hedge, every breach in a wall, every sagging strand in a barbed wire fence is stored in his memory, for each is a possible bolt-hole which may at some time be needed to assist his retirement from some intruder on his solitary walks, a bull or a bishop, or some fellow out rabbiting who might talk of the weather. From whatever quarter the winter winds may blow, he will lay his course along some valley where the bleached grasses scarcely stir on the bank. On a spring afternoon he knows to a minute at what hour an ash tree will throw the prettiest shade, and on the way thither he will forewarn one of the nettles. And however bare and bleak the down from which one sees the storm cloud hurried on by the March gale, he will have led one to a hay-stack or a bramble-thatch before the first volley of sleet rattles on the windward side of the shelter. Long knowing this, my trust in Theo's guidance was complete and entire. Yet a time came when that trust was to waver, and that wavering to be proved a blasphemy. It was a November afternoon when he took us over West Chaldon Down to overlook the valley of Mockery Gap. The air was mild, and to the south-west a vast cloud was sucking up the sunset, and we stood for a long while watching the dusk grow in the valley. In that dusk the Mockery wood seemed to enlarge itself, and as the light went from the sea, movement went with it, till it lay heavy and glum as a leaden shield. As we turned back along the coastguard's path the darkness of the cloud came after us, and overtook us. For a while there was still a glimmer of broken chalk at the cliffs edge, but presently even that was gone, and we were walking by foot-feel alone. As a rule the coming of darkness is to some extent balanced by the increase of cats-sight, but this was a night when even a cat would have stretched her pupils in vain. It was the thick darkness that rested on the land of Egypt. While we kept to the coastguard's path, with Theo's footsteps going in front of us we were well enough, but in order to reach home by the route he had appointed, it would be necessary to turn off, and traverse a quarter of a mile or so of bramble patch and waste ground and so strike into the track which leads down into Rat's

Valley. In my mind's eye I had a fair picture of the terrain, I also had lively recollections of how scratched and shaken I had been in crossing the bramble tract once before. But when Theo, speaking out of the darkness, remarked that there was a little patch through the brambles, used by him and a few rabbits, which he thought he could lay hold on, I lost my faith, and began to murmur. Theo kept on. At first I thought that he would never know where to turn off into his rabbit-path, then I began to feel sure that we must have passed it, for we seemed to have been walking for ever through the dark air, our feet shuffling on the beaten turf. Then, when I had lost interest in my fate, and was prepared to walk on until we came to Lulworth, or fell into the sea, I heard his feet hesitate, and his stick probe the tangle of briars and grasses for a moment or two. Then he put out his hand, took hold of me, and drew me into the path. My feet told me that I should have been hard put to it to find it by day.

We were too much awed to comment, and Theo took his achievement too much as a matter of course to say more than that in about five minutes time we should be passing some hurdled sheep; my graceless murmurings, though, were not to be taken as a matter of course and he must have decided that a little magnanimity would not be amiss; for when we were on the cart-track, and our heels striking sparks from the flints, he politely requested me to take the lead. At the end of this visit one thing was certain—that I should pay another.

Four novels have been written – *Innocent Birds, The Market Bell*, which he does not intend to have published, *Mockery Gap* and *Mr Weston's Good Wine*. With the exception of the second, each of these shows decided individual modifications and the last such a deepening of content and treatment as almost sets it apart from the rest. Yet they are all bound together by their subject-matter and continuity of feeling, so much so that I suppose the only other author who has achieved the same diversity in unity is Jane Austen. And though Theo speaks very rarely of his work and seldom reveals his own view of it, I believe that his novels were consciously though not deliberately written as a series of connected works, and that in *Mr Weston's Good Wine* he set himself to sum up the import of the whole.

In January 1926 he wrote to me: 'I shall try once more – with Mr

Weston's Good Wine, a short novel (But it is one of his longest). And then I shall rest.'

And again, when I asked him if he thought of writing about the Chaldon people any more or if he had finished his Wessex Novels he said that having brought Christ to Ringstead in *Mockery Gap* and God himself to sell His Good Wine to the people of Chaldon, he considered he had done as much as was feasible for his neighbours. 'For the Devil would be no novelty to them, they are quite familiar with his tail. They handle it in as friendly a way as the sexton handles a bell-rope.'

As he had said, after *Mr Weston's Good Wine* he rested. The phoenix, when its time is come flies away into the desert, and to the artist not to be producing is to be in a desert, even though he may assure his friends that it is very restful there. *Mr Weston* was finished in 25/26. In February 1927 I went to Chaldon and found that Theo had started to write again. He was writing fables. He had not done with the people of Chaldon however, for many of them appeared in the fables, conversing with ash-trees, cuckoo clocks, glow-worms and old hats; and harking back to one of the names he had given to Chaldon in his novels, he suggested that if he went on with the fables and did enough of them to make into a book the title might be The Madder Fables[16]. There was an element of truth in such a title which made me a trifle doubtful if it were a wholly suitable one. But the madness of the fables was of a kind that made me very anxious that Theo should write more of them. . . .

T. F. Powys's books grew like stalactites and stalagmites. He deposited them, secretively and methodically – a process taking place in a cave. After breakfasting, rather late, and leisurely, he went off to the parlour, sat down before a large solid table, read for half an hour (usually in the Bible) and then set to work. He wrote uninterruptedly for three hours or so, put his work back in the table drawer, and began again, where he left off, on the following morning. He told me, when I questioned him about this, that he always wrote consecutively, that he would have felt uneasy if he had not done so. 'I should not like to lose my place.' When I happened to pass the window, I saw the same grave, dispassionate countenance, the pen moving steadily over the paper, dipping at regular intervals into the inkpot.

I think he never discussed a book while he was writing it. His secretiveness and reserve forbade enquiries. Occasionally – but rarely – he would speak of a book he had it in mind to write. But this was as an intimation though it might be politely couched as an enquiry. 'Do you think it would be proper for me to introduce Death into a story?' was his intimation of *Unclay*. In fact, as far as planning went, he had already done so: for when, a few days later, he asked me how, if I were writing a story about John Death, a stranger, coming to a village, I would begin it, and I said that perhaps it might begin with a scythe hung outside the inn door and flashing in the summer sun, he said with gently malevolent satisfaction, 'Unfortunately, I have begun the book in October.'

Titles, however, he was always pleased to discuss – though in the end he always chose them for himself. Sometimes the title engendered the story. *Unclay*[17], for instance, was deposited round the verb, to unclay, which he had found in some seventeenth-century religious author. One of his short stories, *I Came as a Bride*, was similarly deposited round that phrase, which had been used to me by a very old woman, relating how she had first come to the farm where she had lived ever since. The phrase happened to take his fancy: what he deposited round it was something so entirely different that I should not have known I had supplied the title if he had not told me so. The Book of Amos supplied him with *Naughty Figs* as a title. He was much pleased with it, but the story failed to deposit.

I doubt if he ever sought for material. He lay in wait for it. He was, however, exceedingly selective, and discarded with infallibility. 'I like to think about an old gate,' he remarked. He wouldn't have given a thought to the Arc de Triomphe. He liked lumber-room material. Once, when we were sitting with a hedge between us and the wind, he turned to me and said with great earnestness, almost urgency: 'Tell me about your aunts.' None of my aunts happened to serve his purpose; but a cousin much-removed, who after several northern winters of dining alone under his family portraits had taken them down from the walls and made a bonfire of them on the grounds that they were all so damnably ugly, reappeared, transmogrified, as the short story, *Squire Pooley*, in *The White Paternoster*. Most of T.F. Powys's friends could recognise similar appropriations and transmogrifications: but these are trifling debts. Violet, returning from the village post-office, or from a journey to Dorchester in the bus, or reading bits of local news aloud from

The Dorset Echo, would bring him infinitely more, and better. Observant, speculative, credulous, unaffectedly interested in her neighbours, naturally talking the local dialect yet just enough removed from it to have an ear for its idioms, and with a memory ramifying into every local pedigree and bygone event and oddity, she was an inestimably good purveyor – with the crowning merit of remaining unconscious of it. I doubt if such an idea as 'This is just what will do for Theodore,' ever crossed her mind. She purveyed; perhaps she even determined. Under any circumstances, TFP would have been a writer; but I suspect his bent towards theology and contemplation would have kept him writing about God and Theodore Francis Powys if Violet had not drawn his attention to humanity. . . .

After his morning of work, and his lunch, TFP went out for a walk, a long walk sometimes, at other times a constitutional. If it was to be a long walk, when he would want to sit down and rest, he carried a small square of pale mackintosh to put between himself and grass that might be damp. Once, when I had arrived at Chaldon in the middle of a drought, I remarked, seeing him folding up this square and putting it in his pocket, that I did not think we were likely to find any damp grass. In the voice of goblin benevolence he employed when administering a snub, he replied, 'No, my dear. But we may find thistles.'

His constitutional walks were determined by some chosen goal – a bush, a gate, a particular telegraph post. If it were the telegraph post he would give it a sort of nudge with the end of his walking-stick, as much as to say, 'I've got here. Observe it.' He also took a walk after dark, by preference alone. I remember him coming back from one such walk, but sooner than usual, and looking troubled. 'I heard a noise in the hedge. I said to myself, It's only a rat. But then I thought, Who made that rat?'

I remember the relation of a daylight walk. 'I was coming down the side of High Chaldon when I saw a white patch by the hedge; and I wondered if it were Nelly's petticoat. As I got nearer, I saw it wasn't that, so I thought it might be a newspaper. But it wasn't that, either. It was – a dead seagull.'

Lust or death, in fact. In either case, violence. TFP spoke of himself with touching wistfulness as 'a quiet man', 'a harmless man'. He liked to think of himself as a Mr Solly 'who lived at Madder in a quiet sort of way', or as a compendium of those innocent eccentric clergymen in the Powys

Crockford. While leading a virtuous methodical life, while drinking tea or admiring the snowdrops in the churchyard, it would be difficult to speak of oneself as a man of blood and rapine but he could equally well have done so, he was quite capable of entering into Farmer Mew as into Parson Hayhoe. He would not, as one says, have hurt a mouse; but there was a vein of cruelty in his nature and of a cold goblin malevolence, which he was quite aware of and in a way rather proud of. It seems to me significant that he elected to be old, that he imposed himself as elderly when he was still middle-aged. The imposture fitted him like a glove. He may even have been taken in by it: he certainly found it convenient. But I believe that a psychoanalyst would have found out that he was an impacted adolescent, simultaneously entranced and horrified at feeling so many irreconcilable things at once, and all so violently. In those solitary walks he was not only engaged in shaping and deepening what he would write down so composedly on the morrow, he was engaged in assimilating himself to his writings, in becoming a character by T. F. Powys.

There was not, in fact, a great variety of characters open to him. The characterisation in the novels is limited and arbitrary: one remembers the people by their traits, their humours; their part is allotted to them, and they must play it in keeping, as in the Commedia del Arte. There is a girl who must be ravished, a livelier girl who will marry a quiet man older than she. There is a greedy farmer, who is likely to have a lustful son. There is a rancorous old woman. They reappear under different names, they inhabit a village called Madder, or Dodder, or Maids Madder, or Dodderdown, where there is a vicarage or a rectory, much as Cezanne arranges his apples sometimes on a blue dish, sometimes on a napkin. Powys likes monotony. At some time or other, Powys has been in all of them. But there is also a rather mysterious character who has a mysterious influence on the other characters, while remaining detached from them, who is called Jar or Weston: and TFP seems almost to settle down in them: but not quite: they are at once too responsible and too free from human care. He hesitates towards a character who is detached and influences nobody. He felt himself very much at home in Mr Grobe. But I believe he moved on, and this time marked his elected dwelling-place, a character in one of the *Fables* called Nathaniel Crew. Nathaniel, a Hebrew name, has the same significance as Theodore.

THE PORTRAIT OF A TORTOISE
(Introduction to *The Portrait of a Tortoise*, 1946,
extracts from the Journals and Letters of Gilbert White)

'Young Hirundines cluster on the trees. Harvest bugs bite the ladies.'

If one is a lady this record of August 14, 1790, may seem a little heartless in its serene objectivity. But a naturalist penned it. A child of his most social century, Gilbert White, Curate of Selborne in Hampshire, complied with his social obligations, whether as friend, host, or member of the White family (descendants of the *Jutae* or *Viti* to whom King Ina gave a grant of settlement). There were gifts of pheasants, cucumbers, and melons; there were tea-parties at the Hermitage (his gothic summerhouse on Selborne Hanger) where Brother Harry, cowled and bearded, 'appeared to great advantage' as the Hermit; there were supper-parties when 'at one in the morn the gentlemen and us changed Caps and wigs and several minuets were danced'; there were hospitalities to brothers and sisters, nephews and nieces ('I have just ceiled and am fitting up a garret for any young person I may have with me'); there was the over-seeing of stockings being knitted locally for Brother Thomas, the finding of maid-servants for Niece Mary, and later the charge of Mary's baby who came down with his nurse to Selborne and was referred to as The Learned Pig. But through this landscape of Conversation Pieces Gilbert White's private love-affair with Nature runs like a chalk-stream river, pellucid, tranquil, and irresistible. And so when he opens his Naturalist's Journal and sets down the outstanding events of August 14, 1790, the ladies ('Sister Barker, and nieces, Mary and Eliz:') take their place in the realm of nature, rolled round in earth's diurnal course with the harvest bugs and the Hirundines.

But perfect objectivity is difficult to achieve, even by a naturalist. The harvest bugs and their complementary ladies lacked the compelling charm of the Hirundines – the charm of mystery. Harvest bugs ('an insect which

66

is very troublesome and teasing, getting into people's skins, especially those of ladies and children, and raising tumours which itch intolerably') 'prevail only in the hot months of summer.' Ladies, on the other hand, having made some seasonal variations in their plumage, are about at all times of year. But whether the Hirundines migrated during the winter or whether they hibernated was a matter of debate; and to his life's end Gilbert White watched and wondered, seeking, and seemingly on the brink of finding, and never finding, an unequivocal proof of hibernation. A hundred years before him Henry Wotton had written of 'the swift pilgrim's well-daubed nest.' Not till over a hundred years after Gilbert White had looked his last at a swallow was it definitely established that swallows from England had wintered in S. Africa. Between Wotton (for that matter, Shakespeare too) with their carefree poet's guess-right, and the final confirmation of scientific ornithology, the tide of opinion had flowed towards hibernation – in Gilbert White's time so strongly that it collected and carried along with it a considerable amount of irrefutable evidence. English naturalists favoured the belief of land-hibernation, and sent the swallows, swifts, and martins underground into burrows and sandbanks, or into hollow trees or the crannies of buildings. A Reverend Mr Conway of Flintshire said he had looked down into a lead-mine and seen 'numbers of swallows clinging to the timbers of the shafts, seemingly asleep.' Near Whitby some sportsmen, digging out a fox, found 'whole bushels of swallows in a torpid condition.' Other naturalists in Northern Europe preferred to send the swallows under water. 'Dr Wallerius, the celebrated Swedish chemist,' declared he had seen swallows 'assembling on a reed, till they were all immersed and went to the bottom; this being preceded by a dirge of a quarter of an hour's length'; and this theory was majestically supported by Dr Johnson: 'a number of them conglobulate together by flying round and round, and then all in a heap throw themselves under water and lie in the bed of a river.'[18]

Refusing to be immersed with Wallerius, Gilbert White does not seem to have been perfectly convinced in favour of hibernation either. But there is no doubt he hoped to be convinced. As he was what one might call a naturalistic naturalist, relying on his own observations, and as there are always some hirundines who delay their departure or arrive individualistically early, it is no wonder that he found himself observing what seemed to be evidence that swallows wintered in England. Torpidity, that strange power of passing the winter months with every faculty except the minute thread of solstitial consciousness suspended, must also be observed. 'At the Black-Bear inn in Reading there is a stream in the garden which runs under the stables . . . Now all the summer this is full of carps, which roll about and are fed by travellers. When the cold weather comes, these fishes withdraw under the stables, and are invisible for months: during which period, I conclude, they must sleep. Thus the inhabitants of the water, as well as of the air and the earth, retire from the severity of winter.' Heaven and earth and the waters under the earth, all had something relevant to say about swallows; and it was with swallows in mind that Gilbert White first began to be interested in the subject of this biography: 'Timothy, Mrs Snooke's old tortoise.'

'A land tortoise, which has been kept for thirty years in a little walled court belonging to the house where I am now visiting, retires under ground about the middle of November, and comes forth again about the middle of April.' It is thus, at the close of Letter vii to Daines Barrington, after some discursive remarks about birds and ornithologists, that Timothy first steals into public notice. The house where Gilbert White was visiting was at Ringmer in Sussex, and belonged to Mrs Rebecca Snooke, a widow, and his paternal aunt. The date of the letter is October 8, 1770. Gilbert White was fifty, Mrs Snooke seventy-six, and Timothy supposedly nearing his fortieth year. But here we are at once in the realm of supposition, and I do not see how we can emerge from it. In a letter of 1784, addressed to a young lady called Miss Heckey Mulso, Gilbert White, pretending to write in the person of Timothy, asserts that he (Timothy) 'was born in the year 1734 in the Province of Virginia.' Clearly, the choice of this date must be arbitrary, though Gilbert White had been pleased to persuade himself of it, since in a letter of the same year, written to his niece Mary White, he refers to Timothy as 'so old a domestic, who has behaved himself in so blameless a manner in the family for near fifty years.' Admitting, then, that it is not possible to establish the date of Timothy's birth, we must content ourselves with the account (also contained in the letter to Miss Mulso) of how Timothy first became connected with the White family on its distaff side; which is, that somewhere around 1740 Mr Snooke visited the harbour town of

Chichester, where he bought a tortoise from a sailor for half a crown, carried it back to Ringmer, and christened it Timothy. After this impetuous act Mr Snooke lost interest in his purchase, and Timothy, put into the little walled court, became to all intents and purposes Mrs Snooke's tortoise.

Just as the ladies were complementary to the harvest bugs Mrs Rebecca Snooke is preserved for us in her nephew's writings as the owner of some Scotch Pines in which Crossbills appeared, ponds in which he observed 'vast spiders, which dive and conceal themselves on the undersides of plants,' a horse that was struck by lightning, and the subject of this biography. From family papers we learn that in the summer of 1763, being then newly a widow, she was a guest at Selborne, took part in the tea-party which was entertained by the Hermit, and witnessed the minuets when the gentlemen and ladies changed caps and wigs; and that in her eightieth year, having just recovered from a serious attack of gout, she rode out in her chaise in the month of December. Her nephew visited her regularly, and from his *Naturalist's Journal* other facts emerge, peripheral to Mrs Snooke, but nevertheless very much to her credit.

'Fern-owls haunt Mrs Snooke's orchard in autumn.'
'Mrs Snooke has gathered in all her apples, & pears: her fruit is finely flavoured in such hot years. Mrs Snooke's black grapes begin to ripen. No wasps here. The distress in this place for want of water is very great: they have few deep wells in this dry loam: & the little pits & ponds are all dry: so the neighbourhood all come for water to Mrs Snooke's pond.'

To Timothy, secluded in the little walled court, the orchard and the ponds were not significant. But the nature of the soil is a matter of concern to all self-burying animals. 'Ringmer soil is not clay on top but brick-loam: bears good apples, pears, & grapes. Clay under, which holds water like a dish.' Gilbert White usually visited Ringmer in autumn, but in 1773 he was there in December, and realised the inconveniencies of a clay substratum. The tortoise in Mrs Snooke's garden . . . lies in a wet border in mud & mire: with it's back bare.'

This is an affecting picture: but the Ringmer soil must be blamed for it, not Mrs Snooke. Mrs Snooke was very kind to Timothy. She fed him with her own hands, and studied his tastes. He ate of her kidney-beans and of her cucumbers. As for the little walled court, it was not the sort of prison-yard the words might suggest. It had a border in it: in the December of 1773 a wet border, but nevertheless a flower border, for in the Letter xiii to Daines Barrington, Gilbert White describes how Timothy dug his hybernaculum 'beside a great tuft of hepaticas.' In this same letter Gilbert White tells his correspondent not only of Mrs Snooke's kindness to Timothy but also of Timothy's distinguishing affection for Mrs Snooke. 'I was much taken with it's sagacity in discerning those that do it kind offices: for, as soon as the good old lady comes in sight who has waited on it for more than thirty years, it hobbles towards it's benefactress with awkward alacrity; but remains inattentive to strangers.'

Mrs Snooke's attentions to Timothy were not only of the kidney-bean and cucumber kind. She found him interesting – perhaps even taught her nephew to follow suit. It was probably at Gilbert White's request that she kept him posted as to Timothy's winter retirements and vernal reappearances; but the entries in White's *Journals* based on her reports are not mere bald statements that Timothy has gone under ground, Timothy is up and about again: they show that she observed him closely and sympathetically. 'Mrs Snooke's tortoise, after it had been buried more than a month, came forth & wandered round the garden in a disconsolate state, not knowing where to fix on a spot for it's retreat.' In 1777 it was Mrs Snooke's sharp eye that caught Timothy in the act of supplying a most compelling (though erroneous) piece of corroborative evidence for the hibernation of swallows. Gilbert White thought so much of it that he put it in the forefront of his Letter xxxvi to Daines Barrington.

'Dear Sir. You cannot but remember that the twenty-sixth and twenty-seventh of last March were very hot days; so sultry that every one complained and were restless under those sensations to which they had not been reconciled by gradual approaches.

'This sudden summer-like heat was attended by many summer coincidences; for on those two days the thermometer rose to sixty-six in the shade; many species of insects revived and came forth; some bees swarmed in this neighbourhood; the old tortoise, near Lewes in Sussex, awakened and came forth out of it's dormitory; and, what is most to my present purpose, many house-swallows appeared and were very alert in many places, and particularly at Cobham, in Surrey.

70

'But as that short warm period was succeeded as well as preceded by harsh weather, with frequent frosts and ice, and cutting winds, the insects withdrew, the tortoise retired again into the ground, and the swallows were seen no more until the tenth of April.'

Three years later Mrs Snooke died, aged eighty-six, and Gilbert White, travelling to Ringmer for her funeral, was noting along the way that no turnips were to be seen, and that 'Chaffinches sing but in a shorter way than in Hants.' Leaving Ringmer he took with him 'Mrs Snooke's old tortoise, Timothy, which she valued much, & had treated kindly for near 40 years. When dug out of it's hybernaculum, it resented the Insult by hissing.'

Thus a valued family friend passed from the ownership of one generation to another, and exchanged the clay-bottomed brick-loam of Ringmer for the black malm of Selborne. But this was not the only change. A change of mind becomes perceptible in Gilbert White's *Journal*. Timothy is no longer studied as an accessory to swallows. He begins to be studied as a personality.

During the summer of 1780 Gilbert White . . . but the words of today, concentrated, doted, and so on, are too lavish and too indiscriminate for the circumstances: one must revert to the language of his date and say that during the summer of 1780 Gilbert White was exceedingly attentive to his tortoise. Timothy was watched, Timothy was weighed. He was put into a tub of water to ascertain if he could swim (he could not). He was called to loudly through a speaking-trumpet, 'but did not seem to regard the noise.' His excrements were examined, his choice of food recorded. There is a note of rising triumph in these successive entries.

'*July 19*. Timothy picks out the hearts & stems of Coss-lettuce, holding the outer leaves back with his feet.
'*July 24*. Tortoise eats endive and poppies.
'*July 27*. Tortoise eats goose-berries.'

Small wonder that during the course of the summer Timothy's weight increased by eleven ounces.

In the second week of September – the peaches were ripening, and

Gilbert White had just gathered his Bergamot pears – the *Journal* announces: 'The motions of Timothy the tortoise are much circumscribed: he had taken to the border under the fruit-wall, & makes very short excursions: he sleeps under a Marvel of Peru.' This, of course, was just a preliminary sleep, a mere closing of the eyes for better meditation; for a week later comes the experiment with the speaking-trumpet, and the reassuring entry on the following day that Timothy eats heartily. But autumn was coming, and there is a late flock of house-martins, and Gilbert White is in high hopes 'that this late flock at least will not withdraw into warmer climes, but that they will lie dormant among the low beechen oaken shrubs' (this entry, though nothing to do with Timothy, is interesting because it shows Gilbert White in a mid-way frame of mind), and 'men put their hogs up a fatting,' and Timothy, 'who is placed under a hen-coop near the fruit-wall, scarce moves at all.' And Gilbert White, like the good host he is, has turned his mind to that hospitable preoccupation: how to ensure that his tortoise should spend a comfortable winter night.

The second half of the eighteenth century brought great changes to the English garden, new elements of informality, vistas, and romance. To Gilbert White with his love for 'outlets,' evergreens, and 'annuals in the basons down the field,' the little walled court at Ringmer, survival of the mode of Mrs Snooke's youth, must have seemed very poky and unenterprising. To Timothy, on the other hand, the Selborne garden may well have seemed rather draughty. But apart from the draughtiness inseparable from English Picturesque, Gilbert White was justified in thinking (as the *Journal* so clearly shows he did think) that Timothy's change of residence was greatly to Timothy's advantage: affording him more scope for curiosity, more room for exercise, and a free run among the vegetables (at Ringmer he had to wait for Mrs Snooke to bring him his salads). With the oncome of winter Gilbert White feels even more reason to emphasise the superior amenities of Selborne. 'Timothy lies in the border under the fruit-wall, in an aspect where he will enjoy the warmth of the sun, & where no wet can annoy him: a hen-coop over his back protects him from dogs, &c. At Ringmer he used to lay himself up in a wet swampy border: indeed he had no choice.'

But in the following winter Timothy, now having choice, behaved rather oddly; having been put to bed as before in the border under the fruit-wall, on November 8 'the tortoise came out of his coop, & has buried himself in the laurel-hedge.' Perhaps he disliked the coop. Perhaps the soil of the fruit-wall border, being, as Gilbert White boasted, 'very light and mellow,' did not give him a sufficiently quilted sensation to ensure the proper depth of slumber. Perhaps, like many celebrated characters, he preferred to sleep austerely. Perhaps he yearned for something more like the sleeping conditions he had known for near forty years. If it was damp he wanted, he got it. For on March 28, 1782, 'Poor Timothy was flooded in his hybernaculum amidst the laurel-hedge: & might have been drowned, had not his friend Thomas come to his assistance & taken him away.'

Timothy's friend Thomas was Gilbert White's friend, gardener, and factotum, Thomas Hoar. And with this introduction of Thomas we must pause to remark that he was a very unwonted kind of gardener. Even the carnivorous American tortoises are mistrusted by gardeners. Timothy, for all that the sailor said, was a Mediterranean tortoise; and a vegetarian. The *Journals* show that the Selborne garden was a very proper sort of garden, growing fruit, flowers, and delicate vegetables, well-loved and highly cultivated; yet Timothy had a free run of it. We find him asleep in the shade of the monk's rhubarb, or skulking among the carrots and cabbages; he travels about the garden, in the months of high summer he traverses all the garden by six in the morning, he crops the daisies and walks to the fruit-wall border to browse the lettuces, he eats much, he is very voracious, he spoils the lettuce under the fruit-wall but will not touch the Dutch while he can get at any Coss lettuce. And all this takes place without any apparent remonstrance from Thomas Hoar, who not only rescues Timothy from drowning but himself supplies Gilbert White, then visiting in London, with the interesting detail that Timothy prefers Coss lettuce. If Timothy had been the only thorn in Thomas's pillow, Thomas's tolerance would still be remarkable. But it was not so. Thomas had many other things to endure. Mice devoured the crocuses, hares got in and nibbled off the pinks, and on one occasion a strange dog ate the apricots.

To return to Timothy. Having been rescued from drowning under the laurel-hedge Timothy went back to the fruit-wall border and the hen-coop for the winter of 1782-83. But it was for the last time. In the autumn of

1783 he again asserted himself, and made his hybernaculum under the laurel-hedge. The hard winter of 1784-85 he also spent in that vicinity, 'under the wall-nut tree, among the dead leaves,' and so for the three winters following. In the spring of 1789 'Timothy heaves up the sod under which he is buried,' (which suggests a different site, since the earth under a hedge is not usually grassed enough to be termed sod, and noting previous emergences from under the laurel-hedge Gilbert White says, heaves up the earth). Be that as it may, he is back in the laurel-hedge for the winter of 1790-91; but in December 1791 he 'laid himself up under the hedge against Benham's yard in a very comfortable, snug manner: a thick tuft of grass shelters his back, & he will have the warmth of the winter sun.' During the hard winter of 1784 (when Gilbert White's parlour-cat 'was so electric, that had a person stroked her, and been properly insulated, the shock might have been given to a whole circle of people.' – which would have afforded her a great deal of quiet satisfaction, no doubt) the laurel-hedge suffered considerably, and Thomas Hoar was set to shake the snow off the evergreens; and if this became a routine during the spell of snowy winters which followed it is possible that Timothy, discommoded by the vibrations of Thomas's cold stamping feet, may have moved to the hedge against Benham's yard for the sake of a little peace and quiet.[19]

But these migrations from the blue bedroom to the brown bedroom were not Timothy's only assertions of personality. Twice he left the garden altogether. 'May 22, 1784. We have lost poor Timothy, who, being always in a great bustle in such hot weather, got out, we suppose, at the wicket, last Thursday; and is wandered we know not whither. Thomas is much discomposed at this elopement; and has –

> . . . *made as great a coil as*
> *Stout Hercules for loss of Hylas.*
> *He has forced the hangers to repeat*
> *The accent of his sad regret:*
> *And Echo from the hollow ground*
> *His doleful wailings to resound.*

(Thomas presumably had forgotten the experiment with the speaking-trumpet; or his feelings as a friend overcame his natural philosophy.) 'But to be serious, I should be very sorry to lose so old a domestic, who has behaved himself in so blameless a manner in the family for near fifty years.'

A postscript to this letter to Niece Mary adds, 'May 24. No Timothy to be found.' In a letter of June 12 Mary is told of Timothy's return. 'After Timothy had been lost eight days, he was found in the little field short of the pound-field. He had conceived a notion of much satisfaction to be found in the range of the meadow, and Baker's hill; and that beautiful females might inhabit those vast spaces, which appeared boundless in his eye. But having wandered 'til he was tired, and having met with nothing but weeds, and coarse grass, and solitude, he was glad to return to the poppies, and lettuces, and the other luxuries of the garden.'

One can be fanciful in a letter, especially in a letter to a young lady. 'Mrs Snooke's old tortoise' has assumed a new aspect, he is a social being, and part of the Entertainments of Selborne; another Hermit, as it were. During this same summer Miss Heckey Mulso,[20] after a visit to Selborne, wrote a letter in verse addressed to Timothy, 'which, with great labour, and pains, he answered in prose.' This is the autobiographical letter, or Pseudo-Timothy, from which we have the account of how he was bought at Chichester for half a crown. It tells, too, that when Timothy was weighed he was put in the grocer's scales, 'where I sprawl about to the great diversion of the shop-keeper's children,' and that it was a Selborne repartee, to quote from Dryden's Ode on Saint Cecilia's Day, how

> *Timotheus placed on high*
> *Amidst the tuneful quire,*
> *With flying fingers touched the lyre.*

The tortoise of the Pseudo-Timothy is a poor Punchinello of an animal, not comparable to the Timothy of the *Journals*. 'Timothy, contrary to his usual practice, lies out all day in the rain.' Yet a true likeness of Timothy should include at least an impression of Timothy's master; and a letter of 1786, poised between the objectivity of the *Journals* and the benign friskings of a host, vignettes the man and his reptile – the hot-blooded creature, for all its observations, christianity, powers of expression and knowledge of literature, seeming slightly embarrassed in confronting the impregnable mystery of what was going on, coldly and in silence, under that carapace. 'The summer-like weather of last Friday fetched out Timothy. There is somewhat very forlorn and abject in that creature's first appearance after a profound slumber of five months. When a man first rouses himself from a deep sleep, he does not look very wise: but nothing can be more squalid and stupid than our friend, when he first comes crawling out of his hybernacula; so that some farther lines of Dryden's Ode (written he supposes on purpose to ridicule tortoises) might well be applied to him:-

> *Has rais'd up his head,*
> *As awak'd from the dead:*
> *And amaz'd he stares around.*

'Written he supposes on purpose to ridicule tortoises.' Is it Gilbert White and Timothy or is it Monsieur Bergeret and Riquet? Not all the beef and the bullying, not all those deplorable importees from Hanover, can smother the French accent of eighteenth-century English culture.

The midsummer weather of 1787 again transported Timothy 'beyond the bounds of his usual gravity. He was missing for some days, but found at last near the upper malt-house.' The following summer he was 'shut-up in the brew-house to prevent an escape'; and I suspect that a similar confinement befell him in 1789, as the entry 'Timothy begins to travel about, & be restless' is not followed by any record of where he strayed to that time.

But ten years have passed since Timothy was brought in a box from Ringmer and buried in Selborne earth, and 'heaved up the mould, & walked twice down to the bottom of the long walk to survey the premises.' Though in the space of a decade affection may deepen, attention may wander, must wander; for while naturalists grow old Nature still replenishes, continually proffering new objects for investigation or challenging with familiar objects insufficiently observed. There are, for instance, trees. In 1790 Gilbert White began to correspond with Robert Marsham of Stratton Strawless in Norfolk, the arboriculturalist. The *Journal* for that year and the next contains many notes on trees, their girth and their age. There is the Fern Owl. Fern-owls haunted Mrs Snooke's orchard in autumn, they are no novelty; but having at last published the

Natural History of Selborne Gilbert White is maturing a treatise on the Fern-owl, or Churn-owl, or Eve-jar – a bird that Robert Marsham also keeps his eye on. 'Sir, you know the Fern-owl is one of the Spring Birds, and appears here as the latest comer. I used to have many in my Woods; but since the long and severe winter of '88 I have had very few. Is not this a presumptive proof of their torpidity? and that they were destroyed by the severity of the Season?' And always there are the Hirundines, the problem of their behaviour still unsolved. Do they lay themselves up and become torpid, do they fly off to winter 'under the warm and sheltery shores of Gibraltar and Barbary'? 'The cats brought in a dead house-martin from the stable. I was in hopes at first sight that it might have been in a torpid state; but it was decayed, & dry.' In April 1793 'Thomas Knight, a sober hind,' told how he had seen 'several Bank Martins playing in & out, and hanging before some nest-holes in a sand-hill, where these birds usually nestle. This incident confirms my suspicions, that this species of Hirundo is the first to be seen of any;' and gives great reason to suppose 'that they do not leave their wild haunts at all, but are secreted amidst the clefts, & caverns of those abrupt cliffs . . . and, like bats and flies, have been awaked by the influence of the Sun, amidst their secret latebrae, where they have spent the uncomfortable foodless months in a torpid state, & the profoundest of slumbers.' Five days after Thomas Knight's report Timothy comes forth, and weighs 6 lbs. $5^1/2$ oz. As a witness to profound slumbers Timothy could not be bettered; but he is only a tortoise, and in 'the dark but curious business of migration' his witness may be vain.

The spring of 1793, the last spring, unfolds. On May 2 it is 'sad, blowing, wintry weather. I think I saw a house-martin.' On May 3 'the fern-owl returns, & chatters in the hanger,' and the following day 'Timothy travels about the garden.' In the third week of May 'Timothy eats much,' and the white pippin blooms so abundantly that the weeding-woman swept up a bushel-basket of fallen petals, 'and yet that tree still seems covered with bloom.' But in spite of the blossom, it is a cold spring, 'so cold that no species of Hirundine makes any advance towards building, & breeding.' On the First of June 'Timothy is very voracious: when he can get no other food he eats grass in the walks.'

The spring had been cold and dry, and there was no sign of rain. In such a season a gardener naturally defends his greenstuff, his lettuces, Dutch or

Coss (the Dutch are the hardier), in the fruit-wall border. Apparently Timothy's friend Thomas had done something in the way of netting or fencing and Timothy, voraciously travelling about the garden, found himself foiled by Thomas's contrivances, and reduced to browsing the grassed walks. The drought continued into midsummer. When the rows of large kidney-beans were sown 'the ground was so hard that it required much labour to render it fit to receive the seed.' The Provence Roses bloomed, the Dame's Violets were very fine, the Ten Weeks Stocks, that had come into bloom a month earlier, were still in full beauty. But flowers are hardy gipsies compared with vegetables, and will flaunt their way through a drought that intimidates cabbages. That rather sinister entry about Timothy eating the grass in the walks is surely only incidental to a dry season.

But it is the last we hear of him. On June 5 Gilbert White made the last entry in his *Journal* and on June 26 he died; being buried, in accordance with his wish, not in the family vault but out of doors.

Timothy is said to have died in the spring of the following year. Perhaps the piety of family sentiment has ante-dated his demise, and the *ob. 1794* may be as much an intrusion of human caprice as the *nat. 1734* of the Pseudo-Timothy. The sailor who sold him to Mr Snooke, and who is, presumably, the original authority for that *nat. 1734* need not, I think, be taken very seriously. There is no reason why he should have known that Timothy was then about ten years old and every reason (since he was selling him) to assert it, for clearly Mr Snooke would prefer to buy a tortoise with a good expectation of life. On the other hand, between 1789 and 1793 Timothy's weight seems to have been going down, and this might betoken the decline of old age. The where of his death is better substantiated than the when: he must have died in the garden at Selborne, since his carapace was preserved, and is now in the British Museum of Natural History. Though Timothy is an exceptionally well-documented reptile he retains some tortoise-like privacy, he keeps his age to himself. 'And all the powerful Kings, and all the beautiful Queenes of this world, were but as a bed of flowers, some gathered at six, some at seaven, some at eight, all in one Morning, in respect of this Day.' And in respect of tortoises, if John Donne had preached a funeral sermon for a tortoise he might well have said that some complete sixty, some seventy, and some a hundred stanzas of their unobtrusive Hymn to the Sun.

JANE AUSTEN
(Supplement to *British Book News*, The British Council, 1951)

'Mrs. Allen,' said Catherine the next morning, 'will there be any harm in my calling on Miss Tilney to-day? I shall not be easy till I have explained every thing.'

'Go by all means, my dear; only put on a white gown; Miss Tilney always wears white.'

By a considerable leap up in the world Catherine will marry Miss Tilney's brother in the last chapter of *Northanger Abbey*; and without expatiating on the rent-roll of the estate, the number of horses in the stables, the family diamonds and family connexions, Jane Austen must indicate the social level into which that leap will carry Catherine Morland. *Miss Tilney always wears white.* Behind Miss Tilney she sketches in, not the park or the stables, but the laundry-court of Northanger Abbey, the family wash-tubs and the laundry-maids. Her five words do more than that. They illuminate Miss Tilney also. Not only is Miss Tilney so fortunately circumstanced that she can afford always to wear white, she does so from an inherent elegance of mind. At the lodgings in Milsom Street (for the conversation takes place in Bath) where Catherine will presently go to call on her, at the concerts and assemblies, Miss Tilney, unvexed by considerations of how the lawns and muslins will be washed and clear-starched and goffered, unassailed by temptations to appear in pink, will always wear white. With the development of the story we shall learn that she is a dutiful daughter to a taxing father, an affectionate sister, and ready to become an affectionate sister-in-law; but the gist has already been said. We know Miss Tilney.

That does not exhaust the content of this sentence. There is Mrs. Allen, who speaks it. *Mrs. Allen was one of that numerous class of females, whose society can raise no other emotion than surprise at there being any men in the world who could like them well enough to marry them.* The

79

surprising Mr. Allen's gout taking him to Bath, Mrs. Allen has invited Catherine to go with them; and Henry Tilney, conversing with Miss Morland's chaperon at the assembly, conquers her attention by relating his purchase of a dress length for his sister.

'I gave but five shillings a yard for it, and a true Indian muslin.'
Mrs. Allen was quite struck by his genius. 'Men commonly take so little notice of those things,' said she: 'I can never get Mr. Allen to know one of my gowns from another. You must be a great comfort to your sister, sir.'

Mrs. Allen is a completely silly woman, and a very incompetent chaperon; but bringing her milliner's mind to bear, she has realised that a young gentleman so knowing in muslins might be a great comfort to a wife as well as to a sister, and grasping the significance of Miss Tilney's whiteness she thinks that Miss Morland's chance of catching Henry Tilney will be much increased by a white gown.

Northanger Abbey was written in 1797-8. Fifty years earlier, a white gown dazzled the moist-eyed readers of Clarissa Harlowe. Bedford is writing to Lovelace of his visit to the sponging-house, where Clarissa has been imprisoned on a trumped-up charge of debt. *When I surveyed the room around, and the kneeling lady, sunk with majesty too in her white flowing robes (for she had not on a hoop) spreading the dark, though not dirty floor, and illuminating that horrid corner* . . . It is the last of Clarissa's misfortunes, she is near death and apotheosis, she has discarded her hoop: the *neat white brocade robe* of the previous paragraph is of an emblematical whiteness. It is so white that Richardson, who has minutely described every squalid detail of the room, suddenly flinches, and will not allow the floor to be dirty. Dark, but not dirty. Nothing must sully the plumage of that dying swan.

One after another, novelists are subjugated by the sentiment of a white gown.

'Tess!' said d' Urberville.
There was no answer. The obscurity was now so great that he could see absolutely nothing but a pale nebulousness at his feet, which represented the white muslin figure he had left upon the dead leaves.

But Miss Tilney's white gown is cut from a different substance. It is of the world, worldly. Jane Austen is a completely worldly artist: as worldly as Fra Angelico was heavenly, and working with similar conviction and serenity in the field of her choice. Indeed, to some exceedingly distant and transcending eye, so distant and transcending that manner was all it attended to, and matter insignificant, Jane Austen's representations of English country 'good society' at the turn of the eighteenth to nineteenth centuries might seem identically Angelical. Though in her case the saints and the angels are ladies and gentlemen, and the patriarchs are playing whist, and the act of martyrdom has been replaced by the act of marriage – to a worldly talent a theme of prime importance, since the world is peopled by it – both artists display the same unwearied attachment to a sameness of material, present their subjects in the same clear, undramatised lighting, and achieve an effect of untrammelled technical amiability by an underlying austerity of choice. *My Heroine shall not merely be wafted down an American river in a boat by herself, she shall cross the Atlantic in the same way, and never stop till she reaches Gravesend*—so Jane Austen derided the unworldly extravagance of Mary Brunton, authoress of *Self-Control*. With the like austerity of worldliness, her sense of the ludicrous was only allowed to play where she could be sure it was applicable; that is to say, on people in her own walk of life. There are no comic countrymen or comic servants in her novels. To a scribbling niece she wrote: *You are now collecting your people delightfully. 3 or 4 Families in a Country Village is the very thing to work on.* Three or four families, and a visitor coming into the neighbourhood, to quicken the pace of life a little; events and characters that allow for some speculation, but never stretch the bounds of probability; the vicious always subject to the schemes and contrivances of remaining in respectable society, and the virtuous unillumined by any special light; those in between these moderate extremes distinguished by inexhaustible variety of shading; a flower-like profusion of perfectly natural fools; and all these denizens of the Country Village (it is the greatest achievement of her worldly talent) consistently and vitally aware of each other – this is the material from which she made her six novels.

*   *   *

81

The state of life to which, at her birth in 1775, God was pleased to call her, was favourable to a talent for worldliness. Her father was a country clergyman, the rector of Steventon in the county of Hampshire. Though the children of a landowner might grow up knowing the world as no more than a periphery to the stables, though to the labourer's children it was something that went by in coach and gig and hearse beyond the hedge, the children of the parsonage could scarcely avoid knowledge of the world, of the shadings of social position, the indelible heraldry of manners and deportment, the long shadows of small events in a limited society. The world could be studied from Steventon Parsonage with scholarly detachment, as the circumstances of the Austen family did not put them at a disadvantage with their neighbours. Both Mr. and Mrs. Austen were of that class of lesser gentry which, with the growing culture and prosperity of the eighteenth century had become secure and estimable. Poorer than the indigenous Hampshire families of their acquaintance, they were rather better educated, and their connexions were creditable. There is no trace in Jane Austen's *Letters* of snobbishness or social anxiety. Her outward gaze on the world was alert, but cool, there is nothing of the goggle-eyed enthusiasm of the Burney *Diaries.* Her warmth, her admiration, is reserved for the family circle, and, above all, for her elder sister, Cassandra.

It was a family of six boys and two girls, both girls being of the younger half of the family. Jane accompanied Cassandra to two boarding-schools (at the first of these she nearly died of that characteristic eighteenth century malady a 'putrid fever') and came home from the second school when she was nine, still accompanying Cassandra. 'If Cassandra were going to have her head cut off, Jane would insist on sharing her fate', Mrs. Austen said. Thereafter, she remained at home, depending for her education, as many girls of that time did, on being a younger member of an educated family. She studied with Cassandra; in the evenings Mr. Austen read aloud, and needlework and domestic economy came by force of circumstance, for at that date a middle-class country household produced as well as consumed. In the matter of entertainment, too, a middle-class household had to be self-reliant. No doubt there was a good deal of 'improving conversation' – it was a fashion of the time – and there were also gayer diversions. In 1790, when Jane Austen was fourteen, there was a burst of private theatricals. The barn was fitted up as a theatre, and the leading lady in the performances was Parson Austen's niece, Eliza, Comtesse de Feuillide (her husband was guillotined in 1794, and later she married Jane Austen's brother Henry). Little comedies were a pastime at the Petit Trianon as well as in Parson Austen's barn; possibly the visiting cousin introduced them to the latter; if so, we may thank her for her part in Jane Austen's matchless dialogue. Management of dialogue is best learned through the ear, and the ear of a fourteen year old girl is sharply pricked. Miss Bates's tangled garrulity, Mr. Bennet's disillusioned tranquillity, keep their salt because to their author the word was a spoken, not a written, thing.

In this atmosphere of *Vive la bagatelle* and family high spirits she began to write. The three MSS. volumes of her *Juvenilia* are made up of short pieces, equipped with stately dedications. They bear no signs of perseverance (many of them are unfinished, though dedicated – probably the author began with the dedications) or of creative discomfort. One seems to overhear the comment, 'More of Jane's nonsense', and then a burst of laughter. All of them, plainly, were written with delight and *brio*. They have a ringing brilliancy, like the song of a wren. The Austens were a novel-reading family; and these early works show that their author had read more than the contemporary novels of romance and sentiment. Her satiric manner, with its sleek absurdity, its reduction of the sublime to the ridiculous, certainly stems from Fielding; its subjects are some variety or other of pretentiousness: pretentiousness of sentiment, of refinement, of pomposity. *Poor Mrs. Burnaby is beyond measure afflicted. She sighs every now and then, that is about once a week.*

Their dates, given or deduced, run from 1790 to 1793. But they leave a residual impression of being the work of a much younger writer. In spite of the technical skill and the demure management of style in which *clichés* are used to convey the writer's contempt for *clichés*, they remain callow, because they are perfectly heartless. They are more like the writing of a brilliant child than the writing of an adolescent. Family entertainment, and the influence of the family circle, may be the reason; but there is another possibility: that the mask of a brilliant child is held before the face of a young girl because the young girl has not, so to speak, found her expression.

Three years after the latest of these pieces of 'Jane's nonsense' she was writing *Pride and Prejudice*.

When the B.B.C. produced *Pride and Prejudice* as a Sunday serial, the part of the author was spoken as though she were a mature woman. It is hard to remember that she was a girl of twenty-one. But if *Pride and Prejudice* is to be appreciated as well as enjoyed, the age of the author should be kept in mind, since it deals with a theme that is peculiarly a concern of youth: the anguish and embarrassment felt by those who realise that their parents are making fools of themselves. Mrs. Bennet is a gross fool and Mr. Bennet a fastidious one; between them, their eldest daughter nearly loses the young man who loves her and whom she loves; their youngest daughter is seduced by a rascal with sufficient good sense to be induced to marry her only by a large sum of money; and Elizabeth, the heroine, who has refused an offer of marriage practically extorted by her personal charm from a man who cannot endure her family (and whose manifest inability to endure them has prejudiced her against him) realises her love for him at the moment when her sister's disgrace makes it highly improbable that any of Mr. Bennet's daughters will find a respectable match. It is a story in which the sensible characters are at the mercy of the silly ones, and further, at the mercy of their own sillier impulses. Darcy's pride and Elizabeth's prejudice imperil their mating quite as much as Mrs. Bennet's matchmaking, Lydia's headstrong vanity, and Mr. Collins's cousinly contribution of fatuity. By an ingenious stroke, the most monumental fool in the book, the self-important and domineering Lady Catherine de Bourgh, brings about the marriage by being determined to prevent it.

Elizabeth's prejudice is forgiven her by every reader (and it is clear that the author, with her own strong family attachments, does not consider it very blameable). Darcy's pride is another matter. The fact that in the latter part of the story he behaves with magnanimity and modesty is not allowed to atone for his behaviour at the ball, where he stalks about and will not dance with Elizabeth. Indeed, he is at odds with the rest of the book, for he is the only character where the author falters in her worldly wisdom. Young persons who have recently come of age see mankind divided into three groups: those younger than themselves, who are children; those over thirty, who are elderly; those between twenty and thirty, who are grown up. An older author would have remembered to make Darcy more perceptibly a young man, whose shyness and youthful censoriousness are in alarmed revolt at a society to which he is not accustomed. This, I think, is how Jane Austen conceived him, and his development from theory to practice is an essential part of the narrative; but her failure to establish his youthfulness splits him into halves: the unamiable Darcy of the opening, the amiable Darcy of the close.

Pride and Prejudice was completed in August 1797. Two months later, she began to write *Sense and Sensibility*. Some years before, she had begun a story in letter form, called *Elinor and Marianne*. The names, the pair of sisters, and presumably their contrasted characters, reappear in *Sense and Sensibility*, but there cannot be much else, since the Elinor and Marianne of *Sense and Sensibility*, being always together, have no reason to correspond.

Because they have chiming titles and were written within a year of each other, *Pride and Prejudice* and *Sense and Sensibility* are sometimes regarded as a pair of novels. In fact, they have nothing in common except that in both of them Jane Austen availed herself of a device of the time: that the leading figures of a story should exemplify a ruling passion or principle. She used it as no more than a spring-board: pride and prejudice are only elements in Darcy and Elizabeth, and though sense distinguishes Elinor Dashwood and sensibility her sister Marianne, the contrast is between two ways of behaving rather than between two ways of feeling. In *Pride and Prejudice*, however, the 'ruling passion' device is used for many of the lesser figures: in particular, Mr. Collins and Lady Catherine de Bourgh are so consistently 'characteristic' that they would not seem much out of place in a Ben Jonson Comedy of Humours. This glaze of 'characterisation' that contributes much to the effect of brilliant accomplishment in the first novel, is absent from the second, where the character drawing is less assured, but more ambitious. *Sense and Sensibility* is not an attempt to repeat a successful achievement; it is an attempt at something different. Despite its weak passages and occasional lack of elasticity, if it is to be paired with another of Jane Austen's novels, it must be with her last: *Persuasion*.

There is not much in *Sense and Sensibility* that one can quote; but there is a great deal that one can remember, and one thing that is unforgettable. A story of two sisters, both, apparently, destined to lose the exceedingly different young men whom they love with such exceedingly different manifestations of attachment, could easily lapse into a morality, a

Hogarthian record of the discreet and the foolish virgin; and the tendency of the narrative to split in half is increased by Marianne's Willoughby stealing all the limelight from Elinor's Edward Ferrars – who is so nearly a nincompoop that her sense must be called in question for falling in love with him, however sensibly she conducts herself afterwards. Two things hold the narrative together: one, the process of a hundred feather-like details by which the reader becomes convinced of the intimate affection, the two cherries on one stalk relationship between the sisters; the other, the structural contrivance by which, after a sustained crescendo of emotion, the climax of feeling occurs in a scene between Elinor, the representative of sense, and Willoughby, who, loving Marianne with a sensibility equal to her own, has yet jilted her. This encounter, so unforeseen, so skilfully led up to, and developed with such unwavering control, is the unforgettable thing in *Sense and Sensibility*.

The third novel, the last of the group of three which Jane Austen wrote in her early twenties, is *Northanger Abbey* [21]. It is hard not to think of *Northanger Abbey* as a point of repose after, if not a corrective to, *Sense and Sensibility*. Marianne Dashwood, whose sister in real life is Dorothy Wordsworth, a genuine romantic who loves almost to madness, is followed by Catherine Morland, bewitched by false romanticism, who by falling in love is freed into real life. Henry Tilney, who releases her from her imaginary castle, is Jane Austen's first successful full-length of that difficult subject: a young man who is both engaging and respectable; till then, she had been happier with her *mauvais sujets*. In Henry Tilney she repeats something of Darcy's dilemma: the young man attracted to a girl in a station of life inferior to his own and moving in a company very much inferior; but Henry Tilney has a grace and sophistication that Darcy lacks; it is easier for him to fall in love without seeming to make a favour of it. His father, under the impression that Catherine is an heiress, thinks she will do nicely for a younger son, and invites her to Northanger Abbey. To be staying in an Abbey, however disappointingly modernised and commodious, inflames Catherine's romanticism. Bent on finding skeletons and unravelling mysteries, she makes a sorry fool of herself; and Henry, whose first feeling for her did not go much beyond a smiling acceptance of her infatuation and his father's intentions, finds, having fished her out of her scrape, that he is genuinely attached to her.

Northanger Abbey is the only novel in which Jane Austen allows herself an extra-narrative purpose: to make game of the 'Horrid Mystery' school of fiction. It is the only novel, too, in which she emerges from her private life as narrator, and comments on the narrative. But her most devastating stroke at the 'romantics' is implicit in the development of the story: Catherine's stupefaction when General Tilney, whom she had thrillingly enjoyed as a gothic monster, whose Mrs. Tilney had either been murdered by him, or was kept in a dungeon and fed at night, breaks out as a contemporary monster, and sends her home in a post-chaise because he has discovered that she is not an heiress at all.

* * *

'Sir, I have in my possession a manuscript novel, comprising 3 volumes, about the length of Miss Burney's *Evelina*.' So begins a letter to a publisher called Cadell, written by Mr. Austen, and dated 1 November 1797. The novel was presumably *Pride and Prejudice*. The offer to send it for inspection was rejected by return of post. Mr. Austen inquired no further. He was growing old. In 1801 he gave up the living of Steventon and retired to Bath.

During the next eight years Jane Austen lived a town life, first at Bath, then, after her father's death in 1805, at Southampton. During those eight years, she achieved nothing. It would seem that in 1803 she essayed to write again. An unfinished novel and a fair copy of an earlier work are both on paper with the water-mark of that year; and in 1803 *Northanger Abbey* was sold to a publisher called Crosbie for £10. The negotiations were carried out through her brother Henry. Henry, who must be considered the first 'Janeite', may have thought that publication would encourage composition; if so, his kind intentions miscarried, for Crosbie swallowed the MS. and did nothing. The fair copy of this date is *Lady Susan*, a short novel in letter form, and a lion in the path of those persons who would call Jane Austen charming, soothing, refreshing, etc. G. H. Lewes, when he recommended Charlotte Brontë to 'follow the counsel which shines out of Miss Austen's mild eyes' was unaware of *Lady Susan*, where Miss Austen's eyes are those of a hunting cat. Lady Susan Vernon is a high-bred Tartuffe: insinuating, malicious, depraved, and merciless; her victims are either willing dupes or weakly resentful dupes; her daughter, whom she intends to discard in a marriage of convenience, is shown as the fact of the fictional oppressed heroine: insipidly well-meaning and weakly reckless; and when in the upshot Lady Susan marries the dolt she designed for a son-in-law, and the young man she has excited into loving her is *talked, flattered and finessed* into transferring his affections to her daughter, no more emotion is aroused than by a change of partners in a quadrille.

When *Lady Susan* was first written is unknown. In harshness of plot and nakedness of satire it looks back to the *Juvenilia*; in controlled grimness it looks forward to a masterpiece never written – a masterpiece that even without her untimely death, the intervention of nineteenth century optimism might well have made impossible. Whatever the date of its composition, it suggests that Eliza de Feuillide had previously mettled her cousin by an introduction to Mme de Merteuil in *Les Liaisons Dangereuses*. That it was considered as a possible next in line to *Northanger Abbey* seems out of the question; but gravelled authors know the stimulus that can come from the mere act of fair-copying, the sense of writing resumed; so probably the fair copy of *Lady Susan* was undertaken as a preliminary to the novel that was begun and never finished.

In *The Watsons* (the title is editorial: the MS. is a first draft, untitled and unchaptered) it is plain that she intended a full-length novel, and began it with her characters securely in mind. *The first winter assembly in the town of D. in Surrey was to be held on Tuesday, October 13th, and it was generally expected to be a very good one. A long list of county families was confidently run over as sure of attending, and sanguine hopes were entertained that the Osbornes themselves would be there. The Edwards's invitation to the Watsons followed of course.* Such an opening, that in three sentences establishes the *milieu* of the story, and the relative social standing of the three families chiefly concerned, is Jane Austen in her perfection of worldliness. The sanguine hopes raised by such an invitation are not substantiated; the assembly is not a very good one. One must allow for the awkwardness of a first draft, especially in the case of Jane Austen, who, in her own words, *lop't and crop't*; one must allow for stiffness, straggling, the tendency of subsidiary characters to bush out and smother the main characters; these are present in *The Watsons*, but only to a small extent, and her technical serenity flows over them but as the story extends, one becomes conscious of a failure – as opposed to faults: a failure of impetus. The story goes on, but does not become airborne. This is reflected in the startling intensity of certain passages where the narrative gets going: Emma dancing with the little boy at the ball, Lord Osborne's afternoon call, and Tom Musgrave, a gentleman's hanger-on, masking his social incertitude by a show of bluff eccentricity, who when his grandées remove the light of their countenances from the ballroom announces his brave decision to retire with a barrel of oysters *and be famously snug*. Tom Musgrave is enough to give the lie, once and for all, to the people who say that Jane Austen cannot 'do' men. How could she bear to leave him?

Her nephew, James Edward Austen-Leigh, looking back from 1870, hazarded his guess 'that the author became aware of the evil of having placed her heroine too low, in such a position of poverty and obscurity as, though not necessarily connected with vulgarity, has a sad tendency to degenerate into it; and therefore, like a singer who has begun on too low a note, she discontinued the strain'. This is scarcely tenable; authors as clear-headed as she do not wander into the wrong *tessitura*. But there is such a thing as not being in the vein; there are singers who, in certain circumstances, cannot sing. It is said that when Jane Austen heard of the family decision to remove to Bath, she fainted away. Fifteen years later, in *Persuasion*, she described Anne Elliot, confronted with a similar decision: *tho' dreading the possible heats of September in all the white glare of Bath, and grieving to forego all the influence so sweet and so sad of the autumnal months in the country. . . .* While it is debatable how far she was an autobiographical novelist, there are some matters in which all novelists are autobiographical, and one of these is physical pleasure. All Jane Austen's sympathetic characters take pleasure in the country. Little may be said of it: only Marianne Dashwood expresses that pleasure with eloquence: but who could doubt the sincerity of Anne Elliot's farewells to Kellynch, who could imagine Mr. Knightley glad to go to town? And if Anne Elliot had been a novelist, she might have grieved as much again to forgo the leisure for contemplation, the uninterrupting fostering climate of a native countryside.

Cassandra, from whom her sister had no secrets, destroyed all the more intimate of Jane Austen's letters to her. Even so, truth slides out of them here and there. About to quit Steventon, Jane Austen tries to console herself by looking on Bath as a place to make excursions from[22]. *The prospect of spending future summers by the sea or in Wales is very delightful* ; and, when her brother Henry is visiting his family in Bath, *he talks of the rambles we took together last Summer.*

One of these rambles – recalled for use in *Persuasion* – was to Lyme Regis. On another such – possibly at Teignmouth in Devon – Jane Austen had her only serious affair of the heart. This seaside stranger who fell in love with her, and whom she might have married, only exists in family recollections of what Aunt Cassandra told, long after her sister's death. According to these recollections, he was a clergyman, and died soon after their meeting. If this is so, it is another example of Jane insisting on execution if Cassandra had her head cut off, for Cassandra had authentically been betrothed to a Revd. Mr. Thomas Fowle, who died of yellow fever in the West Indies in 1797. It seems reasonable to suppose that this is a family conflate between the stories of two maiden aunts. An earlier approach to matrimony has sharper outlines. In 1802 Cassandra and Jane, who were visiting at Steventon, where the living was now held by their brother James, paid a further visit to a neighbouring county family. Early one morning they reappeared at the parsonage, 'unexpected and in agitation'. On the previous day Harris Bigg-Wither, a son of the family, had proposed to Jane Austen, and she had accepted him. During the night, she began to doubt: whatever his merits and recommendations – and a home in Hampshire must have been powerful among them – she found she could not have him, and fled.

Mr. Austen's death left his widow poorly off. She and her daughters quitted Bath, and settled at Southampton in a joint household with Francis Austen (who was in the Navy) and his wife. There, Jane Austen began to develop her talent for being an aunt (she is recorded as having been a particularly agreeable aunt): and there, in October 1808, arrived two nephews from Winchester, who needed all her kindness. They were the sons of Edward Austen, and their mother had just died.

Edward Austen, Jane Austen's third brother, had been adopted as heir by some wealthy relations, who sent him on the Grand Tour, married him advantageously, and left him two properties, Godmersham in Kent and Chawton in Hampshire. Though adoption had taken him out of the family circle, Edward Austen seems to have retained a good deal of Austen family-heartedness. Cassandra and Jane were often at Godmersham Park, visiting alternately; and as we owe many of Jane Austen's letters to these separations, one must feel grateful to Edward Austen for being so hospitable. The fact remains, however, that when his mother and sister fell on hard times, he did nothing for them until after his own wife's death. This may have been due to a natural anxiety to provide for his own children – he had a family of eleven; or his wife may not have shared her husband's family affection for two unmarried sisters not quite of her own world. Fanny, the eldest daughter of this marriage, may have been echoing a maternal voice when she wrote, looking back on her youth from the mid-Victorian eminence, 'Yes my love it is very true that Aunt Jane from various circumstances was not so *refined* as she ought to have been from her *talent*, and if she had lived so years later she would have been in many respects more suitable to *our* more refined tastes. They were not rich & the people around with whom they chiefly mixed, were not at all high bred. . . . Both the Aunts (Cassandra & Jane) were brought up in the most complete ignorance of the World & its ways (I mean as to fashion, &c.) and if it had not been for Papa's marriage which brought them into Kent . . . they would have been, tho' not less clever and agreable in themselves, very much below par as to good Society and its ways.' Be this as it may, in the autumn of 1808, Edward Austen, the widower, offered his mother the choice of two small houses, one on his property in Kent, the other at Chawton. They chose the latter, and in 1809 moved to Chawton Cottage. And immediately Jane Austen began to write again.

*   *   *

She meant to; she was sure of her intention. Before the move took place she wrote, under an alias, to reclaim the MS. of *Northanger Abbey* from the do-nothing Crosbie. It is the letter of a woman who knows her own mind, and is sure of the value of what she is reclaiming. With the intention to write, went an intention to publish. It may have occurred to her that the author of a published work is in a stronger position to write others, or it may have been that she felt she must get her first brood out of the nest before she hatched again. This seems the likelier, as she began by revising her first two novels, and the addition of Scott's poems to Marianne Dashwood's reading shows her careful to bring them up to date. *Northanger Abbey*, making game of an entirely out-moded school of fiction, could not be brought up to date, and was put by, though later on she drafted a foreword to it, saying, *The public are entreated to bear in mind that thirteen years have passed since it was finished.* In fact, it was not published until after her death.

In 1811 *Sense and Sensibility*, by a Lady, was published at Jane Austen's own expense. *Pride and Prejudice* followed in the New Year of 1813. In a letter she tells of getting her first copy of *Pride and Prejudice, my own darling child*, and goes on to say: *Now I will try to write of something else, & it shall be a complete change of subject – ordination.* This threat was not substantiated. Ordination is not the main issue of *Mansfield Park*, though enough is made of it, perhaps, to account for the fact that Mr. Gladstone found this the most enjoyable of her books. Of all Jane Austen's unthematic works, *Mansfield Park* is the least thematic, and the most completely unified. Its characters are presented so convincingly that they are sufficient in themselves to hold the reader's attention – what happens to them is of less interest than how they will adapt themselves to circumstances. Whether Edmund Bertram, however fascinated by Mary Crawford, will hold to his purpose and go into the church; whether Sir Thomas will come back from Antigua in time to frustrate the private theatricals; whether Henry Crawford's intention of *making a small hole in Fanny Price's heart* will lead him into a real attachment; whether Fanny will wear the chain or the necklace at the ball, accept or refuse Henry Crawford, hold out or give way under the strain of her exile – the suspense is not merely to know what will happen, but how it will happen, and what will happen then. And when the house of Bertram is smitten in the midriff of its respectability, when Maria runs away from her husband with Henry Crawford and Julia elopes, the quickening of action only quickens the reader's curiosity as to how everybody involved will take it.

On the surface, *Mansfield Park* is less ironical than the previous novels. The irony lies beneath, in the fact that it is the good and guileless Fanny who brings calamity on the family that adopted her. *Had Fanny accepted Mr. Crawford, this could not have happened.* This reflection, so irreproachably true, Jane Austen gives to the odious Mrs. Norris; but leaves it to the reader (*I do not write for such dull elves*, she light-handedly misquoted, *As have not a great deal of ingenuity themselves*) to reflect that if it had not been for Mrs. Norris's own penchant for contriving good deeds at other people's expense, Maria would not have been married to a husband she could not respect, nor Fanny settled at Mansfield Park, to meet, and charm, Henry Crawford. Mrs. Norris is Jane Austen's only creative expression of hate; other of her characters are unpleasant, despicable, disagreeable – but still not, in the eyes of their author and creator, damned. Mrs. Norris is indubitably damned. The whole force of Jane Austen's condemnation falls on this prating, bustling, insensitive skinflint; and with the coolness of perfect hate, she shows her as just the sort of person who on a slight acquaintance is considered a notable, amusing old body, and uses her to furnish the comic relief.

Hate is a serious passion; and *Mansfield Park* is a serious novel. Even at their most innocent or most frivolous, its characters recall certain Conversation Piece figures, strolling, or drinking tea on a sunlit lawn; behind them is the family mansion; and behind the family mansion hangs the purplish dusk of an impending storm. There are no such skies in *Emma*, the novel that followed. The storms in *Emma* brisk out of April skies: everybody gets a drenching, and immediately the sun comes out again. *I am going to take a heroine whom no one but myself will much like*, Jane Austen announced. One does not make these excluding announcements unless one is already in love: Jane Austen was in love with Emma Woodhouse, and Emma Woodhouse has been loved by most of Jane Austen's readers ever since.

The portrait painter can convey charm, that mysterious quality, objectively; he delineates it in the turn of the head on the shoulders, he slides it with a stroke of the brush into the corner of an eye or the tip of a nose; the writer cannot go to it so straightforwardly – at any rate, he should not; he must convey charm obliquely, refracted by the words and actions of the surrounding characters. It is by means of Pierre and Prince Andrew, and Denissov, and Maria Dimitrievna, and the Little Uncle that Tolstoi enchants us with Natasha, and Emma is charming by the same method. Like Natasha, she has the elasticity of perfect health, the robustness of the rose. Such constitutions are not prone to second thoughts. Affectionately disposed towards everybody, and untouched by sexual love, Emma at twenty-one is sure of her future. Her elder sister being married to the younger Mr. Knightley of Donwell Abbey, she will remain Miss Woodhouse of Hartfield, the darling companion of her gentle sickly father, the natural first lady of Highbury society. She will always be busy, and

93

happy, and the other Mr. Knightley (who is unmarried and must remain so, for the good of his nephews) will always be at hand, to talk to her father and be talked to by her. Meanwhile, there is the happiness of others to see to: there is Harriet Smith, whose happiness would be so much increased by encouraging young Mr. Elton to make her the mistress of Highbury Rectory. Emma devotes herself to this project. But the encouraged Mr. Elton has other views. *'Miss Smith! – I never thought of Miss Smith in the whole course of my existence . . . Miss Smith, indeed! – Oh! Miss Woodhouse! who can think of Miss Smith, when Miss Woodhouse is near!'*

The candour that left her unconscious of Mr. Elton's intentions, renders her equally blind to Frank Churchill's lack of them. When it becomes known that his pursuit of her was merely a pretext to be in the same neighbourhood as Jane Fairfax, to whom he is privately engaged, every one is deeply concerned on Emma's behalf – everyone but Emma. The vocation to remain Miss Woodhouse, though not forbidding a spirited flirtation, had preserved her from any serious inclination. It is the luckless Harriet she feels for; for Harriet had confided a romantic secret devotion, and though she named no name, it could only be for Frank Churchill. Emma had encouraged her to hope – and now must tell her to hope no longer. But Harriet echoes Mr. Elton. *'Mr. Frank Churchill, indeed! I do not know who would ever look at him in the company of the other.'*

The other is Mr. Knightley. *'Ah! je vois clair dans mon coeur!'* Emma, so hopefully misunderstanding other people's hearts, suddenly and painfully understands her own. *Why was it so much worse that Harriet should be in love with Mr. Knightley, than with Frank Churchill? Why was the evil so dreadfully increased by Harriet's having some hope of a return? It darted through her, with the speed of an arrow, that Mr. Knightley must marry no one but herself!*

Of all Jane Austen's novels, *Emma* most fully conveys the exhilaration of a happy writer. As the arabesques of the plot curl more intricately, as the characters emerge and display themselves, and say the very things they would naturally say, the reader – better still, the re-reader – feels a collaborating glow. Above all, it excels in dialogue: not only in such *tours de force* as Miss Bates being grateful for apples, Mrs. Elton establishing her importance when she pays her call at Hartfield, but in the management of dialogue to reveal the unsaid; as when Mr. John Knightley's short-tempered good sense insinuates a comparison with his brother's dryer wit and deeper tolerance; or as in the conversation between Mr. Knightley and Emma about Frank Churchill, whom neither of them then know except by repute: Emma is sure he will be all that he should be, Mr. Knightley's best expectation is *'well grown and good-looking, with smooth, plausible manners'* – and by the time they have done, it is plain that Emma is not prepared to fall in love with Frank Churchill, and that Mr. Knightley has been, for a long time, deeply and uncomfortably in love with Emma.

By November 1815, when Jane Austen was staying with her brother Henry in London seeing *Emma* through the printer's hands, *Sense and Sensibility* was in a second edition, *Pride and Prejudice* in a third, and *Mansfield Park* (published in 1814) sold out with a second edition in contemplation. Her anonymity was lost in something like celebrity – Henry had been too proud not to boast a little of his kinship to the *Lady* of the title page. Among her admirers was the Prince Regent. Learning that she was in town he sent her an invitation to visit the library of Carlton House; and during her visit the librarian, a Mr. Clarke, intimated that His Royal Highness would be very willing to receive the dedication of her next book. H.R.H. was modestly content to suggest nothing beyond a dedication page. Mr. Clarke's patronage was more searching. He hoped that she would 'delineate in some future work the life, character and enthusiasm of a clergyman', and 'describe him burying his own mother – as I did'. When this hope was gently quashed, he wrote again to say that 'any historical romance illustrative of the august House of Cobourg, would just now be very interesting', and that it might be dedicated to the Prince Leopold, to whom he had just been appointed chaplain. Replying, Jane Austen softened the refusal by congratulations on his appointment, and added hopes that it might lead to something still better: *In my opinion, the service of a court can hardly be too well paid, for immense must be the sacrifice of time and feeling involved.*

'You judge very properly,' said Mr. Bennet, *'and it is happy for you that you possess the talent of flattering with delicacy. May I ask whether these pleasing attentions proceed from the impulse of the moment, or are the result of previous study?'* It must have pleased Jane Austen to find Mr. Collins appearing in real life and promoted from a Lady Catherine to a Prince Leopold.

Toadies are a steadfast type; but the twenty years that had gone by since *Pride and Prejudice* had brought many changes, notably in what was expected of women. Under the growing influence of the Evangelical religious revival, women lost much of their liberty of speech and of action: they could assert themselves less; on the other hand, they were allowed to feel more. In *Emma*, Jane Austen chose a heroine who no one would much like but herself. In *Persuasion*, the novel that followed, she complied with the taste of a new generation. To a representative of that generation, her niece Fanny (of the subsequent, 'Yes my love, it is very true' epistle), she wrote, *You may perhaps like the Heroine, as she is almost too good for me.* Perhaps it was less the quantity than the quality of the goodness that provoked this reservation. Elinor Dashwood was good, and prudent, too; Fanny Price was both good and dutiful; but it is impossible to imagine either of them giving way on a point of conscience or a point of heart, as Anne Elliot of *Persuasion* did, submitting to family displeasure and prudent counsels from a family friend, and breaking off her engagement with Frederick Wentworth because he was poor and must depend on his own merits to make a career in the Navy. At the opening of the novel, Anne is twenty-seven, sad, vainly wiser, and a thing of nought in her family except when she can be of use to them. It would be expiation enough; but Frederick Wentworth reappears. . . . *'he said, "You were so altered he should not have known you again".'* Resentment had kept her alive and lovely in his mind; but finding her so unlike the girl who had jilted him, his resentment vanishes, and he feels no more than an acknowledging pity for the actual Anne. With Anne thus doubly lost to him, *He had a heart for either of the Miss Musgroves, if they could catch it; a heart, in short, for any pleasing young woman who came in his way, excepting Anne Elliot.* Anne, committed to a useful visit to the sister whose husband is brother to the Miss Musgroves, is compelled to exchange the passive regret of a lifetime for active loss and mortification. Taking part in the Musgrove gaieties, the rambles and excursions, during which Captain Wentworth's heart is caught by Louisa Musgrove, she sees Louisa loved for strength of will and assertiveness – the very qualities she had failed in. But when Louisa's strong will to be jumped down the Cobb at Lyme Regis involves her in an accident, and Captain Wentworth, mistaking concussion for dying, cries out, *'Is there no one to help me?'* only the negligible Anne shows presence of mind and self-control.

Jane Austen writes of Anne Elliot with a solicitude not called out by any of her other characters. They fall into their scrapes and misfortunes, and their uncomfortable remorses are described with a pardoning understanding, but without much change of voice. In the case of Anne Elliot – whose only fault has been a submissiveness which by new standards of female behaviour was praiseworthy, not blameworthy – there is a degree of sympathy that almost amounts to special pleading. This makes *Persuasion* both the most compelling and the weakest of Jane Austen's novels. Every stage of Anne Elliot's transition from resignation to fortitude, and every detail of her relations with Frederick Wentworth, is registered as though with Anne's own sensibility; elsewhere, the narrative is thin and almost perfunctory. Mrs. Clay, and Lady Russell, and both the Walter Elliots, and the barefacedly expedient Mrs. Smith are shadowy figures. One sees them, in fact, through Anne's eyes. They do not hold her attention, and they do not hold ours. If Anne Elliot is *almost too good*, nothing of that sort can be urged against Frederick Wentworth – the limberest and best-studied of all Jane Austen's heroes. His recoil from the dead-alive Anne Elliot who has replaced the girl he angrily remembered, the candour and realism with which he sets off to find a new love, his affectionate animal enthusiasm when he supposes her to be found in Louisa Musgrove, are part and parcel of a vigorous character that has learned adaptability in a dangerous profession. Without a breath of *avast* or *ahoy*, he is psychologically a sailor. Sailor on shore enough to find that his heart has returned to Anne at the very moment when he is confidently expected to offer marriage to the convalescent Louisa, he sails out of the predicament by going to stay with a brother in Shropshire – a strategy justified in the event, and convincing one that he had been an excellent commander of the *Asp* and the *Laconia*. Jane Austen, with two brothers in the Navy, loved a sailor; bringing this one to his mooring, she parts from him with an affectionate dig in the ribs. *'Edward . . . enquired after you very particularly; asked even if you were personally altered, little suspecting that to my eye you could never alter.'*

If *Persuasion* is a work of unequal accomplishment, in one point it is uniquely satisfactory to admirers of Jane Austen: it shows her as her own critic. It had been finished, but she was dissatisfied with its winding up. Discarding the whole of a penultimate chapter, she wrote in its stead the two chapters before the last of the text as we know it. The cancelled chapter happened to be preserved, and is printed in the Austen-Leigh *Memoir*. The difference between it and the final text goes far beyond revision or variant; it is a complete re-making. Incidentally, it shows Jane Austen too modest in her estimate of her technique – *the little bit (two Inches long) of Ivory on which I work with so fine a brush, as produces little effect after much labour*. That the brush was fine, no one can deny; but in the light of this textual evidence, it is equally undeniable that the mind directing it was firmly aware of the difference between well-enough and well, and bold in establishing it.

A last book contains a valedictory significance that in most cases the author did not intend. The fact that *Persuasion* (a posthumous publication) is slightly out of line with the novels that preceded it, and that before its completion Jane Austen was already in poor health, has led some critics to treat it as a sort of swan-song – pensive because its writer was pensive too – and others to see it as the first example of a new manner which she would have pursued if it had not been for her untimely death. These interpretations are not supported by the last piece of writing she undertook, an unfinished untitled novel that we know as *Sanditon*. *Sanditon* is a work of great gusto, totally objective, and promising to be more akin to *Emma* or the unfinished *Watsons* than to any other of her novels. It shows no sign of declining health, or of farewelling the world, for it is conceived on a large scale, with a great number of characters, and its only recognition of sickness is a spirited and derisive study of the genus *malade imaginaire*. Had she lived to finish it, no doubt she would have toned down some of the rawer absurdities and an almost girlish enjoyment of fools; but no amount of revision could alter the conception of the book, etherealise Mr. Parker's feverish promotion of a seedling watering-place and Miss Diana Parker's twin passions for being at the point of death and being devotedly busy for the good of others, or make its chief woman, Charlotte, anything but an exemplar of slightly satirical common sense.

The first page of the MS. is dated *Jan. 27, 1817*, and *March 18* is noted where the narrative breaks off. By then, she was seriously ill. Two months later she went with Cassandra to be under the care of a doctor in Winchester. There, on July 18, she died in Cassandra's arms. Her body lies in Winchester Cathedral[23].

* * *

Two years later, another figure of English literature was in Winchester, observing that the side streets were *excessively maiden-ladylike; the doorsteps always fresh from the flannel*, and feeling *all the influence so sweet and so sad of the autumnal months in the country*, that Anne Elliot had grieved to forego, that Jane Austen knew no more. 'How beautiful the season is now', he wrote to a friend. 'How fine the air – a temperate sharpness about it.' It is as though John Keats were inditing the first, the most discriminating, of all subsequent praises of Jane Austen's prose; but it was the *Ode to Autumn* that he had in mind.

THE BOOK OF MERLYN
(Prologue to *The Book of Merlyn* by T. H. White, 1977)

The dream, like the one before it, lasted about half an hour. In the last three minutes of the dream some fishes, dragons and such-like ran hurriedly about. A dragon swallowed one of the pebbles, but spat it out.

In the ultimate twinkling of an eye, far tinier in time than the last millimetre on a six-foot rule, there came a man. He split up the one pebble which remained of all that mountain with blows; then made an arrow-head of it, and slew his brother.

The Sword in the Stone
Chapter 18, original version

'My father made me a wooden castle big enough to get into, and he fixed real pistol barrels beneath its battlements to fire a salute on my birthday, but made me sit in front the first night – that deep Indian night – to receive the salute, and I, believing I was to be shot, cried.'

Throughout his life[24] White was subject to fears: fears from without – a menacing psychopathic mother, the prefects at Cheltenham College 'rattling their canes,' poverty, tuberculosis, public opinion; fears from within – fear of being afraid, of being a failure, of being trapped. He was afraid of death, afraid of the dark. He was afraid of his own proclivities, which might be called vices: drink, boys, a latent sadism. Notably free from fearing God, he was basically afraid of the human race. His life was a running battle with these fears, which he fought with courage, levity, sardonic wit, and industry. He was never without a project, never tired of learning, and had a high opinion of his capacities.

This high opinion was shared by his teachers at the University of Cambridge. When tuberculosis tripped him in his second year, a group of dons made up a sum of money sufficient to send him to Italy for a year's convalescence. He took to Italy like a duck to water, learned the language, made some low friends, studied pension life, and wrote his first novel, *They Winter Abroad.* The inaugurator of the convalescent fund recalled: '. . . he returned in great form, determined to have the examiner's blood in Part II; and sure enough in 1929 he took a tearing First Class with Distinction.'

In 1932, on a Cambridge recommendation, he was appointed head of the English Department at Stowe School.

It was a position of authority under an enlightened headmaster who allowed him ample rope. His pupils still remember him, some for the stimulus of his teaching, others for the sting of his criticism, others again for extracurriculum rambles in search of grass snakes. He learned to fly, in order to come to terms with a fear of falling from high places, and to think rather better of the human race by meeting farm labourers at the local inn. After a couple of years he tired of Stowe, and decided on no evidence that his headmaster meant to get rid of him. With poverty a fear to be reckoned with, he constructed two potboilers and compiled another. An Easter holiday fishing in rain and solitude on a Highland river showed him what he really wanted - to write in freedom, to land a book of his own as well as a salmon.

At midsummer 1936 he gave up his post and rented a gamekeeper's cottage at Stowe Ridings on the Stowe estate. The compiled potboiler, made up of extracts from his fishing, hunting, shooting, and flying diaries and called *England Have My Bones*, sold so well that its publisher undertook to pay him £200 a year against a yearly book.

The gamekeeper's cottage stood among woodlands – a sturdy Victorian

structure without amenities. It was by lamplight that White pulled from a
shelf the copy of the *Morte d'Arthur* he had used for the essay on Malory
he submitted for the English tripos, Part I. Then he had been concerned
with the impression he would make on the examiners. Now he read with
a free mind.

One of the advantages of having taken a First Class with Distinction in
English is a capacity to read. White read the *Morte d'Arthur* as acutely as
though he were reading a brief. The note in which he summarised his
findings may be his first step toward *The Once and Future King*:

The whole Arthurian story is a regular greek doom, comparable to that of
Orestes.

Uther started the wrong-doing upon the family of the duke of Cornwall, and it
was the descendant of that family who finally revenged the wrong upon Arthur.
The fathers have eaten sour grapes etc. Arthur had to pay for his father's initial
transgression, but, to make it fairer, the fates ordained that he himself should also
make a transgression (against the Cornwalls) in order to bind him more closely
in identification with the doom.

It happened like this.

The Duke of Cornwall married Igraine and they had three daughters, Morgan
le Fay, Elaine and Morgause.

Uther Pendragon fell in love with Igraine and slew her husband in war, in order
to get her. Upon her he begot Arthur, so that Arthur was half brother to the three
girls. But he was brought up separately.

The girls married Uriens, Nentres and Lot, all kings. They would naturally
have a dislike for Uther and anybody who had anything to do with Uther.

When Uther died and Arthur succeeded him in mysterious circumstances,
naturally Arthur inherited this feud. The girls persuaded their husbands to lead a
revolt of eleven kings.

Arthur had been told that Uther was his father, but Uther had been a vigourous
old gentleman and Merlyn had very stupidly forgotten to tell Arthur who his
mother was.

After a great battle in which the kings were subdued, Morgause, the wife of
King Lot, came to Arthur on an embassy. They did not know of their relationship
at this time. They fell for each other, went to bed together, and the result was
Mordred. Mordred was thus the fruit of incest (his father was his mother's half

101

brother), and it was he who finally brought the doom on Arthur's head. The sin was incest, the punishment Guinever, and the instrument of punishment Mordred, the fruit of the sin. It was Mordred who insisted on blowing the gaff on Launcelot and Guinever's affair, which Arthur was content to overlook, so long as it was not put into words.

> *En trentiesme année de mon aage*
> *Quand toutes mes hontes j'ai bues*

White was thirty when he rented the gamekeeper's cottage. He had done with his past, he was on good terms with himself, he was free. His solitude was peopled by a succession of hawks, a rescued tawny owl, a setter bitch on whom he unloosed his frustrated capacity to love. Now in the *Morte d'Arthur*, he had a subject into which he could unloose his frustrated capacity for hero worship, his accumulated miscellany of scholarship, his love of living, his admiration of Malory. It is as though, beginning a new subject, he wrote as a novice. Instead of the arid dexterity of the potboilers, *The Sword in the Stone* has the impetus and recklessness of a beginner's work. It is full of poetry, farce, invention, iconoclasm, and, above all, the reverence due to youth in its portrayal of the young Arthur. It was accepted for publication on both sides of the Atlantic, and in the United States was being considered by the Book of the Month Club – who took it. But it was 1938, the year of Munich; the pistol barrels in the toy fort were charged for more than a salute. Fear of war half choked him when he was fitted with a gasmask, retreated when Chamberlain bought peace on Hitler's terms, but could not be dismissed.

White's thinking was typical of the postwar epoch. War was a ruinous dementia. It silenced law, it killed poets, it exalted the proud, filled the greedy with good things, and oppressed the humble and meek; no good could come of it, it was hopelessly out of date. No one wanted it. (Unfortunately, no one had passionately wanted the League of Nations, either.) If, against reason and common sense, another war should break out, he must declare himself a conscientious objector. In the first lemming rush to volunteer, he wrote to David Garnett: 'I have written to Siegfried Sassoon and the headmaster of Stowe (my poor list of influential people) to ask them if they can get me any sensible job in this wretched war, if it starts. This is the ultimatum: I propose to enlist as a private soldier in one month after the outbreak of hostilities, unless one of you gets me an *efficient* job before that.'

Chamberlain capitulated, the crisis went off the boil, White began *The Witch in the Wood* (the second volume of *The Once and Future King*) and was diverted to *Grief for the Grey Geese*, a novel he never finished. It was conceived in a state of intense physical excitement. He was alone, he was in the intimidating sea-level territory of the Wash, he was pursuing a long-ambitioned desire, intricately compounded of sporting prowess and sadism – to shoot a wild goose in flight. The theme is significant. The geese are warred on by the goose shooters. Among the goose shooters is a renegade who takes sides with the geese, deflecting their flight away from the ranks of the shooters. White plainly identifies himself with the renegade, while bent on shooting a wild goose.

In January 1939 he wrote to Garnett, who had invited him to go salmon fishing in Ireland: 'If only I can get out of this doomed country before the crash, I shall be happy. Two years of worry on the subject have convinced me that I had better run for my life, and have a certain right to do so. I may just as well do this as shoot myself on the outbreak of hostilities. I don't like war, I don't want war, and I didn't start it. I think I could just bear life as a coward, but I couldn't bear it as a hero.'

A month later he was in Ireland, lodging in a farmhouse called Doolistown, in County Meath, where he proposed to stay long enough to finish *The Witch in the Wood* (published shortly thereafter) and catch a salmon. It was his home for the next six and a half years. For six of them he never heard an English voice and rarely a cultivated one. Provincial Ireland swallowed him like a deep bog.

He had escaped his doomed country, but he could not avoid being in earshot of it.

Diary, April 26th, 1939

Conscription is now seriously spoken of in England, and everybody lives from one speech of Hitler's to the next. I read back in this book at the various tawdry little decisions which I have tried to make under the pressure of the Beast: to be a conscientious objector, and then to fight, and then to seek some constructive wartime employment which might combine

creative work with service to my country. All these sad and terrified
dashes from one hunted corner to the next.

Meanwhile he tried to protect his peace of mind by dashes in new
directions. Lodging in a Catholic household and treated as one of the
family, he considered becoming a Catholic. Because his father had
happened to be born in Ireland, he deluded himself with an idea of Irish
ancestry. He read books on Irish history, with scholarly dispassionateness
reading authors on either side of that vexed question; he tried to learn
Erse, going once a week to the local schoolmaster for lessons and 'doing
an hour's prep every morning'; he looked for a habitation, and rented a
house called Sheskin Lodge in County Mayo for the shooting; later, he
made researches into the legendary Godstone on the island of Inniskea.
More to the purpose, being involuntary, he was captured by the sombre
beauty, the desolate charm, of Erris – that part of County Mayo lying
between the Nephin Beg range and the sea.

It was at Sheskin Lodge, embowered in fuchsias and rhododrendron
thickets and surrounded by leagues of bog, that he heard the last English
voices. They were saying Good-bye. War had been declared, the visiting
Garnetts were going back to England.

The tenancy of Sheskin ran out, he returned to Doolistown and listened
to the news.

October 20th, 1939
There don't seem to be many people being killed yet – no hideous
slaughters of gas and bacteria.
But the truth is going.
We are suffocating in propaganda instead of gas, slowly feeling our
minds go dead.

October 23rd
The war as one hears of it over the wireless is more terrible than
anything I can imagine of mere death. It seems to me that death must be
a noble and terrible mystery, whatever one's creed or one's circumstance
of dying. It is a natural thing, anyway. But what is happening over the
wireless is not natural. The timbre of the voices which sing about Hitler

104

and death is a sneering, nasal mock-timbre. Devils in hell must sing like this.

By then he was preparing for *The Ill-Made Knight* (*The Witch in the Wood*, delivered to his publisher six months earlier, had been returned with a request that it might be rewritten) and making an analysis of the character of Malory's Sir Lancelot – with traits akin to his own: 'Probably sadistic, or he would not have taken such frightful care to be gentle. Fond of being alone'

In the analysis of Guenever, where he had nothing personal to go on, he speculates, and does his best to overcome his aversion to women. 'Guenever had some good characteristics. She chose the best lover she could have done and was brave enough to let him be her lover.' 'Guenever hardly seems to have been a favourite of Malory's, whatever Tennyson may have thought about her.'

It was a new departure for White to approach a book so deliberately or write it so compactly. There is no easy-going writing in *The Ill-Made Knight*, where the Doom tightens on Arthur, and Lancelot is compelled to be instrumental in it by his love for Guenever.

He wrote it in Erris, in the small-town hotel at Belmullet, between researches into the Godstone, lying out on freezing mornings waiting for the passage of the wild geese, local jovialities, and drinking fits after which he would lock himself in his hotel bedroom in terror of the I.R.A.

On October 1st, having completed *The Ill-Made Knight*, he put Erris behind him and went back to Doolistown to write *The Candle in the Wind*. This, the last *Morte d'Arthur* book, in which the doomed king staggers from defeat to defeat, already existed as the skeleton of a play. White was incapable of writing slowly. By mid-autumn the play was brought to life as a narrative, and he was considering titles for the complete tetralogy: The Ancient Wrong . . . Arthur Pendragon . . .

November 14th, 1940

Pendragon can still be saved, and elevated into a superb success, by altering the last part of Book 4, and taking Arthur back to his animals. The legend of his going underground at the end, into the badger's sett, where badger, hedgehog, snake, pike (stuffed in case) and all the rest of them can be waiting to talk it over with him. Now, with Merlyn, they must discuss war from the naturalist's point of view, as I have been doing in this diary lately. They must decide to talk thoroughly over, during Arthur's long retirement underground, the relation of Man to the other animals, in the hope of getting a new angle on his problem from this. Such, indeed, was Merlyn's original objective in introducing him to the animals in the first place. Now what can we learn about abolition of war from animals?

Pendragon can still be saved. Another salvation was involved. White had gone to Belmullet assuming himself to be at home in Ireland. He came away an Englishman in exile. He had been received, and welcomed as something new to talk about; he had never been accepted. Another Ancient Wrong forbade it – the cleft between the hated and the hating race. He was believed to be a spy (the rumour of an English invasion had kept most of Belmullet sitting up all night); his movements were watched; he was reported to the police and not allowed to leave the mainland; he had joined the local security force, but was asked not to attend parades. His disillusionment may have been rubbed in by the parallel with *The Candle in the Wind,* where Arthur's goodwill is of no avail against his hereditary enemies. Now another winter lay before him, a winter of intellectual loneliness, with only himself to consult, only himself to feed on. He had a roof over his head, a room to be alone in, regular meals, the hedged landscape of County Meath to walk his dog in, nothing much to complain of, nothing to go on with. War had imprisoned him in a padded cell.

It was his own salvation he leaped at.

On December 6th, he wrote to L. J. Potts, formerly his tutor at Cambridge, continuously his Father Confessor in Letters: 'The next volume is to be called The Candle in the Wind (one has to add DV. nowadays) . . . It will end on the night before the last battle, with Arthur absolutely wretched. And after that I am going to add a new 5th volume, in which Arthur rejoins Merlyn underground (it turns out to be the badger's sett of Vol.1) and the animals come back again, mainly ants and wild geese. Don't squirm. The inspiration is godsent. You see, I have suddenly discovered that (1) the central theme of Morte d'Arthur is to find an antidote to war, (2) that the best way to examine the politics of man is to observe him, with Aristotle, as a political animal. I don't want to go into all this now, it will spoil the freshness of the future book, but I have been thinking a great deal, in a Sam Butlerish way, about man as an animal among animals – his cerebrum, etc. I think I can really make a comment on all these futile isms (communism, fascism, conservatism, etc.) by stepping back – right back into the real world, in which man is only one of the innumerable other animals. So to put my "moral" across (but I shan't state it), I shall have the marvellous opportunity of bringing the wheel full circle, and ending on an animal note like the one I began on. This will turn my completed epic into a perfect fruit, "rounded off and bright and done." '

On the same day he wrote to Garnett, asking what book it was in which Garnett alleged having read that Malory raided a convent, and continuing, 'So far as I can see, my fifth volume is going to be all about the anatomy of the brain. It sounds odd for Arthur, but it is true. Do you happen to know, off hand, of a pretty elementary but efficient book about brain anatomy in *animals, fish, insects, etc.*? I want to know what sort of cerebellum an ant has, also a wild goose. You are the sort of person who would know this.'

Though White uses the future tense in his letter to Potts, it is unlikely that he waited from November 14th to December 6th before beginning *The Book of Merlyn*. Book 5, taking up where the original Book 4 ended, has an immediacy of plain statement that could not have brooked much delay. Arthur is still sitting alone in his tent at Salisbury, awaiting his last battle in the final insolvency of his hopes, and weeping the slow tears of old age. When Merlyn enters to renew their former master-pupil relationship and sees the extent of Arthur's misery, he is not sure whether he can do so at this late hour. His assurance that legend will perpetuate Arthur and the Round Table long after history has mislaid them falls on inattentive ears. He invokes their past relationship. The pupil has outgrown the master and puts him off with a *Le roy s'advisera*. Nowhere in the four previous volumes had White made Arthur so much a king as in this portrayal of him defeated. In *Farewell Victoria*, his novel of the early thirties, he hit on the phrase 'the immortal generals of defeat.' In the first chapter of *The Book of Merlyn* he substantiated it.

But the scheme of Book 5 is to take Arthur underground, where the animals of Book 1 are waiting to talk to him, and where Merlyn is to subject him to the contents of White's notebook so that he may discover what can be learned from animals about the abolition of war.

Since animals avoid warring with their kind, this could be a good subject to examine.

But the discussion is slanted from the first by Merlyn's insistence on the inferiority of man. *Liber scriptus proferetur . . .* Merlyn has opened White's notebook, and finds small evidence that man deserves to be placed among the two thousand eight hundred and fifty species of mammalian animals in the world. They know how to behave befittingly, existing without war or usurpation. Man does not. Merlyn weakens the denunciation by adding the insult that man is a parvenu.

At this point no one present is impious enough to suggest that man may do better in time.

At a later stage of the discussion Arthur, the representative of the parvenu species, suggests that man has had a few good ideas, such as buildings and arable fields. He is put in his place by the achievements of coral animals, beavers, seed-carrying birds, and finally felled with the earthworm, so much esteemed by Darwin. The distinction between performing and planned performance is not allowed to occur to him, and the conversation sweeps on to nomenclature: *Homo ferox* (*sapiens* being out of the question), *Homo stultus, Homo impoliticus.* The last is the most damning; man must remain savage and dunderheaded till, like the other mammalian species, he learns to live peaceably.

It is easy to pick holes in White's rhetoric. *The Book of Merlyn* was written with the improvidence of an impulse. It holds much that is acute, disturbing, arresting, much that is brilliant, much that is moving, besides a quantity of information. But Merlyn, the main speaker, is made a mouthpiece for spleen, and the spleen is White's. His fear of the human race, which he seemed to have got the better of, had recurred, and was intensified into fury, fury against the human race, who make war and glorify it.

No jet of spleen falls on the figure of Arthur. Whenever he emerges from the torrent of instruction, he is a good character: slow to anger, willing to learn, and no fool. He is as recuperable as grass, and enjoys listening to so much good talk. When Merlyn tells him that to continue his education he must become an ant, he is ready and willing. Magicked into an ant, he enters the ants' nest which Merlyn keeps for scientific purposes. What he sees there is White's evocation of the totalitarian state. Compelled by his outward form to function as a working ant, he is so outraged by the slavish belligerence and futility of his fellow workers that he opposes an ant army in full march, and has to be snatched away by Merlyn.

For his last lesson White consigns him to what by then must have seemed an irrecoverable happiness: the winter of 1938 when he went goose shooting.

It is an insight into how many experiences White packed into his days and how vividly he experienced them that little more than two years had elapsed between *Grief for the Grey Geese* and *The Book of Merlyn*. He had taken the goose book with him when he went to fish in Ireland, and Chapter 12 of *The Book of Merlyn* opens with its description of the dimensionless dark flatness of the Lincolnshire Wash and the horizontal wind blowing over it. But now it is Arthur, become a goose, who faces the wind and feels the slob under his webbed feet, though he is not completely a goose as he has yet to fly. When the flock gathers and takes off for the dawn flight, he rises with it.

The old patch shames the new garment. In that winter of two years before, White was at the height of himself, braced against an actual experience, his senses alert, his imagination flaring like a bonfire in the wind. 'I am so physically healthy,' he wrote to Sydney Cockerell[25], 'that I am simply distended with sea-air and icebergs and dawn and dark and sunset, so hungry and sober and wealthy and wise, that my mind has gone quite to sleep.'

At Doolistown his mind was insomniac, vexed, and demanding. It allowed him to extend the vitality of the old patch over the few pages where Arthur watches the geese. But with Chapter 13 the intention to convince drives out the creative intention to state, and with but one intermission – when the hedgehog leads Arthur to a hill in the west-country, where he sits looking at his sleeping kingdom under the moon and is reconciled to the bad because of the good – the book clatters on like a factory with analysis, proof and counterproof, exhortation, demonstration, explanation, historical examples, parables from nature – even the hedgehog talks too much.

Yet the theme was good, and timely, and heartfelt, and White preserves an awareness of persons and aerates the dialectics with traits of character and colloquial asides. It is clear from the typescript that he recognised the need for this, for many of these mitigations were added by hand. Whenever he can escape from his purpose – no less aesthetically felt for being laudable – into his rightful kingdom of narrative, *The Book of Merlyn* shows him still master of his peculiar powers. It is as though the book were written by two people: the storyteller and the clever man with the notebook who shouts him down.

Perhaps he went astray in that stony desert of words and opinions because he lacked his former guide. In the final chapter, Malory has returned. Under his tutelage White tells how, after Arthur's death in battle, Guenever and Lancelot, stately abbess and humble hermit, came to their quiet ends. These few pages are among the finest that White ever wrote. Cleverness and contention and animus are dismissed: there is no place for them in the completed world of legend, where White and Malory stand farewelling at the end of the long journey that began by lamplight in the gamekeeper's cottage at Stowe Ridings.

This is the true last chapter of *The Once and Future King*, and should have its place there. Fate saw otherwise. 'I have suddenly discovered that . . . the central theme of Morte d'Arthur is to find an antidote to war.' To give weight to his discovery by making it seem less sudden, White incorporated new material into the already published three volumes. In November 1941 he sent them, together with *The Candle in the Wind* and *The Book of Merlyn*, to his London publisher, to be published as a whole. Mr. Collins was disconcerted. He replied that the proposal would need thinking over. So long a book would take a great deal of paper. The prosecution of war made heavy demands on the paper supply: forms in triplicate, regulations, reports, instructions to civilians, light reading for forces, etc. White insisted that the five books should appear as a whole. After prolonged negotiations, in the course of which White's demand to see *The Book of Merlyn* in proof escaped notice – a grave pity, for he was accustomed to rely on print to show up what was faulty or superfluous – the fivefold *Once and Future King* was laid by.

The Once and Future King was not published till 1958. It was published as a tetralogy. *The Book of Merlyn*, that attempt to find an antidote to war, had become a war casualty.

NOTES

1   These indulgent recollections of Powys and life in Chaldon Herring, c1930, were to be published as *Animae Effigies*, but Powys never really approved of the venture and the idea was dropped. Despite occasional inaccuracies they remain a valuable reference

2   Old Harrovian, sculptor and Warner's charismatic London friend

3   In the form of a religious confession, published in 1916

4   A line of round barrows north of the village

5   Warner's poem 'Nelly Trim' appeared in her first collection, *The Espalier*, 1925

6   Beth Car, West Chaldon

7   Wife of Theodore Powys

8   Bea Howe, sister of Old Harrovian George Howe and friend of Stephen Tomlin. She and Warner became life-long friends. Tomlin, Warner and Bea Howe had stayed at the Weld Arms, East Lulworth, in 1921 from where Tomlin discovered Chaldon Herring

9   Not known, presumably a friend of Stephen Tomlin

10 *Chaldon Herring: Writers in a Dorset Landscape*, 2004, by Judith Stinton, provides a fascinating account of the village and the Powys circle

11 The village drunk according to Stinton

12 Characters in David Garnett's novel *The Sailor's Return*, 1925, written after visiting the pub. He was instrumental, with Warner, in getting Powys published

13 Much loved vicar from 1885 until his death in 1902

14 According to Stinton the house, begun in 1874, was unfinished when Cope died

15 Hardy's brother worked in the area but there is no proof he built Beth Car

16 These stories were published as *Fables* in 1929

17 T. F. Powys' last novel, 1931

Notes 18-20 are those provided by Warner in her Introduction

18 E. M. Nicholson, in his Introduction to the *Nat. Hist. of Selborne* (1929) remarks that it is a striking fact that the majority of naturalists supporting migration were 'very out-of-date seventeenth-century men.' This seems just about what one would expect if one takes into consideration the way thinking varies from one generation to another. 'To us it seems more probable that they fly away into hot Countries, viz, Egypt, Aethiopia, &c.,' says the seventeenth-century Willughby, in his forthright seventeenth-century way; and adds that Herodotus 'witnesseth, they abide all the year in Egypt, understand it of those that are bred there (saith Aldrovandus) for those that are bred with us only fly thither to winter.' Bacon's materialism had taught the seventeenth century this confident approach to probabilities. By Gilbert White's day the Age of Reason had set in, and thought proceeded more cautiously, supporting itself by analogy instead of laying violent hands on Herodotus. By analogy with known hibernants, swallows also must be supposed to hibernate. By analogy with mankind (the Age of Reason was singularly self-regarding) some swallows might be strong enough to fly to Africa, but the weakly or the late-fledged birds must remain behind. By a comprehensive exercise of the powers of reason, swallows, not strong enough to fly to a warm climate from

Northern Europe, and equally not strong enough to spend the winter in frozen ground, must go under water.

19 I hope this enquiry into Timothy's dormitories is not out of proportion. Antiquarians comment on beds where Queen Elizabeth spent but a single night. Timothy spent from four to five months in his beds.

20 Niece and name-child of Mrs Chapone 'who, in defiance of prejudice and fashion, made the archbishop a good man'.

21 See also Warner's Introduction to the novel, p.241

22 See also the Bath chapter, p.313-14, from Warner's *Somerset*

23 Warner, who was often compared with Jane Austen, intended to write a longer book of criticism, the *Six-fold Screen*, on Austen's novels, but it never materialised

24 Warner's acclaimed biography of White appeared in 1967

25 Sir Sydney Cockerell, Curator of the Fitzwilliam Museum, Cambridge

DISPATCHES

ROSA LUXEMBURG
('Women of Yesterday No 2' in *Woman Today*)

Surviving from one's dark-lantern, 'let's play at conspirators,' childhood is a notion that it is pretty good fun to be a revolutionary, that though such a life is full of danger and privation it is full of excitement too.

The story of Rosa Luxemburg gainsays that sanguine notion. She was a lifelong revolutionary, lived hard and uncomfortably, was several times in prison, and in the end was murdered. But probably the greatest sacrifice she made to the cause she had chosen was the resolute patience with which she submitted herself to boredom.

She was born in Poland, in the year of the Paris Commune, 1870. Her father was a merchant, cultured and Liberal, his sympathies were with the oppressed nationalities, and Rosa grew up hearing talk about freeing Poland from Tsarist tyranny, freeing Europe from its cumber of monarchies.

She grew up in the old world, and was of the new, as though in her cradle she had heard the message of the Commune, its bitter debunking of the fallacy that because ardour and high motives can begin a revolution they can also carry it through against the counter-attacks of society. In her teens she was studying Socialism, studying it as though it were engineering or chemistry. Such thoroughness was too much for the authorities. She had to escape from Poland.

Crossing a frontier is one of the highlights of a stock revolutionary romance. Rosa Luxemburg did it quietly enough, availing herself of a modest efficient lie. A Jewess, she said she was running away from home because she wished to be baptised in the Christian faith.

Leaving Poland, she left the oppressed nationalities behind. Thirty years before the beginning of Fascism she was acutely-sighted enough to realise that an oppressed nation, freed as such, is freed from an external tyranny to an internal. She turned to the international oppressed, to the working-class. She studied working-class conditions and Labour movements of different countries. She studied law, in order to know how and where law made a barrier against working-class progress, how and where loopholes could be found in that barrier. She studied economics, in order to understand the working of a system which kept the king in his counting-house, the queen in her parlour, and the maid (who was a daughter of the working-class) in the garden hanging out the clothes. She studied political economy, in order to understand how the workings of the economic system are solidified in governments and state-craft.

It was necessary for her to know these things exactly and perfectly because, as a revolutionary, it must be her function to explain them exactly and perfectly to a working-class which was kept in ignorance.

The time was past for appealing to people's feelings, playing on their consciousness of being oppressed. Such tactics might make a revolt here or there, a revolt to be followed by a tighter grip of the iron hand, with or without the velvet glove; but such tactics would never build Socialism.

She was young: she was only twenty-three when she attended the International Socialist Congress of 1893; she was highly thought of, both for her achievement and her promise; she was respected; but she was not much loved.

It seems likely that many of the established Socialists of that day saw in this young woman with her clear head and her trenchant tongue, and her power of seeing through Utopian theories, a sword that was almost as dangerously sharpened against them as against the capitalist order. However, there was nothing for it but to accept her, as one accepted those then new and dangerous forces, electricity and the internal combustion engine. And she, for her part, must accept them; in some instances as one accepts those old incommodities, the oxydisation of metal, the smells inseparable from the tribe of cabbage. For she was to work with them and argue with them for the rest of her life.

In 1899 she settled in Berlin, joining the staff of *Vorwärts*, the Socialist daily newspaper. And immediately she, who had mastered theory as a preliminary to action, found herself up against a section of Socialists who had apparently mastered theory as a means of proving, scientifically and at immense length, that action need never be taken.

All around lay Europe: peaceful – at least peaceful except for some necessary colonial wars; prosperous – at least with every indication of prosperity in the moneymarkets; industrialised: basking in the late summer warmth of a century of brilliant exploitation of material, machinery and men.

In this genial atmosphere the Revisionists, the Right Wing of the German Labour Party, laid themselves down to bask also, prepared for a long intellectual picnic of pamphlets and congresses, and expositions of their theory that, since the working-class was becoming more prosperous (and therefore stronger) and the exploiting class immensely more prosperous (and therefore milder) they would presently melt into each others arms. Why interrupt this beautiful, inevitable and after all not too gradual process by harsh talk of Marxism and class warfare?

For they overlooked in these calculations the fact that, even if becoming immensely more prosperous may make the exploiting classes temporarily milder, the growth in prosperity makes them immensely more powerful.

Lulled by the long crescendo of industrial expansion they would not look forward to a day when industry along capitalist lines could expand no further, when a slump would come, when the exploiting classes would forget to be mild and only remember to be powerful.

Against these people Rosa Luxemburg fought tooth and nail. These stout shepherds, piping their ditties of Socialism without tears, painless birth of a new order, were fatally likely to lead the working-class up the path to the slaughter-house. Nine people out of ten (in Germany and England, perhaps ten people) would rather wait for their rights than fight for their rights. Those who spend their strength in field and factory would rather hear that their emancipation is bound to come than that it is something to be hazardously purchased by struggle and sacrifice.

The Revisionist doctrine was another 'opium of the people.' It must be proved such, not only to the people themselves, but to the handers-out of the dope. Pen, tongue, endless patience, endless listening and discussing, must be used.

In 1905 Rosa Luxemburg had a brief holiday from the Revisionists. She went, with a false passport, to Poland, to help in organising a revolt among the workers. For a while she could be engaged in action instead of in theory, be among the workers themselves. In 1906 she was arrested and imprisoned in Warsaw. She escaped from prison. It was a year of what

117

romantic convention considers the typical life of a revolutionary. But her intellect would not sanction this brief escape into excitement. A revolt here, a revolt there, however striking, would do no good. She analysed her Polish experience in a book on the mass strike as a working-class weapon, and she took up a post as teacher of economics.

This idea of the mass-strike she put forward against the first rumour of the war of 1914, calling on the workers to strike unitedly against war, should war come. War came. And not only did the workers not strike, but the leaders of Left Wing Socialism, her friends and adherents, stampeded by talk of patriotism and the hereditary German bogey of invading Cossacks, voted for participation in the war. It seemed as though everything had failed. Rejecting jerry-built revolts she had spent her life in trying to build German Socialism on a solid foundation. The storm came, and the house went down as though it had been founded on sand.

She, however, did not fail herself. She went back to her schooldays, she studied the new situation, analysing where Socialism had failed, where it could again take hold. *Vorwärts* was lost, but she wrote in the only paper left open to her: an insignificant little local paper published in Gotha.

In 1915 she was imprisoned, on a charge left over from pre-war days when she was too important a public figure to be clapped into jail. Now she was just public figure enough to be safer out of the way. From prison she took part with Liebknecht in the formation of the Spartakusbund, a new Left Wing Party. In November, 1918, the German Revolution freed her again. She went straight from the prison gate to speak at a demonstration.

With Liebknecht she re-shaped the Spartakusbund into the German Communist Party, and devoted herself to the job of trying to lick into shape the deplorably untidy German Republic. The Revisionist dope now showed its wretched effects in the mass of people who supposed that, once a Republic had been declared, everything would come right of itself. This inertia, this clinging to bourgeois moderation, in its turn exasperated the extreme Left, who clamoured for extreme measures of change to take place at once. It was her thankless task to emphasise that methods successful in Russia could not be implicitly followed in Germany, where the army and the bureaucracy were still powerful forces, that the position must be enfiladed, not rushed. But the copy-cat extremists were too impetuous, the Spartikist rising of 1919 took place and was suppressed, the Majority Socialist Government calling in the only too ready help of the 'Freikorps,' an organisation of German militarists.

She was hourly in danger, but she remained in Berlin, still writing in the Communist *Rote Fahne*, the Red Flag, moving from one hiding-place to another. Finally, at Wilmersdorf, she and Liebknecht were hunted down by officers of the 'Freikorps,' who took them to their headquarters, the Eden Hotel. Rosa Luxemburg, dismissed after three hours questioning, left the hotel as a prisoner.

She walked slowly (she was lame) and one of the escort, a soldier named Runge, lost patience and struck her with his gun. She fell. She was unconscious when they carried her to a car. Probably she was dying then. But to make sure, when she stirred once on the journey, Lieutenant Krull, who had been one of her questioners, shot her through the head with his revolver. The car stopped by a canal. Her body was thrown in.

With permission of the Majority Socialist Government Krull and Runge were tried by court-martial, and acquitted.

JOSEPHINE BUTLER
('Women of Yesterday No 3' in *Woman Today*)

She was young, good, and beautiful and in 1852 she married, most congenially, most suitably and she had a devoted husband, and some charming children, and there was nothing to prevent her from living happily ever afterwards, the happy life of the Victorian middle-class wife and mother, sheltered, graceful, and private, like a rose in a walled garden.

Instead, she chose to live a life by all contemporary standards arduous, odious and painful; a life of scandalous publicity, a life that called down on her continual abuse and contempt. For Josephine Butler, exemplary virgin, wife and mother, 'a pure woman,' 'a refined lady' – to use the praises of her epoch, chose to take up arms for a class of persons neither pure nor refined, women politely referred to as 'unfortunates,' and bluntly dealt with as prostitutes.

She had been brought up in the north country, an upbringing serious and innocent. However priggish one may feel those serious Early Victorian family circles to have been, they had the merit of being sincere and Miss Josephine Grey, of Dilston, learning, in the narrow modicum allowed to a young lady, about prostitution, learned that it was not only a sin, but a moral problem. Marriage released her to the more emancipated society of a university town, and in Oxford she learned that it was a social axiom. She wrote of this period in her memoirs 'When I was distressed by a bitter case of wrong inflicted on a very young girl, I ventured to speak to one of the wisest men – so esteemed – in the university, in the hope that he would suggest, not some means of helping her, but of bringing to a sense of his crime the man who had wronged her. The sage sternly advocated silence and inaction. 'It could only do harm to open up in any way such a question as this. It was dangerous to arouse a sleeping lion.' In other words, it would be highly inconvenient to disturb an established custom, and one which had long found favour with the aristocratic clients for whom Oxford existed. And Mrs. Butler had best run back to her Italian and her needlework.

For a while Mrs. Butler kept those words in her heart. But she was a young woman with a powerful imagination and a powerful will and she had – a rarer qualification – a remarkably considerate husband. When she began working among prostitutes, visiting hospitals and workhouses, taking first one girl and then another into her own house, he encouraged her. When, in her own rather comic words, these acts 'drew down upon my head an avalanche of miserable but grateful womanhood,' he helped her to found a hospice where the incurably miserable could die in peace and kindness, and a rescue home for girls.

All this, if unconventional, not quite the sort of thing one could discuss in the drawing-room, was permissible. Indeed, a little dabbling among prostitutes was rather the fashion at the date, a holy hobby. One sent a quarterly subscription and the weekly washing to the Magdalen's laundry, and if one were very broad-minded one even allowed them to sew one's daughter's trousseau. Mrs. Butler was not so much unconventional in her deeds – though not many British matrons would have a succession of consumptive street-walkers dying in the best spare-room – as in her feelings. She certainly allowed her feelings to carry her rather far, her pity for the unfortunates had a dangerously explosive mixture of love in it, she should not have given up the best spare-room (the poor creatures would really have been more at home in the servants' attics) or filled the coffins with quite so many white camellias (which might have been sold for much and given to the poor). But still she was within the bounds of decorum. She was pitying, but not protesting, she was fulfilling the beautiful womanly mission of softening the hard edges of the wicked world, but not trying to dynamite them.

Meanwhile, prostitution was among the largest and most animated female trades of the day. The good manners of the time, which insisted so strongly that a respectable woman must be sheltered from even a breath of lust, compelled the lustful, even the quite normally and kindheartedly lustful, to carry their appetites elsewhere and the moral code of the time, insisting that 'one step from the path of virtue' was fatal and irrevocable, left no option to those who took this step but to become prostitutes. The market was crowded, even beyond the demand for the wares; competition was keen, prices were low, conditions those of any sweated trade; and as a result, there was an immense amount of venereal disease. Meanwhile, the State had recently become conscious of the bad conditions of long standing in two other professions: the Army and the Navy. The Crimean scandal, and the subsequent Sanitary Commission had done something to open people's eyes (peace-time mortality in the Army was 18 per 1,000 in the line, 20 per 1,000 in the Guards, as against 9 per 1,000 among the civil population of military age). Hounded on by that terrible Miss Nightingale, the War Office enlarged barracks and reformed dietaries. It also seemed desirable to tackle the incidence of venereal infection, and during the 'sixties three temporary Acts of Parliament were passed 'for the prevention of contagious diseases at certain naval and military stations.'

These measures introduced in Great Britain the system of police regulated prostitution and compulsory examination established in France by Napoleon I and adopted by other continental countries. It was a system traditionally repugnant to English thought: to the devout it seemed a legalisation of vice, to the democratic it was an interference with the liberty of the subject. Indeed, it is said that the first Act only passed because there had been previous legislation on the contagious diseases of cattle, and it was not realised by an inattentive House what kind of cattle this new Act referred to.

It is a curious comment on how remote an Act of Parliament could be from a voteless Victorian lady that Josephine Butler did not show fight until after the passing of the third C.D. in 1869. What she did then showed the mettle of the woman. There were already petitions which she could canvass for, societies which she could join, paths reputable for a lady's feet. 'Already many members of both Houses of Parliament, bishops and responsible officials had been appealed to.' And though the appeals had fallen on deaf ears, they could have been reiterated. But in an agony of temper and agitation and female pride (for it was as a woman and scarcely at all as a philanthropist that she resented what she felt to be an intolerable insult to all womanhood) she had her flash of brilliant intuition as to where her appeal should be made.

'I took the train to the nearest large station – Crewe – where there is a great manufactory of locomotives and a mass of workmen. I scarcely knew what I should say, and knew not at all what I should meet with.' It was to a gathering of workmen that she made her first fighting speech, going on to other industrial towns, always addressing people of the working-class – the class which provided the subjects for this legislation, the private soldiers and the prostitutes, the class more deeply affected than any members of parliament or bishops or responsible officials could be, the class to which the ultimate appeal should be made.

Now this step does not seem so very remarkable, so particularly courageous. But in truth what Josephine Butler did then was a thing of revolutionary daring. For a woman to speak in public at all was dubious, for a woman to mention venereal disease was abominable, for a woman to speak in public, to an audience of working men, on that subject, was unheard-of, a turning upside down of all social decorum, a challenge to society. So much so indeed, that even the audiences she chose were in two minds about her. While she spoke her sincerity carried people away; thinking her over there could be two minds on the matter, and her early meetings were followed by meetings of protest. But for all that, she had aimed herself to the right hearers. The working-class, though sometimes puzzled and incensed, stood by the courageous creature, and the lampoons and malice and slanders which followed her till the end of her days came from the ruling class.

122

So bitterly was she resented that when in the following year she went to the garrison town of Colchester, where a by-election was being fought on this issue, no hotel would take her in, and she was warned not to let herself be recognised in the streets. Neither side would tolerate her, for the Government candidate, a Liberal, pledged to the Act, loathed her the more since she herself was, except on this point, a Liberal, and his Conservative opponent loathed her on principle, as a woman who dared to speak in public on a subject which any decent woman would only allow herself to blush over in a bedroom. Law and order, exemplified in a mob of roughs and brothel-keepers, raged through the town, vowed to keep Mrs. Butler away. However, she held firm. A working-class family housed her, disguised she passed through the streets, and spoke at a woman's meeting, straining her voice against the uproar outside. And the Government candidate was defeated, and next year a Royal Commission sat to hear evidence on the Contagious Diseases Acts.

Her subsequent work, both in this country and on the Continent, brought continued opposition, though her action had gathered about her a considerable body of sympathisers and fellow-workers. It brought discouragement too. She learned more, every enquiry, every partial victory even, brought her a heavier realisation of the extent of the evil which she set herself to combat; and by degrees her writings show a tendency to rely less upon herself and less upon the potential strength of the oppressed, more upon the abstract means of public opinion and heavenly aid. She becomes a more eminent public figure, a less dangerous one, she sinks by degrees into committees and prayer-meetings.

Probably at no moment in her life did she properly apprehend the economic basis of prostitution, she was a moral reformer, not a social reformer. And the repeal of the C.D. Acts, though a victory, was not a significant one. Prostitution continued, and continues still, and neither piety nor wit can abate it where the capitalist system continues. She was barking up the wrong tree. But in the decisive moment of her life she transcended all her limitations; in that journey to Crewe, to speak to the railwaymen, she did the right and the only thing as infallibly as though reason and not intuition had guided her. Born into the class of M.P.s, bishops, and responsible officials, her heart, so to speak, was in the right place.

COUNTESS MARKIEVICZ
('Women of Yesterday No 4' from *Woman Today*, September, 1937)

At the end of the last century it was common for the Anglo-Irish gentry to pick up a bit by horse-dealing. Colts and fillies ran wild on their windy acres, and the better looking of these, trained a little, groomed a little, went to the horse show or the races, where they might meet a buyer from England. The same process could be applied to daughters. And in 1888 Miss Constance Georgina Gore-Booth, her beautiful figure supplied with a pair of properly cut stays and her proud head trimmed with the orthodox tuft of ostrich plumes, was presented at court and launched on a London season.

She was handsome, romantic, spirited, a most noticeable animal, and a great many people looked at her. But no one married her. Her father, with a philosophy which may have been the result of three centuries of Irish climate working on English blood, cut his losses without ill-feeling. Constance was allowed to 'take up art.' She worked at the Slade, and then in Paris.

Art, even art in Paris, was tolerated by a certain section of London Society. But any hopes that Constance might yet justify the expense of the white satin and the ostrich-plumes by making a good match were dispelled by her next action. For she married. The details of the gentleman, announced in the society column, did their best for him, but could not do much. 'Casimir Joseph Dunin de Markievicz, a Polish nobleman, of Zyvolavka, Poland.' Actually, he was of Paris, an artist of the type which is pre-eminently described as Bohemian, rather a rake, and the second son of a family of nine.

They settled in Dublin, a cheap city. It was a narrow society, gay and assured, with the gaiety and assurance of those who live habitually on the slopes of a volcano. It was a society that granted a great measure of freedom, everybody (who was anybody) knew who you were, what you

124

did, what you had. As it was impossible to keep up pretences, one did not try to; one could dance at the Castle one night and walk back from the public-house with a bottle of whiskey the next, and nobody a penny the worse.

And there was always something going on. For one thing, the volcano was always going on, they were living in Ireland. At that time the death-rate of Dublin was twice the death-rate of London, and almost half of those making up that death-rate died in asylums, prisons, hospitals or workhouse. In the depths of the volcano the Irish Republican Brotherhood was going on, and spouting from the crater, along with creameries and the Abbey Theatre, was the Gaelic League, the revival of the Irish language, all the cultural movement arising from the nationalist movement called Sinn Fein, 'Ourselves Alone.'

The cultural aspect of Sinn Fein was fashionable. Irish tweeds and poplins, Celtic knots, the Irish harp and the Irish grammar: if it had not been (oddly enough) for Baden-Powell, the energetic passions of Countess Markievicz might have remained with these. But in 1909 Baden-Powell founded the Boy Scout Movement, and it became a craze. It was suggested that Boy Scoutism might do something for Ireland. It did though with a difference. Sinn Fein, rejecting the kind proposals of the English Scout Movement, set up Boy Scouts of its own, an organisation called Fianna Eireann, whose members were pledged never, under any circumstances, to join the British armed forces.

Constance Markievicz, unloosed by Baden-Powell into all her natural talent for practical energy, took charge of the Fianna. She recruited them, she filled her house with them, she fed and taught and drilled them, she taught them signalling and first aid, and how to shoot. She taught them strictly and well, they learned to shoot with both rifles and revolvers, to drill with fire arms, to clean and dismantle and reassemble fire arms. She taught them, too, though in this she was not the only worker, the theory as well as the practice of shooting. This marksmanship, so carefully taught, was never to be used for the ends of the British Empire. By implication, one did not learn to shoot for nothing. One learned to be ready to shoot for Ireland.

The Fianna had established her among the rebels. A new experience took her further, advanced her from rebel to revolutionary. This was the

125

great Lock-out of the Dublin Transport Workers in 1913. Larkin in Dublin, Connolly in Belfast, had been working since 1907 to organise the Irish workers into Trades Unions and into a fight for better pay and better conditions. Their material was, as one chooses to look at it, deplorable or magnificent. Long oppression, acute poverty, much unskilled labour, ignorance and sectarian passions, the conditions reflected in those significant figures about the Dublin death rate, here was the desperate making of a desperate struggle. Their technique was brilliant. When W. M. Murphy, founding a Dublin Employers' Federation, called the Lock-out he was fighting a defensive battle. And though he might (as he did) win the Lock-out, Trades Unionism had won Ireland.

The struggle was intense, bitter, long-drawn-out. Dublin, so well accustomed to bloodshed, commemorates one of its police charges in the phrase *Bloody Sunday*. The struggle lasted for eight months; through a wicked winter, workers died of cold and starvation, the English Trades Unions sent food ships to Dublin. The struggle was slashed with episodes of wild savagery and frantic humour. James Larkin, wanted by the police, had engaged to speak in O'Connell Street on that Sunday which afterwards came to be called Bloody. He kept his engagement. That afternoon the guests in the Imperial Hotel (proprietor, W. M. Murphy) watched sympathetically the entrance of a venerable and infirm cleryman who presently surprised them by running upstairs at full speed tearing tufts of whisker off his jaws.

The disguise and the stratagem had been arranged by Constance Markievicz. Presently she was engaged in more serious work. She organised a food kitchen for the strikers, a food kitchen in which there was no thought of charity but only a passionate partisanship. All day and day after day she cooked and served and cadged supplies from her old friends of the upper world and heartened her new friends of the lower world.

Rebel and revolutionary both, she worked on now in the double capacity, and with the outbreak of war in 1914 she became linked through James Connolly with that most secret and powerful element of the volcano on whose slopes she had grown up gay and assured – the Irish Republican Brotherhood. She joined the Citizen Army – where she found the fruit of an earlier labour already ripening for those well-drilled, gun-skilled boys of her Fianna were drilling others. She was elected its Joint

Treasurer, and raised money for it; she recruited, spoke, wrote, ran a secret printing press for seditious literature. At the outbreak of war Redmond, the official leader of the Irish Party, had made his sincere irreparable gesture, calling on Irishmen to join in the defence of Great Britain. Sinn Fein, with a policy instead of a gesture, called on Irishmen to boycott Great Britain. Her hour of need was Ireland's opportunity. Irishmen should drill in their own ranks, ready to fight for Ireland, when either assistance from Germany or weakness in Britain should make the moment for a Rising.

As strategy, it was excellent. In practice, it was abominably difficult. To communicate through Ireland was difficult enough, to communicate with Germany harder still. Opportunities seemed to rush by unused, impatience on the one hand, uncertainty on the other, clouded all their counsels. The very day before the Rising MacNeill, commanding the Irish Volunteers (the section of the National Volunteers which, holding out against Redmond's appeal, had remained faithful to Sinn Fein) decided that the moment was not ripe, and countermanded the parade which was to become a mobilisation. Thus, on the morning of Easter Monday, 1916, when the Irish Republic was proclaimed, only in Dublin and a few country districts was the Irish Republican Army mobilised to defend it.

The Dublin force was so small (only 800) that it could not invest the whole city. They seized the centre of the town, occupying its main buildings and sending out forays of attack and communication. 2,000 British troops came from the Curragh that evening, by Wednesday the number was increased to 20,000 (there is no more clinching proof that Great Britain perfectly realised Ireland's will to be free, and was as perfectly determined to keep Ireland enslaved than this massing of numbers, at such short notice, in a time of war). The city was shelled, set on fire, partially destroyed. After five days of this (with aeroplanes, I suppose, five hours would be enough) the end came, and Pearce and Connolly, commanders for the Republic, surrendered themselves and their staff 'In order to prevent further slaughter of unarmed people, and in the hope of saving the lives of our followers.'

With Pearce and Connolly, Macdonagh and Clarke, Ceannt, MacDiarmada, MacBride, Mallin, Plunkett, William Pearse, Colbert, O'Hanrahan, Heuston and Daly, Constance Markievicz was court

127

martialled, and with them condemned to death. Her cell was above the prison yard. For four mornings she heard the footsteps of the firing squad, the volley, and the single revolver shots which finished off those whom the volley had not despatched; and later a friendly wardress would whisper to her the names of the day's dead. Another woman political prisoner managed to catch a moment's sight of her. She said, her face radiant with joy: 'Have you heard the news? I have been sentenced to death.' But the sentence, 'only and solely on account of her sex,' was commuted to penal servitude for life.

In June, 1917, the new Coalition Government released her. She went back to Dublin, to the new leaders who had taken the place of her dead comrades. In May, 1918, she was back in an English jail again, rounded up with other Sinn Fein leaders (among them the widows of MacBride and Clarke), on the Home Secretary's declaration that there was a plot with Germany. Released in March, 1919, in June she was imprisoned for a third time, her offence, making a seditious speech. Between the second and third imprisonment she had been appointed Secretary for Labour in De Valera's first cabinet.

As Secretary for Labour she continued to work for another year, under difficulties, for the Black and Tan auxiliaries were now bestriding Ireland. She lived 'on the run.' It was not safe to spend two nights in the same house. For all that, she attended the weekly meetings of the De Valera Cabinet, going out disguised as an old lady with a bonnet. On one occasion she had the pleasure of being escorted through the traffic by one of these policemen, who, for arresting her, would have received infinite praise and promotion. In September, 1920, she was caught, court martialled, and sentenced to two years hard labour.

With the Treaty between Ireland and Great Britain, an apple of discord was thrown. By the terms of the Treaty the Dail was to include an Upper Chamber, an Irish equivalent of the House of Lords, representing the Anglo-Irish landowning class. The unmixed rebel might be content; it was independence for Ireland. The rebel-cum-revolutionary could not accept so easily. She said, speaking against the Treaty: 'My ideal is the Workers' Republic for which Connolly died. And I say that this is one of the things that England wishes to prevent. She would sooner give us Home Rule than a democratic Republic. It is the capitalist interests in England and

Ireland that are pushing this treaty to block the march of the working people in Ireland and England.'

Long before, Connolly had spoken to her of the ultimate war between 'the Fat Man and his Black flag and the Workers and their Red flag.' She found it true. Under the green flag of Ireland the residual conflict between Fat Man and Worker persisted. She was old, and tired, and as a rebel she could have taken some rest, but as a revolutionary she worked on. She fought an election as a Republican against the Free State candidate, and was defeated. She had another spell of street fighting in Dublin, when the Republican Irregulars entrenched themselves in the Four Courts against the Free State; another spell of editing a seditious paper, a paper whose sedition was directed against the Free State Government; and a final imprisonment as a Republican when she went on hungerstrike.

In England they were talking about the Kilkenny cats, about those impossible Irish who clamour for Home Rule and when you give it them, can do nothing with it but quarrel and fight among themselves. Few English people had the patience to unravel the contest between Free State and Republican. To Constance Markievicz, not an intellectual woman, the issue was clear enough. It lay between the Fat Man and his Black flag, the Worker and his Red flag. Not an intellectual woman, only true-hearted and practical, she did, at the last, the last thing left her to do. She finished her days among the workers of Dublin, a tattered figure, sharing with them her last penny, her last energy, her last jokes. She died in the hospital of the slum district where she had lived, going into the general ward. A friend came to her bedside, saying that she should be moved to a nursing home. She answered: 'if the hospital is good enough for the poor, it is good enough for me.'

Dublin has a tradition of striking funerals. Hers was remarkable for two things. A band of soldiers with machine guns was stationed at her graveside to prevent the volley, proper to a soldier's funeral, being fired over her grave, for she who had fought for Ireland and been condemned to death for fighting for Ireland, must be buried as a civilian. She was followed to her grave by an immense concourse of the poor of Dublin.

RECOMMENDATIONS TO STARVATION
(*The Countryman*, January, 1936)

Supper for five persons; *Fried Eggs*: 4 eggs, 4 pieces of toast. Another such supper; *Cheese Savoury*: 2 slices of bread toasted, 4-6 oz. of grated cheese. A dinner for five persons; *Cornish Pie*: few pieces of cold meat – about 2-4 oz., 1lb. potatoes, 2 onions, 1/2lb. of flour, 4 oz. lard. Another; *Sausages in Batter*: 1/2 1b. of sausages. Skin the sausages and roll them in twelve portions.

These five persons are not, as one might suppose, maniacs thinning. They are a family on the dole, living within the scale prescribed by the Nutrition Committee of the British Medical Association (1933 report), 'if health and working capacity are to be adequately maintained'.

The recipes are given in a booklet called 'Family Meals and Catering,' issued by the B.M.A. with the assistance of the National Training College of Domestic Science, London. The original Report dealt in such terms as calories and carbohydrates. The cookery book (based on diet 16 of that Report, the diet which allows 1/2 1b. of butter a week among five) is designed to show how it works out in real life.

Maybe it would be better to say, 'works out in slow death'. One-tenth of a pound of sausages, one-fifth of 2-4 oz. Of cold meat – these are no dinners to keep adults in 'health and working capacity', or to nourish children.

In addition to its recipes, 'Family Meals and Catering' gives three weekly shopping lists. 'Butter, 1/2lb.; margerine, 1/2lb.; eggs, 3; tomatoes, 1/4lb.; greens, 2 pennyworth; lettuce, one pennyworth.' These proportions are not a week's supply for one person, as a normal housekeeper might assume. They are a week's marketing for five.

'Family Meals and Catering' – how smug this title begins to sound! – is ornamented with three specious colour plates, each showing a week's supply of food. More to the point is the photograph on the front cover.

Here is the food again cooked according to the recipes by the students of the National Training College of Domestic Science. The dishes are set out on a staging covered with a fair white cloth, and the students, covered with fair white overalls, are standing by. In only one instance – and that a slab cake – is one of these dishes which are to feed five persons larger than a student's face.

There is only one thing to be said in favour of this bad book. It is as good a give-away as one can wish for a vile state of things. Science, medical and domestic, all the jargon and apparatus of a cookery book, coloured plates and pious preface, spell but one word, Malnutrition. Or in plainer English, Not Enough to Eat.

On every other count the book is about as bad as it can be. The recipes are unpractical and wasteful of time and fuel, both important considerations in a working-class household. Half an hour's cooking, 'stirring all the time', is laid down to produce a brown gravy made from water, flour, an onion and one ounce of dripping. The shopping lists are drawn up with little attention to real conditions. The quarter of a pound of tomatoes is priced at a penny. Greens are a penny a pound and a half of plums is twopence – interesting calculation for the greengrocer – and, in the sanguine expectations of the B.M.A., two heads of celery – large enough to supply a dish for five, and sufficient outside leaves to flavour two evening meals of soup – can be bought for threepence. By combing the cheapest town markets, vegetables at such prices may be found; but to buy them, as every housekeeper knows, is bad economy, since they will be stale or so badly damaged that a large part of them must needs be discarded before cooking.

Moreover the menus are monotonous and badly balanced. In the first week's shopping list the starch foods (bread, flour, potatoes, rice) amount to 49lbs., as against 12lbs. (uncooked weight) of fruit and vegetables. The voice of the B.M.A. impresses on us the dangers of constipation to the public health, and urges us to eat fresh fruit and fresh vegetables.

I SAW SPAIN
(*The Fight*, February, 1937)

It was our first day in Spain. We were at Port-Bou, in Catalonia, the little frontier fishing town. Our passports had been visaed by the Workers' Committee, we had only to wait for the afternoon train to Barcclona[1].

We sat drinking coffee and staring at the profound Mediterranean blue of the bay, the pale slopes of the Pyrenees, and trying to read the newspaper in Catalan. One of the members of the Committee, a grave grey haired man, speaking a slow, very pure French, came to our table, saying that he had a quarter of an hour to himself, and would have his coffee with us. He helped us with the newspaper, and told us of the situation of the town, its fishers and small holders enrolled in the militia.

He apologised for yawning, saying he had been up all night. There was so much to be done, he said. He looked as though he had been up for many nights. 'Do you ever sleep ?' I asked him.

'With one eye,' he answered.

The Patrol Tug

Just then we heard the hoot of a siren. The children ran to the water's edge, four or five militiamen with old-fashioned muskets or revolvers joined the children, women came out of the houses and stood shading their eyes, looking towards the sea.

'Something abnormal,' said our friend. We too got up and walked down to the water's edge. The siren hooted again, a small tug came round the headland.

'She patrols this coast', he said, 'She must have something to report, she does not usually come in at this hour.'

While we stood watching he pointed to a little hut on the headland. Look-out men were stationed there, day and night. If they saw an enemy ship, or the Italian planes coming from Majorca, they blew a whistle. The alarm would be taken up by other watchers blowing a siren fixed in the church tower, and at that warning the people of Port-Bou would be ready to take shelter.

'We shelter,' he said, smiling rather satirically, pointing to the dark hole

132

in the hillside, the railway track leading into it, 'we shelter in the International Tunnel.'

'Is there any defence for the town?' I asked. He looked at the handful of militiamen, the children, grave and alert, silently watching the tug coming in.

'What you see.'

That group of men and children on the shingle, watchful and resolute, that half-dozen of poor arms, the old tug, hooting like a mother bird giving its warning note . . . this was our first sight of the Workers' Spain against which the weight of Europe is actively or passively engaged. Our friend, bleached with fatigue, haggard with responsibility, nothing bright about him except his clear eyes and the scarlet of the badge in his buttonhole (PSUC, United Socialist Party of Catalonia) was one of those brutal Marxists who endanger, so we are told, the whole régime of civilisation.

Ramona, a Militia Girl

Bright-eyed Ramona, militia girl, aged twenty-four, her solid thighs and round bosom filling out her brown dungaree uniform, a revolver in her belt, her quartermaster's badge on her breast, was, when we met her, already a veteran. She had taken part in the ill-fated expedition to Majorca when volunteer troops were landed on an island where they expected to confront only Spanish Fascism, and found instead the superior forces of international Fascism. The position taken in the first rush was held for three weeks, it was hunger at last which forced it to be evacuated. 'When we saw a cat . . .' said Ramona. 'But at last there was not another cat to be found.'

Above the bright eyes, which had looked death so steadfastly in the face, were a pair of plucked eyebrows. Ramona the veteran, Ramona who could take a machine gun to pieces and reassemble it without a bungle, had not been long enough in the army to grow her natural eyebrows again.

'Before I joined the army I was a shop girl,' she said.

'What did you sell?'

'Mothers of God and ice-creams,' she replied.

'A religious place,' she explained. 'A village in the mountains, like a little Lourdes. It belonged, all of it, to a Fascist, he exploited it, it was his property.

133

'So were we,' she continued. 'We girls, who sold at his shop and waited at his restaurant. If a girl was young, that was enough for him, he would seduce her. But she must be young. When she had a baby, then his mother would dismiss her. She was religious, that old mother, she loved just three things, the church, and money and her son. All night she would pray and weep because her son was a sinner. Then in the morning she would hire another young girl.'

'Were you seduced, Ramona ?'

'Not I! I was in my Trade Union, I was a Socialist, I had ideas. And I was old, too – too old for him. They would not have kept me only I was smart and a good saleswoman, and made money for them.

'I used to talk to the other girls, argue with them, you know, but they were too tired to listen to me, or too much afraid of the boss and the old woman. We slept all in one attic, like in a barracks. At five in the morning she would come in, scolding us for lying so long in bed.

'And they got away,' she exclaimed, beating her brown fist on the table. 'I ran all the way to the Committee in the town, I said to them, "This man is a Fascist, the woman is religious, all their money will go to buy arms to kill us if we do not get it now." And they sent men. But it was too late, they were off, both of them, with their money. Nothing was left but the rosaries and the images, and the girls with their unborn babies.'

'All that money,' she said furiously. 'Shooting us down!' She talked as candidly as a bird sings, there was only one subject from which she would flinch aside, become preoccupied and reserved. It did not do to ask her when the Centuria to which she belonged might go again into the fighting line. For recently the military authorities of loyal Spain had been discountenancing the *milicianas*, no more women were permitted to enlist, those already in the militia were being weeded out. Ramona would need all her prowess and her persuasion, her skill with machine guns, her reputation as a superb quartermaster, if she were to go into the fight again. This unwomaning of the Workers' Militia was given great prominence in the capitalist newspapers of Europe, and attributed by them to one of two causes: that the *milicianas* ran away, or that they spread venereal disease. The actual reason was different, a something unsuspected by the ruling class. It had been found that the sight of a dead or wounded woman tended to set up curious reactions in the men

134

fighting, men, one must remember, untrained in warfare, and for the most part deprived of the rallying effect of being officered by people of the ruling class. These men, seeing their women fellow-soldiers fall dead, or lie writhing, lost their heads. Horror, or furious rage, took possession of them; forgetting caution, forgetting rather that military version of caution which is called discipline, they would rush upon the enemy, calling them Butchers, and Fascists, and get needlessly killed themselves. And since there was no time to train away this working-class chivalry, it was thought best to withdraw the women from the fighting ranks.

So now, though the Fascists have still a good chance of killing Ramona, she is likeliest to be shot in a captured town, or killed as a civilian in an air raid. To the Fascists this will make little difference, a worker dead is a worker dead to them. But it will make a considerable difference to Ramona, so proud in her uniform, wearing her forage cap so jauntily with the tassel dangling above her bright eyes.

A Long Walk from Switzerland

I met him at the Department of Strangers, the office which deals with the affairs of all extra-nationals in Barcelona. He was a large raw-boned man with small grey eyes, his clothes were shabby, his boots were torn. He was sitting on a small gold chair with a red velvet seat (for the Department of Strangers is housed in what used to be a luxury hotel), grim as a man of stone, and in a furious temper.

As I neared him he said in a rasping voice:

'Do you speak French? Well, listen to this. This place is not businesslike.'

'They are very busy,' I said appeasingly.

'Bah! I came here yesterday, and told them that I want to enlist myself in the International Legion. They told me to come again this morning, when they would have made my arrangements. I came this morning, half an hour ago, and I am still waiting.' Leaning forward, squawking his elegant chair on the parquet, he added, 'I find it very irksome.'

'Other people are waiting, too,' I said. 'You must take your turn, even to enlist.'

135

Locking his bony hands, he went on:

'I came here to fight, not to wait. I walk here from Switzerland . . .'

'From Switzerland?'

The exclamation was startled out of me. I had a ridiculous vision of this angry man stalking out of a chalet, setting out on his walk, saying abruptly over his shoulder, in answer to a question cried from within the chalet, 'To Spain.'

He strode over my question.

'I was unemployed, I had no money for trains, so I walked. We have Fascists in Switzerland too, I know them. I come here to fight them, and I am kept waiting. Thirty five minutes, now.'

My name was called. The man for whom I was translating had been summoned for his interview. As I got up the angry man said, in a tone of even profounder resentment:

'If you get a chance, you might mention in there that I have come here to fight.'

When I came out again into the waiting room I looked round for my angry man, to assure him that the word had been spoken, that his affair was already in hand. But he was gone, my angry man. Instead, I saw a beaming stranger, who had borrowed his boots and his travel stained clothes, and who was filling out a form and signing his name in a handwriting full of exultant and stately flourishes.

'It's all right,' he said, recognising me vaguely as something recalled from a nightmare. 'It's all right. I'm going to the Karl Marx Barracks right away.'

BARCELONA
(*Left Review*, December, 1936)

When the soldiers came marching from the barracks of Montjuich into the centre of Barcelona people supposed it was another parade. Parades had been frequent – sabre-rattling gestures supposed by the military authorities to have a sedative effect on the nerves of the populace.

It was not till they opened fire, not till the women out marketing, the breakfasters in the cafés, the street vendors showing their wares, the gardeners tranquilly planting the flowerbeds of the Plaza de Catalonia with scarlet salvia, looked up and saw people falling dead around them, that the sedative effect of this military parade was realised.

It was morning. The workers were already in their factories, safely out of the way. A large body of troops occupied the Hotel Colon, a block-wide building overlooking the Plaza de Catalonia and raking the long, straight boulevard of the Ramblas. Here they sent the guests to the ground floor, the servants to the top floor, and settled themselves and their machine-guns in the remainder of the building. Others continued down the Ramblas, small detachments entering the churches on their route.

What happened then is something which we in England must find almost unbelievable. The police ranged themselves with the people, fighting side by side with members of the middle class, with professors and journalists and intellectuals who left their coffee-cups and their newspapers to make history. The police carried arms already, the others ran to the gun-shops, taking what they could find, sporting guns and automatics, and hunting-knives when nothing better was left them.

Even stranger weapons were utilised. A tram, hastily blinded with some scraps of sheet-metal, was sent at full speed down the Ramblas, through a machine-gun barrage spraying from the heavy Baroque church which has subsequently become so famous and endeared as an exquisite work of art. Where the soldiers had gone in, the tram-cargoes of men with shotguns and pistols followed, though they did not find so easy an access. However, they took the kingdom of heaven by storm, and put the machine-guns out of action. In the sturdily tranquil Barcelona which I saw two months later that tram was running as usual, distinguished, though, from trams of no past by the great wreath of flowers, renewed every morning, which it carried on its bows.

Wearing its proud wreath, it rumbles past the bullet-scarred walls, the trophies of flowers propped here and there against them to mark the death-site of some fighter in the July days, the street-vendors' stalls which line the broad asphalt walk under the trees. Mixed with the old wares, the flowers, the shaving-brushes, the canaries and love-birds, the watermelons, are new wares: militia caps, pistols (toy-pistols to our shame be it spoken), rings and badges and brooches carrying the initials of the anarchist F.A.I. and C.N.T., the Trotskyist P.O.U.M., the Communist P.S.U.C. and U.G.T., the inter-party clenched fist with its motto *No Pasarán* and the hammer and sickle. The bookstalls show new wares, too. Books on political theory, the classics of Marx and Bukharin, Proudhon and Ferrer, the novels of Zola and Rolland and Barbusse. Among them are many treatises – serious, not bawdy – on birth control and sexual hygiene.

On such wares as these the empty sockets of the church windows stare down. They look very queer, these churches, Giant Popes abruptly changed to Giant Pagans: for with their gutted interiors, their unglazed windows, their broken, boarded-up doorways, they carry a sort of dissolute resemblance to Parthenon and Baalbec. Inside them accumulates that peculiar litter which arrives to every derelict building, however made derelict, whether by fire or flood or earthquake or war or the will of man: mortar and rubble, scraps of paper, scraps of clothing, pigeons' dung and pigeons' feathers.

The barrel-organs rattle out the 'Internationale', at intervals the loudspeakers confirm it. Technically, the broadcasts are pretty bad, the loudspeakers blare and rattle; but the quality of the music broadcast, both classical and popular, is good. It was a shock, even remembering what the B.B.C. is like, to return to the 'popular' programmes of the B.B.C.

It was interesting, too, to compare the commercial art posters still remaining on the walls with the new official posters. These are admirable, with a certain stringent and ascetic quality which exactly echoes the *No Pasarán* of a people who, drilling with broomsticks and fighting against the weight of Europe, drill and fight on. Turning from their sober colouring and grim line to the fading Cadum babies, the public statuary, is as much of a shock as returning to the B.B.C.

But to realise fully what sort of taste the new alliance of worker and artist has driven out one has to visit the *torres* – the suburban villas where the upper classes enjoyed pure air and a view over Barcelona. If one is English one can undoubtedly swallow a good deal in the way of architectural delirium, if only because we live in a climate which makes any light-coloured building with a great deal of balcony and veranda and top-hamper seem invigoratingly light-hearted. At heart, too, nests the hereditary feeling that people on the Continent dwell naturally in casinos. But swallowing the minarets and the crenellations, the large bastard-Corbusier bathing-huts and the Fitzjohn's Avenue gothic, the toughest stomach quails before the interior decorations of these villas. They can be perfectly studied by those who have a mind to it since their owners left in a hurry, and the State, taking over, has preserved them intact. Or so I believed till at a local Comité I was shown sheet after sheet of typed lists of the valuables taken from these same dwellings: a dinner-service of 120 pieces, in gold; ten embossed wine-coolers, in gold; a chalice in platinum; a wash-hand set in silver; two grotesque figures, in gold; a coffee service in silver, jewelled.

'Most of them have been melted down. They were of no artistic interest.'

I could well believe it.

Out of the churches a great deal has been taken and placed in museums. Some of these preservations are interesting from other points of view than those of the artist and antiquarian. One church was being burned out when a connoisseur who was present recollected that a certain exceedingly venerable tapestry had been overlooked in the preliminary sifting. He ran forward and beat out the flames which had already begun to consume it. As he did so pieces of charred paper were seen fluttering down. Further inspection showed that the back of the tapestry was wadded with bank-notes.

I heard other stories of non-sacred valuables stored in churches; and it seemed to me extraordinary that a cult sufficiently modern-minded to preserve machine-guns and ammunitions in its churches should not have a more accurate appreciation of the beauties of a bank-balance. I did not discredit the good faith of those who told me these stories, but I supposed that legend, always a quick breeder in a crisis, might have made fifty different versions of one incident.

When I had looked at the rich men's houses, when I had read the lists of the valuables taken therefrom, I revised my opinion. The Spanish aristocracy is in a primitive stage of capitalism, it preserves the medieval brag of possessions, it locks up its money in gold and jewels and keeps the gold and jewels for display.

An amusing example of this was the celebrated boarding-school for young ladies kept by the sisters of the Sacred Heart. No young lady was allowed to enter this establishment (officially sacred to the daughters of the nobility) without a trousseau in which every article of clothing was numbered by a dozen dozen. So valuable was the social prestige of this establishment that the un-enobled rich, equipping their daughters with the requisite 144 nightgowns, bustbodices, etc., strained every nerve and every persuasion to get their daughters received there. So powerful was the tradition of the social prestige that the un-enobled daughters, even when they had been admitted, were not allowed to mingle with the blue-blooded.

The modesty of our English aristocracy, hanging its womenkind with Ciro pearls and synthetic emeralds while the genuine articles repose in the bank, is unknown to them. So strong is this tradition in Spain that the magnates of Barcelona, to seem aristocrats, did the same. That the tradition has its advantages is proved by the number of empty jewel-cases, bare ruined choirs where late the sweet dollars chinked, which they left behind in the villas. If the laity is thus medieval, no wonder that the church is medieval too, only with Christian humility burying its gold beneath the flagstones, lining its tapestries with bank-notes.

The works of ecclesiastical art are in the museums, the churches are bare and barred. Apologists in this country have tended to stress the first statement, but the second is the more significant. Those systematically gutted interiors are the more impressive when one contrasts them with the preservation of the villas. In the villas was as great, or greater, a demonstration of luxury, idleness, and superbity. In the villas were objects infinitely more desirable as loot than anything the churches could offer. Had the churches been sacked, as some say they were, by a greedy and envious mob, that mob would have sacked the villas with more greed and better satisfaction. But the villas are untouched, and the churches are gutted. They have been cleaned out exactly as sick-rooms are cleaned out after a pestilence. Everything that could preserve the contagion has been destroyed.

It is idle, too, to suggest that this work was the result of a policy imposed on the people by a Marxist leadership. One might well wish that it had been. It would be a feather in the Marxist cap. But actually, Barcelona is an anarchist town, and anarchism does not impose policies.

It was the people themselves who, deliberately and systematically, put the churches out of action. So extensive, so thorough a campaign, could not have been carried out unless it were by the will of the people. And it was more than the expression of resentment at finding the churches used as arms-dumps and machine-gun nests. Not every church was so used, but the blameless on this count have not fared any better than the others. It was a longer, a more universal resentment which stripped the walls and burned the pulpits and confessionals, and barred up the doors, a realisation that here, beyond the other strongholds of Fascism and capitalism, was the real stronghold of the oppressors.

I was lucky enough to see one belated example of this. It was reported that in the garden of a suburban villa a religious plaque which had escaped notice was being used as a private praying centre. The local Comité to whom this was reported sent two men with hammers. Seriously, without a vestige of either rage or contempt, they smashed it to bits. Their expressions were exactly those of two conscientious decontaminating officers dealing with a bag of infected linen which had been discovered in a house which was supposed to be free of infection.

A dozen people or so watched the ceremony, and when the plaque had been destroyed one of them drew the men's attention to a garden statue half concealed in bushes. The two men looked at it. 'It's not a saint,' they said, and went away.

Among those lookers-on was a servant girl who had been suspected of worshipping before the plaque. She had had a religious upbringing, she could neither read nor write. While the hammer-blows fell she watched with painful attention. Her face expressed profound animal fear. But it was not on the men that she fixed her terrified stare. It was the plaque itself which she watched with such bewildered and abject terror.

A CASTLE IN SPAIN
(*New Yorker*, January 2nd, 1937)

We took it pretty calmly when, on a fine afternoon in October, William came back to our Barcelona hotel and announced that on the morrow we should all move into a palace. 'Thank God!' said Marion. 'Now we can have afternoon tea.'

I, for my part, asked if Asunción was also invited. Asunción had attached herself to the English Aid to Loyal Spain. As a volunteer cook for the Red Cross, she had transposed herself into a sort of general guardian angel, smoothing our paths with committees, sewing on buttons, and helping me a great deal in the various excursions – excursions ranging from buying large iron frying pans for the hospital kitchen to combing Barcelona for a café where newly arrived English Aiders could be restored with buttered toast, by which, in my humble, stammering way, I, too, helped to combat Fascism.

It appeared that there was plenty of room in the palace for Asunción. There was even a niche for her talents. The palace was already supplied with two maids and a portress, but had no cook.

The government of Barcelona, lacking so much else, had any amount of palaces. Before the revolution, rich men of various nationalities lived around Barcelona in suburbs that look like Hampstead in a fever dream, Hampstead abounding in Moorish crenellations and minarets, palms and bougainvillaea but still unmistakably Hampstead in social smugness and bracing air and classy vistas of the city huddled below. When the rich men departed hurriedly by car or warship, they left their palaces and their servants behind, and palaces and servants passed into the care of the State.

'The *muchachas* – the girls – will welcome you,' we were told. 'It has been dull for them since their family ran away.' We were glad to think that we should be brightening dull lives. Our queer, miscellaneous party had this much in common – that we were all there with the hope and intention of helping Spain, and every little helps. From the start they found us interesting. For the most part they regarded us as being after the nature of the bears in a masque 'framed to astonish and delight,' but the *muchacha* Otilia did some quite serious research work on us. She insisted upon remaining in the dining room throughout our meals, ostensibly to stand at

142

the sideboard ready to hand us another cold plate; actually, as I learned from private information, 'to see how they eat.' At intervals, on the plea of calling for more cold plates, she shouted bulletins of our behaviours through the service lift to the *muchacha* Pilar, and if the bulletins were sufficiently rousing, Pilar would appear from the lift, meek as a Murillo, observing the latest phenomenon from under black lashes. Then, when her giggles were becoming too much for her, she would go politely into the lift again, and vanish.

We, too, could be observant and critical. Marion was a specialist in food values. In her leisure moments she haunted the kitchen to see what atrocities against internal hygiene could be performed with oil and salt fish. Sometimes she watched in silent disapproval, sometimes her feelings would be too much for her, and she would cry for them to be interpreted.

'For goodness' sake, come and tell this girl not to throw away the potato peelings. They are by far the most valuable part of the vegetable.'

'*Las peladuras*,' I began, wishing for the hundredth time that pocket dictionaries might be printed in a type which did not make one feel dizzy.

'*Sí, sí! Las peladuras*,' confirmed Pilar, smiling on my infant steps in Spanish, and peeling rapidly.

'Look! Straight into the garbage pail! Now she's begun on another. Stop her, tell her not to! Explain to her that they are full of vegetable salts, tell her I *must* have those peelings.'

'*Necesiten*,' I said, forsaking the dictionary, falling back upon recollections of all those official notices in Spanish and Catalan which appear on walls and in trams, '*necesiten por l'alimentacion de questa camerade*.' The spirit, if not the letter, of authority had been invoked.

'O.K.,' said Pilar, piously.

I myself have never followed a diet, or followed hounds. But I recognise that either pursuit is, to those who feel like it, the most absorbing passion that life can offer. It was a wonderful sight to watch Marion following her diet, through – so to speak – bush and through brier, to observe how in an alien city already restricted as to food supplies she nosed out the particular products of nature which her diet demanded.

Another fine spectacle, showing what things are possible in an honest-to-God republic, was to see Marion on one side of the kitchen and Asunción on the other, cooking after their respective theories. On

Marion's side all was pure, and almost all was raw. Grated onion, grated carrot, grated cheese, sliced tomatoes, lay arranged on a single plate in a border of lettuce, like a small model of a formal flower bed. On Asunción's side was a welter of mushrooms, sprats, mussels, red peppers, and the bubbling of cauldrons, and the hissing of oil. Sometimes, as an expression of comradely feeling (or perhaps as a demonstration of the lissomeness which follows upon raw carrot), Marion would leave her vegetable plates and run through some gymnastic exercises, extending her chest, touching her toes, or nimbling round the kitchen on all fours. To Asunción, shaped so exactly like a bear, nimbling on all fours was child's play. She would race Marion over the marble from stove to dresser, and beat her by a head. Then they would rise to their feet, clap each other on the back, exchange their bilingual compliments, and return to their cookeries.

Late in the evening, long after English appetites had wilted and fallen away, dinner would be served, and Marion's dishes and Asunción's dishes appeared side by side to tempt us, like Sacred and Profane Love.

The cause of Sacred Love received a grave setback one day when Marion met an English resident, a lady who had resisted all the British consul's pleas that she should depart by warship and, ignoring his threats that if she did not do so he could not continue to be responsible for her, resided still. She and Marion struck up a friendship. One day she came to our palace to drink weak tea. Marion began to expatiate on the martyrdom of vitamins in Spanish cookery, and went on to describe her disappointment when the lettuces she had bought with such triumph were served by Asunción in a broth of oil and vinegar.

'Salads!' exclaimed the English resident. 'My dear, surely you don't eat salads?'

'No, not *salads*. Oil should only be used externally – rubbed on the feet, for instance – The proper channel by which to take oil is the pores. But a raw lettuce is invaluable.'

Marion rallied at this.

'I must tell you at once I'm not an Imperialist. Far from it.'

'Before the British warships come into the Mediterranean,' continued the English resident, 'everyone on board has to sign an undertaking not to touch lettuce. If they do, they are dismissed.'

Marion held her ground pretty well, we thought. She said that such an ordinance was exactly what she would expect of the Admiralty, that preserve of ignorance and petty tyranny. And she added that the Army was just about as bad. But the words had pierced her, the wound festered. By the next day Marion, as far as lettuce went, had joined the British Navy.

Shortly before Marion joined the Navy we developed a second cook. She first became known to us as a deep baritone voice, a voice engaged in making an oration and situated in the kitchen. At first we paid little attention. Spain is a hospitable country we had become fairly accustomed to finding affable strangers using our telephone, children of angelic serenity breathing in the typewriter, puppy dogs in our bedrooms. Some times these visitors turned out to be complementary to our household, relations of Pilar's or of Otilia's; sometimes they were just benevolent strangers, like the two men who arrived with a barrowload of mathematic treatises, proffering them to us, since they were in English, as suitable reading for our leisure moments.

But this voice, so resonant and so persistent, had a disquieting note. It sounded like a sermon.

'Suppose,' said Marion, 'they've got a priest there in disguise. We don't know anything of their real opinions; they may have been harbouring him in the basement for days. It might be very awkward.'

I said I would go to the kitchen and ask if Asunción had come back from market. A pretext is often useful.

The kitchen in our palace was at the top of the house, an odd arrangement, but it now gave me plenty of time to analyse the voice, which, as I approached it, became so remarkably intoning that by the third flight the priest had changed to a bishop. As I opened the door the voice stopped. I saw a massive woman, with sleek gray hair and sleek gray eyes, and a sleek fish-belly skin.

'This is the other cook,' said Otilia.

I said how nice that was, for one has to be careful about people's susceptibilities, – but the thought of another cook brought care with it. Asunción was all the cook we needed. Already she shared the kitchen with Marion and her vegetable plates; three cooks in one kitchen was, from the aspect of housing, congested, and from the social aspect, ostentatious and unsuited to our intention of living, as William had put it, 'as much like proletarians as possible.' Asunción was a Communist, Marion a rigid freethinker, and the new cook was obviously as Church and State as anyone not a bishop could be. Otilia's next remark confirmed this.

'She is the old cook. She used to cook for the family.'

There was a baritone groan, and the gray eyes were rolled upward, and the heavy shoulders heaved in a sigh for a past state of things. Fascism must be combatted on every occasion, so I said, 'Do you belong to your trades union? If not, you cannot cook here.'

The cook put on a look of outraged Castilian sensibility, and said that she feared the lady was talking French, a language she did not comprehend. Otilia kindly rearranged my remark into Castilian. The cook uttered a long and noble collect.

'She says she does not come here to cook. She has come to take away her bed.'

I wished to retort, 'Then she must establish ownership,' but the dictionary did not seem inclined to forward this wish, so I retired.

There now seemed quite a vista of complications. Of course, if the bed really belonged to the cook (which I doubted), the only complication would be that when she had taken it away there would be nowhere for Asunción to sleep. Far more serious was the thought that if the bed did not belong to the cook it belonged, like everything else in the house, to the government. We, as that government's guests, could not countenance the removal of a bed which was, so to speak, a ward in chancery, and I looked forward to vigils and stratagems, and possibly even open strife.

I was glad to think that Asunción was a Communist. Though she could gambol on all fours with Marion or pass away a wet Sunday by tearing about the basement in her combinations and a scarlet sash, pretending to be a bullfighter, she was, like all Communists, serious at heart. She would see that bed in its true light as a part, small but integral, of the political situation.

Another reason for being glad that Asunción was a Communist was that it made conversation between us so much easier. When we had exhausted each other's powers of understanding on such subjects as food and drink, and our relations and health, and the weather, and our acquaintances, we fell back on politics, and became as giants refreshed. Agreement was a considerable aid to conversation, and another thing that helped greatly was Asunción's habit, if she wished to express disapproval, of turning herself into a machine gun and saying, *'Poum, poum, poum, poum!'*

This was one of the things she said about the cook. The cook, it appeared, was a Fascist at heart, and a zealot, and unsyndicated. We must feed her and house her, of course; only in the old order of society could people be shooed from the door like cats. As for the ownership of the bed, that must lie between the cook and the State. The cook must go to the local Committee of Control and lay her claim before them.

What happened between the cook and the Committee we never learned. We did not even know if she went to them. She used to walk out twice a day or so, looking very processional, and sometimes she carried food with her. She also had a certain weakness for brandy. When she had been taking brandy, her gait became even more processional, and her orisons (in which, I fancy, all our sins were remembered) became even more like a bishop's. After a while we saw less of her; in the end she went away. We rather expected to read in the English papers that she had been, on the same day, though in different columns, atrociously martyred by the Reds and received in audience by the Pope – a strange dual fate incident to Spanish bishops in the English press. We epitaphed her with a few *poum, poum, poum, poums.*

Mine were the more vehement; since I had grown accustomed to Catalan sobriety and honesty, those little peccadilloes with the brandy struck me as base indeed. Asunción took a more instructed view. What could one expect of one who was always praying, poor ignoramus, and did not belong to her syndicate? I never dared tell Asunción that in England cooks do not belong to their trades union either. Her interest in England and the English was more warm-hearted than Otilia's; at times, indeed, she took too romantic a view of us. One evening when William and Marion, linked together in our fortuitous party by high senses of duty but not otherwise linked, had gone austerely into a very rainy dusk, Asunción commented on their absence. I explained that they had gone to a meeting. Asunción received this information with the wink of one who knows better.

'Under the pine trees,' she said briefly.

It seemed a pity, since she was feeling like this, that she should not know of a real romance. We told her of another couple from among our group – neither of them, I fear, from her point of view remarkable for youth or beauty – who were linked not only by the prevalent sense of duty but also by a real desire to retire together under the pine trees.

Her jaw dropped; she looked incredulous, and even aghast. But in a moment she had recovered her philosophy, her geniality, her warmth of heart; and raising her fist in the Popular Front salute, she exclaimed, '*Viva la Republica!*'

HARVEST IN 1937
(*New Statesman*, July 31st, 1937)

The road from Valencia to Madrid descends in a series of dramatic hairpin bends to the gorge of the Rio Gabriel; and rises again as dramatically. In those swooping few miles one changes country, leaves behind the orange groves and the olives, the oleanders growing wild along the dried winterbournes, the roses edging the dusty road; and comes into a vast austere tableland that rolls onward towards distant Madrid, and grows corn. Here, as we drove on our way to attend the Madrid sessions of the Second Congress of the Writers in Defence of Culture, the harvest was being reaped, reaped with a sickle.

It is a beautiful gesture, if one cares for the picturesque. As the reaper stoops, grasping the locks of corn, and swings the sickle with a movement made elegant by centuries of hereditary use, and casts the swathe behind him, and stoops and grasps and swings the sickle again, it is as though one watched a series of caresses. And along with him his shadow, small under the midday sun, repeats the movement in a contracted perspective.

Women reap among the men. Looking closely, one sees how these groups acknowledge war. Women of all ages, old men, children, make up the greater part of these bands. The babies sit along the edge of the corn-strips, sometimes there is a dog with them, or a tethered mule or donkey, chewing at the harsh stubble.

The reapers are too sunburned to look hot. Faces and bared arms are dark, shining with sweat they look like oiled wood. The men wear broad-brimmed straw hats, the women muffle their heads in thick kerchiefs, sometimes they have a white cloth bound over the mouth. This prevents the rasping straw dust from irritating the throat. The dust settles on faces and bared arms, the flies buzz.

Mile after mile the beautiful reaping gesture persists, tireless, identical. And one begins to remember the feel of corn, to remember that those locks of corn which seem so yielding as the reaper gathers them are in truth harsh and spiky; that to tread on corn-stubble is like treading on metal filings; that along with the sweet scent of corn flies the teasing, tickling corn dust. Among the corn are the sharp, low-growing thistles, the small aggressive weeds of a dry soil, clawing and scratching the feet of those who tread them.

There are many weeds among the corn. By our English standards it is a poor crop, short in straw, light in the ear. Scanty as is the corn, the reapers are scantier yet. As the road goes on over the interminable plain one begins to wonder if the corn will ever be reaped, the landscape is so large, the little groups of reapers so widely spaced.

At intervals along the enormous horizon mountains appear. The plain is a general sunburned tawny colour, the rock of the mountains is painted by distance to a lovely colour like lavender. But in spite of the tender colour given to them by depth of air, these mountains have an inimical aspect, they seem to have the watchfulness of tyrants, not of guardians, as they overlook this landscape of poor corn and scattered reapers.

And where do they live, these reapers? Bound to the soil, it is as though they rose out of it to serve the corn, and, the harvest gathered sank into the ground again. The villages lie leagues apart, sometimes there are not even villages, only long barrack-like farmsteads, what old Scotch husbandry called 'a town', the bailiff's house, and the barns and stables and granges, and the field-workers' quarters all enclosed within one wall. No lesser roads, no lanes, branch off the main road, only a few tracks and footpaths. A signpost is an eye's wonder on this journey.

It is the harvest of 1937, the first harvest these peasants have ever reaped for themselves. When the great landowners fled these melancholy miles of corn-land were allotted among the workers. This year, like every

149

other year, the harvest goes on, the harvesters repeat their gesture, the babies, docile with heat, sit patiently along the edges of the corn-strips. The harvest goes on, the sickle swings forward. And as though it were a groundbass in a piece of counterpoint the rhythm of harvest after harvest becomes apparent, is a recurring gesture like the movement of the reaper, stooping to grasp the locks of corn, swinging the sickle, casting the swathe behind him. Subdued to this rhythm, working on under the heavy sun, the corn-dust flying, the flies buzzing, the beat of the swollen vein, the ache in the loins . . . to those who reap it can this harvest of 1937 seem so very different from the harvests of other years?

There is a heavy sound on the road behind us, an imperious klaxon. Our car draws to one side, and one of the new Government lorries tears past. The reapers lift themselves from the corn, with stiff, awkward movements they straighten themselves, the sweat pouring off their faces with the effort of wrenching themselves so suddenly upright. They hold up their clenched fists in the salute, they cheer and shout greetings, and the soldiers salute and shout in answer. The lorry passes, the reapers stoop to the corn again. All along the road the groups of reapers, one after the other, straighten themselves out of the corn to salute and cheer as the lorry sweeps on towards Madrid.

WHAT THE SOLDIER SAID
(*Time and Tide*, August 14th, 1937)

'In the name of the soldiers of the Sixth Army Corps, I am come to say a few words to you. We are defending the legitimate cause of the Republic, and the cause of justice. We will defend them with courage and with all the strength that is in us. Now we, the Sixth Army Corps, say this to you. We fight in defence of justice and culture. We will fetch peace and culture at the point of the bayonet for the sake of our own happiness and that of our children. That's all. Greeting, comrades.'

It was July, 1937. The International Association of Writers in Defence of Culture was holding its second congress. War had not, as we feared it might, deflected our intention of holding that congress in Spain. The Spanish Government had confirmed the original invitation of the Spanish members of the Association. War had not affected, either, the arrangements for that congress. We held our sessions in Madrid; it was in Madrid that the delegate soldier from the Sixth Army Corps made us his speech. His was not the only military voice to be raised at our congress. Many of the writers in defence of culture who took part in our sessions came to us on special leave, fighters in the defence of culture as well as writers: Ludwig Renn, Jef Last, Ralph Bates, were among these. And through all the various languages of the delegates from twenty-six countries sounded the international language of cannon; for we sat discussing questions of culture and humanism within earshot of the battle.

'What the soldier said is not evidence.' This dictum is by now almost an axiom of British thinking. Even in the improbable event of a private soldier of the British Army addressing a congress of writers, it seems unlikely that his speech would be received as evidence. His interest in culture must be felt as one of two things: a private idiosyncrasy of extraordinary force, or an indication that the War Office had issued orders that at such and such a moment interest in culture should be manifested.

The hypothetical soldier in the British Army should, ideally, be better equipped for interest in culture than the Spanish soldier who addressed us. He would have learned, at any rate, how to read and write, whereas it is quite possible that our Spanish soldier had learned neither of these arts, or was but just now learning them, in the schools staffed by the Cultural Militia of Spain – an organisation of the lettered classes whose duty it is to teach the fighting men, in the barracks, and in the actual trenches.

But we could feel no doubt but that what the Spanish soldier said was evidence. His speech, as you see, expressed no subtlety of thoughts, no yearning for culture; it expressed a more solid appreciation than yearning, an intention to have and to hold. And what the soldier said to us was borne out by a hundred speeches we heard in Spain.

One of the long discontents of Spain has been its illiteracy. The Spaniard has a natural appreciation of culture; this shows itself in a hundred manifestations, in the decoration of a wayside inn, in the turning of a phrase, the lingual consciousness of those who use dialect (a cook in Barcelona said to me, 'This is our Catalan word. In Castile you must say *manzana*'), in the common people's appreciation, passionate and passionately critical, of points of style in such things as the singer's coloratura or the gestures of the bullring. Even such affairs as the arrangements of wares on market stalls are stylised: a novel juxtaposition of fruits will call out interested comment and discussion.

But these people who have preserved a traditional culture and preserved it alive and kicking, have been in great number denied any education. In the streets one hears the clacking of typewriters, and the clacking comes from the public letter-writers' booths, where men and women whose faces bear the unmistakable imprint of intellect and thought wait in a queue to dictate the letters they are not able to write for themselves.

The Government of 1936 came into office pledged to carry out a programme of education. In spite of the war, this programme is being steadily carried out. New schools have been built and are a-building, every month the Cultural Militia render their figures of the numbers of soldiers who have passed from being analphabetics to being literates (the figure for May 1937, was over 4,000). Other war-time Governments might have hesitated to offer hospitality to eighty literary delegates, people who would consume food and petrol and accommodation and care. Going from Barcelona to Valencia, from Valencia to Madrid, we had no doubt that this hospitality of the Government of Spain was the hospitality of the people of Spain also. Hotel-workers, shopkeepers, people in villages[2], harvesters in the fields, welcomed us, not as curiosities, not even as possible propagandists, but as representatives of something they valued and understood. To us, the British delegates, this unfeigned and natural welcome was a particularly interesting experience. We learned to hear ourselves spoken of as *los intelectuales* without dreading words usually so dubious in good intent, without feeling the usual embarrassment and defiant shrinking. We were released from the old fear that by giving one's support as a representative of culture to a cause one had at heart one might be doing that cause more harm than good.

The experience was the more impressive in contrast to a recent experience in our own country.

For we had applied for permits to travel to Spain as delegates to the second congress of our Association, and had been refused them. With patience and firm serenity an official of the Foreign Office had assured us that there was no political bias underlying this refusal; it was merely that as representatives of culture we were not included in the Foreign Office's *Weltanschauung*, cultural reasons are not among those reasons recognised as valid reasons for wishing to travel to Spain. If you go (so he explained) as an accredited journalist, yes. If you go on a humanitarian errand, yes. If you go as a man of business, YES! But if you go for purposes of culture, no.

THE DROUGHT BREAKS
(*Life and Letters Today*, Summer, 1937)

Rafaela Perez went a step or two into the street, pulling her shawl closer around her. A drizzling rain fell out of the winter sky, by midnight that rain would be snow. A cat came along, nosing in the gutters. It would not find much there, this was a poor street and the poor had no food to throw away.

In the rich quarter there was feasting and waste. The German soldiers, the Italian soldiers, were eating as they had not eaten for years. Last week a German lieutenant, tipsy, very affable, had said to her in his halting, clumsy syllables, 'Spain, fine country. Much eating, much wine. Pouf!' And he had distended himself, and thumped his stomach, smiling candidly, showing his bright young teeth. '*De nada*,' she had said – 'It's nothing' – the conventional phrase with which one puts off a thanks or a commendation. For it did not do to give no answer at all, one must at all costs seem civil to these invaders. And she had gone on scrubbing the floor of the café, wringing out the cloth stinking of chloride of lime.

Now the cat was licking up rain-water. It would not find anything else, drink water if one can fill the belly no other way. Curious to think at all about a cat, curious to be so attentive to a grey cat slinking through the grey dusk. Ah, but life was so empty, so hideously empty, one would think of anything now, of a cat, of a cobweb.

Two days after the town was taken by the Nationalists her husband had been shot. They had not even troubled to find the gun in the chimney, the bullets padded in the mattress. His Trades Union card had been enough. One glance at it, and they were driving him out of the house, up the narrow street towards the church. A dozen other similar groups converged thither: a man, struggling, or walking in silence (Diego had walked demurely, without a word, without a glance back), and about him the soldiers and Civil Guards, and, trailing after, a woman, two women, a woman with her children. There, by the church, the firing squad was waiting, trim and powerful. And so – and so – the men were lined up against the wall, and the word was given to fire.

The bloodstains were still on the church wall and the flies buzzing round them when the church was solemnly re-sanctified. New confessionals, new hangings, new pictures and images, arrived in furniture vans and were carried in. Then had come the procession, soldiers and choir-boys, the bishop under a canopy, priests and gentlefolk and more soldiers. They, the people of the quarter, must kneel on the cobbles while the procession went by. Inside the church everything was smart and fresh, there was a smell of incense and of flowers and of varnish from the new confessionals. Outside there was the stain of blood and the smell of blood. The religious people came clustering and buzzing back as fast as bluebottles, as though they, too, came wherever there was a smell of blood. And now, more than ever, it was impossible to escape them, impossible to say them nay, whether they came demanding alms or children.

If one's husband had been shot, then one's children must be taken also.

'Holy Church,' said the Reverend Mother, her black robes seeming to fill the room, her eyebrows bristling, 'Holy Church will not leave these innocents where they can be contaminated. You have three children, I think. See that they are ready by eight tomorrow morning.'

The convent was far away, at the other end of the town, a heavy building with barred windows, a garden surrounded by a high wall topped with spikes. For many days the mothers of the lost children haunted there, hanging about, watching the barred windows and the spiked wall; for though there was no chance of seeing the children one might perhaps hear a voice on the other side of the wall. But there were never any voices. Twice a day one could hear a clatter of small feet, marching, marching. And so, after a time, one lost hope, did not go so often, did not go at all.

Every week the nuns came round to collect the money. They knew to a peseta how much one earned. 'Your children are well. They want no other mother than the Mother of God. But they cannot be kept for nothing. We ask you in the name of the Lord and his little ones.' Then the hand would glide out of the sleeve and the downcast eyes would scan the pesetas.

From the loud-speaker further up the street came the accustomed sound of the hour. A drunken vaunting voice, Queipo de Llano's, saying that Madrid would fall in a couple of days, that Valencia had been bombed, that the Catalans would not fight, that everywhere the Reds were falling back, without food, without arms, without hope. Then would come the singing, and the shouts of *Arriba Espana*!

It was four months and twenty-one days since the children had been taken away, and now she was standing in the rain, looking at a cat – no looking where the cat had been, for it had long ago sneaked on its way. The street was dark and silent, as though dead. Indeed, it was half-dead, depopulated. This neighbour dead, that neighbour in prison, that neighbour gone off. People would be there in the evening, and in the morning they would have disappeared, leaving no word, no trace.

The wireless brayed on, presently there would be the national music, humstrum of guitars, snap of castanets. In the cafés of the rich quarter the foreigners would lean back in their chairs, wag their heads, stir their haunches, eye the prostitutes trailing past, say to themselves, 'We are in Spain.'

Later still, a noise not broadcast, there would be cries, hooting laughter, rattle of a volley. Every night, even now, they were shooting in the prisons.

In the Calle de Rosas no one stirred. Those who were left in the tall houses sat, cold and scattered, like the last leaves on a winter tree. The houses were so much colder, being half-empty: no steps on the stairs, no smells of cooking, never a laugh or a song, not even a quarrel to liven up the air.

She shook her head and sighed. Like an echo there came the noise of the wind awaking in the mountains.

The voice on the wireless bragged on. Madrid had again been bombed, a sally of the Reds had been wiped out with great slaughter, five hundred prisoners had been taken on the Basque front, an ammunition dump had blown up. One did not listen, but yet one heard. One did not look at the placards, but yet one saw. One pulled one's shawl over one's ears, turned away one's eyes; yet through one's mind marched the newly-arrived battalions, one saw their grand equipment, one heard their strong marching and the words of command shouted in foreign tongues. A scrap of newspaper, wrapped round a bit of salt fish or a handful of olives, jabbed at one's eyes with a threat or a sneer.

And yet Diego had said that it was good to know how to read, good to take an interest in the affairs of the country.

Sometimes out of her stagnating cold misery a flash of rancour would explode like a marsh-gas. If Diego had been content to work and to eat, like other men! – then, though this had come, though there had been hunger and cold and terror, there would still have been husband and children, a clue to living; and the church wall would have been only what it had been, a wall much thicker than those of the flimsy tenements around it.

The wind was rising, desolate among the stone crags. *Arriba Espana!* chorused the voices on the wireless, a wolfish pack-howling. Overhead a window opened softly, a head peered out.

'Rafaela! Is that you? What is it, what are you waiting for?'

'Nothing.'

Without comment the head withdrew, the window was closed again. There was nothing to wait for. She must go in, chew her slow supper, lie down cold on the bed. The wind blew stronger, its voice among the mountains trembled with intensity, it was like a wild singer. The wind throbbed, came closer with its throbbing voice.

Ah! What was that? – that rending crash of sound, and after-rattle, and another and another crash? What were these jarring wings over the city?

Windows opened, doors opened, the street was full of voices. Blind Adela was wailing. 'It's them! Mother of God, it's them! They're going to bomb us now!'

'No! It's us, it's us! They're *ours*!'

She tore off the dripping shawl, waved it upwards in greeting, turning

156

up her face, her heart, to the death falling from the air, as though to a greeting from the dead, as though to a greeting from life.

All around were voices, voices hushed, broken, excited; gasps, cries caught back, questions and exclamations. It was like the noise of earth, thirsty with long drought, clucking with parched lips as it drinks the rain.

SOLDIERS AND SICKLES
(*The Countryman*, October, 1937)

It is unusual for writers to hear such words as 'Here come the Intellectuals' spoken by working class people and common soldiers in tones of kindliness and enthusiasm. And it was a new experience to see a harvest being reaped with sickles, and trodden out upon threshing floors.

This harvest on the long plain east of Madrid is significant in many ways. While the strange workings of Non-Intervention impede even foodstuffs from reaching that part of Spain which is loyal to the government, every ear of corn is important. I was told a story about this, while we sat quenching our midday thirst in the inn of Utiel, sitting in a large, bare, half darkened room, while, silhouetted against the blazing, light of the open doorway, the children of the town came in, at first shyly, then confidently, to walk exploringly around us, murmuring to each other those words we had already learned not to flinch at, 'These are the Intellectuals.' It was a writer who told me the story, Jef Last. But he spoke as a soldier, for he has been fighting since the outbreak of the Franco revolt. This year, he said, the corn had ripened early. His regiment was holding a section of the line which runs through cornfields. The men, very many of them peasants, watched the corn with interest; presently, with passionate concern. For it was ready to reap, and in these acres dominated by war, there was no one to reap it. They watched the corn as patriots, too, knowing the important of the harvest. They held a meeting, and decided that they themselves would reap it. Sickles were got and the corn behind the lines was reaped and stooked. But there was corn in front as well, in

157

no man's land. Crawling out on their bellies, under threat of fire always and often under fire, working in the time allotted to them for rest, they reaped the no man's land corn also. Between them and the enemy was an array of neat stooks. But who was to carry it? Each soldier is equipped with a blanket, and they carried the corn in their blankets, carrying the treasure back behind the lines to where common life began again, to where the mules trudged on the threshing floor and the barns could store the harvest.

That story was in my mind as we drove all day across the melancholy plain, with its few huddled villages. Scattered groups, elderly men and women mostly, stooped over the corn, repeating that movement that looks so harmonious, that in reality entails such ruthless fatigue. So they reaped when the corn was carried to the windmills of La Mancha against which Don Quixote aimed his spear.

But this year's harvest was different. It is the first of a new lineage of harvests, the first these peasants have reaped for themselves. But it is also the last, if things go as they should, of the old lineage of harvests. Those leagues of corn-land, immemorially fertile, vast rolling stretches of shallow tilth, demand a stronger technique of agriculture. It would be a perfect country for tractors. When the Spanish government can beat its swords into plough shares there will be deep ploughing here, the internal combustion engine will take the place of the mule and the donkey, science will reinforce the patient traditional skill of the *campesino* (peasant). When those days come, I thought, these lands will show a harvest worthy of those who will reap it. And afterwards, as though it were a promise of what should be, I saw, stepping down a hillside in the early golden dusk, a rank of pylons, ghostly silver, their delicate geometrical beauty most perfectly assorted to the austere landscape of Castille.

How would they seem to Don Quixote, these strange apparitions? They might pull him out of his romances by what they could promise, a stranger news in this countryside than any romance, speaking of power and light coming to the darkened and the exploited, of education in the stead of ignorance, of houses for hovels, of the lives of free men for the lives of anxious bondage. But it is the children of Sancho Panza and Maria Gutierrez his wife who will best understand these promises.

WARDS OF THE PEOPLE

(unpublished ms, Warner/Ackland Archive, Dorset County Museum)

With the outbreak of the civil war in Spain the government and the municipal authorities had to take charge of a lot of objects, animate and inanimate, whose previous owners and guardians had no further use for them. The objects ranged from rare exotics to foundlings, from canvasses by Velazquez to old family servants, so much more like friends than servants that their wages had not allowed them to put any money by. There was, in fact, something for every taste.

Naturally, the inanimate objects were the easier to deal with, though one must not suppose that all the objects of value and beauty left behind have been as gratifying as the involuntary bequest of the Duke of Alba. Cataloguing connoisseurs have had some terrible times with family portraits of the late nineteenth century, they have grown faint trudging along library shelves stored with the curious literature of the rue de Rivoli and large bound price-lists of the London Army and Navy Stores, they have groaned under heavy burdens of stuffed wolfhounds, life-size St Josephs in painted cast-iron, and groves of baronial antlers.

But however distressing an inanimate object, it is, at any rate, inanimate. Far more painful were the early experiences of the educationalists detailed to take over the various charitable institutions abandoned by the religious orders. One of these institutions, an orphanage, had always been celebrated for a high standard of teaching; but the standard of discipline had been higher still, and it distressed the newcomers to find themselves among children who never laughed or played. They sought to persuade by force of example. They laughed, they bounded along the polished corridors; and the orphans, accustomed from the age of six to put away childish things, looked on with silent civil horror. Even more plaintive is the first report of the explorers of a home for children with tuberculosis of the bone, now the *Sanatori d'Infants Angel Guimerá*. 'They are terrified of water, they refuse to eat fruit. Their pockets are crammed with cigarettes made of dead leaves and every sort of trash. They have no love for each other, and each one of them is a tell-tale.'

Many of the grand houses had aquariums or aviaries. Obviously one cannot travel with the family carp as easily as one travels with the family jewels; so the aquariums and the aviaries have passed into the keeping of the new order, have changed their status from private to public property; and if the mansion is granted to an administrative committee or something of that sort the new inhabitants become responsible for the livestock. An aquarium is a peaceful responsibility, the fountain splashes, the goldfish nose around, it is soothing to leave one's desk and stroll out for a glance at the goldfish. Even though they may have as little mutual affection as the children at the *Sanatori d'Infants Angel Guimerá* few will grieve for it.

An aviary can be much more insistent.

I had been told to go to a committee of anarchists who from a suburban villa controlled the destinies of a great quantity of fascist furniture. I was to ask them if they had a gas-cooker to spare. In the ante-room there was the usual crowd of babies pestering the sentry, who sat in a wicker chair with his gun across his knees, loading a pea-shooter for them. Some of the babies no doubt had been dumped by their mothers, mothers visiting with similar errands to mine. Others had just strayed in from the street, moved by that impulse to club-life which is so strong a feature of Spanish character. Comrade Emilio, said the sentry, was in there.

Comrade Emilio was in a stately and tidy drawing-room, seated behind an elegant writing table. But despite the stateliness and tidiness of the drawing-room, and the impression of hush given by a very thick carpet, his drawing-room was as uproarious as the ante-room; for in the window was an aviary, and the aviary was full of love-birds. In a halting yell I asked him for a gas-cooker. And he, sparing his vocal chords, nodded, and began to turn over the pages of a ledger.

While he looked for a gas-cooker I looked at him. He was everything in appearance that the most alarmist aunt could wish – a rough swarthy dangerous-looking man. His face was weary and needed shaving, he had a revolver on his hip. Meanwhile, the love-birds screeched louder and louder. It was impossible to resist the thought that they were full of aristocratic resentment at seeing this coarse fellow in their drawing-room.

160

At intervals he gave them a glance of hopeless resignation. Then, shaking his head as though to shake the noise out of his ears, he turned back to the ledger. It seemed to me I should give him a chance to say something about them. It would do them no harm to hear the opinion of the other side.

'You have birds,' I said.

The face of this dangerous bloodthirsty man lit up with a smile. 'They sing loudly,' said he. Adding with pride, 'They are in splendid condition.'

Humbler than the love-birds, and pleasanter, were the wards of the *Alianza de Intelectuales Antifascistas* in Valencia[3]. The *Alianza* has its headquarters in a narrow street of old houses, a street called the Street of the Knightly Jewels. The house is in the old style, the inhabited part begins with the first floor, below is a large, dusky, stone-paved hall, whose wide doors open onto the street. Here, in the old days of knightly jewels, the lackeys sat in waiting. Here, now, a kitten keeps house with two doves. At first it seemed to me that the strange trio must have wandered by chance, but examining round more closely I saw that they were part of the establishment. For there were two saucers on the floor. One saucer contained indian corn for the doves, the other bread-sop and some fish trimmings for the kitten.

The doves were plump and self-satisfied. The kitten was a small tabby with a thin peaked face, large anxious ears, large pale eyes and an earnest expression.

Spanish cats of any age are a serious hard-working breed, the only cat I have met in Spain who was not a cat that worked for its living was a black cat that lived in a café in Barcelona; and even that cat was clearly nothing like a parasite or a rentier, it must have owed its easy life to some intellectual distinction. There are a great many cats in Spanish proverbs, and these proverbs exactly place the position of cats in Spain. *The Rat knows much, but the Cat knows more*; *Rats don't jest with the Cat's son* – sayings like these acknowledge both the functions and the capacity of cats. On the other hand, *One eye on the Pot and the other on the Cat*, conveys the fact that cats are expected to live by their wits.

But this kitten at the *Alianza* with its peaked face and its anxious air embodied something more than the usual working-class cat's admission that life is a serious matter, the battle to the strong, the race to the swift. It was, I suppose, about four months old. It was a war-time kitten, it had known bombardments and air-raids. And without any fantasy at all it was easy to recognise on the face of this kitten, living so queerly with two doves, the expression of strain and a serious outlook on life which was also on the thin faces of the Valencia children.

I was glad to think that it was under the wardship of the Anti-fascist Intellectuals. It needed kindness, and I was by no means sure of the kindness of the doves. It seemed to me that they cold-shouldered it. Not, I think, from any racial feeling; but partly because they were a pair and it was a unit, and more because they were less affected by war conditions, their nerves were in better order. Though there had been an air-raid overnight there was not a feather out of place on those doves, and their bright flat eyes twinkled with the usual arrogance of these birds, so oddly supposed to be tender and holy.

Five days later, returning from Madrid, I saw the kitten again. This time it was rather happier, it was playing, in a cautious unobtrusive way, with a cork, whisking like a small striped shadow about its shadowy domain. And there were the doves, conversing about their own affairs, and there were the two assorted saucers. No milk, of course. Milk must be kept for the children and the sick.

I should not see this queer household again. I looked round on their home, and that was queer, too. Beyond the door was the assassinating July sunlight, the cars honking down the narrow Street of the Knightly Jewels. Within was this vast shadowy hall, with the wide flight of steps leading up from it to the life of the intellect going on so fiercely and freely above-stairs. The hall was unfurnished, but not empty. In one corner stood a large faded dolls-house, a relict of some much earlier inhabitation, too battered to be given to any play-centre, and leaning against it some oil painting on stretchers. At the back of the room, pale in the dusk of a recess, was a plaster cast of a piece of memorial statuary – a shallow oblong, and within it, in bas-relief, the figure of a militia-man, lying in the negligent sleeping posture as death had tumbled him.

162

THE POLICEMAN AND THE DEAN
(*Time and Tide*, 1927)

In one of Mr. Rudyard Kipling's dashing early works there is a description of an encounter between a policeman and a prostitute (at least if I remember Mr. Kipling's insinuations rightly that was her profession, but I won't be positive; she may have been a policewoman), in the course of which the policeman austerely remarked: 'My Good Girl, Cover Your Breasts' (or words to that effect). But though my memory continually plays me false, I feel sure that I have correctly remembered the ethos of this passage, and that I am right in supplying all those capitals; for the policeman spoke as one delivering a Moral Judgment. Not all breasts are beautiful; but no aesthetic considerations underlay his recommendation, nor was he concerned to prevent the woman from catching cold by unaccustomed exposure. Breasts, he said, not chest.

In taking this view of the affair the policeman was basing himself upon a considerable rock. Had he been called upon to do so, he could have brought forward the names of many eminent moralists, quantities of divines, congregations of saints, and the Fathers of the Church, all of whom had at different times delivered similar judgments. And even when he had done this, he would still have had a trump card up his sleeve (unless he kept it, like the baton, down his trousers); for no less a personage than St. Paul had forestalled him in that *locus classicus* where women are bidden to cover their heads 'because of the angels'. The reason why they were to do this was lest the sight of their tresses should inflame the sexual passions of aerial beings and bring about a repetition of those regrettable mismarriages between the angels and the daughters of men which preceded the Deluge.

It is then the considered opinion of Europe that in a street the first duty of a woman is to cover her breasts, to observe feminine modesty, to dissimulate her sex. The policeman might have said: 'Pull yourself together and behave like a reasonable being'; or, if he were of a more philosophical turn of mind: 'My dear Mrs Badalia, you're a good creature; compose yourself to the Police Station, for to the Police Station you must come'; or even: 'Stop tearing your rival's hair out'. But any of these remarks would have been issued as riders, subsequent and subservient to his Prime Decree. That men should hold this opinion is not surprising; for it is undeniable that the course taken by civilisation has made men more sexually dependent upon women than women are sexually dependent upon men, so that feminine modesty is to be encouraged as a form of insulation, which protects men from the inconvenience of being reminded of their dependence when they wish to attend to their own affairs. But it must be pointed out that most women would also agree with the policeman. An ancestress of mine once jumped into a canal and rescued a drowning man. The moment she had hauled him to land she fled from him, and hid herself in some bushes lest her drenched petticoats should discover to him the contours of her legs; and there she sat and trembled till she was dry enough to walk home in decent obscurity.

This word, *legs*, brings me to the turning point of my article. It is, so to speak, the link between the Old Covenant of the Policeman and the New Covenant promulgated by the Dean of Westminster. Addressing the members of the Girls' Friendly Society at their recent Festival at the Royal Albert Hall, the Dean of Westminster said (I quote from the report in the *Sunday Times*, July 3rd): 'I hope that you will one day appreciate that a woman's hair is beautiful and learn that all ankles are not beautiful.'

These words have aroused a fair amount of comment already; but it seems to me that commentators, whether they comment favourably or unfavourably, have missed the really significant thing about the Dean's aspirations which is, that in the stead of a moral criterion, he has set up an aesthetic one. Perhaps this is because the intelligence of the public has been blunted by reading too often of the advice which is given to women for their good by public characters – advice so continuously imbecile that no one can continue in the habit of giving it any serious consideration. Let me try to make clear the exciting novelty embodied in the Dean's words by a transposition of the sexes. Suppose that Miss Maude Royden, addressing the members of a Theological Training College, had said; 'I hope that you will one day appreciate that a man's moustache is beautiful, and learn that all calves are not beautiful.' Surely this implication that those ambitious of becoming Deans and Bishops should take into consideration their fitness or unfitness to appear beautifully in gaiters would not pass unnoticed? I think not.

Speaking for myself, I have nothing but enthusiastic welcome for the

New Covenant of the Dean. Both as an artist and a woman I infinitely prefer it to the Old Covenant of the Policeman, and I rejoice that I have lived to see the day when a public character has publicly declared that the hem of my garment is to be measured by what is spiritual, instead of by what is animal. But further, I regard this memorable saying as a test case; not only does it determine between those who, like Dr. Foxley Norris, are artists and those who, like the policeman, are still but moral monkeys, but also it is an infallible touchstone to discover the true believers in the equality of the sexes. If they unfeignedly believe that what is sauce for the Gander is equally sauce for the Goose, then they will see no difference between calves and ankles, short skirts and gaiters. But if they will not admit this parity, then I am sorry, but I must consider that they are still in Egypt.

NOTES

1   Warner and Ackland were already members of the British Communist Party when they were sent for by Tom Wintringham in Barcelona during the Spanish Civil War. On arrival in September 1936 they worked for three weeks in a Republican Red Cross unit
2   On its way from Valencia to Madrid the convoy stopped in the village of Minglanilla where they were entertained by the mayor to an impromptu meal
3   The Second International Congress of Writers in Defence of Culture was held in sequence in Barcelona, Valencia and Madrid. In Valencia Warner gave a short speech in French

LIFE LINES

PRIVATE LETTERS IN OLD INK
(the *Spectator*, March 21st, 1969)

To make Inke. Four ounces of Gaules Two ounces of green Copperice one ounce and half of Gum Arabick: break the Gaules; the Gum and Copperice must be beaten in a Morter & put into a quart of white wine or Strong Stale beer (or as others say Smaller beer least it grow to thick) with a little double refined Suger: it should be stood in a Chimney Corner for a fortenight at least & be well shaken twice or thrice a day the Longer its Kept the Better.

Chimney corners at Claydon[1] must have held many such bottles. 'There are about 30,000 letters in Claydon House from the seventeenth century,' says Sir Harry Verney in his preface to *The Verneys of Claydon*. In the 1860s Parthenope Verney, his step-grandmother, had the enterprise to begin reading them. An enormous task of systematically reading, ordering and transcribing them was continued and carried to completion by her daughter-in-law, Margaret Verney. The resultant four stout volumes have now been abridged by Margaret Verney's octogenarian son into this single volume – a work carried out with filial devotion, albeit with a sense of filial impiety. 'It has been a dreary job murdering my mother,' he wrote to a friend.

Some unrecorded dullard endorsed one bundle 'Private letters of no interest.' The special glory of the Verney hoard is its richness in private letters, letters which cast on public events the revealing illumination of how those events affected contemporary individuals. 'When my mare Lea hath foaled, let the foale bee knockt on the head, and the mare taken to Howse, for I cannot spare her this summer.' Lea's foal was a preliminary casualty of the Civil War. A few months after this letter to his steward, Sir Edmund Verney, the King's Standard-bearer, was killed in the battle of Edgehill. Sir Edward Sydenham wrote to Ralph Verney, the heir: 'For all our great vicktorie I have had the greatest loss by the death of your nobell

169

father that ever anie man did . . . the battell was bloody on your syde, for your hoorss rann awaye at the first charge, and our men had the execution of them for three miles.' There was no malice in Sydenham's comment on Lord Essex's cavalry. It was a sort of 'Bad luck, old chap.' For the outbreak of the Civil War found both sides inadequately prepared to hate each other, perplexed and socially embarrassed.

Sir Edmund fought for the King but not for the King's cause, which went against his conscience. Sir Ralph was a Parliament man and Member for Aylesbury. A year later, his conscience compelled him to refuse to sign the Covenant. Foreseeing that Claydon would be sequestrated, he did what he could to protect its revenues by leases and trusteeships – he had three brothers and five young sisters to think for – and exiled himself to France, taking his personal family and the Vandyke canvases with him. Exile was poverty and fret. 'Noe English maide will bee content with our diet and way of liveing' (Lady Verney's Luce and Besse stayed, for all that). 'There are noe Protestant masters allowed to keepe a schol heere.' 'Let not the wig part behind, charge him to curl it on both sides towards the face.' For in France it was considered clownish to wear one's own hair and Sir Ralph was put to the expense of a periwig and its upkeep.

As a wife is not accountable for her husband's debts, Mary Verney (whose nickname in happier days was Mischief) spent eighteen months in England as Sir Ralph's agent – a double exile, for she loved him – visiting Claydon, where 'Ratts' had gnawed the feather beds, lobbying their London friends to have the sequestration taken off, shopping for the family – not always satisfactorily ('As for Mun's grey stockings they are about a handful too short and almost an inch too Little, soe I have laid them upp for your sonn John'), giving birth to a boy child which died – while in France, unknown to her, her young daughter was dying. The sequestration was lifted. She returned to France, to a slow death by consumption. Sir Ralph's day-book of letters received and replied to is interrupted by an outcry of woe. 'Oh my deare deane.' He was thirty-seven, an affectionate fireside man. But in that most remarrying age, he stayed a widower.

He let three more years go by before going back to Claydon. England was a Commonwealth, the battle of Worcester had been fought, bygones were bygones – or best treated as such. Landowning gentry were busy restocking their pillaged woodlands, mending their boundaries. Sir Ralph set a nursery of young fruit-trees, planted firs, limes and walnuts: the latter an act of faith, for walnuts are slow-growing. He ordered vegetable seeds and vinestocks from France, and two thousand sweet briars for hedging – an example to be commended to the National Trust.

He complied too with Marvell's other prescription: *A Stately Frontispice of Poor*. The old and destitute had weekly allowances of 3d and 6d, apprentices were portioned, fuel distributed among widows; though the poor were not so rewarding as the plant-kind and frustrated his scheme for improving their cows. Above all, Claydon House had a stately frontispiece of relations. Sisters and their husbands, aunts, nephews and nieces, a spreading cousinry, family friends and their cousinries, turned to him for advice and aid, invited him to stand godfather, relied on him to ease them out of their troubles, find husbands for their daughters, horses for their coaches, told him the latest news from London, urged nostrums on him when he was ill, knew no beer comparable to Claydon beer. 'I live by the strenth of your malt.' They lived by the strength of their confidence in him. 'I have filled the paper,' one letter ends, 'therefore should think of a conclusion, but I fancy myself with you all this time and that is so great a plesur that I forget it is but a fancy.' On one occasion he was asked to spare a wig. 'It 'tis to help away a frind. You shall know all hereafter.' The friend was a young cousin of many removes who had taken to highway robbery. Another request was to find a milch ass for Lord Rochester who, repentant and sickly, had been prescribed asses' milk.

In this frontispiece of relations, the figure of Mun Verney (whose grey stockings had been a handful too short) seems to have been portrayed by an artist of a later date, an artist who had studied Watteau's Gilles. Educated in France and something of an intellectual, Mun had married a local heiress and was the squire of East Claydon. He had inherited his mother's sweet temper, but to his undoing. Calamitously matched to a madwoman, bogged down in debts, flouted by disorderly servants, grown unmanageably fat, to all outward seeming a Sir Tunbelly Clumsy, he accepted his lot with the gentle civility of a superior mind, writing to his tailor, 'My Coate is too scanty in the circumference, a fault a man should not have committed who had ever seen me.' In 1672 he tried to hoist himself out of his squiredom by volunteering to fight the Dutch, and appealed to his father to help him. 'Mun, I pray say noe more of your desire to goe into the Fleet, unless you have a mind to render me & your children miserable.' Mun subsided: he did not want to render anyone – short of a Dutch admiral – miserable. *'Je choisirai d'ofirir violence à mon genie, et ainsi passer ma vie comme un Faisnéant plus, tôt que comme mu fils desobeissant.'* Later he recouped by writing some stern admonishments to his two own sons. They and he all predeceased Sir Ralph. Title and estate went to Mun's brother John, as presumably the stockings had done.

Another family appurtenance passed to Sir John: Tom Verney, the Standard-bearer's second son. Tom's career included three expensively subsidised trips to Barbados where it was hoped he might settle (he didn't); a brace of deserted wives; various imprisonments; trailing a pike impartially for either side; a spell on board a warship, where 'noe damned bayliff, nor hellish sergeant can or dare disturb my abode'; a project to become very rich by mining – if Sir Ralph would put up the money; acting as an *agent provocateur* for Cromwell and possibly as a spy for Charles II; and cultivating every branch of begging letter writing – beguiling: 'my dayly study now is to serve God and to avoid the banquier apprehending mee'; blackmailing: 'Your refusal will caus me to forsake my colours and in so doing I may be liable to a councell of warr, and even be punishable'; lofty: 'Time was, when I have equalized my friends in curtesies, and though I have hitherto been clouded and am brought to a very low ebb, yet their may come a floud of prosperitye, which may inable mee to express my self gratefull. All of us knowes our beginnings, but God knowes our endings. I referer the application to your one sweet self.' Tom's ending did him credit. He lived on in Wales, a family pensioner, till 1707 and died 'merely of old age, his speech and memory perfect to the last.'

Sir Ralph had died eleven years earlier, directing that he should 'be burried as privately and with as little pomp as may be' – a wish unusual at the time but characteristic of the man. He would have been surprised to learn that his unobtrusive steadfastness in well-doing is as real today as it was to the relations – and neighbours who gathered on a tempestuous morning in October 1696 to see him laid in the grave. Surprised; but not, I think, displeased. Other amiable Verneys – in their authenticity of 'private letters of no interest' survive with him. They were his dearest concern.

ALEXANDER POPE

(*Alexander Pope*, Edith Sitwell; *Time and Tide*, March 28th, 1930)

During the last decade so much biography has been put forth under the device 'I come to unbury Caesar, not to praise him,' that Miss Sitwell's readers should be grateful for the enthusiasm shown in her study of Alexander Pope. Pope, indeed, is both as a poet and a person a highly suitable subject for enthusiasm. So superb and sensitive a technician that a no less eminent example of the school of criticism Miss Sitwell deplores than Thackeray must describe him as 'the greatest literary artist that England has seen', he was in character desirably faulty – for who cares to panegyrise a prig? Warm-hearted, generous, courageous, humane, the most admiring biographer must yet present him as waspish, suspicious, endlessly embroiled, or descending to unseemly shifts and falsifications in order to add a twopenny lustre, a sticking-plaster security, to his radiant and impregnable reputation. His friends were Swift, Bolingbroke, Peterborough, Arbuthnot, Gay; his hatred stooped to Cibber, Dennis, Curll, and Mr. James Moore Smith. In an age of corruption and place-seeking he kept his independence, more truly indifferent to the world in his compliance, than Swift in his scorn of it, and faithful to the spirit of the *Ode on Solitude* even while showing duchesses round Twickenham; yet he planted a revised version of a correspondence with Wycherley[2] in Lord Oxford's library with the hope that it would be stolen thence and pirated and adopted even more discreditable and ungainly shifts to get back his letters to Swift, that they also might appear in a re-touched form and be a credit to him, while Swift, the darkened Polyphemus, yet lived, but would not know.

Discrepancies such as these put enthusiasm on its mettle. 'To this fine and sensitive artist, inferior poetry and clumsy texture in verse were an agony, and must have had almost the effect of a physical rupture.' No doubt; *Fools rush into my head, and so I write.*

This is a perfectly satisfactory explanation of the attacks on Curll, Dennis, Cibber and Co. (Dr. Keate was affected in a rather similar manner by a false quantity) but it is no explanation of the letter business. It is scarcely tenable that Pope's ignominious dodges in order to repossess himself of his letters were due to the fear lest these should fall unamended into the hands of his enemies, for the dodges were just as likely to become enemy property, and could have been used much more damagingly. Nor does Miss Sitwell's general defence for her hero's eccentricities – the outraged sensibility of a passionate soul in a deformed and mocked-at body – convince, however much it may move, for outraged sensibility is hardly able to sustain a stratagem of months. Defence, moreover, is beside the question. It is the duty of a biographer to explain, not to exculpate. In the passage quoted above the explanation is so satisfactory that it is a pity that a similar approach was not made to the difficulty of the letters, which, surely, falls into place when Pope's solicitude to titivate his reputation is seen as the superfluity and overflow into private life of the indefatigable solicitude which perfected his poetry.

The account of that perfection, and the analysis of how it is achieved, is the finest part of this book. Indeed, I do not see how it could be bettered, unless by being extended. Pope's was an art-concealing art; or perhaps it is that the flashing excitement and vigour of the thought conveyed, blinds readers to the delicacy of the versification; but henceforward there should be no excuse for those people who hold the view that Pope is a poet but not poetical. It is upon the purely poetical, almost the romantic, aspect of his genius that Miss Sitwell concentrates, and rightly so. There can be no need to insist upon the wit and spirit of such lines as:

> *One solid dish his week-day meal affords,*
> *An added pudding solemniz'd the Lord's;*

Or,

> *Flow, Welsted, flow! like thine inspirer, Beer,*
> *Tho' stale, not ripe, tho' thin, yet never clear;*
> *So sweetly mawkish, and so smoothly dull;*
> *Heady, not strong; o'erflowing, tho' not full,*

174

but even if the ear tells one that the line

High on his helm, celestial lightnings play,

is superior to the earlier version of

Bright from his beamy crest the lightnings play,

we need the acuteness of Miss Sitwell's analysis to show us that 'the alliteration and the emphasis on one-syllabled words before the caesura give the effect of height, because of their emphasis' – and may I suggest further that the constancy of vowel sound in *helm*, and *celestial* lengthens those lightnings almost into a garland, thus reinforcing the word *play*?

It would be pleasant if one could discuss Pope without being obliged to mention her whom I recently heard an authority on the eighteenth century refer to as 'that besom, Lady Mary Wortley Montagu.'[3] But I must join issue with Miss Sitwell over her statement, in the matter of those lines,

From furious Sappho scarce a milder fate,
Poxed by her love, or libelled by her hate,

that 'the only reason for connecting furious Sappho with Lady Mary Wortley Montagu lies in that lady's not otherwise very active imagination.' Such remarks as *Sappho's diamonds with her dirty smock*, square too certainly with the lines

You laugh, if coat and breeches strangely vary,
White gloves, and linen worthy Lady Mary,

and with Lady Mary Wortley Montagu's reputation for personal uncleanliness, to allow for much doubt as to whom Pope intended by Sappho on the slut count; and he was constant in his nomenclature.

(*Samuel Richardson*, Brian W. Downs, *New York Herald Tribune*, 1929)

Short, rather plump than emaciated, notwithstanding his complaints; about five foot five inches, fair wig, looking directly foreright, as passers-by would imagine, but observing all that stirs on either hand of him without moving his short neck; of light brown complexion, teeth not yet failing him; at sometimes looking to be about sixty-five, at other times much younger; a regular, even pace, stealing away ground rather than seeming to rid it; a gray eye, too often overclouded by mistiness from the head, by chance lively – very lively it will be if he have a chance to see a lady he loves and honours – his eyes always upon the ladies; if they have very large hoops he looks down and supercillious, and as if he would be thought wise, but perhaps the sillier for that; as he approaches a lady his eye is never fixed first upon her face but upon her feet, and thence he raised it up, pretty quickly for a dull eye, and one would think that from her air and (the last beheld) her face he set her down in his mind as So or So, and then passes on to the next object he meets; only then looking back if he greatly likes or dislikes, as if he would see if the lady appear to be all of a piece in the one light or the other.

This is Samuel Richardson's description of his person, a description which was to identify him in the eyes of an admiring female correspondent who sought a meeting with the author of *Clarissa*. It might well be a description of his genius, too. 'A regular, even pace, stealing away ground.' What is that but the style, so artfully flat, so methodically meandering, which bears the reader through the two volumes of *Pamela*, the seven apiece of *Clarissa* and *Sir Charles Grandison*? 'His eye always upon the ladies.' That eye, rising from the ankle to the countenance and turned back to make sure, but justly, of its prey, was the eye which could read so clearly into the niceties of a female heart, and that could dally, too, even in the moment of his heroine's abduction to scan the niceties of female costume, the embroidery from her own needle, the little muffs (for it was winter, and waiting in the copse Lovelace's wig had stiffened with the hoar frost) upon either wrist. And that age, varying its appearance from sixty-five to something much younger, does not that throw some light upon the problem of how this elderly printer, who wrote to show how virtue was rewarded and vice dismayed, whose aim was to advance religion and household laws, should have described with such convincing gusto the raptures, the stratagems, the self-glorifications of a libertine?

The truth is that even in this letter Richardson had begun to dramatise himself; he is, even in these few lines, already a character in one of his books. Without moving his short neck he could leap into the souls of those passersby whom he so intently observed and in a moment be seated in their hearts, knowing them better than they knew themselves. And so, irresistibly propelled, they move into the texture of one of his enormous romances. Outwardly they remain as he saw them – a little, or even more than a little, prosy; still, of limited intelligence, slightly artificial, as people in real life must be, lacking the authentic homogeneity of people in art; poor creatures, botched together by the makeshifts of mortal mating, but inwardly they live beyond questioning, their small merits and failings, their whims and passions, their momentary thoughts and half thoughts smelted into enduring shape by the rapt interest of this short, plumpish gentleman who disliked large hoops and whose teeth were not yet failing him.

It seems to me proper to indicate that Richardson was a genius before coming to an account of Mr. Brian W. Downs's book on him, because that book, though admirable as a well manipulated account of his life, works and influence, does not happen to mention the fact. In a way Mr. Downs writes almost as though he were one of his subject's contemporaries. They questioned as to whether Richardson's novels were really likely to do what their author averred they were intended to do; to raise the standard of chastity among servant maids by the story of Pamela, who by a judicious mingling of not giving warning – always such a faulty trait in domestic servants – and not giving leave bowed her seducing master into marrying her; to teach by the misfortunes and epiphanal death of Clarissa the double lesson: *Children, obey your parents in all things. Fathers, provoke not your children to wrath.*

Mr. Downs is seriously concerned that: 'Richardson, in fine, would seem to be far out in a general estimate of his own work'; that having promised in his preface to teach us a moral lesson, he should have turned so far aside from his purpose as to present us with that wilder fowl, a work of art. Mr. Downs, clearly, has an exact mind; elsewise he would not have moved so deftly through the entanglements of his subject; his study would have been as messy as most biographical and critical studies are; and so, I suppose, he cannot be quite easy that Richardson should have grown a trifle confused in reconciling his intentions and his achievement. That gray eye for Mr. Downs is 'too often overclouded by mistiness from the head.' It seems to me a matter of small importance whether Richardson was in or out in estimating his own works; the exciting thing is that he wrote them. For surely, it is exciting, quite apart from the slow boa constrictor excitement of the novels themselves, that at the age of fifty a perfectly respectable and rather priggish tradesman, owning a suburban villa, a thriving business, two wives (one dead, of course), a family, a fair wig, should have become from the 10th of November, 1739, to the 10th of January, 1740, a young servant maid with a waist that her wicked master could span with his hands (and here I must break off, to the ruination of my paragraph, to mention that such was the earnest concern of Richardson's admirers as to the effect of his writings that this detail about the waist laid him open to a charge of encouraging tight lacing, a charge that he rebutted in a later edition). Yet this does seem to be more or less what happened; Richardson shut himself up for two months and became Pamela, writing not about her but through her, for her (for of all the forms of narrative the letter form is the one demanding the closest identification between the creator and his creation); pouring out day by day to his, her, aged parents, her persecutions, her hopes, her schemes, and going to bed, one may think, night after night, in fear of being raped by Mr. B. So violent was this assimilation between them that Pamela transcended his first impressions of her, forcing him willy-nilly to disclose herself (and this is well pointed out by Mr. Downs) not only a heroine, but also an intuitively calculating little slut.

Mr. Richardson's next incarnation was longer and more complex. By October, 1746, he had been that young lady whose magnamimity and misfortunes drew tears from Europe, the amorous rascal who undid her, his confidant, her confidant, several members of the aristocracy and the keeper of a bawdy house. In *Pamela* Richardson's female self surprised him into being a little less admirable than he intended; in *Clarissa* it surprised him into the sublime. He was avowedly an enemy to enthusiasm, to the romantic; but as Clarissa he soared up from a virtuous, accomplished, early-rising young lady to a being as loftily, as movingly, as heroically romantic as that other phoenix of this kind, Stendhal's Armance. And then, taking up a fresh page and dipping his quill again into the ink, he became the character whom Mr. Downs sums up as 'this consummate cad' but to whom the general opinion of posterity, less gentlemanly in prejudice than Mr. Downs but possibly more appreciative of the creative purpose, has awarded the sinister honour of making his name a by-word and letting Lovelace be synonymous with libertine.

So powerfully did Richardson's appearance as Lovelace threaten the public weal, so corrupting was the energy with which the virtuous tradesman, who on his own admission 'never, to my knowledge, was in a vile House, or in Company with a lewd Woman, in my Life', argued in favour of debauchery, that in his last incarnation he set himself to behave better, and emerged as a truly Christian gentleman and two honourable ladies (though he did contrive to have a short run for his money as Sir Hargrave Pollexfen, who carries off Harriet Byron from a masquerade, dressed as an Arcadian shepherdess with 'a little feather perking out above the left ear', and shows for a moment like the first adumbration of Charlotte Bronte's Rochester). Nothing is here for tears from any moralist. 'Virtue' in the words of Mr. Downs, 'simply brings with it an increment of Virtue'. This sounds intolerable; but if one can once bring one's self to grant that virtue is not necessarily as uninteresting as its own reward, *Sir Charles Grandison* may be read and re-read (I speak from experience) with interminable pleasure. Perhaps Clementina suffers from the fact that Clarissa came before her; but Harriet Byron, that silken twist of feminine scruples, is the subtlest of all Richardson's female impersonations, and, though it is an accepted legend that the faultless baronet is a bore, there is more discrimination in the remark of one of the acutest living Richardsonians that he always feels great pleasure when Grandison comes into the room.

'They both wept, courtesied and withdrew.' *They* were Grandison's two sisters, exquisitely rebuked by their brother for incivility to their dead father's mistress. But it is not going too far to say that *they* were also the most sensitive, the most fashionable minds of the time, who heard with reverence and compunction the voice proceeding from the

awful cell
Where sober Contemplation loves to dwell

179

– in other words, from the grotto or garden house of the villa at North End near the Hammersmith Turnpike Road. A strange chance, a queer whim of destiny that made the sickly and in common life rather dull and sheepish printer the arbiter of European sentiment. Psycho-analysts have a name – I'm sure I do not know it – for those folk who absolve the dullness of their days, the sheepishness of their actions, by a continual passionate day-dreaming. They sit at their desks, they go home to their suppers, they lie with their wives ('A very worthy Woman. She has suffered all her life from low spirits'); and meanwhile they abduct or are abducted in chariots, drain the intoxicating cup of calamity, die majestically meek on well attended death beds. It is quite a common phenomenon, does no harm and comes to nothing. But now and then something happens – some concatenation of chances, a gray eye peculiarly piercing, an unusual variety of mistiness in the head – and the dream takes hold of the dreamer, speaks through his lips, teaches his right hand wonderful and terrible things, annihilates his age, his sex, his waist measurement, drives him out into the world again, a creator.

LUDWIG VAN BEETHOVEN

(*The Unconscious Beethoven*, Ernest Newman; *Beethoven*, Harvey Grace
Time and Tide, March 25th, 1927)

Like a very superb bramble-patch the ruling and noble families of Germany and Austria tangled and extended, struck root, branched again, blossomed and cross-fertilised over the Europe of the Rhine and the Danube. So when a swarthy, stocky, red-faced young man from Bonn arrived in Vienna in the November of 1792, with a certain reputation as a keyboard virtuoso, some aptitude as a composer, an album containing a flattering inscription by Count Waldstein, and a promise of financial support – not fulfilled, though; the French Revolutionary Army put a spoke in that wheel – from the Elector of Cologne, he could be fairly sure of finding patrons, employment and (what a young man wants most) attention. This was not his first experience of Vienna. He had visited the city five years before, had met Mozart and improvised before him. Now, Mozart was dead, and the untimeliness of his death emphasised the fact that Haydn was sixty-one. People were looking round for a new composer. They were to get him.

But there is no reason for that rather menacing cadence, for indeed they were delighted to do so. Beethoven's case gives a rude jolt to the convention that a great composer must inevitably be slighted by a generation of deaf adders. From the first year in Vienna he was honoured, sought-after and well-paid. His concerts were crowded, he made friends almost as fast as he could be disillusioned in them, and publishers queued up for his new works. It is sometimes said that the fickle Viennese public neglected him in his later years. This is not true. The fickle portion of the Viennese public, virtuoso-gapers, turned their attention elsewhere when deafness compelled him to give up his career as a performer; but the true music-lovers were true to the end. It is a testimony to the worth of their constancy that the late string quartets were attentively and appreciatively received (op. 127 was 'so much in request among the most celebrated players of Vienna that I [Beethoven] have granted it to some of them for their benefit'), and that with the exception of the *Grosse Fuge*, which was demurred at on grounds of technical difficulty, there was none of that boggling and bunkum which afterwards made 'Beethoven's last manner' such a word of fear.

But for all this, I suppose there was never a more distressful genius, and certainly never one so self-tormenting. Ten years after his arrival in Vienna, years of success, comparative freedom from rumpusses and untrammelled musical development (and there can be no satisfaction to the artist anywhere approaching the satisfaction of feeling himself go from strength to strength) Beethoven was writing in the Heiligenstadt Testament: 'Providence, let me have at last just one pure day of *joy;* it is so long since true joy resounded in my heart.'

He had already had attacks of deafness. His fears and self-pity were acute, his distress frantic. But those who pity Beethoven for his deafness should pity him accurately. In his letters and diaries he bewails that deafness will cut him off from his fellows, from an active musical life, from the outer world; not from his music, which was within him.

With The Hunted

Mr. Newman in *The Unconscious Beethoven* – a study so luminous, concise, sympathetic and level-headed that it should become a classic, not only in Beethoven literature, but in the difficult craft of writing of music – treats Beethoven as an extreme example of that welling-up from the unconscious mind which is called inspiration, in that 'in his greatest music head-work was carried on at the same level of incandescence as inspiration.' The truth of this saying must be appreciated if one calls to mind that most characteristic, non-musical quality in Beethoven's music, the impression it gives of intense sincerity and integrity. Even when the music seems to be saying nothing in particular, or something rather foolish, there can be no doubt for the hearer that whatsoever is said, is meant. It is significant that it comes natural to speak of his music saying something. At its remotest and most austere it is not abstract but extract music, it is Beethoven speaking to us in his native tongue.

But I would go further. It seems to me that this incandescence has fused the whole man, and that Beethoven's worldly life, so incompetent, so fretful and perturbed, and apparently so utterly at variance with the power, the constancy and deliberate purpose of his creative life, was but a reverse, was the dark side of the moon. One reads the letters about his nephew's upbringing and they are so fussy and so teasing that the exclamation 'Old Granny!' rises to one's lips. And one turns to the letters about proof-corrections and finds the same fuss, the insistence upon jots and tittles. But one has half-circled the moon meanwhile, a solicitude which is misapplied to Carl's underwear is not misapplied to op.132. Again, the vacillations and dilly-dolly which preceded the 1824 concert can be oddly paralleled in the eighteen versions of the opening of Florestan's Aria. Lodgings and servants were discarded as ruthlessly as a superfluous quaver or a modulation which belied his true thought. Even that suspicion, that dreadful hankering to discover a fault in a friend which is the most painful trait in the letters, becomes in the scrutiny and revision of his creations the just exigence of one who is driving in rivets for eternity. The faculty for self-tormenting made him what he was, both as man and musician.

It must have tormented others too. His friends had a good deal to put up with. Yet they endured his rude speeches, the 'Ah coom fra' Yorkshire' airs of his early manhood, his violent temper and his table-manners, his

182

superhuman clumsiness, his puns, his priggishness (he was a sexual prig), even the infirmities and miseries of his later years; and endured them, as far as one can see, not because there was such greatness in his music, but because there was something to love in the man. He, too, loved his fellows and none the less sincerely because he could not get on with them. He found it easier to get on with nature. He liked sitting under trees, 'that splendid May rain,' wandering about in rough weather. Five years before his death he succeeded in getting himself arrested as a tramp. On the day of his death, as he lay unconscious, there was a violent clap of thunder, such as sometimes comes with a March snowstorm. He looked up. He seems to have heard that, though he had never heard the drums leap out in the Scherzo of the Ninth Symphony.

SIMPLE ANNALS
(*The Brothers Grimm*, Ruth Michaelis-Jena
the *Spectator*, July 25th, 1970)

'The black coffin, and the bearers carrying yellow lemons and rosemary . . .' Lemons and rosemary are traditionally associated: they embellish roast pork; they combine in a hairwash. Rosemary has long been a funeral herb, carried, not for remembrance but to countervail the smell of churchyard mould; perhaps the lemons were carried as abettors. There is a great deal of botanical folklore waiting to be inquired into; meanwhile it is tempting to speculate on their strange occurrence as a funeral garnish.

In the black coffin was Philipp Wilhelm Grimm, Amptmann of Steinau in Hesse and father of Jacob and Wilhelm Grimm – but for whom one's mind might not swivel so easily from funerals to folklore. Jacob and Wilhelm were still children but their futures were decided on. Philipp Wilhelm intended them to study jurisprudence, that solemn creaking vehicle which would convey them to the creditable status of Justiciary, Burgher-master even. And as they were eminently 'good' children, biddable and industrious, they would have obeyed his wishes. From the point of view of posterity the Amptmann of Steinau died in the nick of time. The family fell into poverty. A mother and an aunt, with six children to fend for, were too busy scrambling through the present to have much authority over the future; and though both the elder boys went to the Lyceum and duly on to the University, and were model pupils there, they developed ideas and intentions of their own.

Napoleon, too, to whom Europe owes more than it acknowledged or acknowledges, had a hand in preserving the Grimm brothers for folklore. The Napoleonic Code had replaced the Teutoburgerwald of German jurisprudence in which they had intended to make their careers. It was a fine pretext to look elsewhere. Jacob became librarian (with quite remarkable ease) to Jerome Bonaparte, King of Westphalia. Wilhelm studied mediaeval manuscripts. Sharing in the nationalistic romanticism which was overturning the sedate notions of the waning Enlightenment and looking back to the age of minnesingers, they were already collecting songs and stories of the past; these they offered to Brentano, joint-editor with von Arnim of *Des Knabens Wunderhorn*, a publication as crucial as Percy's *Reliques*.

'All that we have is yours,' wrote Wilhelm and a collaboration over the next volume of the *Wunderhorn* was adumbrated. But in regard to the offered *Maerchen* what was theirs became too exclusively Brentano's. He was a fantasist, seeing the bare folk narrative as a framework to clothe with his own inventions. These *droit de seigneur* proceedings shocked the bourgeois integrity of the Grimm brothers. They set themselves to take down stories as though they were taking down evidence, preserving regional idioms, including unconsidered trifles such as proverbs and local sayings, recording nonsense-jingles without attempting to put sense into them. It is the practice of every folklorist nowadays; but whereas the modern folklorist single-mindedly pursues folklore, Jacob and Wilhelm were basically preoccupied with establishing the development of the German language and German literature. Writing down what they heard from country servants, nannies, pedlars, shepherds, farmhands, children, 'an old soldier who bartered his tales for gifts of discarded trousers', they listened for echoes of an earlier story-telling, echoes of the Nordic saga, the Christian legend, of Orpheus and Osiris even. And when the *Kinder- und Hausmaerchen* came out in 1812 it was offered as a work of scholarship with notes and appendices.

It had a mixed reception. Romanticists deplored the inelegance of the narratives, the burden of the annotations. Moralists thought the stories unsuitable for children. It was the children who decided. Scorning the erudition with their heels, they welcomed the rough, adventurous, vitaminous diet of what was unsuitable for them. True, being children of that date, they had the Old Testament – those nourishing plagues of Egypt, Jezebel, Simpson *alias* Sampson. But the *Household Tales* were brisker and could be enjoyed without impiety.

As it seems to us, the brothers had got there. To their contemporaries, they seemed to be continuing their journey along the plateau of respected eminence – so respected and eminent, indeed, that when Jacob, considered to be the ringleader in a professorial opposition to Ernest Augustus, King of Hanover, was sent into exile under an escort of dragoons, his students demonstrated in protest. They studied, they taught, they wrote, they published. Wilhelm edited early German texts, Jacob systematised German grammar (he was Grimm's Law, too), worked on a dictionary. They produced two more volumes of folk-stories; Jacob published legal treatises and *Reynard the Fox*. Apart from that brush with Ernest Augustus, their lives were tranquil, industrious, brotherly.

There is not much here for an unfalsifying biographer. But the Grimm Brothers were members of the Grimm family. Their admirably unfalsifying biographer has availed herself of this – which was undoubtedly of central importance to Jacob and Wilhelm. The fatherless children, scattered hither and thither, maintained a deep family affection, a mercury-like faculty of cohesion. Wars swept past them, dynasties fell, fashions changed, armies advanced and retreated: what was happening to other Grimms remained their chief concern, their most engrossing topic. During the invasion of France, Ludwig Grimm in bivouac heard himself greeted by another soldier. 'Oh, what a joy, it was my brother Carl'. The word one scunners at, can only use in derision, *Gemuethlichkeit*, is redeemed into decency by their honest delight in a domestic circle.

Ruth Michaelis-Jena's rendering of this small-town, small-state domestic chronicle is enhanced by the domesticity of the illustrations, almost all by Ludwig Grimm, the artist of the family, and drawings of household articles of the time: baking-dishes, ink-stands, moulds for gingerbread cookies, 'a small hammer belonging to the Grimm family'. Her unostentatious research is so substantiating that by the end of the book I felt myself taking leave of Jacob as though I had known him:

Uncle was always so cheerful that we were apt to forget his age. At times he was in very good spirits, as when last August we were preparing to travel to the Harz mountains, and he sat quite seriously at the dining-room table, wearing Mamma's straw hat with ribbons over his long white locks. And how happy he was when the weather was bad, and he did not have to go for a walk, but could sit at his desk from early morning till late at night.

THE INSPIRED OLD BUSTARD
William Blake, 1757-1827
(*Time and Tide*, August 12th, 1927)

> *If Hayley knows a thing you cannot do*
> (If, mark you. It is characteristic.)
> *That is the very thing he'll set you to.*

Hayley, who wrote the 'Triumphs of Temper,' all about maddening Serena, fancied himself as a Benefactor. So do quite a number of us, but luckily for our comfort of mind inspired bustards are rare birds, and we are not likely to pitch upon them as the objects of our bounty. A country cottage is a tempting cage, and when Hayley chirruped, his bird flew down to Sussex in a most obliging fashion, and sang as follows:

> *The Bread of sweet thought and the Wine of delight*
> *Feed the village of Felpham by day and by night;*
> *And at his own door the bless'd hermit does stand,*
> *Dispensing, unceasing, to all the wide land.*

This song of innocence (and one of the most misleading things about bustards is the peculiar artless warble they have when they please to) was composed in the second week of September, a season when, as those who have lived in the country cannot fail to have learned, the dispensations of bless'd hermits take the form of runner beans and vegetable marrows. However unceasing, these dispensations alone would hardly have brought about a rupture between Blake and Hayley; for they would have been directed upon Catherine Blake, a wise woman who knew how to keep domestic annoyances out of her husband's way. Unfortunately the hermit also dispensed exhortation and good advice. William's Prophetic Books were very fine; so now would he try his hand at some miniatures?

I cannot quite forego a slight tea-cosy tenderness for Hayley. For one thing, he loved the poet Cowper; for another, he has been, for some time, safe dead. But I am ready to lift up my voice and roar very loud indeed against the tribe of little Hayleys, who for the last twenty-five years and more have been pilfering the bustard's feathers to line their own nests. I came on a fine specimen the other day – a woman, I *should* say, a lady, with a sweet wistful grin, who was trailing her draperies round the Blake Exhibition, and omitting, with a touching gesture of incompetence, to replace the covers over the show-cases of the illuminated books, 'Ah, dear Blake !' said she. 'Such a wonderful poem, this! Such a favourite of mine! I quoted it in my little private *Anthology of Comfort* that I made during the war.'

It cannot be said too firmly or too plainly that Blake's poetry was never intended for use as private poultices. He whose tears were 'an intellectual thing' shed them that they might scorch the brain, and rouse it to thought; he did not shed them for an irrigation system that should rear crops of mustard and cress on mental flannel – mustard and cress that would come in nicely for afternoon tea. Nor did he mean his poems to be seized upon as conveniently undenominational hymns, to be taught to defenceless school-children and sung on Empire Day. When Blake speaks of building Jerusalem he does not refer to the establishment of forced, native labour in African colonies. Neither does he refer to Welwyn Garden City.

I suppose those *Songs of Innocence* have, innocently, a deal to answer for. Yet one would have hoped that even sheep might have suspected that though the Lion should lie down with the Lamb, he will be a Lion still. Perhaps only black sheep take this cynical view. I have always nursed great hopes of the character of a burglar, who removed from my parent's

187

house, together with a purse and some jewellery, a copy of the *Songs of Innocence.*

And of late I have been much cheered by the behaviour of some Lambs. Flocks of Lambs from the Harrow Road pass down my street on their way to Kensington Gardens, and one afternoon three of them saw fit to climb over the railings which guard my front garden. Perhaps they were after my zizanias. Several respectable persons on the pavement saw this unlawful act, and raised their voices in reproof and admonishment. One respectable person indeed would have come in by the gate and driven the marauders out, if I had not leant from my window and threatened him very briskly with a Prosecution for Trespass. And while the Lambs were at their Un-covenanted leaping and skipping, they sang, very loudly and rejoicingly, as though they sang a war-song. And the words they sang were these:

> *Bring me my Bow of burning gold:*
> *Bring me my Arrows of desire:*
> *Bring me my Spear: O clouds unfold,*
> *Bring me my Chariot of fire.*

And when I heard these words I knew that the inspired old bustard had escaped the net of the fowler even the fowler Hayley.

PORTIA

(*Abigail Adams: The Second First Lady*, Dorothie Bobbe,
New York Herald Tribune, 1929)

Women lend reality to history by being themselves so unhistorical. They travel through life like the gypsies, an unchanging nomadic race, cloistered in their domesticity as in a caravan. They hang up the washing on the boughs of the virgin forest, they go brambling along the edge of the battlefield. They bear their uninteresting children at the most unsuitable moments; at coronations, in earthquakes, in revolutions, in solar eclipses.

No catastrophe is sacred to them, they will rummage for a darning-needle in the dissolution of empires. I have a specimen in mind who, if the Day of Judgment were just getting into its stride, with the graves opening and people with a proper sense of the situation calling upon the rocks to cover them, would walk into the room with a tea-tray. And I, for one, should be glad to see it.

For the Day of Judgment is a mere flash-in-the-pan episode in the human epic; striking because of its singularity, but by reason of that same singularity non-significant and ineffective compared to the continuous social pressure of tea-drinking. It is, biologically speaking, a sport; the exception and not the rule; the Bearded Lady and not the Eternal Feminine. Even a Bearded Lady must be in a booth to be at her most arresting; in her home she would cease to arrest and fall to doing, and her Barker would forget to bark in asking her for a second helping of steak and onions or bidding her to keep those children quiet with a fairy-tale. It is our childishness that writes the histories, filling them with Bearded Ladies and Days of Judgment, Destructions of Sennacherib, Rome Burning and Nero Fiddling, Gunpowder Plots, Great Frosts, Massacres of Saint Bartholomew, Tea-Parties in Boston Harbour – the bloodier the better; for though man lives many days and dies on only one of them, his mind is excited by the thought of death as a collector's mind is excited by the thought of an auction, distinguishing in the common lot his chances of a unique experience, his own personal rarity. It is this same raree-show spirit which puts forth the Bills of Mortality. It would be interesting, I think, to have Bills of Vitality as well. This week so many have discarded patent razor blades, read Shelley's 'Ode to a Sky-Lark', lost their umbrellas, bought a bowl of goldfish, planted a tree. But if it is our childishness which writes the histories, it is our sophisticated and philosophic strain which in reading them is pleased to light on 'such arresting nouns as *small-pox, pony, or boots and shoes,*' which pricks up its ears when a woman strolls on to the page.

But it must be some ordinary humdrum housekeeping woman, some smooth-chinned unhistorical creature, securely rooted in her own present. Once let her stray into the extraordinary and the spell is lost. Such women as Cleopatra or Mrs. Besant may lend romance to history; we cannot say that they lend it reality. And if the woman strolling on to the page is to have

189

her due effect there, she must not stay on it too long. Her function is to walk by on some errand of her own, to appear with a preserving pan or in widow's weeds, transient and actual, a symbol of the everyday living she succours and upholds. If she hangs about too long it is at the peril of being turned herself into one of the permanent wax-work exhibits of history.

As an illuminant of her time Abigail Adams, wife of the second President of the American Republic, is well-nigh perfect. I say well-nigh for, living to us as she does in her letters, she had as a letter-writer one grave defect; she wrote her letters twice over, once as a draft, once as the finished composition. John Adams does not seem to have objected to this formality in a spouse; but we may be allowed the regret of posterity in that, knowing this memorable lady, we may not know her more intimately. It is painful to think that where we are given a considered opinion on British tyranny we might have had a little scandal about General Burgoyne, that a quotation from Dryden has usurped the place of an impromptu from Abigail. Something of the wary decency of these letters may be attributed to the fact that there was no certainty that they would not be intercepted, and read by unfriendly eyes; but more, to the writer's lofty notion of what, and what not, befitted a New England lady, who signed her letters *Portia* and aimed to do all 'after the high Roman fashion'. How inflexibly the Massachusetts matron observed her code of discretion, duty, self-command, can best be gauged, not from the record of her own letters, but from those of her husband. The John Adams, lawyer, who wrote in 1765, when the first kicking against the Stamp Duty had led to the retaliatory measure closing the Massachusetts Law Courts: 'So sudden an interruption in my career is very unfortunate for me . . . I have groped in dark obscurity till of late, and had but just become known and gained a small degree of reputation, when this execrable project was set on foot for my ruin as well as that of America in general, and of Great Britain', was to write as Delegate in 1775: 'But all these must go, and my life too, before I can surrender the right of my country to a free Constitution,' as President, on the eve of his inauguration: 'I have not the smallest dread of private life nor of public'. One suspects that a husband had felt the necessity of becoming a hero to his wife.

And this was not a wife to be cheaply provided with a hero. She carried the touchstone in her own well-kerchiefed bosom. 'If danger comes near

190

my dwelling, I suppose I shall shudder,' says she; and there is something almost grim in the nonchalance with which this young woman, awaiting a bombardment, with four small children at her skirts, envisages, not the danger of danger, but the danger of shuddering. And at the first defeats of the new Independent American States, while others still covered up bad tidings with patriotic hallooings, her dauntless mental integrity flashes out with: 'If our army is ever in so critical a state I wish to know it, and the worst of it. If all America is to be ruined and undone by a pack of cowards and knaves, I wish to know it.' This letter bears no subscription; perhaps Arria would have been more proper for the nonce than Portia. 'If it is necessary to make any more drafts upon us', she continues, 'the women must reap the harvests. I am willing to do my part. I believe I could gather corn, and husk it; but I should make a poor figure at digging potatoes. There has been a report that a fleet was seen in our bay yesterday. I cannot conceive from whence, nor do I believe the story.' Reading these imperious, high-hearted, cool-headed laconics it is borne in on one that their writer was scarcely likely to be outmatched by a potato.

When people can present themselves as superbly as this, the biographer is in danger of making his presentment of them a water-colour rendering of the original etching; and it must be admitted that Dorothie Bobbe's *Abigail Adams: The Second First Lady* gives a somewhat weakened and diffused version of its subject. It is the technique of the book which is to blame for this; the intention, the stratagem of attack, is praiseworthy. For Miss Bobbe has recognised the prime importance of showing Abigail Adams, not as a heroine of the American Revolution, but as an heroic woman who happened to be alive at that time. So she would have behaved, so suffered, so endured in any other troubled epoch, in any other country. So would she have behaved, suffered and endured had she been, during the years of the American Revolution, a royalist and a tory. For the upkeep of daily living must go on, and wool be carded and spun, whether for children's blankets or soldiers' uniforms; molasses provided for the household, whether it come from the West Indies or be distilled from Independent rye-stalks. But though remembering that Abigail Adams was, as a woman, an unnoticeable figure in the affairs of her time, a private soldier whose marching orders kept her out of every engagement, Miss Bobbe has not been able to resist the temptation to drag her in, a mute inglorious participant, a moral victor in every actual victory, a close-up registrar of emotion in every national discomfiture.

The Continental Congress had disbanded, closing its deliberations with nothing more than a certain resolution. Sam Adams and Hancock had come to Boston with the others. But where they had disappeared to after that, it seemed no one could inform Mr. Gage. Abigail was amused, but aloofly.

It was rumoured that Gage had now eight thousand in his army. They were drilling night and day, and landing arms and powder. Abigail's answering enquiry was obvious. What of the patriots? They were drilling also? They were preparing?

The red line stopped; huddled a little, went on. Gage would not give up Boston at the loss of a few hundred lives. Gage knew – what Abigail knew, what the British generals down there must know – that patriotic powder must be running low.

This is the expedient of the cinema, not of history or biography. There is no earthly reason why Abigail Adams should be included in the Battle of Bunker Hill. Her presence on the battlefield, even though the British generals are hastily mobilised to be her chaperons, is misplaced.

Miss Bobbe has clearly taken pains to be acquainted with her subject, she has the letters at her fingers' ends and weaves them into her narrative dexterously; she has, as I said above, gone the right way to work in perceiving her subject as a woman in real life and not a figure in history; she writes briskly and vividly for those who like that style of writing (personally I find the plethoric Ludwigian paintings very wearing); but in her misplaced anxiety to keep Abigail Adams in the spotlight she gives the unfortunate impression that, with the spotlight once removed, Abigail Adams would fade from the reader's mind. There is no such likelihood to fear. 'In large and mixed companies she is totally silent, as a lady ought to be.' Thus wrote Abigail Adam's husband of Mrs. Hancock, in Philadelphia; and we may be sure that his views of what a lady ought to be were shaped by what his lady was. There is no call for Miss Bobbe's heroine to gesticulate on battlefields like a baggage-wagon trollop. It is offering her an indignity thus to hale her in by the neck to the large and mixed assemblies of her countrymen, there to put into her mouth answering enquiries that are obvious. When she spoke for herself, she did not speak so. Perhaps it is best to leave these vital and reserved people to speak for themselves, or perhaps Miss Bobbe has been misled by a confusion between the two Portias. For it was no gad-about Italian young lady that the Massachusetts Shakespearian invoked, one who would put on man's attire and quibble in a law court; but that other, who once only unloaded her great heart; and then to Brutus.

A CLASS DISTINCTION
(unpublished ms, Warner/Ackland Archive, Dorset County Museum)

Monday 14 February. In the evening went to a concert of Mendelssohn's chamber music in St. James's Hall. Began with the posthumous quintet, which is exquisite, especially the andante. Still, one cannot quite away with the wiriness of even the best violin playing. Music, to be perfect, should have no artificial medium: or at least the medium should not obtrude itself upon one's notice. Yet in fact one cannot help thinking of *it*, as well as of the music.

It is rather sad to see how mere physical comfort or discomfort is able to weaken and destroy the purest spiritual and highest sensual delight. At first, the music was all in all to me: then I began to have a sense of being comfortable, and the music ceased to be absorbing, and became the accompaniment and the ground-tone to my melody of reveries: then again, after long sitting, one began to have a sense of being uncomfortable, and it seemed an insult to the music to stay longer.

The listener was Arthur Joseph Munby (1828-1910). The year was 1859. He was the first-born of a Yorkshire family of local importance. His father was a solicitor; when Munby left Trinity College, Cambridge, his future lay in wait for him. He obeyed as a son and read for the bar. Cambridge was pious (as opposed to Oxford which was religious). While there, he was influenced by F.D. Maurice. The Working Men's College, Maurice's foundation in Central London, expressed conviction that charity included a duty towards the ignorant – that the well-read equally with the well-fed should share their fullness with the poor. After going to

193

London, Munby became a voluntary teacher there and tutored a class in elementary Latin. Later he was elected to the Council where he met Ruskin and Rossetti.

In 1859 he grew a beard and began to keep a diary. The beard was a declaration of modernity. To his frosty-cheeked father it must have seemed proof that Arthur was neglecting his profession. He was; he disliked the Law. The Working Men's College had admitted him to a society of wider speculations, livelier ambitions and a dash of carbonari fellowship. It was serious-minded – 'G took me to the Cosmopolite, talking by the way of protestantism and prostitutes' but it was confident and exploratory: 'visited the Circus, sat in taverns, went to the cheap days at the Crystal Palace where fireworks, bals musettes and the Hallelujah Chorus evoked a Christian society when people did not rejoice in compartments.'

Among these new acquaintances Munby shed his provincialism but kept his sharp provincial eye. A.J. Froude[4] with his 'wavering sardonic smile,' Swinburne 'waving his arms and writhing his little legs,' 'Ruskin in one of those moods of desolate frivolity which forecast his madness rising up and down on his toes with his hands in his tail-pockets' as he derided the followers of Adam Smith, 'and finally jaunting downstairs in the same springy fashion, with the prim smile of Sir Oracle on his dry lips' flash through the Diaries with the authenticity of pre-biographical life.

Derek Hudson, who has traced, transcribed, edited, and established Munby in the canon of English diarists, subtitles his book *Man of Two Worlds*. If it did no more than record Munby's acclimatisation to the world of mid-Victorian intelligentsia it would still be notably interesting.

But the world to which God had been pleased to call him lay considerably further down.

It was a world peopled by women who earned their bread regardless of sex: dustwomen, mudlarks scavenging naked-thighed in the Thames, pithead lasses, crossing-sweepers, fisher-girls, milk-women harnessed in yokes, farm-hands, waggon-loaders.

Behind one of the farms in the village, pumping water in the yard, appeared a creature truly worth seeing: tall and strong as a man – short thick neck and square massive shoulders – square broad back, straight from shoulder to hip with no waist to weaken it – stout solid legs, and arms as thick as legs, bare and muscular throughout. A noble creature, refreshing to behold.

I found my path to the cliffs cut off by a large saltwater pond which was rapidly widening as the tide came in. An old fisher woman came up, and proposed that her daughter, a stout pêcheuse de crevettes who was wading with her nets near by, should carry me across. The daughter was called and came striding out of the waves to us. She took off her creel and laid down her nets, and replied with bland contempt to my fears that I should be too heavy to carry. Only she hoped I should sit firm on her hips, and clasp her shoulders with both hands. I sprang into my seat. Her strong legs stood the shock like pillars: she plunged through the water, which was above her knees, with the firm easy tread of a carriage horse.

One of those well-known figures came up the street – a woman in flannel trousers, waistcoat and pink shirt, and lilac cotton bonnet. She was quite clean, for besides working at the pit brow she is employed to run errands from the coal office, and her dirty work had not begun yet. Her dress was not noticed in the streets: in Wigan, a woman in trousers is not half as odd as a woman in crinoline.

Of the bait-gatherers at Filey (also in Yorkshire) hauling themselves and their loads up the cliff face, he wrote that he loved them 'as passionately as I love the grand country where they dwell.' Exhilarated by their strong striding legs, their weather-beaten skins and great red hands, their prowess and their professional tribalism, he sought out such women as though he were travelling in foreign parts, and like a traveller sketched them and photographed them. He felt no lust and no philanthropy, and his social conscience approved of them. He could talk about them to his parents.

He could talk to no one about Hannah Cullwick. He could barely admit her to his diary, cutting out passages about their meetings, referring to her as Juno or Reine. She was a domestic servant, her place was below-stairs.

Met my Juno at the Haymarket Theatre. We went to the gallery, of course. Poor child! She did not presume to recognise me in the street, but waited alone in the crowd. As for me, to stand in the mob at the gallery door, to sit in the gallery among the 'roughs' by the side of a maid of all work and drink with her out of the same bottle between the acts – is not that the very idea of vulgarity and degradation?

Is this the companion and the sphere I have chosen for myself? Looking over the rails down on my equals in the stalls and boxes, I am sensible of a feeling of placid, half-contemptuous indifference: but how if they should look up and see me thus? Should I feel ashamed, worthy of their contempt? I think not; yet if not, would it not be only because I know that she is worthy to be one of them? And so we get back to class distinctions.

Munby at the Mendelssohn concert, Munby drinking out of the same bottle as the woman he loves and with whom he has stolen this meeting, mislays pleasure in a fumble of analysis. Left to himself, and beginning to feel uncomfortable he might well have forsaken her with a high motive. The diaries show several such tentatives. But he was dominated by a character stronger and simpler than his own. Hannah was unvexed by class distinctions. They were as actual to her as the kitchen where she worked and slept, the drawing room where she cleaned the grate before her mistress got up. That Munby's hands should be gloved and hers raw, that if they walked together she should walk behind and have remarks addressed to her over his shoulder, was as fundamental to her love as their relative sexes. At his bidding she wrote fragments of autobiography.

The kitchenmaid and me had our meals in the kitchen and at tea one day i saw a man's face as clearly as could be in the fire, and i showed it to Emma she said, 'Ah one of us will see somebody like that some day' – it was such a nice manly face with a moustache – i little thought i should see such a face, much less love such a face, but in 54 i *did* see it – it was the day after i'd turned 21. i'd my lilac frock – a blue spotted shawl and my black bonnet on, and an apron. When i was crossing for the back street on the way to Grosvenor St. a gentleman spoke to me, and i answered him – that was Massa's face that i'd seen in the fire but i didn't know it again till a good while after.

Now, it is not easy to understand why it was so painful, so peculiarly forbidden, to fix one's love on a kitchen girl – why even to speak of marrying her would break one's mother's heart. Nor is it easy to realise the girl's surroundings – darkened, grimy, verminous, the stink of drains and garbage, the squalor of her basement lot. She existed as an adjunct to dirt and in total lack of honour, for society refused to see any dignity in such labour.

When the year began i was general servant to Mr Foster the beer merchant, i was kitchen servant like, and did all the dirty work down stairs, besides the dining room and hall and steps and back stairs. There was 12 steps to the front door, and it took me an hour to clean crawling backwards and often ladies that came in while i was a-doing 'em and their feet close to where my hands was on the steps. i liked that and made foot marks wi my wet hands like they did wi their wet feet, it made me think o the contrast. i cleaned all the boots and knives and some o the windows and the grates – and i cleaned the watercloset, privy and the long passage and all the rough places downstairs and my wages was 15 lb a year. All that is my sort of work and i *love* it, but i had to wait at breakfast, what i couldn't do well, cause there was no set time and i couldn't keep myself clean enough to go up any time in the morning – to go before my betters and be star'd at, and the Missis told me once or twice of it. But i couldn't be clean, besides i'd liefer be dirty, and no grand folks to stare at me – at last i got warning, the Missis said to me when i was clearing away the things, 'Hannah, your Master and me think you'd better leave and get a place where you've no waiting to do' – i looked surprised, and she says, ''you're a good hard-working servant, she says and we like you, but that strap on your wrist, your Master can't bear to see it nor yet your arms all naked and black'd some-times and you so dirty.' i felt hurt to be told i was too dirty, when my dirt was all got making things clean for them, and as for the leather strap i couldn't leave off *that*, when its the sign that i'm a drudge and belong to Massa. But after all i was glad to be sent away for being dirty, for then Massa may know i *am* dirty.

The strap was worn to strengthen the wrist for hard scrubbing. The dirt was a heraldry.

For Munby, trying to reconcile his love with its object, it was not so straightforward. Slinking down the area steps, he applied Christian Socialist specifics, reading aloud 'simple bits out of Kingsley and Allingham which she seemed to enjoy' and seeing to it that she was confirmed. Going off on a different tack he tried, since he could not make a lady of her to approximate her to the bait-gatherers and pit-head lasses he had loved with refreshment because he was not in love with them, and preached the doctrine of the nobility of labour, the beauty of strong legs and a dirty face. She complied with all her heart. Drudgery was natural to her, she was strong and a hard worker, and took pride in it. Though she could not work for Munby, she could work as a love-offering. When she foresaw a particularly grimy job she summoned him to come and see her 'in her dirt'.

There was her hair, once massy and flowing, now cut short like a man's for mere cleanliness' sake: there was her fine face – once girlish and blooming now reddened and soiled with work and weather: there were her hands – delicate and shapely by nature, but now grown broad and coarse and unseemly, in so many years of scrubbing.

Photography at that date had not learned to flatter. From three photographs of Hannah at work which Munby had taken professionally (cleaning boots, washing dishes, down on the floor scrubbing) it is evident that she was tall and well-made, that the fine face had regular features and a commandingly clear-cut profile. A photograph of Hannah 'in her noblest guise' – that of a chimney-sweep, 'blackened from head to foot' and standing 'almost nude before that phlegmatic little German' compelled him to a fit of self-examining scruples. 'Do I respect her the less because I allowed such degradation?'

Derek Hudson suggests that the photography sessions were motivated by Munby's 'sub-conscious urge to de-feminise the opposite sex.' It might have been an urge to re-masculinise his own. The Evangelical Revival, sweeping through the middle-classes, had brought about a marked decline in sexual hilarity, and this in turn had shaken men's appreciation of their sex. They moulted their nuptual plumage, lost confidence in their power to please or be pleased, and resentfully venerated female delicacy. Munby had escaped the worst infection of this mortifying change in sexual balance. He melted before his mother, otherwise his interest in women of all sizes was rational and humane. It was only with Hannah that he showed these traits of sentimental sadism; but he didn't dare marry her, hadn't bedded her (she had given him opportunities, which he attributed to her innocence); his highmindedness must have looked like half heartedness. Did she respect him the less?

6. April 1872. To Her Majesty's at Drury Lane, and heard Fidelio . . . Seeing it at least once a year, this must be about the 20th time I have seen Fidelio.

The sub-title of *Fidelio* is *Die Eheliche Liebe* (Conjugal Love). Leonore, aliased Fidelio and dressed in man's clothes, has hired herself as servant to the jailor of the fortress where she suspects her husband lies captive. On her first entry she staggers under a load of wood. Telling the jailor she is strong enough to help him dig a grave, she follows him to a dungeon, and saves her husband by pistolling his oppressor. Thanked for all she has dared and suffered, she exclaims 'It's nothing, nothing!' *Nichts, Nichts, mein Florestan*! It was Hannah in her noblest guise, Hannah who insisted on calling him Massa, Hannah vouched for by Beethoven.

By the time of the twentieth *Fidelio* he had resolved to marry her and make an honest man of himself. Meanwhile, he installed her as his housekeeper at Fig Tree Court, Inner Temple. They were married by special licence at 9.a.m. on a January morning. He was 44, she was 39. His duty as a son to conceal the marriage from his parents supplied the illusion of a clandestine amour. By day, Hannah was his servant below-stairs. In the evening she cleaned herself and came up to his chambers.

Home to Hannah . . . sitting in her red frock and white apron and neat cap, sewing; with the cat asleep on the hearthrug, and the kettle singing, and the old poets and other worthies looking down on her from the shelves around, and the evening sun shining in on the linnet in its cage and the myrtles and primroses growing in the window. I sat down, and looked thankfully on this sweet homelike picture, and on her central figure.

I went home at 4, but my dear wife in her servant's dress came forward demurely as I opened the door, and said aloud 'The carpenter is in the bedroom, Sir.' However, we got rid of him.

My Hannah, like Selene, has three aspects: the lady-like and etherial, as at Dorking on Sunday; the neat and homely – not too good for human nature's daily food – as this evening; and the Hecatish or laborious . . . In each she is equally charming to me, but though her sweet nature underlies them all, her manners and her talk are influenced by her dress and appearance, and are appropriate to it. Drest as a lady, her speech and attitudes and ways are all grace and dignity; dressed as a drudge, she works with manlike vigour, rough, and black, and silent; drest, as tonight, like a servant after work is over, she uses kitchen ways and talk, eats her supper with her fingers' aid, wipes her mouth with the back of her hand.

It was the first aspect of Selene he wanted to see more of. His parents were not immortal; a day would come when he could live openly with Hannah as his wife – his lady-wife, facing a new existence with composure. Her dexterity in leading a double life in Fig Tree Court had enchanted him, but Fig Tree Court would not do to practise being a lady in. He persuaded her to country excursions. Dressed as a lady, cloaked as a servant, she met him at the railway station, shed her disguise, changed her hood-bonnet for a feathered hat, hauled on a pair of gloves; and Mr and Mrs Munby arrived at their hotel to enjoy a few days in country air. In August they went for a tour in Normandy.

But wherever they went, she was always glad to be back, glad with an animal gladness, falling ravenously to work; and wherever they went, the only people she felt drawn to were servants; and though she sat so happily with Munby in the evenings, she demurred at sitting at table with him, and ate with a plate on her knees, or escaped to eat in the kitchen; and at every incident which acknowledged her servanthood – when Mr Rees, the revising barrister on the ground floor, tried to kiss her, when Mr Thornbury gestured to her to pick up his letters for him, when the carpenter commented on the muscle in her arm, measured it and found it larger than his, when her brother-in-law, Fred Munby who had stayed the night, tipped her a shilling she reported it with triumph.

'I have loved her for twenty years as a servant, and this year, now that I am her husband, I learn to love her as a lady too,' he wrote after the holiday in Normandy.

The proposal was chivalrous and self-regarding (these qualities go arm-in-arm more often than people suppose). It was also impracticable. He records her progress with fond attentiveness, and it is as though he were recording the progress of a child. Hannah was forty, she too had loved for twenty years, and now she had got him, a gentleman-husband to love and serve. Being a lady was play-acting, nothing to the purpose; a reality of it would subject her to the worst requirement at Mr Foster the beer-merchant's: 'to go before her betters and be stared at.' Munby saw her unwillingness, pitied it, lost heart. She saw his discouragement with peasant insensibility and worked more vehemently than ever. When he imported a couple of under-servants, to spare her strength, she gossiped with them and did their work as well as her own. And all the time their love persisted, and each tried to please.

In August 1877 Hannah went to stay with her brother in Shropshire, while Munby travelled in Switzerland. On her return, she cleaned everything, had an illness (unspecified, probably menopausal), behaved, in some unspecified way, outrageously. Munby consulted a doctor. 'He advised me to send her into the country at once.' She went, a servant dismissed from her place.

Later that same day Munby went to look at a vacant farm-house in Surrey he thought of renting. It was one of Fate's exaggerated ironies: ten years before, during one of his tentatives to love a marriageable Hannah, he believed he had found her there.

The old Munbys died, their hearts intact. Their son lived between his Surrey home and his friends in London, writing a narrative poem in Clough's hexameters about a girl farmworker, which was admired by Browning. In 1882 he must have visited Hannah. Her subsequent letter was copied by him.

. . . One thing dear, I feel *happy*, and that's what I haven't done for many a day, I was singing this morning quite merrily, and I go to bed and get up again with a lighter heart nor I have had for a good while. You didn't say anything to make me *permanently* happy . . . but I enjoyed your visit – you was very nice and as sweetmouth'd as ever, for kissing, and I enjoy'd working for you and waiting on you – so perhaps you'll wonder what's made me happier – It's this darling – I see you love me as much as ever your nature will let you, and I see also that you enjoy being alone as a bachelor, and having no inclination like other men for a wife it's decidedly better that you shouldn't be bothered with one about you, and so my mind is more settled and it would be weak and foolish of me to fret for what we have as it was done on purpose, tho' *I* was quite innocent as to the consequences of such a long engagement, but I must say I used to wonder how ever it would end,

201

and I used to feel every year that the rod was soaking for my own back – so it has proved, though I didn't expect this sort of suffering – to be alone in the world – that is of all things the worst thing that a *woman* can have to endure I am sure, still dear, I do not complain and indeed you will not let me – so I will not seem to –

They wrote; he invited her to London – never to Wheeler's Farm. In 1888 he rented a cottage in Shropshire for her where for long stretches of time they lived together on a married footing.

Thursday, 27 August 1891. This morning Hannah said 'You mun let me soap you all over, Massa; it's good to get the sweat off, I always soap myself.' And, as I stood in the bath, she did this for me, with vigour and address, rubbing me down afterwards with equal skill.

She stood there, tall as myself nearly, drest humbly in blue cotton frock and large white cap and coarse white apron, her loving face and her bare strong arms glowing red with the work: an obvious servant, yet an obvious wife, for none but a wife might do such a thing . . . At bedtime, she went upstairs to have her bath. For she had said this morning, 'I shall use this water again tonight, to wash myself all over; only I mun spit in it first, else we shall quarrel': it being well known in Salop, that if two wash in the same water, they will fall out, unless that rite be observed.

When she was ready, I joined her, and did for her what she had done for me in the morning. To me, it is nothing carnal or voluptuous, but a thing of infinite sacredness, the sight of the fair pure body: still plump and firm and strong, the healthy skin soft and pink-white everywhere, except on her face and neck and her robust round arms and roughened hands. And even all these were softened and made more delicate by the bath. I saw her safe into bed and came down again to write.

In the village they had given up all pretence of concealment. Married or not, nobody minded: they were a loving old couple.

The strong woman died in 1909. He, frail and almost blind, died six months later. He had time to dedicate a last book of verses 'to the gracious and beloved memory of HER whose hand copied out and whose affection suggested all that is best in this book,' and to dictate the inscription on her grave: Hannah, for 36 years the beloved wife and servant of Arthur Joseph Munby.

SOME THINK HIM ILL-TEMPERED AND QUEER

(*Edward Lear: The Life of a Wanderer,* Vivien Noakes,
the *Spectator*, October 25th, 1968)

Illyrian woodlands, echoing falls
Of water, sheets of summer glass,
The long divine Penellan pass,
The vast Akrokeraunian walls
You shadow forth to distant men . . .

One may not immediately associate these lines with the Jumblies who
went to sea in a sieve; but E.L., the travelling artist of Tennyson's
dedication, was Edward Lear, artist of nonsense.

Painting was his livelihood. Before he was sixteen he was colouring
prints for booksellers, 'making morbid disease drawings,' painting fans.
His *Illustrations of the Family of Psittacidae, or Parrots* brought him a
commission to paint the inmates of Lord Stanley's private menagerie at
Knowsley[5]. Grandee households of the 1830s affected tame cats, and Lear
might well have remained at Knowsley, an odd young man with an
enormous nose who was such good company and whose comic rhymes
and drawings were so popular in the nurseries, if he had not become
alarmed about his health, and restless. Lord Stanley sent him to Rome.
Rome was full of artists and visiting patrons. Those who travelled, those
who stayed at home, wanted pictures of foreign lands. Lear published
seven illustrated travel books, seeking his material in the wilder, more
picturesque, more verminous fringes of the Mediterranean.

His pattern of life was established: in winter he travelled and made
sketches; in summer he came back to England, finished his sketches, sold
them, stayed with friends. He had many friends and they were kind. His
talent was kind, too. He had a clever hand, a true eye, a delicate
perception of contours and perspectives. More remarkable, he painted

without a vestige of rant. And if, in his later years with the coming of photography and the drawing-room stereoscope, he lost his market, he kept his old friends, made new ones, and was recognised as a master of nonsense.

But concurrently with this pattern of a busy and fortunate life ran an undertow of apprehension and blighted sexuality. He was an epileptic and homosexual. He endured the one laconically, going into hiding when he felt his attacks coming on, recording them, sometimes as many as twenty a month, with a little cross in his diary. The attacks of the other were more insidious, coming in the guise of friendship – ideal, total friendship; then smiting him down with the realisation that friendship was not what he wanted, that love was not what the other wanted. At intervals he peered at the expedient of marrying; but he was an epileptic.

> *There was an old man in a fix,*
> *Who said, I can't possibly mix.*

It seems permissible to summarise Lear's tragic quandary like this. Though he did not invent the limerick, we think of it as his. It is typical, though, not personal. His personal self, his perforce acceptance of his tragic quandary, dictated the later *Nonsense Songs*[6] and made them as mysteriously, indisputably poetical as the poems of Edgar Allan Poe; which they strangely resemble.

It is the signal merit of Vivien Noakes's biography that she conveys the continuity of Lear's discordant life without a single false emphasis. Her narrative is like his best drawings: clear, orderly, perceptive, detailed and without a vestige of rant. The scholarship of her researches is exemplary. So is the index.

ESCAPE FROM THE SUET CRUST
(The Tale of Beatrix Potter, Margaret Lane,
the *Spectator*, September 27th, 1968)

Margaret Lane's *The Tale of Beatrix Potter* was first published in 1946. Now she has the deserved good fortune of being able to make a good book better. Since 1946 new material has come to light, notably Beatrix Potter's journal, written from 1881 to 1897 in a cipher of her own invention, which Mr Leslie Linder transcribed after a four-year struggle to break the code. This new material does not affect Margaret Lane's first reading of her subject, but it substantiates it and casts a sharper light on the traits which underlay, like rock strata, a sombre life and a happy ending. For like all true portraits *The Tale of Beatrix Potter* enforces the mysterious enigma of a personality.

In the book-famine period during which *The Tale of Beatrix Potter* first came out I met a careful mother of young children who was trying to reconstruct from her own memory and the memory of others the Peter Rabbit Books of her childhood. The illustrations were beyond recall. The stories she could give an account of. It was the text, the exact word-by-word text she was after.

And, of course, she was right. The wording is essential to the magic, though it clothes the narrative so economically, so inevitably, that it is almost imperceptible. Only when one looks more closely at this art which conceals art does one begin to see how the few words fall into place with unerring precision, how they shape the action and define the characters without commenting or explaining, how exactly they comply with the wild objectivity of a child's mind; and how spontaneously the stories begin – and end (to appreciate the spontaneity of Beatrix Potter's best endings one has to turn to *Ginger and Pickles*, of a date when a pre-occupation with real life betrayed her into postscripts).

Her authorship began with equal spontaneity. In September 1893 (her twenty-eighth year) she wrote to a small boy, an invalid: 'My dear Noel. I don't know what to write to you, so I shall tell you a story about four little rabbits, whose names were Flopsy, Mopsy, Cottontail and Peter.' And there they are, and there the story and the illustrations are, without a stumble, without an erasure. Eight years later *The Tale of Peter Rabbit* came out in print. During the following eleven years she produced a book or a brace of books yearly. Apparently all she needed to do was to look in her heart and write.

The heart, like Faithful Henry's, had been bound with iron bands. From childhood the sheltered, negligible, dutiful daughter of wealthy, respectable, middle-class parents had been packing it with the industry of a lively mind imprisoned in idleness, with a prisoner's vehement observation of the geometry of a cobweb, the eye of a mouse, the neatness of a pin. Twice a year, when her parents left London for holidays in the country, the ticket-of-leave prisoner might add a nettle, a duck-pond, a cottage kitchen. It must be allowed to the Potters that the ticket-of-leave prisoner returned with actual bats and snails, that she was permitted the company of a rabbit, a hedgehog, a pair of mice – provided, of course, these did not appear downstairs; and that she was encouraged to paint their portraits with minute accuracy. Perhaps while her brother was at home this scanty childhood was (quite by accident) congenial to her turn of mind.

Shades of the prison house closed on the young lady. When she was fifteen she began a journal in cryptogram and kept it into her thirties. It is a scrupulous record of suffocation: daily doings, hearsay of public events, Papa's comments on them, family stories, items of information such as fill up gaps in provincial newspapers. Only very occasionally is there a brief wail for the loss of childhood, a brief outcry of terror at the prospect of the boredom blackening ahead, an icy diagnosis of what ails her. 'It is somewhat trying to pass a season of enjoyment in the company of persons who are constantly on the outlook for matters of complaint.' The family stories came from a north-country ancestry. A granite resignation underlies the journal.

There is no resignation in the stories, and the morality is of a business acumen kind. Meanwhile, the success of the stories had put a little golden key into her hand. In 1905 (the year of Mrs Tiggy-Winkle) she bought a small farm[7] in the Lake Country. She could not live in it – yet; but it gave her a standing with her parents and an admissible pretext for leaking away during some part of those seasons for enjoyment, family holidays. She bought stock, she added acres, cottages, another farm. She made a friend of Mr Heelis, a local solicitor. He asked her to marry him. He cannot have known what a turmoil of conscience, disapprobation, family jurisdiction and wrath her acceptance exposed her to – if he had, I hope he would have abducted her. But she held on for two years and in 1913 they married. I think it is not for nothing that *The Tale of Mr Tod* and *The Tale of Pigling Bland*, written during those years, admit to a grimmer world than she had acknowledged before.

The Tale of Beatrix Potter has a happy ending. Like Peter Rabbit, she had heard Mr McGregor hard on her heels; like Tom Kitten, she had been destined for the family table, bundled in suet crust, tied up in a pudding cloth with very hard knots; but she escaped and lived happily ever after with a comfortable husband and under a roof of her own. She wrote little more, and that without distinction, turning her mind to Herdwick sheep, on which she became an authority.

THREE VOICES

(the *Spectator*, November 29th, 1968)

Mrs Beer's House, Patricia Beer
The Incense Tree, Diana Hopkinson
Birdless Summer, Han Suyin

Mrs Beer's husband was a railway clerk, her house was a small red brick house in an outlying suburb of Exmouth. Her younger daughter's account of a small-town childhood conveys with pre-Raphaelite intensity the sensation of life in a matriarchate. The sensation was not painful, but it was unremitting. Mrs Beer did her duty in the state of life she had got herself into (she felt she had married beneath her) and did it with a swing. But her vitality was funnelled into her intentions. She had been a school-teacher, so her daughters must be school-teachers. She belonged to the Plymouth Brethren, so her husband must become a Plymouth Brother. An early memory of Mrs Beer's daughter was seeing her father cycling off to be baptised by total immersion. 'It was a summer evening, and he was carrying a change of clothes rolled up in a towel, an unpleasantly fraught version of someone going bathing.'

It takes the shock of adolescence to crack the detachment through which children observe their world. It takes a disciplined memory to recall those observations without falsifying them. Patricia Beer's recall of the Plymouth Brethren variety of religious experience rings true because she has the candour to remember enjoying as well as observing. Hymns, of course, are always enjoyable. There is an animal release in hymn singing. Of the hymns she quotes I myself particularly enjoyed

> *Twas vain for Israel bitten*
> *By serpents on their way*

for the evocation (not however intended) of serpents snatching a quick bite *en route*. But this small closed society of the Saved, positive of its salvation, faithful to its tenets with the faithfulness of those who go only to one grocer because he is the best grocer, also afforded a release from the pressure of Mrs Beer's intentions by a reassuring mundanity, a kind of righteous going bathing – though her daughter is too loyal to say so outright. The truth giveth life: *Mrs Beer's House* could be a trivial book, in fact, it is oddly enthralling.

Diana Hopkinson was born to the relative freedom of wealth. She learned customs not conventions, she was not expected to become anything in particular, she was blessed with a mother who had a life of her own. But the significance of *The Incense Tree* is due to the fact that she was born a mischling, the child of a Gentile father and a Jewish mother, and had her predominant ancestry from a race which depends for its continuance on intellect, adaptability, sensibility, knowledge of the world, family connections and the unquenchable Jewish talent of perceptiveness.

In intervals of schooling she was duly travelled about – to Belgium, to Italy, to Geneva, where the flower-beds had bloomed to order and she felt that 'everything was for the best in a wonderful Europe.' When she was nineteen she was sent to spend a summer in Munich on her own. It was 1931. '"One day," said Frau Hey, "Hitler will come and take away my grand piano."' And one day 'I joined a group of students who were making a light-hearted demonstration outside the Braune Haus. We laughed at the Brown Shirts strutting outside the building and mocked them by imitating the Hitler salute.' But this was a side-show affair among the riches Munich had to offer: the new art-form of films, Modernismus in decoration, Mozart evenings in the courtyard of the Residenz, Palestrina in the Theatinerkirche, sailing, being looped the loop by moonlight, love and new friends and freedom all round in the *Davidsbundlertanz* of the Weimar Republic.

After Munich, Oxford, autumnal and unwelcoming and Lady Margaret Hall at the end of Norham Gardens 'like a railway terminus.' At a Labour Club dance her partner jolted her against a very tall young man – a German Rhodes Scholar whose name was Adam von Trott zu Solz. He proved to be disappointingly more serious-minded than her Munich companions ('When we stood on the steps, admiring the starry skies. he asked me if I had read the works of Jean-Paul'), so less single-minded than the Labour Club implied. But a laughing love grew into a perplexed triangle where the third party was Germany. His patriotism was filial and protective. He was appalled by the spread of Hitlerism, knew it must be combated, idealistically believed that it could be overcome. But the evil must be fought, the true Germany defended, from within. So, loving honour more, he went back to Germany.

Censorship froze their letters. Each time she visited him he was more uneasy, more withdrawn. They had to meet where he was not known. She must observe every regulation, or her landlady would be penalised for housing a Jewess. With an averted head he had to walk her past houses badged with the Yellow Star, walls daubed with *Juden heraus*. He kept to his purpose, was not suspected, had a position. 'Adam made several journeys to England during the last summer before the outbreak of war. His movements and his objectives were wrapped in a secrecy which alienated many of his friends.' In 1944 he took part in the attempt on Hitler's life and was hanged. With her unquenchable Jewish perceptiveness, she saw his fallacy and never lost her faith in him.

Birdless Summer is also by a mischling. Han Suyin, born Rosalie Chou, was the child of a Chinese father and a Belgian mother. It should be an interesting reminder to broad-minded whites that in China her European blood was her disgrace. In his kinder moments her young husband would overlook this. 'Your blood is Chinese, blood comes from the father, the mother is only a receptacle.' More often, he struck the face which was not adequately egg-like and submissive, and when they met his fellow officers or officials she was under orders not to speak, not even to agree, since he had a reputation to keep up and a career to make.

They met in 1938, returning to China on the same boat, she a medical student, he an army cadet, and as it then seemed to them to serve a China which at last held a promise of fighting back the Japanese invasion. The promise was Chiang Kai-shek, a leader, a spellbinder. Like his European counterpart, even to having Shirts (Chiang's were Blue), he was a fervent Nationalist. China must be saved, not by force of arms or private negotiations but by a mass return to Confucian ethics, a sacred pyramid of subserviences, of people knowing their places and paying their taxes, where from base to summit a woman's place was to be a receptacle. When Wuhan (placarded with *Wuhan Must Be Defended to the Last*) was unobtrusively evacuated by the General Staff, the young couple went on to Chungking. Here there was ample time for the military cadet to polish his loyalty and climb his ladder; for his wife to practise calligraphy (calligraphy, for those who could write, was a national duty), to play mahjong with other wives, to whiten her husband's gloves (white gloves were a military obligation) and to meditate (meditation was in vogue, commanders went off to meditate in temples) on the filth and starvation of that crowded stronghold, the avarice and intrigue and fatuity of the official camp-followers who creamed it, and on the conscript troops roped together and driven on with whips to another inattentive defeat.

Two things saved her reason, visits to her uncle's house in Chengtu, traditional in ceremonials, family pieties, concubines, and spells of working as a midwife in the Chengtu Missionary Hospital, untraditional in its endeavours to save unwanted female babies from being thrown away, ended with a mallet-blow, preserved long enough to be saleable as a slave or prostitute. 'Before this pitiless, pitiful unending story of suffering, my own dwindled into nothingness.'

THE VICTORIAN PSYCHE

(*Marian Evans and George Eliot*, L. and E. Hanson,
Britain Today, 1952)

To sit for one's portrait to an amateur artist who is also a friend or a relation is to put oneself in jeopardy of disclosures. With a stammering earnestness, with the mildest intentions, and often failing to catch anything resembling a likeness, the portraitist will scarcely fail to show what the sitter is like. It was a brother who recorded the dogmatic set of Charlotte Brontë's lips. In 1842, Miss Marian Evans, then in her twenty-third year with fourteen years to run before she became George Eliot, was painted in watercolour by her friend Caroline Bray. The head is disproportionately large, with a massive brow, an interminable nose, a heavy and protuberant mouth. Extended by ringlets bunched over the ears, it has the portentousness of a gargoyle, and a gargoyle's discrepancy to the gothic of slender torso and crimped muslin fichu below it. The countenance shows a sullen melancholy, and an obstinacy that could become obtuse; yet the residual impression is of mingled timidity and sensibility.

Now, only a few years short of the centenary of her first novel[8], we view George Eliot enskied in fame and time, a large-headed, large-accomplished female bust attached to the temple of English literature. At this distance from the eye, the expression of timid sensibility is not easily seen. But if it had not been for what that expression denoted, the large-headed woman might not now be attached to the edifice. Instead, her name would be recorded in some crypt or lean-to: Evans, Marian. Journalist: translated Strauss's *Life of Jesus* and Feuerbach's *Essence of Christianity*. Obstinacy, and a sullen resignation to being saddened at the bidding of the intellect, took her just so far. Then obstinacy, and no doubt the bidding of the intellect, but also the bidding of the flesh, and the ambiguous bidding of the world, which while demanding female chastity jeered at old maids, took her across a Rubicon, and she left England with

211

G. H. Lewes, a married man without even the hope of a divorce to cover his nakedness.

After eight carefree uncensored months of travelling in Germany, they returned to England; and immediately the change of climate began its work. Lewes came back from a scouting expedition through their former London circle saying it would be wiser for them to live quietly in the suburbs. She and Lewes could not go visiting together. She signed her letters Marian Evans, but letters to her could not be so addressed without alarming landladies. And though she still got commissions to write articles and reviews, she must write anonymously. Her desire to improve and elevate mankind was as sincere as ever, her ability to do so considerably limbered by living with a man who had not a vestige of prig about him, but she could no longer reinforce what she wrote by who she was. Circumstances had unfrocked her. 'I shall say nothing of sorrows and renunciations,' she wrote in a letter of this period. In truth, she was increasingly depressed, and wincingly conscious of slights and handicaps. It was Lewes who drew her from this Slough of Despond and directed her towards being a novelist, working on her with little tweaks and shoves and perhaps – he knew her well besides loving her well – with provocations, doubts as to whether she could manage dialogue of dramatic tension. At last, she wrote in her journal, 'I am anxious to begin my fiction writing.' One might not augur very hopefully from this dutiful approach. But the novels of George Eliot came of it.

The vitality of Laurence and Elizabeth Hanson's *Marian Evans and George Eliot* is greatly due to the care and insight with which they have burnished the Marian Evans side of the medal. The long cumbrous development of her character, in which deliberation was so oddly traversed by wilfulness, is related with such narrative skill that when Lewes enters the story his impact on the reader explains (what contemporaries found so perplexing) his impact on George Eliot. A biography of George Eliot must needs be a period study also; her subjectivity to society made her a sociological novelist. Here, too, Mr and Mrs Hanson are excellent. But of the many things to praise in this admirable book, I would single out the authors' handling of G. H. Lewes. I wish they would follow this study of their Victorian Psyche by a study of her Victorian Eros.

THE TRUE EAR

(*Thomas Hardy: A Critical Biography*, Evelyn Hardy, *Britain Today*, 1954)

A small-sized boy with a capacious back to his head, and that head ringing with dance tunes, ballads and psalm tunes, Thomas Hardy 'could tune a fiddle when he was barely breeched,' and to the end of his many days remembered a toy concertina which had been given to him when he was four years old.

An outstanding merit of Evelyn Hardy's *Thomas Hardy: a Critical Biography,* is her recognition of Hardy's sensibility to music and of the way his latent musicianship crops up in his writing, whether as a passion that helps to shape the plot, or as a fineness of ear which catches and defines the minutest sounds of nature, or as a metrical inventiveness which gave such variety to his lyrics. It was an accurate sensibility, moreover. Hardy is one of the few English writers (Shakespeare is another) who cannot be faulted in his musical technicalities; and where he makes use of this technical *savoir faire* – as for instance in the metaphor of tonalities in the Apology to *Late Lyrics and Earlier*[9] – one feels that he has a peculiar satisfaction in doing so, as though, wedlocked to writing, he were keeping clandestine assignations with his first love.

That Thomas Hardy should have been born at that moment when Stinsford quire was dying [writes Evelyn Hardy] is an odd prank of fortune, for no one would have been a more fervent player than he. Yet we might have been the poorer: his ardour might have evaporated in evanescent music-making rather than in preserving for us 'the old musicianers.'

Possibly the speculation might be carried further. The power of music was a power which Hardy accepted without demur, for in music there was nothing to vex his sense of justice, nothing to deplore or gainsay: one tunes the fiddle; and the tuning of a fiddle is something under a man's control, unlike the fall of events, the way of the world or the ways of a woman. The pleasure of playing in the church band might have kept Thomas Hardy at least an acquiescent churchman. He would have questioned the right dealings of the parson, no doubt, and imagined his funeral; but perhaps not God's Funeral.

But Hardy was apprenticed to architecture, wrote poetry by inclination, lost his faith, married a canon's niece, was for thirty years a novelist, and wrote on Christmas Day, 1890, 'while thinking of resuming "the viewless wings of poesy" before dawn this morning, new horizons seemed to open, and worrying pettinesses seemed to disappear.' Seventeen years later he had completed *The Dynasts*[10].

It is by its treatment of *The Dynasts* that any critical book on Hardy must stand or fall. Evelyn Hardy is here at her best. She begins with the initial advantage of a stroke of sound common sense, for she does not attempt to summarise the action. It is the workshop aspect she deals with: the long preoccupation, the almost instinctive gathering of material to cohere round the first material of all – the reminiscences and hearsay of Hardy's childhood; and then the strange fusion of Dorset anecdotes, old pike-heads, and uniform buttons with Aeschylus and the Immanent Will; and then, after the assemblage, the construction, the enormous fabric built up like a ship and complemented with its thronging *dramatis personae*. At the same time, she does not forget to relate *The Dynasts* to the rest of Hardy's work. Commenting that 'by comparison his stories, poems and novels, even the finest of them, seem puny and somehow lacking in masculine virility,' she suggests that 'this is because, for the first time, the writer allows himself to conceive, and to express, robust thoughts and matter which hitherto he had been forced to conceal, or suppress, to placate an over-pudentious public. It had been his plaint more times than one that if what he wrote had been set in verse no one would carp or criticise. Now he took the full liberties which blank verse proffered.'

It was Hardy the novelist who took charge of the construction. 'He set down his thoughts in plain prose, altering it to blank verse later.' Quotations from the first draft with the subsequent emendations show, too, a setting down of plain blank verse which only a last revision fired into poetry; but the speeches of the in-prose characters, common soldiers and countrymen, are little altered, if at all, from the first draft. *The*

Dynasts, in short, was a synthesis of Hardy the poet and Hardy the novelist, working together, and neither of them thwarted or deprived. This may be the reason why *The Dynasts*, for all its fatalism, its Spirits Sinister and Ironic and the outcries of its Spirit of the Pities, has never been much of a target for those who write about Hardy's pessimism; for it was where the poet was at odds with the novelist that such arrows had been aimed in the past. The Hardy of *The Dynasts* had no such chinks in his armour.

Evelyn Hardy's last chapter carries a well-argued refutation of the tedious and dishonest cliché of Hardy's pessimism, but she would have done better if she had not allowed a note of special pleading to creep in, leaving it open to the reader to conclude that it was because of a train of circumstances impacting on a character of great sensibility that Hardy's integrity might look like pessimism. Hardy's integrity looks like integrity. Apart from this, and from making perhaps rather too much of her three Ladies of the Manor, the author is to be congratulated on a careful and judicious book.

THE LAND OF GWENT
(The Aylesford Review, Vol.V, Spring, 1963)

'All my life,' Arthur Machen[11] said to me, 'I have been trying to write well. And I have never succeeded.' This was in Pembrokeshire, in 1928. He had taken me to look at an ash tree whose curious shape attracted him, and we were standing beneath it when he spoke, breaking a long silence.

There are no consolations for Lucifer. Though I could have cited weightier opinions than my own, or disproved him by quoting passages from his books which are indisputably very well written, it wouldn't have availed, it wouldn't have applied. I knew from his *Hieroglyphics* what he meant by writing well, and how sparingly, and how arbitrarily, he granted that patent. In any case, the remark was addressed to the ash tree rather than to me. He plainly felt a particular intimacy with it, or with what was behind it.

In *Far Off Things* Arthur Machen recalls his youth in Gwent and how, out of the child's first marvelling acceptance of its new world there had

215

grown an acknowledgement of indwelling mysteries, both good and evil. This acknowledgement impelled him to write, governed the course of his writings, determined much of his taste in letters. I remember him saying, apropos of his preference for the 17th century, that Shakespeare knew what grew on his bank, and that it was a fine bank in its way; but that there was nothing underneath it: Vaughan and Traherne would have seen the bank very differently. As with banks, so with books. It is usual for books to be written with an eye for what grows on them – characters, incidents, turns of narrative. Arthur Machen's concern was with what would be underneath the book. It was his ambition to write a book, a great book, that should have the quality of an incantation, and so convey the ecstasy that he insists upon in *Hieroglyphics*; and as part of that ambition he wanted to write well – that is, absolutely well: because being a practical man he knew that this was the only means by which the book he wanted to write could be written.

He wrote with difficulty, with anguish, with stubborn perseverance, with sudden glories of hopefulness and long tracts of disillusioned industry. His ambition continually disabled his intentions. He says of *The Hill of Dreams*: 'I sat down every night for three weeks with blank paper before me, trying to get the second chapter.' If, as an exception, 'I set about this task with the utmost relish and enjoyment. For once, I knew what to write about', the task is the Epilogue for a book not yet begun, a flourish of fancy and nothing to do with what he ambitioned. 'For once, I knew what to write about. There is a sharp difference, a difference in kind, between that and knowing what one wants to write, between knowing what grows on the bank and invoking what may lie underneath it, kingdom of Elfin, pit of iniquity, buried temple'. It is easy for an outsider to see this distinction; I doubt if Arthur Machen was aware of it. What he saw was the image of the book he had wanted to write; and that he had not succeeded in writing it.

He was not embittered by his failure. He was not even embittered by the success of his *Far Off Things* and *Things Far and Near*, epitaphs, as it were, of the ambition he had put away. 'I have always had a kindly feeling for the two books of reminiscences, partly because they recalled old days, and partly because I wrote them with comparative ease, which has not been a common fortune with me.'

216

EDMUND FELLOWES AS EDITOR
(*The Musical Times*, February, 1952)

'It was the most extraordinary stroke of luck – .' Those who knew Edmund Fellowes[12] will remember the note of appreciative astonishment in his voice as he narrated some editorial achievement, some discovery or solution, which a less spontaneous nature might have attributed to personal causes such as hard work or technical skill. Luck, undoubtedly, played its part. It was lucky that in his fourth year at Oxford a suggestion that he might make himself useful in transcribing a Dunstable manuscript set him to study early notation (though the matter got no further). It was lucky that during a tennis tournament in 1911 a conversation should turn to music and a lady of the party should ask him why, though there were complete editions of all the poets of the Shakespearian epoch, no such service had been done for the madrigalists. It was lucky that having gone to Durham in search of material to complete a deficient text of some Gibbons anthems he should discover in the Cathedral library eight of the ten voice-parts of Byrd's 'Great Service', a major work whose existence was till that moment unsuspected. It was lucky that besides living more intensely than most men, he also lived longer, and was able to see to the finish his complete edition of the works of William Byrd. But the willingness to study something quite unremunerative, the decision to rescue the madrigalists, and the decisive recognition (and immediate transcription) of a new work by Byrd, were matters, not of luck, but of character: the disinterestedness, enterprise and acumen which marked his career as an editor.

He himself ranked high among his 'strokes of luck' the fact that he turned, having finished his 'English Madrigal School', to an exploration of the solo songs of John Dowland – an exploration which led to his edition of 'The English school of Lutenist Song-Writers'. It can be claimed that this is his most important contribution to English music. The

217

works of the madrigal composers, even if neglected and misunderstood, had always been granted a lip-service recognition. Choirs had thumped their way through the 'Triumphs of Oriana' and 'Now is the month of maying', though their renderings had done all that was humanly possible to disguise the quality of what they were performing. But the work of such song-writers as Dowland, Campian, and Robert Jones was not even 'pyramidally extant': and consequently the original editions were so little valued as *collectors' items* that, in some cases, only one example had survived. The rescue of this exquisite variety of English music is certainly the most romantic, and probably the most important of all the things that Edmund Fellowes did for music.

It shows the neglect into which the Elizabethan composers had fallen that when Fellowes, B.Mus., went to the British Museum to begin scoring the madrigalists, he had only the vaguest notions what the original texts would look like. It shows the scope and capacity of his intentions that his first act was to make a list of all the available material, and to draw up a scheme for a complete edition in thirty-six volumes. And it shows his astonishing industry and clear-headedness that within a year of setting out he had decided on his editorial method (including the then novelty of irregular barring), and scored four volumes of Thomas Morley. It is not, perhaps, so remarkable that he could find no music publisher to undertake their publication unless the editor guaranteed the cost of production, and no public body prepared to take over this financial responsibility. He issued a statement of his project, and within a year enough English and continental music-lovers had subscribed to it to make publication possible.

Other editors have possessed energy and discrimination, the power to conceive an ambitious project and the industry to carry it to a conclusion – together with the necessary extra industry required to do so on a subscription basis. Yet their work may have remained no more than an effort of scholarship. The Sleeping Beauty, so painstakingly awakened, is allowed to fall asleep again. Fellowes did not consider that the task of an editor ceased with the last corrections to proof; he worked ever harder to make known than to make knowable. He taught, he lectured, he demonstrated. He sang the lute songs to his own accompaniment on the lute. When, in the early twenties, the English Singers sang English madrigals in Berlin, German critics supposed that their renderings were 'the fruit of centuries of carefully preserved tradition'. They were the fruit of ten years work by Fellowes, and of his insistence that the madrigals were of absolute musical value.

As an editor, he was free from the slightest arthritis of antiquarianism. Such words as 'quaint' or 'meritorious' were not in his vocabulary; he could be critical, but he was never condescending. Here, one may allow a little credit to his luck: he was fortunate in his approach. The fiddle was his instrument, he had played much chamber music; thus he came to Elizabethan polyphony via the secular freedom of the string quartet. During the ten years' preparation of the critical edition of Tudor Church Music it was my privilege to meet him in the close and constant association of an editorial committee, and I saw how naturally his mind fitted itself to the texture of a music 'apt for voice or viols', and how, when it came to a conjectural reading, his suggestions expressed a contemporaneity with composers uncircumscribed by 'four-part vocal harmony', so that, while others might be puzzling how to supply a missing part in some refractory passage, his mind would have flown to the possibility of half a bar's rest. Quick and supple in the solution of problems, he was also inexhaustibly and obstinately conscientious. Nothing would satisfy him but to be satisfied. Though he might seem to give way, or pass over, he never mislaid a scruple. Hours later, or at a subsequent meeting, he would say, 'I'm still uneasy about . . .' – and the amazing memory would find the place on a particular page among so many pages, and the finger, slightly shaking with excitement, would point, and his face, reddened with an interior conflict between amiability and integrity, would work with honest woe until the right answer had been found. No one, seeing him at such moments, could miss the clue to his distinguishing merit: that he brought to his editorship the sensibility and conscience of the creative artist.

JOHN CRASKE: FISHERMAN AND ARTIST 1881-1943
(*Exhibition Catalogue, The Aldeburgh Festival*, 1971)

When John Craske[13], aged thirty-nine, emerged for a few months between his recurrent comas and thought he would like to do a painting, he faced the problem of what to paint with, and what to paint on. Paper would cost money. Fortunately, his home supplied flat surfaces. He painted on door-panels, window-boards, box-lids, trays, the back of Laura Craske's pastry-board. Not until he had exhausted these did he buy paper – cheap and regrettably flimsy, as the *James Edward* shows. For paints he used the only paints he knew: heeltaps of housepaint, distemper, poster-paint.

Laura Craske's story of his first needlework records the same kind of necessitous inventiveness. At this time, they were lodging with her mother. Craske, now discovered to be a diabetic, had been ill again.

'One evening, John was so distressed, he would not settle to anything. I said "Shall we try to make a picture?" Mother found an old frame, and then I said, "Mother, have you a piece of calico?" Mother replied. "Only my new piece which I bought for my Christmas pudding." I looked at her and she looked at me, and then said, "Oh – let John have it!" We tacked it onto the frame, John drawed a boat on it. We found some wools, and I showed John the way to fill it in. He did it, then when we came to the sky we had no wool suitable and no money to buy any with. I remember, I mixed some distemper in a saucer, gave him a brush, and with mother's blue bag he made the sky. It takes a lot of money in sickness.'

But as to what he would paint, Craske was never in doubt. He would paint what he knew: ships, because he understood their behaviour, the north Sea whose behaviour he had experienced, the East Anglian coast. As a fisherman and a fishmonger he knew about fish, so he used fish and shells in his few still-lives; and the frames of some of his earlier watercolours he decorated with a bold *rocaille* of shells and pebbles.

Ships and the sea . . . They were life and death matters to him, and he painted them as such, seriously and truthfully; dramatically, when the situation – being a life and death situation – called for it, but never romantically. He painted like a man giving witness under oath to a wild story. Marriott, the *Times* art critic, praised the veracity of his pictures[14]. Veracity was a discerning word. Whether it be a shipwreck, a blizzard, a fair wind, a string of smoked bluefish, boats on a slipway, a parson dropping a letter in a pillarbox, Craske gives you his word for it. The veracity came by experience and weather-eye. Most artists know the sea from its edge. Craske knew it from the middle, from experience of being a small upright movement in a vast swaying horizontality.

Another ingredient in his veracity is his awareness of the gravity equation between sea and ship. When Coleridge wrote:

> *. . . idle as a painted ship*
> *Upon a painted ocean*

he showed himself a landsman by that *upon*. Craske's ships make their way through the sea, are supported by it, founder in it; his pictures never let one forget their vital relationship with it, part contest; part connivance; he conveys the posture of a boat riding at anchor, the relative weights of the tug and the two boats on tow in the *Red Bridge*. One might say, he goes to sea in his ships. I once heard him express this participation. He had an elaborate needlework almost finished – a seaward view of a ship entering a bay round a headland. When I saw this again, on a later visit, the whole centre, sea and sky and ship, had been unpicked. Respectfully – he was a man who imposed respect – I asked why. 'That ship,' he said, 'She couldn't have got in on that tack.' The strange thing is, that the final version with the ship on the right tack was the better composition. Not all his revisions were so scrupulous, though. He showed me an album into which he had stuck a number of his smaller water-colours – to keep them tidily together, he explained. Among them was a painting of a fishing village, glumly facing an unmistakeable east wind. Several pages further on was another section of the same village. As the picture was too long for the album and the album his pleasure at the moment, he had bisected it; subsequently making an honest picture of the second half by signing it. He did not sign as boldly as he usually did; but both signatures can be seen in the *Fishing Village* water-colour.

Yet I wonder whether the ship's tack reason was not just a reason he adduced to himself to account for an intuitive process. As there are Primitives, there are Intuitives. If Craske is to be put into a category, he must be placed with the Intuitives – a companion to John Clare. At first

221

sight, in the *Rescue by Breeches Buoy* the men in yellow oilies, seeming so much out of proportion, might suggest the naivete of the Primitives. But in fact, they are in proportion to the event. Their disproportion to the boat declares the height of the cliff and makes the rescue something to attend to. Slavish perspective would have made an ungainly diagram of the composition. Craske took an intuitive solution; but he might have told himself he was saving a great expenditure of filoselle.

With one exception, he was, as far as I know, uninfluenced and uninfluenceable. Till he thought he would like to do a painting, he had accepted pictures as a variety of pious furnishings in a respectable home. After Laura Craske had shown him the way to fill in the boat he had drawn on the pudding-cloth, he developed his stitch technique unguided. He liked approval, and was pleased with earnings, but neither affected him. The one exception was his dreams about the sea. A particular dream of a tempest with much lightning was so compelling that when he woke and asked what day it was, and heard it was Sunday, he broke through the Sabbatarianism of a lifetime and worked all day, making sure of the lightning. That picture he gave to his wife.

But in a truer sense, all his pictures were hers. But for her devotion, they would not have come into being. Against all reason, all regulations, she set herself to get him, lying senseless as a log, out of the Norwich Asylum.

I used to go three times weekly to see him. One day I was so distressed, kneeling down in my front bedroom – Oh, how I pleaded with God to let John come home again.

And I remember I asked God to let me know when he would be home, and I opened my Bible to Ezekiel, 34 chapter, 27 verse. The whole verse comforted me. I read: *And the tree of the field shall yield her fruit, and the earth shall yield her increase, and they shall be safe in their land and shall know I am the Lord.*

In my mind I reasoned: there is not much left in the earth nor on the trees after October.

I took my Bible down to John's father in the shop, and told him John would be coming home in October. Father said, "I hope you may be right, child."

An orderly brought him home the last day of October.

NANCY CUNARD

(From *Nancy Cunard, Brave Poet, Indomitable Rebel*, 1968)

A contribution to *Authors Take Sides*[15] was my first link with Nancy Cunard. We had some correspondence about Spain, but we did not meet till the winter of 1942-43, when Morris Gilbert's work brought him on a visit to Dorset and she came with him. They, Valentine Ackland and I met for lunch at a hotel in Dorchester. Slender, long-legged, walking with a neat, slightly tripping gait, like a water-wagtail's, she came in carrying with elegance a large onion. At that date every scrap of paper was needed for making Heads of Departments; it was ordinary for purchases to be unwrapped. But Nancy carried her onion with a difference. That same evening she and Morris dined with us. As they were leaving, she slid the heavy African ivory bracelets off her wrists and asked us to look after them. They would be safer in a Dorset village than in London. She looked sadly at her wrists when they were off. She would have felt much less denuded if she had stripped off her clothes.

Possibly the bracelets drew her back, for she came for several weekends that winter. She prided herself on travelling light. Nothing was forgotten, nothing was crumpled, everything was fitted into the smallest possible compass: a tartan haversack, supplemented perhaps by a Dick Whittington spotted handkerchief. Settled in, she began to preen: a button was made fast, a lining re-stitched; the bracelets were fetched and devoutly polished; after that, she would polish her nails or do a little washing. On a desert island, in a jail cell, she would have kept herself spruce, well-kept, clean as a cat. Her temper was notorious, her life was wilful and erratic – and she was compellingly respect-worthy. Loyal, industrious, thorough, she had the qualities that make the sublimely good servant – a good servant in French, at that, for she was *courageuse*: an indomitable worker. She had another domestic merit: she was punctual. I have cooked many meals for Nancy and never known her late for one of them. Whatever she had been doing, however absorbing it had been, she would be ready – brushed and combed and creditable; and sitting upright and slightly formalised, she would converse agreeably, as a guest should. This frosting of social convention made her peculiarly entertaining, since it co-existed with a wide range of violent opinions and violent language. Even when she was drunk, it persisted, though *allargando* into solemnity and owlishness. 'Nancy, you're tight.' 'Only a little, darling' – flawlessly enunciated. And when an explosion of feeling broke through this habitual *bel canto*, the effect was formidable.

Yes, she was formidable. But as it happened, I was not afraid of Nancy and we never fell out. Each of us sometimes found the other exasperating; but we saw eye to eye about Spain. It was that which cemented us. Her engagement with Spain, her implacable loyalty to what the democracies had allowed to become a lost cause, made her take a rather *de haut en bas* view of Britain's protracted series of Finest Hours. When she talked of life in London, it was muddle and officialdom she complained at, not danger and privation. Air-raids were no more than what we had asked for when we turned a deaf ear to *Arms for Spain* and a wall-eye on Guernica. The only air-raid I remember her referring to was one when incendiary bombs set fire to dumps of domestic fuel stored in Hyde Park. Among these was a dump of those singularly incombustible pellets called Boulet Bernod. 'Actually burning,' she said with enthusiasm. 'What a strange sight!'

She had an eye to notice such details – it was part of the good servant side of her character, as was her power to nail a personality in a phrase. I asked her – she was then working for the Free French – what General de Gaulle was like. In a flash she replied: 'Froid, sec et cassant.'

This dash and dexterity in the spoken word flowered from the pains she took in writing. Her French translations of the *Poems for France*[16] anthology were arrived at after countless expedients and discardings and considerations and consultings. I remember a postscript, the handwriting enlarged by triumph. 'Darling! Got it at last, de croupi longuement.' This was poetry, and she was a poet. But she would be as self-exacting over something she was unconcerned by. Once, when she was staying with us, she brought down a commissioned translation of an article about French painters. It was quite unimportant, it was plain sailing, until a painter of marine subjects involved a technical term in rigging. Dictionaries were fetched, and failed. Sea-going authors were looked through, in case one of them came up with the term she needed. Telephone calls were made. The passage was really not of the slightest importance, but she must have spent over an hour on it. And reading through the final version, her face assumed the particular grimace of such moments: wary, censorious, bleak.

For though the application might be the same, the mood was totally different. Her concern with poetry was carnal and passionate: she pursued the word, the phrase, with the patience of a weasel, the concentration of a falcon: When a poem happened to cost her no trouble, she was as pleased as if she'd stolen it out of the church collection. The other achievements were a matter of technical self-respect, to be classed with the packing and the polishing, the type-setting performed with un-inked fingers, the *serpette* slashing with authority among the brambles round her yellow house at Lamothe.

Early in 1944 she came to Dorset in search of a lodging where Norman Douglas[17] would be warmed, well-fed, out of bombs' way and within reach of female attentions. I felt a heartless relief when this project fell through: it seemed to me that if anyone needed the female attentions, etc., it was Nancy. She was thin as a wraith and had a tormenting neuritis in her shoulder. This did not prevent her from walking with great speed and energy over the downs, nor from coming back with such loads of flints in her coat-pockets that silhouetted on a skyline her slender person gave the impression that panniers had been fastened on a cheetah. During the next hour or so, Nancy would be in the bathroom, working on the flints with a nailbrush. Then a towel would be spread over her bed and the flints laid out – to be admired, examined, graded: some for more polishing, others to be rejected. This capacity for magpie delighting was one of her prettiest charms. She used to collect beads (and sewed little bags exactly to contain them), shells, small nonsense. When Valentine, at a rather later date, gave her nineteen mother-of-pearl 'fish' counters, she recorded it in:

A NINETEEN OF PISCES

Nineteen little fishes
(Never been so clean)
Roach and dace

> *And tench and plaice*
> *And dab and brill and bream*
> *Skate and hake*
> *And flounder's mate*
> *And spreckleback in stream.*
> *Herring, grayling,*
> *Whiting, spratling,*
> *All together for an outing . . .*
> *Cod and polk and carp and trout*
> *And that's* nineteen – *no odd man out –*
> *All in a horn – not on a dish –*
> *19's* my *number: I'm a Fish.*

And signed it, with circumstantial exactitude: N. At 2 a.m. Dec. 11, 1953.

From the downs where Nancy collected flints we could see an unusual amount of traffic on the roads: camions and muffled vehicles of odd shapes. Everyone knew that something was going on and creditably few remarked on it. In March of 1944 a frontier was enforced along the South Coast. Non-residents must go outside it, residents must remain within. Once again, Nancy packed with her practised hand; and moved into Somerset. This disconcerted many plans, and she was in no condition to make out alone in a strange neighbourhood. But when we met – and meet we did, for there was a conveniently situated little railway station on the borderline – her *bel canto* was unaffected. Shivering with cold, shrugging the pain in her shoulder, she walked up and down the platform beside me as though we were doing it for pleasure.

I remembered this when, many years later, I saw her good manners shining against a blacker adversity.

> *Pas de carence de vie ici, nenni –*
> *Mais tant de paroles perdues pour dire 'attendre'.*

So ends one of the poems in the group called *In Time of Waiting* which she wrote when she went back to Spain in 1959. They are poems of great force and anguish. Her patience cracked, her bodyguard of practical virtues deserted her, she behaved outrageously. On her return to England she was certified as insane and shut up.

The day we went to see her, the sun shone effusively on her place of detention. We were directed along a series of corridors to a door where we were to ring for admission. We rang, and heard a key turn in the lock; the door was locked after us, and we were directed to a more social corridor where we were put to wait at one of a row of little tables (flowers on it, of course) while an attendant went off with keys under her apron to tell Miss Cunard of our arrival. When she came towards us, she was so unchanged I could not believe it was she.

She was neither harshened nor subdued. She was pleased to see us exactly as she would have been if we had met outside. Her affection rang true. In that hygienic limbo she made us feel welcome, familiar and unconstrained. It was only when she began to talk of plans for when she was let out that I realised, with shock, that something had died in her; and thought, her objective has died in her. Whatever it was, she kept to herself. 'It will have been funny,' she had once written to me, from Port Vendres; where she was waiting, uncertain where to go next, 'my life. How enormously much of it A-LONE.'

NOTES

1 The White House, East Claydon, Buckinghamshire
2 William Wycherley (1641-1715), dramatist
3 (1689-1762), known for her quarrels with Pope and her letters from the continent
4 (1818-94), Regius Professor of Modern History at Oxford
5 Knowsley Hall, Merseyside
6 *Nonsense Songs, Stories, Botany and Alphabets*, 1871
7 Near Sawrey, Cumbria. Bequeathed to the National Trust on Potter's death together with 4,000 acres of land in the Lake District
8 *Adam Bede*, 1859
9 Published 1922
10 *The Dynasts: An Epic Drama,* in three volumes, 1904-08
11 Machen had married Warner's aunt, Purefoy Huddleston, in 1903
12 Warner had served with Fellowes on the editorial board of the Tudor Church Music Project
13 Craske had been discovered by Ackland. She and Warner began collecting his work

which was bequeathed to the Aldeburgh Festival in 1970 as a result of Warner's friendship with Peter Pears. See also the article by Peter Tolhurst in the *Sylvia Townsend Warner Society Journal*, 2001

14 Exhibition at the Warren Gallery, London, 1930
15 *Authors Take Sides on the Spanish Civil War*, 1937, with contributions from Warner and Ackland
16 Edited by Cunard, 1947, with contributions from Warner and Ackland
17 (1868-1952), novelist, travel writer and friend of Cunard. His essay 'London Street Games' appeared in the Dolphin Books series that included Warner's *Opus 7*, 1931

LITERARY CONCERNS

WOMEN AS WRITERS
(The Peter le Neve Foster Lecture
Journal of the Royal Society of Arts, May, 1959)

When I received this invitation, it was the invitation that surprised me. The choice of subject did not. I am a woman writer myself, and it never surprises me. Even when people tell me I am a lady novelist, it is the wording of the allegation I take exception to, not the allegation itself. One doubt, it is true, crossed my mind. It was inevitable that I should remember a book called *A Room of One's Own*, by Virginia Woolf. What had I to add to that? But *A Room of One's Own*, I thought, is not so much about how women write as about how astonishing it is that they should have managed to write at all. As they have managed to, there might still be something I could add. But then I reread my invitation, and became the prey of uneasiness. Women as Writers. *Women* as Writers. Supposing I had been a man, a gentleman novelist, would I have been asked to lecture on Men as Writers? I thought it improbable.

Here was an implication I might or might not resent. Here, at any rate, was an obligation I couldn't dodge.

It would appear that when a woman writes a book, the action sets up an extraneous vibration. Something happens that must be accounted for. It is the action that does it, not the product. It is only in very rare, and rather non-literary instances, that the product – *Uncle Tom's Cabin*, say, or the *Memoirs of Harriet Wilson*[1] – is the jarring note. It would also appear that this extraneous vibration may be differently received and differently resounded. Some surfaces mute it. Off others, it is violently resonated. It is also subject to the influence of climate, the climate of popular opinion. In a fine dry climate the dissonance caused by a woman writing a book has much less intensity than in a damp foggy one. Overriding these variations due to surface and climate is the fact that the volume increases with the mass – as summarised in Macheath's Law:

231

> *One wife is too much for most husbands to hear*
> *But two at a time sure no mortal can bear.*

Finally, it would appear that the vibration is not set up until a woman seizes a pen. She may invent, but she may not write down.

Macheath's Law explains why the early women writers caused so little alarm. They only went off one at a time. If a great lady such as Marie de France chose to give her leisure to letters instead of embroidery, this was merely a demonstration that society could afford such luxuries – an example of what Veblen defined as Conspicuous Waste. No one went unfed or unclothed for it. Nor could she be held guilty of setting a bad example to other women, since so few women were in a position to follow it. So things went on, with now and then a literate woman making a little squeak with her pen, while the other women added a few more lines to Mother Goose (about that authorship, I think there can be no dispute). It was not till the retreat from the Renaissance that the extraneous vibration was heard as so very jarring. By then, many women had learned to read and write, so a literate woman was no longer an ornament to society. Kept in bounds, she had her uses. She could keep the account books and transcribe recipes for horse pills. But she must be kept within bounds; she must subserve. When Teresa of Avila[2] wrote her autobiography, she said in a preface that it had been written with leave, and 'in accordance with my confessor's command'. True, she immediately added, 'The Lord himself, I know, has long wished it to be written' – a sentiment felt by most creative writers, I believe; but the woman and the Lord had to wait for permission.

The French have always allowed a place to Conspicuous Waste, it is one of the things they excel at; and Mme de La Fayette[3] rewarded this tolerance by giving France the first psychological novel, *La Princesse de Clèves*. But Molière was probably a surer mouthpiece of public opinion when he made a game of literary ladies. It is more damning to be shown as absurd than to be denounced as scandalous. It is more damning still to be thought old-fashioned. Margaret, Countess of Newcastle[4], was derided not only as a figure of fun but as a figure out of the lumber-room. (Much the same condemnation fell on Lady Murasaki[5], a most eminent woman writer, whose nickname in the Japanese court of the early eleventh century was Dame Annals.) In eighteenth-century England, a woman of fashion wrote at her peril (I doubt if Pope would have laid so much stress on Lady Mary Wortley Montagu[6] being dirty if she had not been inky). A woman who wrote for publication – by then, a fair number did – sank in the social scale. If she wrote fiction, she was a demirep. If she wrote as a scholar, she was a dowdy. However, as men of letters had also gone down in the world, writing women gained more than they lost. They gained companionship, they approached a possibility of being judged on their merits by writers of the opposite sex.

Too much has been made of Dr Johnson's opinion of women preachers, not enough of the fact that Mrs Chapone[7] and Elizabeth Carter[8] contributed to *The Rambler*[9], nor of his goodwill towards Mrs Lennox[10], and the hot apple pie he stuck with bay leaves in her honour. In the case of Fanny Burney[11], Johnson showed more than goodwill. He showed courage. Fanny Burney was his friend's daughter, and a virgin. And Fanny Burney had written a novel. Not even a romance. A novel.

The speed with which women possess themselves of an advantage is something astonishing. Such quantities of virtuous women turned to novel-writing that Jane Austen was able to pick and choose among them, to laugh at Ann Radcliffe[12] and Mary Brunton[13], to admire Miss Edgeworth[14]. It was an Indian summer, the last glow of the Age of Reason. Jane Austen could inscribe her title-page with that majestic, *By a Lady*. The Brontë Sisters, not so. They were born too late. The barometer had fallen, the skies had darkened. They grew up in an age which had decided that women had an innate moral superiority. As almost everything was a menace to this innate moral superiority, it was necessary that women should be protected, protected from men, protected from life, protected from being talked about, protected from Euclid – Mary Somerville[15] the mathematician has recorded how hard put to it she was to expose herself to Euclid – protected above all from those dangerous articles, themselves. You couldn't have women dashing their pens into inkpots and writing as if they knew about life and had something to say about it. Determined to write and to be judged on the merit of their writing, women put on men's names: Aurore Dudevant became George Sand, and Mary Ann Evans, George Eliot, and Emily Brontë consented to the ambiguity of Ellis Bell.

I think I can now venture a positive assertion about women as writers. It is a distinguishing assertion; if I were talking about Men as Writers I could not make it. Women as writers are obstinate and sly.

I deliberately make this assertion in the present tense. Though a woman writing today is not hampered by an attribution of innate moral superiority, she has to reckon with an attribution of innate physical superiority; and this, too, can be cumbersome. There is, for instance, bi-location. It is well known that a woman can be in two places at once; at her desk and at her washing-machine. She can practice a mental bi-location also, pinning down some slippery adverb while saying aloud, 'No, not Hobbs, Nokes. And the address is 17 Dalmeny Crescent'. Her mind is so extensive that it can simultaneously follow a train of thought, remember what it was she had to tell the electrician, answer the telephone, keep an eye on time, and not forget about the potatoes. Obstinacy and slyness still have their uses.

But I have sometimes wondered if women are literary at all. It is not a thing which is strenuously required of them, and perhaps, finding something not required of them, they thank God and do no more about it. They write. They dive into writing like ducks into water. One would almost think it came naturally to them – at any rate as naturally as plain sewing.

Here is a non-literary woman writing in the nineteenth century. She wrote under her own name, for her sex was already notoriuos:

There were three separate registers kept at Scutari. First, the Adjutant's daily Head-Roll of soldiers' burials, on which it may be presumed that no one was entered who was not buried, although it is possible that some may have been buried who were not entered.

Second, the Medical Officer's Return, in regard to which it is quite certain that hundreds of men were buried who never appeared on it.

Third, the return made to the Orderly Room, which is only remarkable as giving a totally different account of the deaths from either of the others.

I should like to think that Florence Nightingale's work is not yet done. If it could be set as a model before those who write official reports the publications of Her Majesty's Stationery Office might grow much leaner, much time and money might be saved. But this is by the way.

Her is another, writing in the seventeenth century:

Take a pint of cream, three spoonfuls of rice flour, the whites of three eggs well beaten, and four spoonfuls of fine sugar. Stir these well into your cream cold; then take a few blanched almonds and beat them in a mortar with two spoonfuls of water, then strain them into your cream and boil it until it comes from the skillet. Then take it up and put it in your custard, and let it stand until it is cold.

From a cookery book, as you will have realised – but a piece of tight, consecutive writing.

Here is a woman writing from Norwich in July 1453[16]:

And as for tidings, Philip Berney is passed to God on Monday last past with the greatest pain that ever I saw a man; and on Tuesday Sir John Heveningham went to his church and heard three masses and came home never merrier; and said to his wife that he would go say a little devotion in his garden and then dine; and forthwith he felt a fainting in his leg and slid down. This was at nine of the clock and he was dead ere noon.

Here is another Norfolk woman, writing, or possibly dictating, towards the close of the previous century[17]:

And after this I saw God in a Point – that is to say, in my understanding; by which I saw he is in all things. I beheld and considered, seeing and knowing in sight, with a soft dread, and thought: What is sin?

I really have not cheated over these examples. The two notable women, the two women of no note, I chose them almost at random, and went to their writings to see what I would find. I found them alike in making themselves clear.

As far as I know, there is only one certain method of making things clear, and that is, to have plainly in mind what one wishes to say. When the unequivocal statement matches itself to the pre-determined thought and the creative impulse sets fire to them, the quality we call immediacy results. Immediacy has borne other names, it has even been called inspiration – though I think that is too large a term for it. But immediacy has this in common with inspiration, that where it is present the author

235

becomes absent. The writing is no longer propelled by the author's anxious hand, the reader is no longer conscious of the author's chaperoning presence. Here is an example; it is a poem by Frances Cornford:

> *The Cypriot woman, as she closed her dress,*
> *Smiled at the baby on her broad-lapped knee,*
> *Beautiful in a calm voluptuousness*
> *Like a slow sea.*

One does not feel that the woman has been written about. She is there.

Women as writers seem to be remarkably adept at vanishing out of their writing so that the quality of immediacy replaces them. Immediacy is the word in *La Princesse de Clèves*, that masterpiece of emotion laced up in the tight embroidered bodice of court dress. Madame de Clèves's heart is laid open before us, and we hang over it; not even pity is allowed to intervene between us and the demonstration. Immediacy is the word when Jane Austen keeps a bookful of rather undistinguished characters not only all alive at once but all aware of each other's existence. In *Wuthering Heights* immediacy makes a bookful of almost incredible characters fastened into a maddeningly entangled plot seem natural and inevitable, as if it were something familiar to us because of a dream. When the goblins fasten on Lizzie and press the fruit against her clenched teeth; when Orlando finds the man in Mrs Stewkley's room, the man who turned his pen in his fingers, this way and that; and gazed and mused; and then, very quickly, wrote half a dozen lines – and no more need be said, with our own eyes we have looked on William Shakespeare; when Murasaki's Genji takes Yugao to the deserted house where the ghost steals her away from him; when, at the close of Colette's *La Chatte*, the girl looks back from the turn of the avenue and sees the cat keeping a mistrustful eye on her departure and the young man playing, deftly as a cat, with the first-fallen chestnuts, it is not the writer one is conscious of. One is conscious of a happening, of something taking place under one's very nose. As for Sappho, I cannot speak. She rises in my mind like a beautiful distant island, but I cannot set foot on her because I haven't learned Greek. But I am assured that immediacy is the word for Sappho.

While all these splendid examples were rushing into my mind, I realised that a great many examples which could not be called splendid were accompanying them: that when the gust of wind flutters the hangings and extinguishes the solitary taper and Mrs Radcliffe's heroine is left in darkness, it is a darkness that can be felt; that in George Sand's writing, for all its exploitation and rhetoric, George Sand may suddenly be replaced by the first frost prowling under cover of night through an autumn garden; that the short stories of Mary Wilkins[18], a New England writer of the last century whose characters appear to be made out of lettuce, can remain in one's mind and call one back to a re-reading because one remembers a queer brilliant verisimilitude, the lighting of immediacy.

There is, of course, George Eliot. She makes herself admirably clear and her mind, such a fine capacious mind, too, is stored with things she wishes to say; but in her case, immediacy does not result. We remember scenes and characters, but do they ever haunt us? She dissects a heart, but something intervenes between us and the demonstration – the lecturer's little wand. There is a class of women writers, praiseworthily combining fiction with edification, and among them is Mrs Sherwood[19] of *The Fairchild Family*, Mrs Gatty[20] of *Parables from Nature*, Mrs Trimmer[21] ... it seems to me that George Eliot insisted upon being a superlative Mrs Trimmer. Still, George Eliot apart – a considerable apart – I think one might claim that this quality of immediacy, though common to either sex, is proportionately of more frequent occurrence in the work of women writers. And though it is impossible in judging the finished product to pronounce on which pages were achieved with effort, which came easily, the fact that even quite mediocre women writers will sometimes wear this precious jewel in their heads seems to indicate that it is easier for a woman to make herself air and vanish off her pages than it is for a man, with his heavier equipment of learning and self-consciousness. Perhaps this is really so, and for a reason. Suppose, for instance, that there was a palace, which you could only know from outside. Sometimes you heard music playing within, and the corks popping, and sometimes splendid figures came to an open window and spoke a few words in a solemn chanting voice; and from time to time you met someone who had actually been inside, and was carrying away under his arm – it was always a man – a lute or a casket or the leg of a turkey. And then one day you discovered that you could climb into this palace by the pantry window. In the excitement of the moment you wouldn't wait; you wouldn't go home to smooth your hair or borrow your grandmother's garnets or consult the Book of Etiquette. Even at the risk of being turned out by the butler, rebuked by the chaplain, laughed at by the rightful guests, you'd climb in.

In something of the same way, women have entered literature – breathless, unequipped, and with nothing but their wits to trust to. A few minutes ago, or a few centuries ago, they were writing a letter about an apoplexy, or a recipe for custard. Now they are inside the palace, writing with great clearness what they have in mind to say – for that is all they know about it, no one has groomed them for a literary career – writing on the kitchen table, like Emily Brontë, or on the washstand, like Christina Rossetti, writing in the attic, like George Sand, or in the family parlour, protected by a squeaking door from being discovered at it, like Jane Austen, writing away for all they are worth, and seldom blotting a line.

Do you see what we are coming to? – I have put in several quotations to prepare you for it. We are coming to those other writers who have got into literature by the pantry window, and who have left the most illustrious footprints on the windowsill. It is a dizzying conclusion, but it must be faced. Women, entering literature, entered it on the same footing as William Shakespeare.

So if women writers have what might appear an unfairly large share of the quality of immediacy which is sometimes called inspiration – and in the case of Shakespeare we all agree to call it so – it is not, after all, original in them – like sin. It derives from their circumstances, not from their sex. It is interesting to see what other qualities, also deriving from circumstance, the circumstance of entering literature by the pantry window, they share with Shakespeare. I can think of several. One is their conviction that women have legs of their own, and can move about of their own volition, and give as good as they get. Lady Macbeth, and Beatrice, and Helena in *All's Well*, could almost be taken for women writers' heroines, they are so free and uninhibited, and ready to jump over stiles and appear in the drawing-room with muddy stockings, like Lizzie Bennet.

Another pantry window trait is the kind of workaday democracy, an ease and appreciativeness in low company. It is extremely rare to find the conventional comic servant or comic countryman in books by women. A convention is *pis-aller*, a stop-gap where experience is lacking. A woman has to be most exceptionally secluded if she never goes to her own back door, or is not on visiting terms with people poorer than herself. I have said before – but as the remark has only appeared in Russian I can decently repeat myself – Emily Brontë was fortunate in being the daughter of a clergyman, because the daughter of a clergyman, with her duty of parish visiting, has wonderful opportunities to become acquainted with human passions and what they can lead to. Another trait in common is a willing ear for the native tongue, for turns of phrase used by carpenters, gardeners, sailors, milliners, tinkers, old nurses, and that oldest nurse of all, ballad and folklore. Just as Mme de Sévigné was always improving her French by picking up words and idioms from her tenants at Les Rochers, Colette listened to every trade, every walk in life, and kept dictionaries of professional terms beside her desk—while Edith Sitwell's poetry reaches back through centuries of English poetical idiom to *Nuts in May* and Mother Goose.

These traits, as you will have noticed, are technical assets. They affect presentation, not content. Their absence may be deadening, but their presence does not make their possessor any more eligible to be compared with Shakespeare. The resemblance is in the circumstances. Women writers have shared his advantage of starting with no literary advantages. No butlers were waiting just inside the front door to receive their invitation cards and show them in. Perhaps the advantage is not wholly advantageous; but circumstances do alter cases. It was not very surprising that young Mr Shelley should turn to writing; it was surprising that young Mr Keats did, and his poetry reflects his surprise, his elation. It is the poetry of a young man surprised by joy. So is the poetry of John Clare. But though the male entrants by the pantry window possess the quality of immediacy just as women writers do, are at ease in low company and in the byways of their native language, they do not employ these advantages with the same fluency – I hesitate to use the word *exploit*; I will say, they are not so much obliged to them. I see a possible explanation for this, which I will come to presently.

But first I must come to the present day, when women, one might think, have so well established themselves as writers that the extraneous vibration must be hushed, and the pantry window supplanted as an entrance to literature by the Tradesman's Door. No woman writer should despise the Tradesman's Door. It is a very respectable entrance, the path to it was first trod by Mrs Aphra Behn[22], and many women have trodden it since, creditably and contentedly too. I should be failing my title if I did not remind you that we now have women newspaper reporters working in such vexed places as Cyprus – a signal advance. Yet, when we use the term back-writer, we still feel that it must apply to a man; that a woman is once and for always an amateur. In the same spirit, if she happens to make a great deal of money by a book, well and good, it is one of those lucky accidents that happen from time to time, no one is the worse for it, and she is unexpectedly the better. But if she earns her living by her pen, we are not so ready to accept the idea. If we are polite enough to dissemble our feelings we say that it is a pity that with so much talent she should be reduced to this sort of thing. If we are candid and pure-souled, we say that it's outrageous and that she ought to become a hospital nurse. If she marries – again it's a pity – a polite pity that she will have to give up her writing. So much pity is ominous.

And in fact, the vibration may start up at any moment. Macheath's Law still holds; not for numbers, perhaps, but for area. It is admitted that women may write very nearly what they please, just as, within limits, they may do what they please: though I suppose it will be a long time before they can enter the priesthood or report football matches on the BBC. But this liberty is zoned. It applies to women belonging to the middle classes. You know those shiny papers one reads in waiting-rooms, and how, every week, they show a photograph of a woman of the upper classes, with a little notice underneath. One has just come out. One has recently married. One wins prizes with her Shetland ponies, another has a charming pair of twins, another is an MFH. But despite Edith Sitwell and Dorothy Wellesley, one does not expect to read below the photograph that the lady is a poet. Take it a step higher. Suppose that a royal princess would not tear herself from the third act of her tragedy in order to open a play-centre. People would be gravely put out, especially the men who had been building the play-centre, men who have taught their wives to know their place, and who expect princesses to be equally dutiful.

A working-class woman may be as gifted as all the women writers I have spoken of today, all rolled into one; but it is no part of her duty to write a masterpiece. Her brain may be teeming, but it is not the fertility of her brain she must attend to, perishable citizens is what her country expects of her, not imperishable Falstaffs and Don Quixotes. The Lord himself may long have wished for her books to be written; but leave has yet to be granted. Apart from one or two grandees like Mme de La Fayette, women writers have come from the middle class, and their writing carries a heritage of middle-class virtues; good taste, prudence, acceptance of limitations, compliance with standards, and that typically middle-class merit of making the most of what one's got – in other words, that too-conscious employment of advantages which I mentioned a few minutes ago, and which one does not observe in Clare, or Burns, or Bunyan. So when we consider women as writers, we must bear in mind that we have not very much to go on, and that it is too early to assess what they may be capable of. It may well be that the half has not yet been told us: that unbridled masterpieces, daring innovations, epics, tragedies, works of genial impropriety – all the things that so far women have signally failed to produce – have been socially, not sexually, debarred; that at this moment a Joan Milton or a Françoise Rabelais may have left the washing unironed and the stew uncared for because she can't wait to begin.

NORTHANGER ABBEY
(An Introduction to the Jane Austen novel,
Limited Editions Club, 1971)

She grew on the sunny side of the wall—as it might be, one of those solid cob walls, white-washed and roofed with thatch, such as still enclose Hampshire kitchen-gardens. On such walls, in her day, Moor Park apricots, Bon Chretien and Jargonelle pears, Blue Perdrigon plums were trained and tended and brought forth their fruit in due season. The Rector of Steventon's daughter, growing on the sunny side of the rectory wall, produced in her early twenties *Pride and Prejudice*, *Sense and Sensibility*, and *Northanger Abbey*.

Steventon was a family living—the gift in 1764 of a kind cousin to the Reverend George Austen. He married, and begot five sons and two daughters. Not one of these died untimely, or took to evil courses, or suffered religious doubts: the pyrexia of Evangelical fervour had not yet penetrated the Church of England. It was a happy, healthy, loving family, at ease with the world yet not expecting too much of it, ready to be entertained by it but for the most part relying for entertainment on their own resources.

Mr Austen's contribution was to read aloud in the evenings. Though those who read aloud to a young family tend to choose books which they suspect their children would not read with much attention if left to choose for themselves, from time to time a personal preference will assert itself and an old favourite be taken from the bookcase. No doubt in these departures from histories, travels, essays from *The Rambler*, Mr Austen used some parental licence as to what he should omit; but I am sure that Fielding was one of the authors he read aloud, and Smollett another. His younger daughter, hemming a handkerchief or stitching wristbands for a brother's shirt, had ears to hear.

For example:

It may now be proper to return to the Hero of this Novel of whom I believe I have scarcely ever had occasion to speak: which may perhaps be partly oweing to his unfortunate propensity to liquor, which so completely deprived him of the use of those faculties Nature had endowed him with that he never did anything worth mentioning.

And again:

Lovely and too charming Fair one, notwithstanding your forbidding Squint, your greazy tresses and your swelling Back, which are more frightful than imagination can paint or pen describe, I cannot refrain from expressing my raptures, at the engaging qualities of your Mind, which so amply atone for the Horror, with which your first appearance must ever inspire the unwary visitor. Your sentiments so nobly expressed on the different excellencies of Indian and English Muslins, and the judicious preference you give the former . . .

The demure brutality of these passages from *Volume the First* of Jane Austen's *Juvenilia* shows what models she had her eye on.

There is also Mrs Austen to be taken into account. She enjoyed reading novels and was a subscriber to a Lending Library:

Her melancholy was assisted by the hollow sighings of the wind along the corridor and round the castle. The cheerful blaze of the wood had long been extinguished, and she sat with her eyes fixed on the dying embers, till a loud gust, that swept through the corridor, and shook the doors and casements, alarmed her, for its violence had moved the chair she had placed as fastening, and the door leading to the private staircase stood half open.

The Mysteries of Udolpho appeared in 1794. It was not the first of its kind (*The Castle of Otranto*[23] had thrown down its Gothic gauntlet thirty years earlier), nor was it Mrs Radcliffe's first novel in that genre; but it was the most compelling. The wind had never sighed more hollowly along gloomier corridors, footsteps had never sounded more alarmingly from battlements, mystery had never been concealed behind a more threatening assemblage of rusty bolts, decaying tapestries, secret stairways, vast echoing halls lit by a single taper, unvisited chambers with dreadful associations, midnight hours. One could say of it that it numbered only midnight hours. It numbered a vast quantity of breathless readers. And three years later, a young untrembling hand dipped a pen in an inkpot and began to make game of it. 'No one who had ever seen Catherine Morland in her infancy would have supposed her born to be an heroine.'

Of Jane Austen's novels, *Northanger Abbey* is the only one in which she shows herself concerned with literature. In the others, she minds her own business and is concerned with writing. The exclamation, ' "Nay, mamma, if he is not to be animated by Cowper! . . . ," ' having served to throw light on Marianne Dashwood and the insensibly sensible Edward Ferrars, Cowper can be dismissed. But in Northanger Abbey she interrupts the narrative with critical opinions. Catherine Morland is not only a girl who makes a fool of herself because of her enthusiasm for *The Mysteries of Udolpho*. Her foolishness involves the foolishness of Mrs Radcliffe, and that of her imitators and that of her betters. For a moment, one glimpses the airy javelin from Steventon Rectory quivering on Goethe's buckskin breeches. Coming after the totally undogmatic narrative tone of *Pride and Prejudice* and *Sense and Sensibility*, these interpolations, these addressings of the reader, sound oddly pedantic. It is the pedantry of youth, however. It was as a young iconoclast, a representative of a *nouvelle vague*, that she assumed the mannerisms of Fielding in order to deride the unreality of the Romantics. But her finest strokes of critical demolition arise from the narrative itself. It is Mrs Allen, that pedestrian dullard, who breaches the mossy walls of the Castle of Northanger.

Wherever they went, some pattened girl stopped to curtsey, or some footman in dishabille sneaked off. Yet this was an Abbey! How inexpressibly different in these domestic arrangements from such as she had read about; from abbeys and castles, in which, though certainly larger than Northanger, all the dirty work of the house was to be done by two pairs of female hands at the utmost. How they could get through it all had often amazed Mrs Allen; and, when Catherine saw what was necessary here, she began to be amazed herself.

Authors are at the mercy of their successes; if it had not been for the swooning piety of Mrs Radcliffe's public, Jane Austen might not have felt the same youthful severity toward Mrs Radcliffe. Whatever the demerits of Udolpho, it was a novel; and in the matter of novel-reading Jane Austen remained her mother's daughter. In the longest of the critical discursions in Northanger Abbey she makes this plain:

If a rainy morning deprived them of other enjoyments, they were still resolute in meeting in defiance of wet and dirt, and shut themselves up to read novels together. Yes, novels. . . . Let us leave it to the Reviewers to abuse such effusions of fancy at their leisure, and over every new novel to talk in threadbare strains of the trash with which the press now groans. Let us not desert one another; we are an injured body. Although our productions have afforded more extensive and unaffected pleasure than those of any other literary corporation in the world, no species of composition has been so decried. From pride, ignorance, or fashion, our foes are almost as many as our readers; and while the abilities of the nine-hundredth abridger of the History of England, or of the man who collects and publishes in a volume some dozen lines of Milton, Pope and Prior, with a paper from the Spectator, and a chapter from Sterne, are eulogised by a thousand pens, there seems almost a general wish of decrying the capacity and undervaluing the labour of the novelist, and of slighting the performances which have only genius, wit, and taste to recommend them.

Of the two young ladies who shut themselves up to read novels together, Catherine Morland was one, and *Udolpho* her reading, with *The Italian* to follow it; and after them the other young lady promises her (she has the names in her pocket-book):

'Castle of Wolfenbach, Clermont, Mysterious Warnings, Necromancer of the Black Forest, Midnight Bell, Orphan of the Rhine, and Horrid Mysteries. Those will last us some time.'

'Yes, pretty well; but are they all horrid, are you sure they are all horrid?'

The opening of *Northanger Abbey* appears to comply with the requirements of such fiction. Catherine, young, unsophisticated, brought up in the country, is taken on a visit to Bath by the Allens, a rich childless couple. She rises another step in the world when she is introduced to 'a very gentleman-like young man,' called Henry Tilney. He in turn introduces her to his sister. They take her for walks, educate her in the Picturesque, have also read *Udolpho*. She falls in love, but without expectations, and without the conviction she would have felt if Henry Tilney had been a dispossessed heir instead of a younger son with a family living. To her amazement, she finds herself vehemently approved of by their alarming father, and invited to visit Northanger Abbey. An Abbey! actually an Abbey, with 'its long, damp passages, its narrow cells and ruined chapel,' and a reasonable hope of 'some awful memorials of an injured and ill-fated nun.' Her anticipations are slightly dashed by the Abbey being comfortable and commodious, but General Tilney's insistence that she should be pleased with it, his deference to her taste, his massive flatteries, reconcile her to well-lit rooms and carpeted floors. Besides, there are a number of corridors and unexplored rooms and these may reveal something very mysterious and very horrid. But the visit comes to a sudden end. Without a word of explanation, she is packed off to make her way home in a hired post-chaise.

As a heroine, she would expect some such startling misfortune. Torn from Henry Tilney, she would be prepared to spend the remainder of her shortened days in melancholy seclusion, walking by moonlight under willows and conifers – for as this is England, she cannot hope for cypresses, and as the daughter of a Church of England parson she can't retire to a convent. But this startling misfortune is no longer appropriate. Foiled at every turn in her quest for the dire secret of Northanger Abbey – perhaps it reposed in the contents of the massive chest, or in the paper that might constitute the 'awful memorials of an injured and ill-fated nun,' and not to mention a compelling suspicion that her host had either made away with his wife or was keeping her in a dungeon on bread and water – Catherine had abandoned all intentions of being a heroine and was thinking about being Mrs Henry Tilney. And with some warrant, in view of the appeal which began with 'Dear Miss Morland, consider the dreadful nature of the suspicions you have entertained' and concluded with 'Dearest Miss Morland, what ideas have you been admitting?'

For a young lady, no longer a heroine, to be packed off in a post-chaise at that point of the story was both mysterious and horrid; but it wasn't in keeping with Mrs Radcliffe.

In fact, Mrs Radcliffe was largely responsible. Jane Austen had taken a leaf out of her book. 'Mrs Radcliffe's method' – I quote from *The Oxford Companion to English Literature* – 'was to arouse terror and curiosity by events apparently supernatural, but afterwards explained by natural means.' The natural means chosen by Jane Austen were the ordinary human failings of cupidity, credulity, boasting, and bad temper.

We have all heard (rather too often) of 'the little bit (two inches wide) of Ivory on which I work with so fine a Brush, as produces little effect after much labour.' Her own words. But she wrote them in 1816, and by that time she may have forgotten how effectively she dealt with the Thorpes when she had newly ripened her fine, brisk, tart flavour on the Rectory wall at Steventon. The Jane Austen who wrote *Northanger Abbey* was not far removed in years from the Jane Austen of the *Juvenilia*; but in the interval she had mastered the inestimable trick of appearing to write without animus. 'Give them enough rope,' she seems to say, 'and they will hang themselves.' Duly, they hang themselves. It is impossible to imagine

246

a deathbed conversion for Mrs Norris, a change of heart for Lucy Steele. The Thorpes will forever be objects of Jane Austen's dislike, and preserved in that implacability they are the most lifelike characters in the book. One sees Isabella writhing her shoulders as she pursues her prey through the crowded Pump-room, one hears John's bragging gabble and loud guffaws, one pities his horse; if his mother were not so flaccidly maternal, one would pity his mother. They are odious, they are paltry, they are beneath derision; she employs none of that affable mockery with which she assailed the romantic conventions. Her dislike is searching, scornful, and serious.

To some degree, it is also social. Jane Austen's class-sensitivity is typically British in the way it distinguishes between gentry and gentility. Seen in one light, the Thorpes are laudably engaged in trying to better themselves, to look out for what may be to their advantage, to get on in the world. Jane Austen sees them as upstarts. The crowning stroke of her dislike is that she disallows their pretensions. Despite their instrumentality in the story, where their ordinary human failings of cupidity, mendacity, etc., subserve Catherine's ignominious dismissal, they remain jostling and insignificant.

For if Thorpe had not believed that Catherine was an heiress and that he was sure to get her – if General Tilney had not believed Thorpe's brag and decided to filch the heiress to fatten Northanger, and had not subsequently believed Thorpe's sour-grapes declaration that she was penniless – there would have been no dismissal. The narrative arches from the credulity of those who crave for castles to the credulity of those who scheme for money. The only disinterested person (for Henry Tilney is not quite above reproach: before he sighed as a lover he was ready to obey as a son) is Catherine. She alone is not a time-server. It was a dream she served.

TWICE AS NATURAL
(*Time and Tide*, November, 1927)

The commission to write upon the Tendencies of Contemporary Literature
was oppressing me. The words, so round, solemn and slippery, were like
three balloons made of black mackintosh. I remembered dear friends I once
had who could hold forth on such a subject for hours, searchingly,
convincingly, unperturbed by the fact that the tendencies they were making
such play with happened to be neither contemporary nor literary. But I am
a dull creature with a conscience that chains me to the foot of the letter.

'Now if it had been the Literature of Contemporary Tendencies,' I
thought as I walked about under the dishevelling trees of Kensington
Gardens, 'I could manage very nicely. For I have read plenty of that;
indeed who can escape it.'

At the moment I noticed a man and a girl who lay side by side asleep
with a newspaper spread under them. It was between ten and eleven on a
fine October morning, a time at which Kensington Gardens are still the
dormitory of many houseless or itinerant folk who have spent the night
walking about the streets. I saw a man come up to the sleeping couple – a
companion, for he greeted them familiarly. They did not wake. Stooping
over the girl he put his arm round her waist, pulled her a little way from
the ground and kissed her several times, rather well. Released, she sat up,
yawning and smiling, as pleased to be woken with kisses as one is pleased
to be woken with early morning tea, neither more or less. Then the other
man woke up and also started to kiss the girl. The first man then strolled
off to a patch of sunlight; and there, putting his fingers in his mouth, he
began to whistle like a blackbird.

This passage was so pleasant and easy-going that it could not have
aroused even the prurience of a moralist. Yet it was not idyllic; it was too
matter of fact for that, having that particular inevitability and life-like
quality which one associates with the ballet. Yes, a ballet certainly;
perhaps a film, if the man in the orchestra would be coerced into playing
his bird-call in the right place – but how about literature? No! Not in these
days. Writers for the many and writers for the few, either could have
managed the kisses, and about equally well; but when it came to the glory
of it, that walking off and whistling like a blackbird (his profession, no

doubt; and like a good artist he kept himself in form) neither could have sprung that surprise. From the one, blood-letting and the embattled male; from the other a great deal of consciousness, starved cats i' the adage, perhaps one of those mental regurgitations which are always so arresting '. . . a broken toilet comb, clotted with grease and hair. How clearly it all came back. His tenth birthday, the sun shone, he had said: "won't use Bert's old comb any longer. I want a comb to myself." But he had gone on using it,' etc.

Suddenly I found myself brandishing a perfectly good Tendency of Contemporary Literature: The Tendency to be Duller than Life by being Twice as Natural. The more I considered it the better pleased I was with my discovery. The tendency is contemporary right enough. George Meredith, for instance, or Charlotte Yonge[24], may be boring, but they are not dull; and of writers continuing into the present day but not of it, such as Kipling, the same distinction holds good. Moreover, the tendency is truly literary, it cannot be shredded off as a tendency of contemporary writers. They indeed show no wish to be Duller than Life. The domestic servants of the day scarcely excuse them in their pursuit of new situations, a pursuit so intoxicating that in many cases (like her) even when they had found a new situation, they can't settle down in it. But the tendency to be Duller than Life is too much for them and at the end of a year's subscription to the lending library one may look back on a distinguished welter of brilliant writing, insight into character, this, that and the other with scarcely a surprise in all those well-printed pages.

Of such surprises is it the biographies which offer the greater number: and the position of biography is one of the significant facts in the literary situation. Twenty years ago biographies were considered 'solid reading,' and as such opposed to fiction. Now this is pretty nearly reversed. More and more readers prefer biographies as being 'more entertaining than novels,' and the same conviction seems to be working among writers too. It would seem that worn out by the strain of being Twice as Natural in their fiction they escape to biography exclaiming: 'Here, at any rate there is no need to be life-like!'

Joseph Smith receiving a pair of spectacles from an angel to enable him to translate the Book of Mormon, Leigh Hunt's[25] embarking for Italy with a goat, Ruskin quitting the house of a friend because it was built in the

Palladian style, the member of the Edinburgh police force whose note-book was bound in the skin of Burke the resurrectionist, Lady Dorothy Nevill[26] fastening whistles to birds' tails, the funeral of Rudolf Valentino – these are situations (the first, perhaps, might need a little glossing over), which uplift and fatten the biographer. In fact, the stranger the fish the more he welcomes them to his net; and very properly, since it is exactly incidents such as these that by their strangeness impart to his book a quality called liveliness – which is an attribute of life.

One might expect the novelist to welcome such situations also, and for the same reason. But the Tendency of Contemporary Literature will not allow him to welcome them so unceremoniously. Cautious before all things to be convincing, to be probable, he will reject the goat and the angel and scarcely allow Rodelinda Baker to tie a whistle to her guillemot without explaining for seven pages the complication of motives which drove her to this momentous step and describing every eddy in her sensations when the bird flew away. It is as though he said: 'As my characters are not real I cannot allow them the licence allowed to mankind. As they never lived, I must make them Twice as Natural!'

It will be interesting to see whether the flippancy of biography will infect fiction, or whether biography too will be forced into adopting the same austere regimen. In any case it will be all the same a hundred years hence. Contemporary tendencies may shape the contours of a masterpiece, but they do not affect its being such, and succeeding generations by accepting the prevalent style of a period discount it. *Werther*[27] is a triumph of sensibility, but none the less a triumph. What's more, the convention of its period may give charm to a book otherwise insignificant. It may be that future readers will say of our period: 'How delightfully dull!' and while carrying about *Ulysses* or a pocket classic find in *An American Tragedy*[28] (say) the same rather snuffy fragrance which lingers in the pages of *Ivanhoe*.

DEFOE AND *MOLL FLANDERS*
(the *New York Herald Tribune, 1929*)

The automobile, I thought, has carried us back into an earlier stratum of time. Where the traveller by rail substantiated the name of a country town, not important enough to stop at, by a view of the gasworks, a laundry that also keeps hens, a yellow brick institute or a blue brick bethel, and the semi-detached houses all along the Station Road, the motorist pierces this integument and is for a few minutes in the world of people who travelled by stage coach. The narrow streets, so narrow that one can look into the houses on either side, catch a glimpse of the cornchandler's cat asleep in a bin, or recognise through the drawn blinds the silhouette of a pot of geraniums, decant one into the wide market square, over which the rival inns hold out their signs. The market still holds, groups move conversationally over the cobbles, the cheapjack postures under his flare, and countrywomen sit on the pavement-edge with plucked and trussed chickens, ornamented with epaulettes of liver and giblets, laid on the stones besides them.

Or perhaps the traveller may find himself skirting the village green; on one side of it are the gentry houses, conscious but not self-conscious, officially protected by a chain looping from low posts, and raised in the social scale by a flight of steps to the front door. The inn has red blinds, and standing a little apart is the church, being everything one could expect of it. It is all traditional and unremarkable, the alphabet and daily bread of the English nightingale area – south of the Trent and east of the Severn. One might live here, in any of these unnumbered and passingly-seen heres, very respectably, very cosily and prosily; and yet the mind experiences a faint impression of romance, as from viewing the parthenon or the Alhambra, places in the present once but now in the *passé défini*; for one is not cosy or prosy nowadays, barely respectable.

These sights, these thoughts, still possessed me when I reached home, and, too sleepy for a new book, pulled an old one from the shelf. There are some books, as there are some personalities, which one can open anywhere and be sure of an interest. This, I knew, was one of them. I read:-

With this stock I had the world to begin again; but you are to consider that I was not now the same woman as when I lived at Rotherhithe; for, first of all, I

251

was near twenty years older, and did not look the better for my age, nor for my rambles to Virginia and back again; and though I omitted nothing that might set me out to advantage, except painting, for that I have never stooped to . . .

Roxana, with her Frenchified name, might paint; famous Moll Flanders never fell so low as that. 'Born in Newgate, twelve years a whore, five times a wife, twelve years a thief,' she yet kept her face honest, used no whitelead or ceruse. Cosy, prosy, respectable. All that small, remote, stage-coach world I had been prying into rose up perfect from the page before me, from the cornchandler's cat – faithful, for all her rapscallionly midnight matings, to the fireside, the cushioned chair, the creamjug, and an admirable mouser and mother – to the church, standing a little apart and being everything that one could expect of it; for Moll, despite her handling of two of the Commandments, received all the Thirty Nine Articles of Religion, and always married if possible. She visited a gaming-house but once, she did not run into debt, the probity of her budgets is beyond reproach.

Balzac has been praised by no less a critic than Mr. Strachey[29] for the proper insistence he lays upon money matters in his novels. I daresay *La Comedie Humaine* could be audited; I have no doubt that *Moll Flanders* could be, though perhaps its heroine was mistaken in supposing that she 'might board very handsomely at a town called Manchester for about £6 a year.' But this information she had from a north-country gentlewoman, 'and nothing was more frequent in her discourse than her account of the cheapness of provisions, and the easy way of living in her country; how plentiful and cheap everything was, what good company they kept, and the like'; others of us may have heard similar pious brags from that part of the world.

It is noteworthy that the most highly wrought emotional scene in this book hinges on £.s.d. Moll, beginning the world again at two and forty, allows a match to be made by this same north-country gentlewoman between herself and a man who passes as a man of fortune. But the go-between has lied to both parties; he is as much of a fortune-hunter as she, as, a little after their marriage, they discover. Ruefully, for they have been happy together, but sensibly, they agree to separate and go on their several dubious ways.

252

I pulled out a bank-bill of £20 and eleven guineas, which I told him I had saved out of my little income; that if it was taken from me, I was left destitute, and he knew what the condition of a woman must be if she had no money in her pocket; however, I told him, if he would take it, there it was.

It is true that on the next page we hear of another bank-bill, not disclosed. At two and forty one has learned a little hard sense – hard sense which can run concurrently with the pain of a last passion. But when, rejecting the thirty-one pounds – no, let me follow Defoe's example and be accurate: £31.11.; – Moll's fortune-hunter sets out alone, passion routs hard sense, and Moll, endowed with the pathetic, school-boyish, parting, amends of 'ten guineas, his gold watch, and two little rings, one a small diamond ring worth only about £6, and the other a plain gold ring', is as genuinely in love, as genuinely distracted, as any woman need be.

This is the fourth husband. He is succeeded by a worthy bank clerk with whom poor Moll is as cosy, prosy, and respectable as her true heart could desire. But he dies, ruined by the failure of a fellow-clerk, and Moll, too old now for marriage or keeping, is forced to thieve for a living.

All this book is golden, but there is no doubt that the thieving part is the best. From the moment of yielding to temptation – ' 'twas like a voice spoken over my shoulder, "Take the bundle; be quick; do it this moment,"' to the arrival in Newgate, Defoe's narrative sweeps on with the force and circumstantial thoroughness of a river in flood. Each successive larceny is invented with such art and described with such relish that one might almost suppose that the moral purpose of the book had been a little lost sight of, and that its author was saying to himself: 'Now what shall I steal next?' Be it a child's necklace, a parcel of Flanders lace, a horse, or the periwig of a gentleman overcome by love and liquour, he snaps it up so perfectly that the reader must feel a naughty delight in such accomplishment; and I defy the best regulated mind not to applaud when the lady at the country opera house 'who was not only intolerably merry but a little fuddled,' is lightened of her gold watch, or the bullying mercer brought to his bearings, or when Moll, grown a great lady at her trade, speaks of 'mere picking of pockets'.

For even as a thief Moll's estimable qualities are, so to speak, too much for her. Shrewd, industrious, reliable, steadfastly ambitious, she can no more help thieving successfully than she can help thieving; it might be said of her as was said of the virtuous woman in the Book of Proverbs: 'She seeketh wool and flax, and worketh willingly with her hands.' So trudging further and further into the morass of crime, while all the time her native integrity and her stout heart delude her on, she reaches Newgate, where the hardened wretches that are there before her give her an envious and merry welcome.

It is with a shock – so time-abolishing is true art – that one realises that this is the small, remote, stage-coach world where a woman was hanged for stealing a porringer or two ells of linen. Fortunately the scheme of this work precluded hanging – for no sentimental cause, but for the sound practical reason that a woman with a broken neck cannot write her autobiography. Morality, too, must receive her dividends; and it would be a mistake to suppose that Defoe did not pay them in good faith, though a two-century shift of perspective does for us rather dim 'the beauty of the penitent part'. So, abjuring the past, Moll is transported to the New World, there to 'grow rich, live honest, and die a penitent'. The order of the first four words is significant.

THE WEEK-END DICKENS
(introduction to *The Week-end Dickens*, 1932)

When I was young – I do not know how it is now – an insensibility to Dickens was almost a touchstone of culture. They did not dislike him, those altifrons of that day; they remained unmoved, modelling themselves upon the demeanour of the family in Thomas Haynes Baily's[30] Ballad:

> *Oh, no, we never mention her,*
> *Her name is never heard.*
> *Our lips have quite forgot to speak*
> *That once familiar word.* ·

When asked, as I, brought up on Dickens, and much impressed by this lofty dismissal of him, sometimes asked them, for their reasons, the reasons they gave were curiously, were indeed contemptuously beside the point. One could not read Dickens, he was always dragging in the Poor Law; or, more impressively recondite yet, he was always lapsing into Blank Verse. But the impression left on my mind was that they thought him Low; much as if they were Mrs. Jarley thinking of the Punch and Judy.

But, indeed, I believe they condemned him from exactly the same standpoint as that from which their parents had applauded him – a standpoint of morality. Nothing alters the deep English preoccupation with morality, though the idea of what is, and what is not, moral alters with every generation. Victorian morality was concerned with conduct, and to such a morality Dickens appealed like a Bishop – a Bishop reinforced and embellished with all the arts and persuasions of a cheapjack. Pure water, pure women, a humanitarian broadmindedness that never went too far – he was exactly what such a morality could make into exactly what it wanted. But the Edwardian morality – that at any rate of the Edwardian altifrons of my recollection – had changed its battlefield from conduct to art, and with a more ascetic faith embraced pure English, pure linen, and an artistic intolerance that stopped short at the Channel; for in the same breath that condemned Dickens they would approve the much untidier and more rodomanting Balzac.

To such minds, moving always under the shadow of that tormented and tormenting artist, Flaubert, Dickens must have been a painful phenomenon; a melodist as fluent as Verdi (Verdi they abhorred), and as popular among the whistling classes; a man bristling with axes to grind (and to write with any dogmatic purpose was anathema); above all, a slapdash, carpet-slippered fellow whose blank verses were almost as unblotted as Shakespeare's, a man who could say with the utmost calmness: 'My views being deferred to, I thought of Mr. Pickwick, and wrote the first number.' The crime did not lie in the thinking of Mr. Pickwick, but in thinking of him and putting him into execution without a twinge, without one of those lockjaw pangs which should be the doom and glory of the artist. Glorified by the palm without the pang, seated in the front row of English Letters with scarcely a scratch to show how he got there, it was no wonder that Dickens was a spectacle on which such eyes would prefer not to rest, such lips to mention.

'*Et j'attends le coit de ces beaux volatiles,*' wrote Flaubert, who, having decided to put a peacock's mating as an incident into *Bouvard et Pécuchet*, ordered the birds in a crate, and sat down with pen and notebook to await the event. 'I thought of Mr. Pickwick.' From a moral point of view the contrast is flagrant, and I do not see how the congregation of good Edwardian altifrons could have felt other than they did.

Now morality has shifted its battleground again. Whatever, in the smoke of the fray, it may be concerned with, it is certainly not concerned with conduct nor with art. Conduct and art, it may be hoped, will get on the better for lacking its attentions; at any rate a considered judgment of Dickens should be easier, since time has swept him beyond the reach of its excessive limelight and its excessive blacking-out.

There is a description of a stew in *The Old Curiosity Shop*, which would stand as a tolerable account of the Dickens novels. 'A stew of tripe – and cow-heel – and bacon – and steak – and peas, cauliflowers, new potatoes, and sparrow-grass, all working up together in one delicious gravy.' The ingredients are common enough, cow-heel and tripe are positively vulgar, and to a delicate palate perhaps the whole might be rather rich; but then there is the grace of that 'all working up together in one delicious gravy.' So, in the novels, the common ingredients of the English Romance, love, and the comic countryman, and deathbeds, and missing wills, and wicked uncles, and appetising young women, and babes in the wood, are all worked up together in that persuasive simmering juice of Dickens' imagination.

It is not a speculative imagination – the story-telling imagination rarely is. It is the possessive imagination of a child, the power, the gravy-like power, of mouthing and moulding and melting and permeating things intently-seen, half-understood, and long-remembered. Reading Dickens with this thought in mind, it is strange to see, emerging from the novels he wrote, like fumes from a cauldron, the vague, cloudy emanations of the novels he never achieved. There is that novel about the Marshes – attempted in *Great Expectations*, but mislaid among the plot and the characters. 'I see the marshes once. I don't know where they are, but I see 'em, guv'ner. They was flat. And miste.' The words are those of an incidental character in *Bleak House*; but it is Dickens who speaks through

256

him, using a disguise of accent like a false beard. Once, as a child sees, he must have seen the marshes –– a more imminent neighbour to London in his day than now – have seen that they were flat, and moist, and secretive; and the imagination aroused began to work upon them, to brood over them like their own mists, sucking, as a mist does, or a gravy, their juices out of them. Later, to Dickens the novelist, it might seem that the marshes were a good background for incidents of a gloomy or sinister kind – a good place to be benighted in, to be murdered in; or to that other man Dickens the reformer, they might seem a social menace and something that should be drained; but use or misuse them as he might, his imagination still wandered there, fastened to that first aspect.

Akin to the novel about the Marshes looms up from the cauldron the other ghostly unwritten novel about London. It is the London of a child's mind also; dark with fog, daubed with the rich colours of cheerful taverns, or red blinds screening warm parlours; a London of tangled alleys, lost graveyards, solemn deserted wharves at night, with the mysterious river running through it. This London obsession is particularly potent. Sooner or later, all the Dickens people come to London, drawn, like the rustic peas and new potatoes and sparrowgrass, to simmer in that powerful gravy.

But the London novel, like the Marsh novel, was never written. Perhaps it never could have been written. For together with these childish influences Dickens carried to his grown man's work another influence of childhood, as implicitly accepted by him, and much more implicitly accepted by the world he wrote for: the traditional English Novel, with its meat-and-two veg. canons of a hero and a heroine for the hero to win, plenty of well-marked subsidiary characters, a great deal of bustle, and an unlimited amount of robust right feeling. We, when we think of the novel, look back on the standard novelists we read in our childhood, Dickens large among them. He looked back upon those novelists of *his* childhood, Fielding and Smollett. How faithful he was to them, the conventional estimate of Dickens, still based upon the estimate of his own day, does not sufficiently admit; since he was destined to cast them, in contemporary estimation, so deeply in the shade. But we, far enough away from Dickens to see beyond him, can see clearly how filial he was to these masters, how willingly, for instance, he brought his characters to an inn, or plunged them into some buffoonery of circumstance; how, even when he wrote as a reformer, pluming himself as one who had constantly written with an intent to better the housing of the poor, the voice raised on behalf of the unfortunate spoke with the high spirits and gusto of a blunter, and more carefree, age.

It is by his precursors that Dickens claims to be measured. Happy as he was in his illustrators (and how happy the reader of these unpictured pages should realise), who has not dallied, sighing, with the idea of a Dickens illustrated by Hogarth? If we allow to those precursors that, though their sentiment was sometimes pumped-up, their humour sometimes over-emphatic, their Gods shot rather too abruptly from the flies in the last scene, they are yet masters of their trade of story-telling, a similar allowance must be made for Dickens. By an irony of time, it is by his very advantages over them that he falls short of them. His delicacy weakens him into occasional namby-pamby, his constructive conscientiousness betrays him into artifice, his passion inflames him into bow-wow. And writing, as they did, to please a public his public diluted his genius with a trickle of its falseness and pusillanimous thinking. Yet, despite the haunting sense of a pleased public, that sickly waft is blown away by the overpowering impression of a pleased author. It is Dickens's delight we feel as much as our own, when we read him. No cook could hang stirring over his stewpot with greater gusto than he snuffing up that delicious gravy, watching the ingredients come bobbing and twinkling to the surface, and working up all together. There is a story told by one of Dickens's children, that, falling asleep in his father's study, he woke to find himself in the company of a homicidal maniac – a man who gnashed his teeth, pulled faces, snarled, and griped the air. It was the inventor of Quilp, if I recollect rightly, inventing him. To be thus in love with one's trade, at home in it, possessed by it, is the secret – if any one secret there be – of good writing, of that true good writing which makes good reading. And even in the least meritorious, or the slightest of Dickens's work, this ardent and possessive fervour of the convinced imagination will suddenly flash out on one, real and insinuating as a scent of flowers or good cooking, or a strain of music, as enhancing to the sense of life as a circus or a horse jumping. How the happy author must have beamed, then, with Micawber, postured with Crummles, thwacked Squeers and soused Stiggins! It is thus he comes to us, profuse, frank, loud-voiced, with a thump for this and a sugar-plum for that, rejoicing in his strength, striding over the broad acres of his fancy, a Squire Western of Letters; with the earnest consequence of a child who has thought of a story, and must tell it out.

HARD TIMES
(unpublished ms, Warner/Ackland Archive, Dorset County Museum)

When Charles Dickens wrote *Hard Times*, he had already written ten major novels, and in all but two of these he had attacked social abuses of his day. His attacks are passionate and outspoken. They are also entertaining. While exposing the abuse, he makes sport with those who profited by it, setting up his unforgettable Aunt Sallies – Mr Bumble drawing his consequentiality from lording it over helpless paupers, Mr and Mrs Squeers conjugally battening on their starved pupils at Dotheboys Hall, Mrs Gamp and Mrs Prigg making themselves comfortable beside a dying bed. A Smollet-like gaiety attends Dickens's forays against the forces of corruption, tyranny, and hypocrisy. One feels he is so sure of his strength that he can whistle as he goes to the attack.

Childe Roland to the Dark Tower came . . . There is very little entertainment to be got from *Hard Times*. In his previous onslaughts, Dickens's objectives had been a State of Things. In *Hard Times*, it was a State of Mind. Slums, the Yorkshire Schools, the treatment of paupers, the imprisonment of debtors, the Court of Chancery even, were recognisably abuses or open to abuse. They were things that should be reformed, or done away with, things that the Victorian conscience was uneasy about. They had come about by accident, they were blots. But the State of Mind which Dickens attacked in *Hard Times* was 'cool, classical, and correct.' It was a State of Mind arrived at by enlightened thinking, expressed by convincing arguments, popularised by considerations of patriotism, progress, and the greatest good of the greatest number. *Laissez-Faire*, the theory of the Manchester School of economists, had been accepted, not only by get-rich quick employers, but by a mass of earnest, puzzled, plain sensible men, to whom it appeared as the guiding and coordinating Light of Reason, shed on the confused violence of the Industrial Revolution.

Precisely because the evils of the Industrial Revolution had always been patent, the theory of *Laissez-Faire*, Non-Interference, was the more persuasive, since it accepted and justified the evils as necessary constituents in the progress and prosperity which would insure the greatest good of the greatest number. A sixteen hour working day? But the steam engine that powered the factory would work a twenty-four hour day, its time was money and must not be wasted. Starvation wages? But if wages rise, the cost of living will rise too, exports will cost more and not sell so readily. An unnatural enmity between rich and poor? Not at all; the natural antithesis between Capital and Labour. 'Wagon-loads of crippled factory-children'? A fly in the general amber, since the majority of factory-children remain uncrippled while early learning the lesson of industry. Look at the figures. Consider the facts. Don't be run away with feelings.

If *Hard Times* had attacked a state of things, it would have been somewhat out of date, for by 1854 sufficient feeling had been aroused for Commissions to have been held and Acts of Parliament passed. But the State of Mind persisted, and was honestly adhered to by honest men. This compelled Dickens to a new approach. Such men could not be Aunt-Sallied, they must be shown as they were; and Dickens shows us Mr Gradgrind. Mr Gradgrind of Coketown is an honest, conscientious, unpleasing man, who believes in facts and figures, and is horrified when he finds two of his carefully brought-up children peeping through the gap of a circus tent; for in a well-ordered life there is no more place for fancy, sentiment or circuses than in a balance sheet. With such beliefs, he is the natural prey of his friend Bounderby, a wealthy mill-owner and banker, and a coarse braggart whose constant boast is that there is no nonsense about him. Bounderby wishes to marry Gradgrind's daughter. The daughter, brought up on facts and figures, can find no statistical reason for saying No, and after a courtship 'in the form of bracelets', and urged on by her wastrel young brother who knows it would be easier to get money from Bounderby's wife than from Mr Gradgrind, marries. Mr Gradgrind, who wants a reliable *Laissez-Faire* M.P. for Coketown, imports a glossy cad, and introduces him to Bounderby, who will back his candidature. The glossy cad finds it more to his taste to canvass Louisa Bounderby. On the brink of being seduced by him, she makes a desperate flight from lover and husband both, and goes back to her father. Her return forces Mr Gradgrind to a stupefied realisation that facts and figures are not enough to nourish a well-ordered life – a conclusion hammered home when the young brother is discovered to have robbed his brother-in-law's bank.

It is a bleak story, bleakly told; and the underplot of Steven and Rachel, two haplessly virtuous mill-hands, is perfunctory and oddly clammy. It is as though Dickens were embarrassed by the working-class of the industrial North, as if he had read too many blue-books about 'factory operatives'. Only in Mrs Sparsit does he allow himself a truly 'Dickensian' character; and set in the midst of this austere narrative, she is perhaps not so much Dickensian as Balzacian. Odious and ludicrous, she pursues a self-appointed mission to undo the all-powerful Bounderby, whose housekeeper she condescendingly is, by showing him up as 'a Ninny'. Shown up he is, but not by Mrs Sparsit. A foolish old woman, a poor one at that, is the instrument appointed to overthrow this Dagon. A younger Dickens would have shattered Dagon entirely. The Dickens of *Hard Times* was not so sanguine. Mr Bounderby, his reputation chipped but his money-bags plump as ever, goes bragging on, and makes a vainglorious will, designed to keep alive for evermore the name of Bounderby, and which from the moment of his death began 'its long career of quibble, plunder, false pretences, vile example, little service and much law.'

RASSELAS

(*Rasselas, Prince of Abyssinia* by Dr Johnson
Introduction by G.K. Chesterton, woodcuts by Douglas Percy Bliss, 1926)

. . . The sound of a cough close behind me, made me turn my head. I saw a girl sitting on a stone bench near by; she was bent over a book, on the perusal of which she seemed intent; from where I stood I could see the title – it was *Rasselas*; a name that struck me as strange, and consequently attractive.

'Is your book interesting?'

'You may look at it,' replied the girl, offering me the book.

I did so; a brief examination convinced me that the contents were less taking than the title: *Rasselas* looked dull to my trifling taste; I saw nothing about fairies, nothing about genii; no bright variety seemed spread over the closely-printed pages.

So Jane Eyre handed it back again: perhaps Charlotte Brontë would not have kept it much longer. It is amusing to speculate what the characters of another Jane thought of *Rasselas*. Edward Ferrars, who could read aloud even Cowper without animation, might have delivered the measured opinions of Imlac more successfully, if Marianne could have been brought to listen to them. Mr. Bennet certainly delighted in it, and I fancy that there was a well-bound, well-worn copy in the library at Donwell.

I suppose it was a classic even then; indeed, it is hard to conceive of *Rasselas* ever being other than a classic. There are few works in the English language having more the air of one in authority than this small, perfect, unimportant fable, this rounded, translucent blob of gum that oozed from the tree of vast stature and rough bark which was Johnson. Written in 1759, the author did not look at it again until more than twenty years after, when he was within four years of his death. He read it in a travelling carriage, and seemed, Boswell says, 'to be intensely fixed.' Little wonder. It is sad enough to cry out: 'What a genius I had then!' – yet there is a kind of flourish in the cry. It is with a deeper and more irremediable pang that the wise man says to himself: 'Ah, had I come to these conclusions already?'

It would be affected to write of *Rasselas* without some reference to the traditional comparison between Johnson's irony and the satire of *Candide*. It seems to me that the crux lies in the opposition of those words – irony and satire. *Rasselas* is both more sober and more crushing than *Candide*: it is, as Mr. Chesterton says in his introduction to this edition, the work of a stoic. Voltaire was not a stoic. He was an idealist, and had all the idealist's savagery. His satire is directed against this infamy or that; it is purposeful, he squirts it out like a corrosive fluid against whatever offends his views for humanity. Johnson's irony is shed as dispassionately, searchingly and quenchingly as rain. It is as harmless as rain; it may even be as beneficent; but to the mental picnicker it is as ruthlessly discouraging.

"'You seem to forget,'" replied Rasselas' – to Nekayah, who had drawn a black picture of the disadvantages of the married state; "'that you have even now, represented celibacy as less happy than marriage. Both conditions may be bad, but they cannot both be worst.'"

This refusal to admit the possibility of two worsts is a degree of steadfast pessimism to which Voltaire in his satire on optimism never approached.

No bright genii are spread over these closely-reasoned pages. Jane Eyre's disappointment is not very surprising. But if she had seen this *Rasselas* of 1926 she might have received the text for the sake of the pictures, for Mr. Bliss's woodcuts have a curious quality, florid and at the same time sinister, which would have exactly hit her fancy. The dancers in the Happy Valley exhibit a scorched cat agility, as though they were dancing in hell-fire. Rasselas, Imlac, Nekayah and Pekuah Visit a Hermit amidst explosions of tropical foliage, Visit an Astronomer whose telescope is like an instrument of mental torture reared against a sky which swarms with comets and nebulae, thick as bacteria under a microscope, Meet an Old Man in a landscape more threatening than the jungle landscapes of Rousseau for being black and white, a Rousseau jungle seen by lightning.

Mr. Bliss's illustrations are not, it will be seen, just what one would call in keeping with Johnson's sedate narrative. I doubt if any woodcuts could be, for the woodcut gets its effects by emphasis and trenchancy, and the effects in *Rasselas* are got by sobriety and understatement. One may regret that Mr. Bliss did not undertake, say, *The Pilgrim's Progress* instead; personally, I think he is wantonly hobgoblinish, even for Bunyan, in his observance of the Caliban element in the woodcut tradition – an element merely due to callous craftsmanship and cheap production; for instance, I can see no reason why Nekayah and Rasselas in the Invocation of the Nile cut should appear, the one a harridan, the other a moron: but his wisdom in electing to be true to his medium instead of attempting a compromise between medium and subject is well justified in a set of full-page illustrations all of which are notable and one – Pekuah among the Arabs – beautiful.

Pleasantly, though perhaps fortuitously, this, the best of the woodcuts, is also the most relevant. A woman seated in a fierce and fruitful landscape, who meditates while two other women lay their heads in her lap – it is too melancholy, too romantic for Pekuah; as an allegory of Johnson's thought it is better, though still too romantic; but as an expression of his title it is admirable. *Rasselas* – an enchanting word, evocative and unmeaning! No wonder Jane pricked up her ears. When I first read the book it was a surprise to me to find that Rasselas was a person; I had thought of it, being so beautiful, as the name of a place, a happier valley, perhaps, wearing the rich stillness of autumn; or an island. It is said that Johnson wrote this story in the space of a week, to earn money enough to pay for his mother's funeral. One might wait for years before finding such a word. It remains in our minds, and if we are asked about it, we reply that it is the title of Johnson's one work of fiction. But it is more than that. It is his only lyric.

SOLDIERS, WEEDING-WOMEN AND LINNETS
(*Good Housekeeping*, 1945)

But what became of . . . ? Cinderella's coachman, King Alfred's cakes, the little pig that didn't have real meat? It is not only children who insist that no loose ends should be left hanging at the end of the story. The same tidy mind persists in the grown-up literary public. It was to comply with those *what became ofs* that the Elizabethan dramatists slaughtered so many minor characters before the fall of the curtain, that the Victorian novelists rang such peals of marriage bells in their last chapters, pairing off the curate and the governess, the valet and the lady's maid, the old aunt and the family lawyer, leaving not a celibate behind. 'There is, sure, another flood toward, and these couples are coming to the ark. Here comes a pair of very strange beasts.' The speaker is the melancholy Jacques, but for a moment one hears Shakespeare himself, poking fun at an artistic convention even while he complied with it.

Historians achieve the same satisfying tidiness by different means. Armies are annihilated, cities levelled with the ground, whole native populations vanish before the invading colonist in a sentence or two, flattened into a macadamised surface down which the muse of history proceeds as calmly as a steam-roller.

But the reader of memoirs, diaries, collected letters, must forswear the pleasures of a tidy mind, and prepare to be haunted by ghosts that cannot be laid, minor characters that appear but once, exist only in half a dozen lines – but for all that, exist. Sometimes they are of incalculable importance, like the Person from Porlock who interrupted Coleridge while Coleridge was writing *Khubla Khan*. 'At this moment he was unfortunately called out by a person from Porlock, and detained by him above an hour'. And so the thread of the poem was broken, and Coleridge 'found to his mortification that though he retained some vague and dim recollection of the general purport all the rest had passed away like the images on the surface of a stream into which a stone has been cast, but, alas! without the after restoration of the latter.' Unfortunate Person from Porlock, poor speechless ghost whom every lover of poetry has abused for being so haplessly talkative for above an hour! He can say nothing in his defence. Perhaps he visited Coleridge with some philanthropic intention of telling him about a house to let, a copy of Sir Thomas Browne's *Pseudodexia* which could be bought cheap in a second-hand bookshop. Perhaps he brought strawberries or asparagus (for it was in summer that the ill-timed visit took place). No doubt Coleridge did quite half of the talking, perhaps the Person from Porlock's whole life went awry because of some engagement he missed through being delayed by that talkative Mr Coleridge. Perhaps, he ended his days in shame and remorse, having bought a copy of the *Collected Poetical and Dramatic Works*, having begun to read *Khubla Khan* with rapture, having turned the page, and found the poem unfinished, and followed by that accusing foot-note. It is quite possible. But it is impossible to know. The ghost can neither answer our questions or be laid.

The Person from Porlock is, so to speak, a public ghost, as one is a public statue or a public nuisance. But if you begin to attend to the ghosts of this kind, ghosts of no importance will waylay you, and haunt quite as efficiently as any ghosts of good standing. Only last week I added another to my repertory. He started up from the Journal of Miss Jane Hester Reilly[31], in which she recorded her journey from Dublin to London in the year 1791.

Miss Reilly was seventeen, a rather pert young lady, and somewhat of a

265

Jacobin, to judge by her reactions. 'We were there for some time before the procession began, which was as grand as a parcel of ugly old Dukes, Lords, and Bishops could make it. The Duke of Gloucester came in the procession with his train held up by two attendants . . . I should have known him by his likeness to all the halfpence and guineas I ever saw to be one of royal family'. This was at Westminster Hall, where the trial of Warren Hastings was proceeding. *My* ghost rises up from the side of the Finchley Road, and is one of those common persons from whom the use of History constructs her smooth surfaces. 'About four miles from London we observed a soldier, he had sat down on a stone and appeared so ill that my mother stopped the carriage and called him over to give him some trifle; she asked him what regiment he belonged to, he said the 30th, that he had been discharged for illness, and that he had long lain in a hospital in London unable to begin this last journey to his own country to die with his friends, which he now scarcely hoped even to accomplish. Where was he going to? – to Liverpool. What was his country? – Ireland. What part? – the County Down. Oh!, whereabouts? – a town called Banbridge. He then described exactly the spot on which he was born, it was my father's estate and he gave him a blessing before he knew how welcome that blessing was to us. It was an odd and pleasant adventure to us and I hope a lucky one to the poor man who was enabled by it to pursue his journey more comfortably.'

At first sight it is a charming vignette: the ladies in their plumed hats leaning from the carriage, the soldier's face lighting up at this news from home, the three voices becoming more and more Irish as the conversation proceeds. It could be drawn by Morland[32] and engraved by Bartelozzi[33], and called *Benevolence, or the Soldier's Fortune*. At first sight. But then the questions begin to scribble over the vignette. How much did they give him? How far did it take him? Did he achieve his last military ambition, the close of all his marches and counter-marches: to reach home and die there? The carriage bowls on towards London and Westminster Hall and the Duke of Gloucester who is so like a guinea – or a halfpenny. The soldier goes limping up the Finchley Road. And that is all we know of him, nor should we know that if Miss Jane Hester Reilly had not happened to keep a journal.

Some diarists have a sort of cedar-wood-chest quality, and sweeten what they preserve. The ghosts that wander in and out of Gilbert White's

266

Journal have caught a particular serenity and charm from their dwelling-place. Goody Hammond is my favourite. Goody Hammond was his weeding-woman. She came in the spring, like a cuckoo or a brimstone butterfly. At the beginning of harvest she went away to work in the harvest fields and when the harvest was gathered she came back. She is not, of course, so interesting as a cuckoo or brimstone butterfly to Gilbert White the naturalist, and he is not quite sure of her exact nomenclature, for sometimes he calls her Goody Hampton. But there she is, grubbing about in the garden among the pinks and the Dames Violets and the Crown Imperials; and in the spring of 1793 'my weeding-woman swept-up on the grass-plot a bushel basket of blossoms from the white apple-tree; and yet that tree seems still covered with bloom,' And yet Goody Hammond seems still to be brooming away under gnarled apple trees that were apple-pips in that spring of 1793.

A cousinly contrast to Goody Hammond is Mrs Mule. 'There is something to be very softening in the presence of a woman – some strange influence even if one is not in love with them. I always feel in a better humour with myself and everything else, if there is a woman within ken. Even Mrs Mule, my fire-lighter – the most ancient and withered of her kind, and (except to myself) not the best-tempered . . .'

It is Byron who writes. Mrs Mule was a charwoman, of unbelievable ugliness, whose witch-like countenance lightened upon him in his Bennet Street lodgings. She was the mock and marvel of his friends; but when he moved to the Albany Mrs Mule moved with him. Even when he married, and lived in Piccadilly with a household of proper respectable servants, Mrs Mule was taken along, and marked her rise in the world by a new wig in which she looked even uglier than before. And when Byron quitted England in a storm of pride, rage, debt, frustration, and mystery, though he left his friends unfarewelled he found time to say goodbye to Mrs Mule. 'The poor old devil was so kind to me,' he said. He said it at a time when every woman in London society was hell-bent on being kind to Byron; but Mrs Mule's was the only kindness he acknowledged as such. If we could have Mrs Mule's account of Byron we might be nearer to understanding him. But she is a ghost. She flits before us with her broom and her duster; she stands in the deserted Piccadilly mansion listening to the last sound of those limping departing footsteps; she goes off shaking her hideous head, an old woman who doesn't hold with gossiping about employers. There's been a sight too much talking about his lordship already, if you ask *her*.

One can be haunted by apparitions even more shadowy and insignificant. From Swift's *Journal to Stella*, its pages embossed with statesmen and men of letters, rustling with the silk trains of duchesses and the silk cassocks of bishops, such an apparition peeps out.

London. January 4. 1711. I went last night to put some coals on my fire after Patrick had gone to bed; and there I saw in a closet a poor linnet he has bought to bring over to Dingley: it cost him sixpence, and is as tame as a dormouse. I believe he does not know he is a bird; where you put him, there he stands, and seems to know neither hope nor fears: I suppose in a week he will die of the spleen.

Swift shuts the cupboard door, and makes up his fire, and thinks that Patrick's linnet will be something to tell Stella. He is in the flush of his ambitions, in the thick of his schemings; he is that remarkable Dr Swift who is so witty and so learned and so savage and so mysteriously commanding. And the sixpenny linnet, bought by a foolish man-servant, has won its minute immortality, even though it will die in a week, losing what knowledge it had may have had that it was a bird. Down it goes into the *Journal to Stella*: a trifle, trifles please women; a trifle and a portent. For thirty-four years later Swift too will die of the spleen, not knowing he is a man, shut up in the dark closet of his madness.

THE HISTORICAL NOVEL
(Lecture to the Third Congress of the League of American Writers
from *Fighting Words* ed. Stewart, Donald Ogden, 1940)

When I was young I read everything in the house, including historical novels, and two things struck me. First, that historical novels had usually long and frequent descriptions of scenery – I supposed in order that the author might have a spell of taking it easy. Oaks and brooks get along through the centuries without much fuss about being 'period.' Second, that the period quality of the characters in these novels was a class distinction. The upper class characters were fully period. But the servants and the peasants and the social what-not had scarcely a period rag to cover them, except for an occasional 'zounds' or 'gadzooks', and getting into a morris dance every now and then. They belonged to the date of the author.

This period class distinction has pretty good authority. It is the method of Shakespeare.

And I think you will agree with me that in almost every piece of historical fiction it is the characters of the ruled that come bursting out of the texture. But the reason for this class distinction? There are three reasons which might be put forward. First (and we can dismiss it forthwith), that the author wasn't going to bother with such small fry. He was too aristocratic. Second, that authors of historical novels are all near-Marxists, and were expressing the view that the closer you are to the economic, bony structure, the hungrier you are and the harder you work, the more permanent are your class characteristics; or, to put it another way, it is only the rich who can afford to be up to date, who can display strong period characteristics, whereas the poor get along with the minimum of fashion.

The third reason, which seems to me the likeliest, is this: if you examine the historical novel you will find that it is the working-class characters who fill the role of the commentator, the analyst, the person who sums things up. The noble sentiments, the villainous sentiments, go into the mouths of the ruling characters; but when it comes to a piece of plain common sense, it is the ruled who speak. So I would suggest that the authors kept their working-class characters contemporary because of this structural function of pinning the story together by comment and analysis; or, if you prefer, of keeping it from going bad by salting it. A wise word in the mouth of a lifeless character is no longer a wise word; it is just a moral maxim; and these commenting characters were kept contemporary because writers felt it the safest way in keeping them life-like.

All this, of course, applies to the traditional historical novel. More recently there has been a revolt against this, and *all* the characters in historical novels are of the present day, contemporary in speech, in behaviour, in motive, in psychology. But the talisman is not infallible, and these characters straight out of modern life may make up a perfectly lifeless book. There must, it seems, be some recognition, of history in the historical novel. The writer of the historical novel cannot escape the obligation of a period.

We can cast 'gadzooks' and 'by our lady' behind us. They mean nothing. It is not the manner of speech that matters; but the matter of the speech, plus, – and this is crucial – the manner of thinking. In all ages, the prime motives are the same; fear, love, anger, hunger, necessity, ambition – the old gang. Nor has the economic structure altered that much. To get some work to get enough to eat to get some work – it is a song of the ages. And the reactions to the economic structure are pretty constant too; but constant with a qualification. There were strong men before Agamemnon. There were tolerable Marxists before Marx. But they were before Marx. And an historical novelist who includes (and I think the historical novelist should) the economic ground-base, must simultaneously recognise the social-economic variations which move above that ground-base. Thomas More and Latimer, for instance, wrote as socialists; but they were Christian socialists. Oliver Cromwell had the career of a fascist leader; but he was a fascist before imperialism (though not before possibilities of European empires, as you can read in Marvell's 'Horatian Ode').

The historical novelist cannot dodge the obligation, so it seems to me, of knowing pretty accurately how people clothed their minds. Human nature does not change, etc., but human thinking alters a great deal, is conditioned by what it has been taught, what it believes, or disbelieves; what it admires in art or nature; at what age it marries; to what extent it has outwitted weather (it was the medieval winters, cold, dark, and boring, that taught the troubadours to praise the spring); what careers are open to it; whether it reads Aristotle or Plato; whether it believes in witches or planets. If you know these things, then you may have a chance of knowing *all* your characters, that is to say, a chance of making them life-like, or bringing the whole of your book to life.

And to do this there is nothing for it, I think, but to be historian enough to do a little research. There is no need to haunt museums, in fact it is sometimes better not to haunt museums. You may not be able to see the showcases for the other historical novelists. And finally, after you have gathered your material, use a fruit-press. It's the juices you want.

SAKI

(Short stories by 'Saki' [H.H. Munro]
The *New York Herald Tribune*, 1929)

There is a form of behaviour idiomatically described as 'cutting off your nose to spite your face'; and ten years ago this interesting self-mutilation was the fashionable sport all over Europe among those who had survived from the 1914 class. Ordinarily one does not lose one's youth in four years; in England, especially, where the national temper is so casual and procrastinating that the normal person in the early twenties is only just beginning to shed the seriousness of adolescence, it was a considerable shock to find one's self in one's fifth lustre a quaint survival from a vanished past, a kind of moral mastodon. Consequently the sport of face-spiting was practiced there with peculiar devotion and dexterity. The remnant of a lost generation, suddenly confronted with the appalling prospect of living out their natural span of years and dying in their beds, uncontemporaried, for all remaining time an anachronism, historical Ishmaelites, gathered up the only youthful qualities left to them – cynicism and despair – and set to work at making the worst of a bad job. Since they could not be young, they would be old; surviving, they would impose themselves as survivals; the irrecoverable pre-war world, now remote as another world and only to be viewed through a telescope, should be viewed through the wrong end of the telescope, reduced by an exaggerated historical perspective to the dimensions proper to a world that could slip and had slipped, from their grasp.

Great artistry was brought to this sleight of mind; soon the performers were almost perfect, their youthful audiences wholly convinced that by four years' seniority one could conjure a forgotten civilisation out of a hat. To have witnessed the coronation of King George V was a boast and historical as to have witnessed the coronation of King George IV; to recall Mrs. Pankhurst demanding to be enfranchised was tantamount to recalling

Mrs. Pankhurst wearing a crinoline; to have hired a chair in Hyde Park for a penny made one as venerably interesting as to have been carried thither in a sedan chair; everywhere antediluvians of twenty-five were putting on their shrouds to sit to the portrait painter, were assuming the smock-frock of the Oldest Inhabitant, were rapidly qualifying themselves to become the Club Bore.

There was only one flaw in the impersonation, one rent in the shroud whence an aspect of youth peeped out; they forgot that it is the prerogative of age to have known a Golden Age. While their fathers and grandfathers were using the adjective 'pre-war' to bless pre-war manners, Stilton, butlers, barometers and what-not: 'The gum on pre-war postage stamps was so much gummier' – they used it to damn or to ridicule. The forgotten civilisation they conjured out of their hat was displayed as something rather fantastic and wholly deplorable: a blight that never was on land or sea. They turned bitterly against the peace and prosperity which had nurtured them, they looked back and saw the parks and lawns and playing fields only as the pastures where they were fattened for the slaughter-house.

Since then there have been revivals of the past which may well be considered in the light of religious revivals. Successful campaigns were conducted by Sir Nigel Playfair[34] and the Rev. Montague Summers[35]; Mr. Lytton Strachey, who might be described as the English Aimée Semple Macpherson[36] (and I verily believe that the reason why Mrs. MacPherson fell so flat in London was that the rival evangelist is so strongly entrenched there) has revived the reign of the Good Queen, and converted the word Victorian from a term of abuse to an endearment; but the most intrepid, the most desperately famishing revivalist would scarcely hazard himself to revive the English decade 1904 -14. The taboo of the face-spiters still lies upon that decade. It is the haunted room, the room that no one goes into. Of course, we say, walking quite calmly past that door, of course there is no reason why any one should go into it. There is nothing in there of the least significance; the furniture is of the worst period, there was never any view from that window; it gave on to the tennis court, the stables that were never properly converted to a garage, a glimpse of the vicar's pergola festering all over with pink Dorothy Perkins. It was a stupid room, rather stuffy. No one goes into it now.

This decade is exactly covered by the five volumes of 'Saki' (Hector

272

Hugh Munro) which have been given me to review. The first sentence turned the door-knob, the first rustle of a turned page closed the door behind me. I was back in the room that no one goes into, and everything was there exactly as it used to be, and seeing it there I remembered that was exactly how it was. The same persons were there, and when they spoke their voices had the forgotten familiar inflexions. They spoke in the same way still, rather slowly, choosing their words like persons who have time to spare. They were a leisurely lot and seem, compared to us nowadays, sure of themselves and strangely sure of each other; they might all be relations, relations insulated by being distant relations; there is a kind of family resemblance among them. They converse with a studied flippancy, a deliberation of understatement that might become pompous if it were not fielded back into safety by some sudden trait of absurdity. There are some children in the room, too, whom they love respectfully; and quantities of animals, whom they admire. They say:

This bread and butter is cut far too thin; it crumbles away long before you can get it to your mouth. One feels so absurd, snapping at one's food in mid-air, like a trout snapping at a May-fly.

He conveyed the impression that if a destroying angel had been lent to him for a week it would have had very little time for private study.

One of the chief reasons why there are so few really great poems about Russia in our language is that you can't possibly get a rhyme to names like Smolensk and Tobolsk and Minsk. Of course you could rhyme Omsk with Tomsk; in fact, they seem to be there for that purpose, but the public wouldn't stand for that sort of thing indefinitely.

Then he had gone into Parliament, possibly with the idea of making his home life less dull.

The woman creates a positive draught with the number of bazaars she opens.

Waldo is one of those people who would be enormously improved by death.

The German governess told Lanner more about Schiller than he had ever heard in his life about any one person; it was perhaps his own fault for having told her that he was not interested in Goethe.

273

These sentences, combed swiftly and at random from Saki's pages, should be enough to give some idea of the irony and wit that found him such devoted readers in his own day, and by which, I suppose, he finds most of his readers still. It is slightly disturbing to discover that the delicate fabric of this wit should be so durable a material; it is as though one should learn that butterflies live as long as buffaloes, a certain mental priggishness resents such possibilities. But Saki's writings have more than the salt of wit to keep them fresh; though we must place him among the little writers – and indeed he seems by a fastidious observance of his own limitations to insist that he should be placed so – he has one quality in common with great writers; a personal constancy, a slant of the mind which is as authentically Saki as other slants of mind are Marvell, or Proust or Gogol. It is as important in aesthetic criticism to remember that this element of personal constancy – call it individuality or flavour or originality, what you will – is not contaminated, but reinforced by responsiveness to national or temporal influences. Marvell is the more Marvell in being also typical of his epoch; a Gogol un-Russianised would have been a lesser Gogol. The originality of Proust transferred to Athens under Pericles would not be originality at all; it would be a mistake. Similarly Saki's personal constancy is conditioned by constancy to his time and country. The peculiar and slightly disdainful imperturbability which marks his style, a refusal to be flustered or surprised or emphatic, is the Sakian rendering of a national code of behaviour, *le flegme anglais*. But this imperturbability is exhibited against a background of the most unlikely events and exotic absurdities; for in that period of accustomed peace and prosperity, that calm in a tea cup, pre-war England, if one was to be imperturbable with any credit one must provide something a little more exigant than the ordinary material for perturbation. In his first, and least estimable book, *'Reginald'*, we see Saki exercising his technique of imperturbability over such subjects as Christmas presents, house parties, besetting sins and the Carlton, as a juggler might begin with balls, who will afterwards go on to knives. In the later stories he is being imperturbable about cats who learn to talk and deliver themselves of home truths; hyenas, who escape from Lord Pabham's park, are christened for the time being Esme and eat little gypsies; Cabinet

Ministers who, being turned into black swans, lapwings and wildcats, have their place supplied by angels; quiet gentlemen informed that an Anglican bishop is making their home the headquarters of his pogrom against Jewish landowners; other quiet country gentlemen who find themselves compelled to adopt the human half of a werewolf; the plight of a commercial traveller who, having allowed himself to be tattooed by an Italian artist with a representation of the Fall of Icarus, is officially scheduled by the Italian government as a work of art.

This is one way of juggling with knives – knives from the armory of Harlequin, shaped and coloured and hilted as no knives ever were before. There is another and a more excellent way. In this case the knives are quite plain; but they are of steel and have a cutting edge. *The Unbearable Bassington* is the story of a young man, the only son of a widowed mother. He is a waster, he is, as the phrase goes, 'nobody's enemy but his own'; he has the charm of a stoat or a weasel, animals considered vermin by all right-thinking British minds. When he might marry an heiress he estranges her affections by borrowing money from her. She loves him, and she does not love her money; but she cannot run counter to the traditional opinion that young men who sponge on their young women are not the sort who should be encouraged. His mother also loves him; but she does not love supporting him, and is not prepared to sell her Van der Meulen in order to have the doubtful pleasure of the society of some one who eats more than his fair share of plovers' eggs. He is packed off to West Africa, is miserable there, and dies. The mother and the heiress remain to be miserable ever after. 'This story has no moral' says the author's note. There are some stories too austere to have morals; for the moral is a form of vegetation that only germinates in a rather gross soil, requiring to be manured by a good dose of sentiment; and *The Unbearable Bassington* is one of these. But here the Sakian imperturbability must master something more dangerous than werewolves – human unhappiness, a situation in which three persons are doomed with classical precision to make wretches of themselves with their eyes open; and raising to this difficulty it passes from imperturbability, a mannerism, however dexterously maintained, to something better; to restraint, and objective detachment.

Hector Hugo Munro was killed in 1916, at the age of forty-six; too old, had he survived, to have taken part in the face-spiting campaign. He was so perfectly a representative of the epoch which that campaign set itself to guy that it seems fitting he should have been in at its death, and died with it. One pre-war illusion was left him, for he wrote shortly before his death of his intention to buy land in Siberia, and settle there, after the war. He died a private soldier, having twice refused the offer of a commission. This seems curiously expressive of his position in English letters. For all his skill, his talent, his industry, his fastidious choice of subject and treatment, he was a modest writer, whose ambition was to do well and not to do importantly. He did all the better for that.

DEATH AND THE LADY
(*The Letters of Katherine Mansfield*
ed J. Middleton Murry, the *New York Herald Tribune*, 1929)

Lonely, unhappy people write the best letters; Dorothy Osborne[37] with her spleen, Madame de Sévigné[38] walking alone in the russet park and seeing black hunting dogs leap out of the bushes, William Cowper sitting behind his myrtles, a damned soul. The shadow of a bird flies over the page, and he looks up to the portion of air where the flight had been; the deliberate pen pauses; for a moment consciousness has expanded, tremblingly still, to a realisation of what it is to be William Cowper, alive this summer afternoon, damned to all eternity; and then he falls to the business of letter-writing again. He writes of his tame hares, of his new wig, of silkworms, or a picnic under a beech-tree with the provisions carried in a wheel-barrow, of the village constable, of the bird that has just flown by. 'William has nothing much to say; but he writes an entertaining letter,' says the recipient. 'He writes as though he were talking,' says another; and we, two centuries after, still read those letters, still hear that gentle voice.

What is it, this especial quality that makes of a letter (ordinarily an affair of information or requests or an untidy scrambling of the emotions on to paper) something that can be read for generations as a work of art is read? Cowper and Katherine Mansfield were literary artists; but Cowper's letters are read while Cowper's books are almost forgotten, and maybe the same measure will be meted to her, one day. It is not a matter of literary artistry, of knowing how to write. There are great writers whose letters have been since the ink dried on them, dead as a doornail. I do not think we should fly to read the letters of Milton, I know we do not fly to read the letters of Wordsworth, it does not require an especial spirit of prophesy to foresee that, although W. H. Hudson[39] had the qualification of being a lonely and unhappy person, *Green Mansions* will outlast his correspondence with Edward Garnett. Dorothy Osborne and Madame de Sévigné are, in their letters, literary artists of the first rank; but it is to be doubted whether, if the one had not had a lover, the other a daughter, they would have written at all. If unhappiness is the qualification for writing good letters, love is the motive. *Take, read. This is my spirit*: that is the device of the great letter-writers. Look, they say. These black signs on white paper, they are me. My blood ran with this ink; here, where I turned the page, it was pain to stem the flow, even for an instant, so strongly the current ran toward you. This is me, here I am. This is what I feel, what I think, what I do. This is the lizard I am seeing, this is the lunch I ate. The sun is shining on me, now it has gone in and I feel the cold. I have put on the painted shawl. To-night what is left of me after I have finished this letter will be unhappy and alone; but I am happy with you, and what I am now is here, is in your hand as you read.

This projection of a self across time and space is in all fine letter writing a curious poignant element; in the letters of Katherine Mansfield it is peculiarly so. In December 1917, she wrote to a friend: 'When I heard the medicine man say: "You ought to go to some place like Teneriffe or Madeira but as you can't go there, Spain or the South of France *will do*!" I would not have swopped my lung with any man alive.' London in the winter of 1917 was not a pleasant place for anyone endowed with unusual sensibilities and little money, who, moreover, was subject to rheumatism and had just had pleurisy. But France was no better; indeed, people with unusual sensibilities must give up hope of being at home anywhere in war time. The journey from Paris to Bandol took thirty-six hours and was a superb example of nightmare; and Bandol was wintry with a fuel shortage, and she had caught 'the most plaguey chill, stiff neck, sore throat, streaming cold that I ever had'. A month later she was reading Keats, and coughing, and looking to see if there was blood still on her handkerchief.

After her first haemorrhage she wrote thus to her husband: 'Since this little attack I've had, a queer thing has happened. I feel that my love and longing for the eternal world – I mean the world of *nature* – has suddenly increased a million times. When I think of the little flowers that grow in grass, and the little streams and places where we can lie and look up at clouds – Oh, I simply ache for them, for them with you. Take you away and the answer to the sum is 0. I feel so awfully like a tiny girl whom someone has locked in a dark cupboard, even though it's daytime . . . You mustn't think, as I write this, that I'm dreadfully sad. Yes, I am, but you know, at the back of it is *absolute faith* and *hope* and *love*. I've only, to be frank, had a bit of a fright. See? And I'm still "trembling". That just describes it.'

'Tomorrow I shall write a gayer letter.'

Tomorrow I shall write a gayer letter. Already the obligation had begun. Cowper, weighed down by God's wrath among his myrtles, sent himself abroad in his letters as he would have wished to be remembered by his friends – whimsical, philosophical, affectionate, idly witty, a pleasant being to remember – he spares them the long misery, the blackening conviction which fate had not spared him. Katherine Mansfield, sitting in her shadow of death, set herself to shine in that shadow's despite. In the letters that follow, the gayer letters that she promised, one feels that an unnaturally vivid light beats and flashes from the page. The seen, the heard thing stabs into her sensibilities, and with a stabbing phrase she transmits it. 'It's a blue and white day, very fair and warm and calm. The sort of day that *fowls* enjoy, keeping up a soft, faraway cackle,' she writes. Or: 'There's such a sad widower here with four little boys, all in black – all the family in black – as though they were flies that had dropped into the milk.' She hears the piano in the house opposite 'braiding its hair in swift, intricate braids.' A woman visiting her 'has left a rather faded taste of white suede gloves in my mouth.' Nothing, it seems, not a transient polite bore, a noise opposite, a change in the weather, the hotel dietary – 'I hate haricot beans. They have no

278

imagination' – can leave her unmoved, can escape the pounce of her sensibilities. She hurls herself hither and thither after the aspects of life, this maenad, whose days are spent for the most part alone, in hotels or in furnished villas, lying in bed, or sitting by the fire (for cold, her adversary – 'I do wish it were not so cold. Cold frightens me; it is ominous, I breathe it, and deep down it's as though a knife softly, softly pressed in my bosom and said "Don't be too sure" ' – pursues her), whose adventures are to go for a little walk, to exchange a few words with a laundress or a gardener, to get a letter from England.

Part of this excitement may be due to the poison of her disease; some measure of her astonishing receptivity to her surroundings may be the mind's response to the menace of death, the keen-sightedness of the drowning man; but it is impossible not to feel that in her letters of 1918-1921 she is constructing, almost with coquetry, a self-portrait that shall by its look of life annihilate the space between her and their reader, the time that will soon have carried her out of the kingdom of the living. Just as a child, suspecting itself to be in disgrace, puts on supernatural airs and graces of goodness, she sheathes herself in vitality and parries every thrust of death with an assertion of how alive she is. She will not be thought of as a dying woman, she cannot bear to forego one moment of the love that we give to the living; she knows, though not a word is said of this, this is one risk which for all her courage she cannot take, how strongly the human heart is moved to animal repugnance by death, how at the sight of disease we grow cold-hearted with fear, how much we dislike it when someone who has been part of our life becomes an intimation of our mortality.

These letters are filled with colours, shapes, lights, noises, people passing the window, fragments of conversation, happenings of all sorts. She breaks off in the middle of one to remark that a fly has just flown into the fire. She tells but little of her thoughts, and those thoughts which she tells are mostly sudden thoughts, impulses of the mind: such reticence, coupled with the vivacity with which she relates every thing that is of the moment, gives to her letters the fascination of a play of light over some reflecting surface. The pool shows everything, every touch of the wind, every chance spangle of the sun, but withholds what lies beneath the surface; it shows us every colour but its own. In her loneliness she had time to polish that reflecting surface. Her writing is spontaneous, but with a deliberate, an achieved, spontaneity, it is never casual. For one does not casually pour out one's heart; such passages as these do not flow from a pen held anyhow.

I walked to a little valley yesterday that I longed to show you. I sat on a warm stone there. All the almond flowers were gone, but the trees were in new leaf and they were full of loving, mating birds – quarreling, you know, about whether to turn the stair-carpet under or cut it off straight. And the trees were playing ball with a little breeze, tossing it to each other.

I sat a long while on my stone, then scratched your initials with a pin and came away.

In 1921 Katherine Mansfield left the Riviera for Switzerland. She arrived in May and immediately it began to rain.

The mountains disappeared very beautifully, one by one. The lake became grave, and one felt the silence. This, instead of being depressing as it is in the South, had a sober charm. I don't know how it is with you; but I feel the South is not made *pour le grand travail*. There is *too much light*.

It is as if this letter set the key for those that follow it. One feels in this admission that there can be too much light, an implicit renunciation; not of life – she worships that still; but of her former passionate gesture of living. Henceforward, she is, not resigned, but a little inattentive. She will admit now to past misery, to present hope; formerly hope wore the face of confidence. The thoughts she tells are no longer sudden thoughts; they are long and rather stumbling questionings.

As I was lying here today I suddenly remembered that: 'O ye of little faith!' Not faith in a God. No, that's impossible. But do I live as though I believe in anything? Don't I live in *glimpses* only? There is something wrong, there is something small in such a life.

But she was not a person for theories of existence, opinions bored her. There must be something more real than opinions, more germane to

280

living; so, she complains that all her new friends are known to her only as writers, 'whether they care personally for the smell of tangerines or not I haven't the slightest idea'. She writes, she lives more and more in her stories, for there she can escape from the half-life of the intellect, she can be with the simple people that she likes and with the small complete existences of birds and flowers and tea-spoons. 'I think my story for you will be called *Canaries*. The large cage opposite has fascinated me completely. I think and think about them – their feelings, their *dreams*, the life they led before they were caught, the difference between the two little fluffy ones who were born in captivity and their grandfather and grandmother who knew the South American forests and have seen the immense perfumed sea . . . Words cannot express the beauty of that high, shrill little song rising out of the very stones . . . It seems one cannot escape beauty . . . It is everywhere.'

When Katherine Mansfield died of consumption in 1922[40] it was a natural impulse to think of what English literature had lost by her fate. These letters turn the mind toward a contrary speculation: it may be that her fate has enriched us. It was from her first exile at Bandol that she wrote saying how her stories now came crowding in on her, pursuing her, plaguing her until they were finished, 'and as good as I can do.' From then on she speaks constantly of the things she wants to write about, the way in which she wishes to write. To the life she saw so glitteringly about her from within her personal shadow there was no response that she could make but creation; had it not been for her sickness she might have created less, or less sincerely, in living more. Whether this is so or not there can be no doubt that her manner of writing, her peculiar style, that shifting, shining, reflecting surface, was in large measure due to the circumstances in which she learned her art. For in a fellow-consumptive she recognises and describes the quality.

He has the same disease himself. I recognised his smile – just the least shade too bright and his strange joyousness as he came to meet one – just the least shade too pronounced, his air of being more alive than other people – the gleam – the faint glitter on the plant that the frost has laid a finger on.

281

THIS TRAVELLER

(*O Lovely England*, Walter de la Mare, *Britain Today*, 1954)

A couple of hours ago, I mentioned during a telephone conversation that I had been asked to write about Walter de la Mare. At the end of the line, nothing happened. I waited, and a cautious voice crept out, saying, 'I remember a poem about a cat.' 'There is a poem in his new book,' I continued, 'about bindweed climbing over an old cannon and its dark mouth of woe.'

'Oh!'

It was the same note of ravished acceptance that I first heard forty or more years ago, when the readers of contemporary poetry in my generation were quoting from *The Listeners*, and *Motley, Peacock Pie* and *The Veil* – and a note remarkably similar to the Oh! uttered by people who look through a diminishing-glass and see the quiddity of an ivy-leaf or a coffee-cup or a shelf of folios.

Unfortunately for my metaphor, diminishing-glasses are not in common use, and people who do not possess one are apt to suppose that as a magnifying-glass makes things larger, a diminishing-glass makes things smaller, and that is all there is to it. If this were so, a diminishing-glass would not have the slightest relevance to the work of Mr. de la Mare, or of any true poet. In fact, while the magnifying-glass is chiefly used by connoisseurs and assessors in pursuit of detail, the diminishing-glass is used by artists in pursuit of the whole. It frames, it states, it places; it gives a kind of spatial immortality to the object seen by it.

> *The longed-for summer goes;*
> *Dwindles away*
> *To its last rose,*
> *Its narrowest day.*
>
> *No heaven-sweet air but must die;*
> *Softlier float,*

282

Breathe lingeringly
Its final note.

Oh, what dull truths to tell!
Now is the all-sufficing all
Wherein to love the lovely well,
Whate'er befall.

Stay, thou art fair. It is not for nothing that one of the poems for which Mr de la Mare is best known and best loved is that *Fare Well* whose last stanza begins

Look thy last on all things lovely
Every hour.

The injunction is immanent not only in many of his poems but everywhere in his technical approach. His vision has the slant of farewell, the particular innocence and penetration of that seeing something standing afar and intact in its moment of being – an aspect which will be familiar to anyone who looks through a diminishing-glass. It is significant that in his prose works he often uses the eyes of children, who possess naturally the faculty of timeless uncalculating attention, who are neither surprised nor accustomed. Miss M., of course, is a diminishing-glass in herself. Lawford, in *The Return*, sees out of his own head with the eyes of a dead man. Even in the anthology, *Come Hither*, it is Mr Nahum who chooses and comments, and illustrates, *How many miles to Babylon?* by a picture of a stone tomb, an earthen lamp, and a 'small owl perched in the lower branches of the thick tree above.'

These manoeuvres for getting himself into an ambiguous relationship with his subject are typical of Mr. de la Mare's work in prose, and perhaps indicate a mistrust of the medium. In poetry, he unmasks, and uses only his own unpretexted sensibility. Nothing stood between him and those astonishing vignettes of his earlier poems, with the particular quality of delicate violence which created the young dog with that one flashing comparison of 'teeth like ships at sea,' or John Mouldy, once and forever spied in his cellar, where

> *Far and near, the drip of water*
> *Went whispering about*

– a lyric of which Forrest Reid[41] wrote, 'It is beautiful and it is horrible, and the beauty is like a flickering zigzag play of lightning by which we see the beauty.' A talent for the macabre is a notable ingredient in the earlier poems, and does a great deal to secure that aspect of farewell, that memorability of actual not factual, which Mr. de la Mare has pursued through all his developments. In his mature poems, only a few slender slips of yew are dropped into the cauldron, and the spell is brewed from technical resources. Analysis will show that the poems in which a man interrogates a revenant, a familiar, a sad bird, an empty house, owe their quality of supernatural to adjustments of scansion; the failure of an expected syllable, a shifted beat – devices which build up a lankness and ambiguity in the stanza, or leave gaps through which a cold air seems to blow.

O Lovely England is prefaced by an Author's Note which mentions that many of the poems 'were written years ago, some of them as far back as the second decade of this century' – and does not mention which. Readers should take the hint, and not speculate over dates, for poets grow like trees and not like sums in simple addition. But the poems are so exceedingly diverse that it is perhaps allowable to range them target-wise, some, like the title poem and *Tarbury Steep* seeming to be on the outmost periphery, others on or just off the bullseye of essential de la Mare. There can be no doubt of the centralness of this:

> *Strange – after so many quiet Springs,*
> *Wherein the ever-dwindling sap uprose –*
> *That swallow should return on death-dark wings,*
> *Should bloom a cankered rose!*

The musing quietude, the one stabbing compound adjective, even the small knot in the syntax, are like a distillation of the poetry which Mr. de la Mare had made his own. Yet there is another English poet who – though with surprise – could have signed those four lines: Walter Savage Landor[42]. For a poet who began as a romantic, and whose admirers have admired him for romantic quality, Mr. de la Mare has gone a long way towards being Parnassian. One of the best poems in this collection, *Outcasts*, is Parnassian *pur sang* in its controlled force of feeling and disciplined advance to a faultless climax.

Admirers, especially that tribe of Faithful Admirers, who have known an artist from his youth up and his bib onward, though they cannot divert the artist's progress, can damagingly misjudge his direction. It would be false, by my reading, to review *O Lovely England* as anything more than what Mr. de la Mare says it is: and the word he chooses – he is a master of words – is *relics*. They are his, but he has left them behind. He left them behind when he chose, or his genius chose for him, to proceed from the author of many hauntingly beautiful small poems to the author of a compellingly beautiful long one.

> This Traveller broke at length, toward set of sun
> Out from the gloom of towering forest trees;

When Mr. de la Mare's admirers have ceased to be faithful, and have put on the impartiality of posterity, it will be, I think, *The Traveller* to which their admiration will turn first, and turn again, and finally settle on. They will see it, not as a new departure, but as a culmination, and as the paradise into which he has conducted all his distinguishing traits. The horrible and the beautiful are there, but fused into one unearthly light. The oddity, the play of imagination, has expanded into the calm incredibility of a dream. The slant of farewell has forsaken everything but mental experience, and so becomes an *Ave* instead of a *Vale*. The diminishing-glass presents a landscape that no one but Mr. de la Mare has visited. The element of questioning and resigned cavilling which has made some of Mr. de la Mare's later lyrics seem as though they had been dictated by a revenant Thomas Hardy is changed into a sort of boding fatalism, unequivocal as a ground-bass, and carrying the narrative as a ground-bass carries the chaconne. Even the smallest true elements reappear. In the course of his life, Mr de la Mare has been a great frequenter of churchyards, has interrogated many headstones, written many epitaphs; the stanza of *The Traveller* is the stanza of Gray's Elegy.

A SPECIAL FAILING

*(Madly Singing in the Mountains: An Appreciation and Anthology of
Arthur Waley, ed. Ivan Morris, the Spectator, April, 1970)*

> *There is no one among men who has not a special failing;*
> *And my failing consists in writing verses.*
> *I have broken away from the thousand ties of life:*
> *But this infirmity remains behind.*
> *Each time that I look at a fine landscape,*
> *Each time I meet a loved friend,*
> *I raise my voice and recite a stanza of poetry*
> *And I am glad as though a God had crossed my path.*
> *Ever since the day I was banished to Hsun-yang*
> *Half my time I have lived among the hills.*
> *And often, when I have finished a new poem,*
> *Alone I climb the road to the Eastern Rock.*
> *I lean my body on the banks of white stone;*
> *I pull down with my hands a green cassia branch.*
> *My mad singing startles the valleys and the hills.*

It is from this lyric by Po Chu-i that Ivan Morris draws the title for this
book – part anthology, part commemoration – about Arthur Waley. 'Mad'
is not a word the Western mind immediately associates with Chinese
poetry; but there is a sacred madness of vocation, a detachment, not a de-
rangement, which the poet was expressing and his translator exemplified.
There could not be a more befitting title. Except for the absence of an
adequate index there could not be a more befitting tribute to the man.

It was in 1918 that *A Hundred and Seventy Chinese Poems* startled the
valleys and the hills with a new voice. The voice was quiet, unaffected,
flexible and persuasive. Above all, it sounded sincere. Quietly and
compellingly, it abolished centuries of falsification and freed Chinese

poetry from an imposed *chinoiserie*.

As I remember it (I am fortunate enough to remember it) the riveting thing about this book of translations was the amplitude and manly reality of the poets it revealed. They were live men in a live world; they saw, felt, regretted, enjoyed, loved their friends and honoured their art with a flesh and blood authenticity. They said with exactitude what they wanted to say, and said it without exclamation. Their feet were planted in a real world, their fans were of use to them. Regardless of time and geography, one became attached to them.

In *The No Plays of Japan*, which was published three years later, the nature of the original forbade any such expansion into reality. One was fascinated by something going on behind glass, and two-dimensionally. No is preoccupied with disembodiment. In their wildest agitations, the *dramatis personae* are like paper puppets dancing on strings; and the dramatist who moves them hither and thither is himself fastened to a convention. The form (No means display, *tour de force*) is ritualistically conventional, a colloquy between a questioner and a recluse or a ghost, who is forced to re-enter the anguish of worldly existence. A non-participating chorus, holding fans before their faces, describe what the actor mimes.

Ghosts and the supernatural also figure in *The Tale of Genji*, the novel by Lady Murasaki, on whose six volumes Waley worked for ten years. But in *Genji* the supernatural is only a fitful apparition in a novel about consistently human beings at the mercy of their human passions in a studiously formalised society. When Waley's first volume appeared, *The Tale of Genji* was variously compared to *A La Recherche du Temps Perdu, La Princesse de Clèves*, the novels of Henry James and Jane Austen (incidentally, in its mixture of passion and a contemporary culture it has a queer resemblance to *The Elective Affinities*) The first chapter was read aloud to the Emperor of Japan in 1008 AD. There is no accounting for marvels: but somewhere or other in all achievements there is an element of fortuity. It happened that Murasaki's husband died: she was appointed lady in waiting to the Empress Akiko. A widow, with knowledge of the world, a taste for writing and leisure to meditate on what to a less speculative mind would have been material to gossip about, she wrote a book.

Waley too was favoured by fortuity. In 1913 be was appointed Assistant

287

in the Print Room of the Oriental Department of the British Museum. In order to make a catalogue of the prints he taught himself to read Chinese and Japanese. His curiosity was aroused by the Chinese poems on some of the prints. 'I soon began to feel that I needed guidance, I went to the recently founded School of Oriental Studies, and consulted an old missionary, who was in charge of Chinese studies. He was not at all encouraging. "You'll find that the Chinese are very weak in that line", he said, referring to Chinese poetry. "They have their ancient *Book of Odes* by Confucius, but that is all". However, seeing that I did not look convinced, he kindly said I might go up to the library and see if I could find anything. There was in those days no catalogue and the books were arranged in a rather haphazard way, but I soon discovered hundreds of volumes of poetry. I began to make rough translations of poems that I thought would go well in English, not at all with a view to publication, but because I wanted my friends to share the pleasure I was getting from Chinese poetry.'

From this beginning, Waley's career flowed with the inevitability of water, China flowed on to Japan, poetry to ethics and Taoism – (*Three Ways of Thought in Ancient China*). He was indefatigably industrious (*The Tale of Genji* is twice as long as *War and Peace*), and lightfootedly learned (among the extracts in this anthology is an account of Chinese mathematics, an inquiry as to whether or no Buddha met his death by eating pork – a matter which might have provoked a schism in a less placable religion – a Chinaman's description of Brighton in 1877, a poem by Kubla Khan). In everything he did, that first motive of pleasure remained; each new undertaking was a green cassia branch, the finishing of a new poem an incentive to take the road to further singing. He climbed alone, for though he had many friends – and their recollections of him in this book prove what affection he inspired – he lived secluded in his own purposes, untainted by duty or ambition. This Taoistic withdrawal from worldly fuss is exemplified by his brother's recollection of Waley as a visitor. 'He used to gaze with mild wonder and sympathy at normal domestic routine and was once heard to exclaim "I hope there is nothing I can do to help".' But when Beryl de Zoete[43] was mortally ill he nursed her single-handed for weeks, to save her from going to a hospital.

The river was never diverted from its course. He never travelled east of

Constantinople and could barely converse in modern Chinese or Japanese. Such creditable doings (failure to perform them has sometimes been cited against him) were outside his purpose – the purpose which seized him when he made those first translations because he wanted his friends to share the pleasure he was getting from Chinese poetry. It was a poet's pleasure. Learning and scholarship sheltered it; but a poet's pleasure is a durable passion, if his technique upholds it. His did so pliably, so limpidly, so unaffectedly, that one scarcely notices that he was a master of his native language, too.

At the end of this anthology Ivan Morris includes a group of Waley's own writings: a prose fantasy, *In the Gallery,* which shows his power of keeping a piece of writing just off the ground while keeping it substantial, and a group of poems, sardonic illuminations of the tragedy and stupidity of war. But what will stay long in my mind is a single line, dating from his tenth year (for he was already a poet) and quoted by him in a BBC interview: 'Long lines of banners, horses, men, move across the plain.' It is as though it were waiting for its Chinese original.

AN ENQUIRY INTO THE DECAY IN THE USES OF POETRY
(*Time and Tide*, April 29th, 1927)

In the foreword to his recent *Anthology of Modern American Poetry*, Mr. Louis Untermeyer[44] tells us that for the last decade there has been published on an average five hundred books of poetry a year in the United States alone. In the face of these rousing statistics it may seem a trifle peevish to enquire into an alleged decay in the uses of poetry. It is obvious that poets, at any rate, continue to find poetry very useful indeed – as a form of exercise, as a repository for those thoughts and feelings which make the heart too hot to hold them, as a vehicle for opinions, as a stimulant, as a febrifuge, and as a method of getting one's own back without unduly exposing one's self to a prosecution for libel. Their publishers, too, must believe in the usefulness of poetry as a warrant of culture, as a means of filling up their Spring and Autumn lists, as a method of securing a lien on an author who may one day take to writing something more profitable, such as detective stories or Popular Encyclopaedias of the Varieties of Religious Doubt, as packing, or perhaps as a propitiatory sacrifice to fortune.

But for all this seeming estimation it cannot be denied that poetry, like the frock-coat, is now being dispensed with in situations where it was once considered indispensable. One of the most ominous symptons is the tendency of the other arts to give poetry the cold shoulder. There was a time when Catalogues of the Exhibitions of the Royal Academy were almost as good as little anthologies; and as far as I can remember Turner was the only artist who had the effrontery to supply his own quotations. Novels too offered up a slight compliment to Apollo at the head of each chapter, and, if they were written in the first person by the heroine, dropped into someone else's poetry on every other page at least. Of course there was not much money in this; but there was publicity, and a very valuable goodwill. Now there is scarcely an Academician left who betrays the least acquaintance with any Muse but his own, and the novelists are equally demure. More serious still is the Ourselves Alone attitude of Music. There, at any rate, it seemed, that voice and verse were complementary to each other. But one of the sphere-born harmonious sisters has turned nasty, and composers who wish to show how truly musical they are either apply their strains to prose, or write long cantatas on the syllables Boo and Bah.

Over the defection of music (for since I write as a poet, such I must consider it) I am not so seriously concerned. The setting of a prose text presents such ungratefully obscure difficulties to the composer that I doubt whether the fashion will be a very widespread or lasting one. I do not expect, for instance, that the lyrics supplied to Mr. Cochran[45] or Mr. de Courville[46] will be prose lyrics. As for the Boo and Bah system, something rather similar obsessed music at the time when Addison complained: 'I have known the word And pursued through the whole Gamut, have been entertained with many a melodious The, and have heard the most beautiful graces, quavers, and divisions, bestowed upon Then, For, and From: to the eternal honour of our English particles.' But as it happened the honour was only temporary; and the particles so singled out for illustration were presently put back in their proper place again.

The chapter-motto, however, is I fear a vantage ground irretrievably lost. It must be admitted that with the exception of Scott and George Eliot (both of them black-legs at whiles, writing their own to taste) the premier novelists of the last century were as churlish as those of today. But Scott's practice alone is enough to ensure the custom a niche in the history of literary manners, and has endowed it with one moving association. Readers of Lockhart[47] will remember the passage which describes the old veteran, broken, dazed with mortal sickness, but writing still; how, on Ballantyne's[48] reminding him that a motto was needed for one of the chapters already finished, he looked out of the window for a moment at the gloomy weather, and penned these lines

> *The storm increases – 'tis no sunny shower*
> *Fostered in the moist breast of March or April,*
> *Or such as parched Summer cools his lips with.*
> *Heaven's windows are flung wide; the inmost deeps*
> *Call in hoarse greeting one upon another;*
> *On comes the flood in all its foaming horrors,*
> *And where's the dike shall stop it ?*

and then, constant to the subterfuges, half modest, half mischievous, of the Author of Waverley, added the ascription 'The Deluge: a Poem.'

Two living authors, faithful among the faithless found, must be mentioned here. One, Mr. Kipling, who having begun with mottoes whose aptness was ensured by them being from the author's own hand, has extended the convention into a special form – the poetical prelude and postlude upon the theme of the prose tale; the other, Mr. C. E. Montague[49], whose novel, *A Hind Let Loose*, is embellished by a very sensitive use of this device. One example in particular remains with me. A chapter describing two rival newspapers, the Eatanswill Gazette and the Eatanswill Independent of a Midland manufacturing town, is preceded by these lines from Mrs. Hemans[50]:

> *They grew in beauty side by side,*
> *They filled one home with glee.*

Such potentialities of irony and innuendo might commend back the chapter motto to its former favour; but I am afraid that it is a lost cause.

Creative artists are a fickle breed, and glorify their inconstancy with the name of Innovation. One might have hoped that the general public, that Giant Sloth, would be more steadfast in their affections; but among them too the Decay in the Uses of Poetry is painfully apparent. This will be seen upon considering a list of the principal lay uses of poetry – which I take to be as follows:

> Mortuary: epitaphs and elegies.
> Commercial: either quotations or original dithyrambs.
> Social: Christmas cards and valentines.
> Punitive: 'write out a hundred lines from the Georgics.'
> Domestic: shaving calendars.

All these, save the second, are markedly on the decrease; and I cannot recall any recently invented use for poetry, unless it be, as I was told the other day, that to repeat rhymed verse so fast that the action became purely mechanical was considered by some to be an aid in the cure of stammering.

No! It is a sad look-out. Though the annual output in U.S.A. should rise to one thousand volumes of poetry we should still have only too good reason for concern. One of the gloomiest aspects of this depressing subject is the apathy displayed by the poets themselves. Their colonies are revolting, their empire is slipping from their grasp, and all they can do is to go on writing poetry. Take, for instance the case of the Ode. Who writes Odes nowadays? And yet what a rich province was there, now neglected and uneared! It is indeed surprising that no one has had the enterprise to revive the polite and gratulatory Ode. I believe that such a revival would be welcomed by those Royal and Eminent Personages at present compelled to receive a Danaan shower of massive pieces of plate, or bouquets of scentless pink carnations. Odes would at any rate be a change and take up far less room. Indeed the more I think of it the better I think of it. And I hereby give the Prince of Wales fair warning that if it is ever my good fortune to be presented to him, I shall come before him with an Ode.

NOTES

1   The author's adventures and amours in the Regency world, published in 1825

2   Teresa of Avila (1518-82), Spanish mystic and saint. Works include her autobiography, *The Life of Teresa of Jesus*, and *The Interior Castle*

3   Comtesse de La Fayette (1634-93), author of *La Princesse de Clèves* (1678)

4   Margaret, Countess of Newcastle (1623-73), wrote verse, plays, letters and a biography of her husband

5   Lady Murasaki (c.973-c.1014), Japanese novelist, poet and lady-in-waiting at the Imperial Court. Best known as the author of *The Tale of Genji*

6   See note 3, p.227

7   Hester Chapone (1721-1801), member of the Blue Stocking Circle, writer of verse, essays and letters and friend of Samuel Richardson

8   Elizabeth Carter (1717-1806), member of the Blue Stocking Circle, classicist and friend of Dr. Johnson

9   Twice-weekly periodical issued by and largely written by Dr. Johnson, 1750-52

10 Charlotte Lennox (1720-1804), novelist

11 Fanny Burney (1752-1840), novelist, diarist and letter writer whose first novel, *Evelina*, was published anonymously in 1778

12 Ann Radcliffe (1764-1823), travel writer and leading exponent of the Gothic novel, notably *The Mysteries of Udopho* (1794)

13 Mary Brunton (1778-1818), Scottish novelist

14 Maria Edgeworth (1768-1849), Irish regional novelist whose work influenced Scott

15 Mary Somerville (1780-1872), Scottish science writer, mathematician and astronomer. Somerville College, Oxford is named after her

16 Agnes Paston to her son John Paston, from *The Paston Letters*

17 Julian of Norwich in *Showing of Love*, written perhaps in 1368

18 Mary Wilkins Freeman (1852-1930), prominent c19 American author

19 Mary Martha Sherwood (1775-1851), prolific author, mainly of children's stories

20 Margaret Gatty (1809-73), writer of children's literature

21 Sarah Trimmer (1741-1810), 'Good Mrs Trimmer', author of children's books

22 Aphra Behn (1640-89), novelist, poet and dramatist. The first Englishwoman, according to Virginia Woolf, to earn her living by writing

23 By Horace Walpole, first of the true Gothic novels, published in 1765

24 Charlotte Yonge (1823-1901), children's author and novelist

25 Mabel Leigh Hunt (1892-1971), American writer of adult and children's fiction, often with Quaker themes

26 Lady Dorothy Nevill (1826-1913), writer, horticulturist and plant collector

27 *The Sorrows of Young Werther* by Goethe, the first great 'confessional' novel

28 A novel (1925) by the American writer Theodore Dreiser (1871-1945) based on a notorious criminal case

29 Lytton Strachey (1880-1932), biographer, essayist and prominent member of the Bloomsbury Group. His *Landmarks in French Literature* appeared in 1912

30 Thomas Haynes Bayly (1797-1839), poet, songwriter and dramatist

31 Jane Hester Reilly lived with her sister in Sandgate, Kent

32 George Morland (1763-1804), prolific painter of animals and rustic scenes

33 Francesco Bartolozzi (1725-1815), London-based Italian engraver

34 Sir Nigel Playfair (1874-1934), actor-manager of the Lyric Theatre in the 1920s

35 Rev'd Montague Summers (1880-1948), eccentric author and clergyman known for his work on c17 English drama and the first translation of the c15 witch-hunter's manual, the *Malleus Maleficarum*

36 Aimée Semple Macpherson (1890-1944), American evangelist. Warner saw her at the Albert Hall on October 10th 1928

37 Dorothy Osborne (1627-95). Letters to her husband were published in 1888

38 Marquise de Sévigné (1626-96). Most of her letters, notable for their wit and vividness, were addressed to her daughter

39 W. H. Hudson (1841-1922), naturalist and novelist brought up in South America. Best known for his novel *Green Mansions* (1904) and *A Shepherd's Life* (1910) about a Wiltshire shepherd

40 Near Fontainbleau at the institute run by Gurdjieff

41 Forrest Reid (1875-1947), Ulster novelist

42 Walter Savage Landor (1775-1864), poet

43 Beryl de Zoete (1879-1962), dancer, orientalist and poet. She had a long relationship with Arthur Waley

44 Louis Untermeyer (1885-1977), American poet, anthologist and critic who did much to promote Warner's work in America. He also edited *Modern British Poetry* (1936)

45 C. B. Cochran (1885-1977), theatre manager associated with the work of Noel Coward

46 Joachim de Courville (d. 1581), French Renaissance composer, singer and lutenist

47 John Lockhart (1794-1854), ferocious critic known as 'The Scorpion', principal contributor to *Blackwood's Magazine* and editor of *The Quarterly Review*

48 Either John Ballantyne (1774-1821), Walter Scott's publisher, or his brother James (1772-1833), Scott's Kelso printer

49 Charles Edward Montague (1867-1928), assistant editor of the *Manchester Guardian*, reviewer and drama critic

50 Felicia Dorothea Hemans (1793-1835), poet, popular especially in America

HOME AND AWAY

FEVERELL'S MIDDLESEX
(*The Countryman*, Autumn, 1948)

Talking of childhood, Feverell[1] said that seeing how homesick the middle-aged can be for the scenes of their early youth, and how distressed at finding those scenes altered and impaired, he was glad to be spared any possibility of such pangs. The countryside of his own childhood existed no longer: Greater London had submerged it; it was irrecoverable as Atlantis.

As he remembered it at the turn of the century it was still obstinately a country landscape, though on a clear day he could see the smoke and the smokestacks of London on the south-eastern skyline. In some engravings of the outskirts of London c.1800 one sees the same sharp imposition of city on country, which now, with the development of ribbon building and residential estates, is scarcely, if at all, to be found. Indeed, if he wanted to recall the scenes of his childhood, Feverell said, it was to such prints and engravings that he turned; and he found very much the same aspect of fields and elm coppices, calm Georgian mansions and squat farmsteads, with a rampart of London behind them. The soil – it was a theory of Feverell's that soil determines most things – was the heavy yellow London clay: an excellent soil for what does well in it. The district had formerly been renowned for its wheat, but by his time it was all dairy-farming and hay. London clay makes bad lawns but excellent hayfields. The first piece of country behaviour he ever learned was not to walk through standing hay, and the second was always to shut gates. But it was a country of footpaths, so he had plenty of opportunities to study Middlesex hay at close quarters and to learn how, from day to day, its colouring developed, the first pure green becoming silvered and silver-purpled as the seed-heads expanded, or golden with buttercup; or stained with clover. Irishmen and tramps used to come into the district to be hired for the hay-harvest. With their coming the ditches became exceedingly

297

interesting (all small children study ditches), enriched with thrown-away boots, waistcoats, kettles and blue enamel saucepans.

Once the hay was cut, he said, the fields seemed to grow smaller, lacking the feeling of perspective which is given by the flow of air-currents over the undulating surface of the standing crop. But in any case the fields were small, and closed in by solid hawthorn hedges, old and well-kept. There were many hedgerow elms too, and elms were planted in the middle of pastures to give shade to the cattle. It was under these elms that the drinking-troughs were placed. Everything was kept in good order. Gates were square on their hinges and closed with wooden latches; the stiles were made of oak, shiny with use; the ditches were kept so clean that water actually ran along them instead of stagnating in puddles. He never saw a barbed-wire fence or a pasture full of thistles. The only exceptions to the common tightness and good husbandry were some of the old barns. They had gone out of use when the farmers turned from corn to pasture, and as they shed their tiles in the autumn gales, or as their mortar crumbled and loosened the bricks, their owners did not always trouble to mend them.

These barns were to him romantic and soul-stirring. They were the nearest thing he could find to a real ruin; and the popular art of that date laid great stress on the beauty of ruin and squalor. A cottage in a Christmas number could scarcely be decently represented without some picturesque holes in it; at the least it had to have a broken-backed roof, little peepy windows set in askew, and a general appearance of decrepitude; just as a church had to be heavily draped with ivy before it was suitable for polite eyes. 'But while the Gothic half of me', said Feverell, 'was shuddering delightfully at ruined barns, my everyday seeing was accustoming me and attaching me to a totally different manner of building: the modest, solid, reasonable tradition of brick. There were no grand buildings within the range of my childish walks; but at least there were very few silly ones. Near the canal there were some wooden shingle houses, such as one sees in Essex. These were painted-cream colour, or buff or pale grey – and, though I naturally longed to live in one of them, I also felt that they were somehow slightly perverse and like summer houses. Otherwise, thank God, it was all brick!'

Brick, and clay tiles, he continued, and timber, were the natural building materials of Middlesex, and as proper to the landscape as elm and hawthorn. Some of the farms must have dated from the seventeenth century, built of small dark brick in a timber frame. Many of the later-built cottages were of yellow stock brick, and had nothing very much to commend them except rectangularity and absence of ornament. For the rest, farms and inns and moderate country-houses were Georgian boxes, with a door in the middle, and two stories of fenestration in the frontage, and dormer windows in the roof – but such fenestration, said Feverell, such just proportion between brickwork and glass, and such roofs, hung with narrow, deeply-rutted tiles, and weathered to the colouring of a bed of wall-flowers! Mixed in with these were some early nineteenth-century 'cottages of gentility' – bowers for retired tea-merchants or ladies in keeping. These adhered to the general pattern of symmetry and sobriety, but added a few mild architectural flim-flams – an iron-work balcony, a green copper hood over the door, ogee windows, or a lunette in the pediment. Some of them still preserved their original stables alongside – and English architecture is at its best when housing the horse. Some were painted in dull delicate tints, like sugar-biscuits.

Even the ungenteel cottages of this date, Feverell said, had a kind of elegance. Often they were built in a terrace, with the central cottage distinguished by some formal element – a pediment, or a special doorway, or a label above the door giving the date of building. Urbanity had touched them, though with the lightest touch of its finger-tip; they looked as if they had been built with consideration. And at that date nobody admired them at all; a shapeless lump of whitewashed cob with a thatch roof was what a cottage had to be before it could be admired. The people who lived in them, however, liked them a great deal, and trimmed their door-steps with pairs of large pink-and-white shells washed every Saturday, or with potted geraniums, and were always touching up the paint or clipping their box borders, or edging the little flower-beds in front with scallop-shells or whitewashed stones or fanciful wire scrollings or rows of stone ginger-beer bottles set in bottom uppermost. It was rare to see a trollopy exterior. As for the gardens, the choice of flowers was conditioned by the stiff clay soil: there was generally a standard rose in the centre of the flower-bed, there was often a lilac in one corner, and for the rest it was wallflowers, Brompton stocks, Canterbury bells, the common iris, London pride, and always white garden lilies, of which the secret was to plant them tight and leave them alone.

Whether in terraces or isolated, these cottage dwellings were placed functionally. 'I mean', he said, 'in regard to need, not by habit. There were no villages in the landscape of my childhood. The former villages had solidified into little towns. So the cottages stood where they were handy for farms, or for small local industries, or as appendages to coaching inns or country houses, or because some one had wanted a cottage just there. One sees the same disposition of dwelling-houses in France often enough. And in the north of England too, for that matter. But it is not recognised as typical of the English manner of life because our experts in rurality are obsessed with the village, and the village community clustering round the manor-house and the church – a more amenable social unit, I daresay, but not the only expedient for living in the country. Speaking for myself,' Feverell continued, 'having grown up under this dispensation, nothing would induce me to live penned up in a village. A plain-headed brick cottage, flowers in front, cabbages at the back, a tarred shed on one side, and nothing round it but the autumn mists rising out of a clay soil – that is my idea of rural domesticity'.

Seeing his friend smile he said: 'Yes, I know what you are thinking – that clay soil. When you cut into it with a spade it was like cutting into a cheese, a Stilton cheese. But one can't remember a clay country without being constantly aware of its soil. It is a ghost that can't be laid. It climbs up in the elm trees, it wanders about at dusk in the smell of the may-blossom or the brickworks; you carry it indoors on your boots, you carry it in your bones as rheumatism, it shapes the landscape and colours it. A clay landscape is always a painting in oils, a landscape of heavy, powerful colours well rubbed into the canvas. And when the autumn fogs varnish it, it looks as rich as a plum cake. But I was talking about a tarred shed. I mustn't forget those intense black notes in my Middlesex landscape. All the wooden outbuildings, from the long milking-sheds in the farmyards to the little tool-sheds and privies in the cottage back-gardens, were tarred a solemn universal black, and often the weather sides of the houses were given a black coat too. The farms, particularly, had a grandly melancholy appearance, their black outbuildings gathered round brilliant slime-green horse-ponds. So it was very appropriate that the bird of the locality should be the rook. Every grove, every spinney, had a rookery. I think I was never out of earshot of rooks cawing. I woke to them every morning, and fell asleep to them every night.

'Except for a couple of months in late spring when all the hawthorns came into bloom, all the lilacs and laburnums, and the red and white horse-chestnuts, and bloomed with the exuberance of a kermesse in Flanders, it was not, I suppose, a gay landscape, and certainly not a picturesque one. But children don't require gaiety, and only understand the picturesque in terms of Wardour Street. In real life they are as indifferent to it as the true artist is. Holidays took me to the sea, to bluebell woods, to mountains in Wales or villages in Devon. I enjoyed the amenities, and returned to be satisfied with flat fields, well-kept hedges, dusty roads, rational houses, brick cottages with tarred sheds, a walk to the canal, a view of the gasworks – and to my special private sensations, which were dear to me because I had come to them entirely by myself. No one bad told me to see with a particular thrill – it was almost a religious awe – the row of poplars along the railway embankment. Except that it was a place where I could pick up chestnuts, no one had directed me into the mossy avenue where I used to feel myself watched and mothered by the broad, mild countenance of a forsaken Georgian mansion – it was in chancery, they said, which meant exactly nothing to me. No one had told me to admire the emphatic blackness of the tarred farm-buildings under the canary-yellow pattern of the October elms against the dove-coloured clouded sky. And certainly no one bad told me to look with intensity at this part of Middlesex because in another thirty years it would be gone for ever.

'I suppose I heard them talking about it. I must have. But the talk of parents is always full of angers and grievances, and as they never do anything about them one soon learns to discount it. For that matter, I could have seen for myself what the future must bring. There were the new houses by the railway station – a little colony of them, all gables and roughcast and fancy timbering. And each had a mangy little lawn and a fanciful gate with a fanciful name on it. And when the evening train had come in – the six o'clock – you could hear all the latches of those gates clicking, one after another, like a clock-maker's shop, as the city gentlemen came home from the city. When I was a little older I used to go that way and watch the new houses being put up, and talk to the builder's men. There was a very friendly plumber, I remember, and once he let me help him to put a bath in. But what child ever puts two and two together? I saw my world being nibbled away, and continued to live in it as though it, and I too, were eternal.'

'And those new houses, with their gables and roughcast and fancy timbering'; said his friend, 'were you so immunised by your Georgian brick that you did not admire them?' Feverell laughed: 'I didn't admire them. But to be honest, I dare say I would have thought them wonderful if my architectural high-mindedness had not been reinforced by a good dose of social snobbery. The people who lived in them, you see, were the sort of people my mother called "mere". They wore the wrong kind of shoes, and bought their groceries at the new multiple store, and used printed invitation cards, and talked about "running up to town". We still said "going to London"'. 'And you have never been back?' 'Yes, once. It was about ten years ago. I went by train and walked about a little. They were still there, those houses by the railway station. They were the only things I could recognise. But I can't say that time had improved them.'

LOVE GREEN
(*The Nineteenth Century and After*, Vol 112, August, 1932)

Described in the county directory as a hamlet, Love Green[2] lies among the seaward-swelling chalk downs, approached by a lane that leaves it only to scramble round a green hill and rejoin the main road. It is an agricultural village, and this may be seen by the architectural predominance of its barns, that rise stone-built and massive among the cottages. Even the ricks and haystacks overtop the roofs of thin slate or threadbare thatch. Being an agricultural village, it is a poor one. Year by year husbandry decays, and the large squares and oblongs of arable that look like carpets tightly stretched upon the contours of the downs show by their colour the invasion of thistles and sorrel and the resurgence of flint. Year by year fewer men are employed upon the land, and the physical standard both of labourers and draught horses grows lower. Upon one farm in Love Green a mule is used; another, for cheapness sake, is worked by old men and boys.

At one end of the village is the church, at the other the inn[3]. Here, two years ago, a badger-baiting was held. From one of the few badger earths in this part of England – a ruinous city of earthy tunnels – a female badger was dug out and carried in a sack to the inn. News of the proposed frolic went round, and every man who owned a dog or loved sport went up to drink that evening. A ring was made and the badger loosed into it. As it turned this way and that from the dogs a kick and a shout stopped its escape, till, fighting sullenly, it met its end.

The inn provides other traditional games, though not such stirring ones. Shove-halfpenny and rings are played there, and, if someone can be found to put up the money, Will Francis will perform his celebrated feat of drinking eleven pints at a sitting. This achievement is interesting as a rarity; but Will Francis is not an enlivened drinker, even upon eleven pints. Intellect tells, even in a country public; and Jimmy Matthews[4], the 'enlightened man' of Love Green, is by far the best company among those who visit the inn. Jimmy is a reader, one who enjoys, as he said himself, 'books of any nature, poetical, historilolical, or Scriptural,' and being lent Lecky's *History of European Morals*, found it much to his taste. He also spent a whole day sitting on the green reading Marcus Aurelius, but did not think so much of him. Theology is Jimmy's forte. When on March 23 he wished me, with every cordiality, a Happy New Year, he added that if I had any religious doubts I had only to apply to him; and if my religion were substantial enough to support doubts, I daresay I would do so. On this occasion he was about half seas over; but I have been assured that when Jimmy is thoroughly glorious he begins to recite the Bible by heart, and cannot be stayed, however urgently his fellow-drinkers protest at this interruption upon the ordinary tavern conversation of scandal, bawdry, the weather, and social injustice.

Few women visit the inn. Those who do so are of the old school. The remainder, who either have pretensions to gentility or ape such pretensions, send there for beer or whisky and drink it at home. It is common too, to make home-made wines – carrot, mangold, elderberry, parsnip – and, more rarely, mead for domestic drinking. These home-drinkers certainly do not drink less than the inn-goers, and from the point of view of social pleasantness the custom is to be deplored, since it increases the suspicion and narrow-mindedness which are cankers of village life.

During the winter Love Green joins with the next village in fortnightly whist drives. But these, since prizes are awarded, cannot be classed as anything so light and trivial as mere social relaxation. They are attended in a spirit of religious cupidity, and on the morrow the winner of a set of pink-handled tea-knives, a china biscuit-barrel, or a cigarette-case walks out with the strained simper of one who has roused the envy and fury of mankind. So solemn, indeed, are these orgies that the unfortunates whose state exposes them to the levy of fortnightly prizes dare not give below the level of expectation; and the level is a rising one, since it is known who gave what, and to give the handsomest prize is equal in glory, if not in satisfaction, to being its winner. A member of the prize-giving class in Love Green pays, I suppose, anything from £3 to £4 yearly upon this score – a ridiculous and unprofitable mulct, since the convention of good manners demands that the prizes should always be of a completely useless nature.

There is, of course, the expedient of giving the booby prize. Once, some years ago, this was awarded to a girl in the neighbouring village, who took the matter so much to heart and was so badly teased about it that she drowned herself.

Such are the diversions of Love Green. The games of its children are even more closely in touch with real life. The smallest among them play, as all very young children do, by pretending to be their elders; but once infancy is outgrown they turn to the traditional rural sports of harrying strangers, teasing the half-wit, and tormenting animals. The nature study learned in the school has put a slightly different complexion upon this last sport. But whether the victim be called a stickleback or a 'minnie' it meets the same underheel end. Meanwhile, in the economy of Nature, the elder boys harry, tease, and torment the children and any half-grown girl they can lay their hands on.

Yet, among the older folk of Love Green, there is a legend that its children were once well-behaved. That was thirty odd years ago, when Mr Pagan[5] was parson here. In Mr Pagan's days every family received at Christmas beer, a joint of beef, and a plum pudding. Each new-born child was inspected and a half-sovereign wedged into its small grasp; any older child who, playing, chanced to butt itself against Mr Pagan's legs or muddy his broadcloth trousers with a hoop was likely to get half a crown, and those who had come to a competent age and attended the confirmation classes were refreshed with chocolates. In Mr Pagan's day no one who went to the parsonage for succour was ever turned away, and the church was always full, for a score at least sang in the choir, and those who were not qualified to do this attended in order to hear the singing and watch the children parading the church behind the gold cross with a crimson jewel in it. Nor did Mr Pagan neglect that most important part of a parson's duty – to give his parish something to wonder at on weekdays; for it was his custom to drive through the village in a swift gig, preceded by eight black dogs leashed together in couples.

A materialistic Eden, no doubt, in the light of present-day use, when few people of Mr Pagan's mind or means go into the church, and when flocks are chiefly edified by the gifts of the spirit. Nor, from those who remember him, have I heard a word breathed that might suggest that Mr Pagan had quickened their spiritual life. He is remembered as a generous man and a stout drinker, just such another shepherd in his own line as is Mr Kid of Love Green – Mr Kid whose sheep always fetch good prices, who never nicks a ewe at sheep-shearing, whose dogs cringe at his enormous bellow, and who, on summer evenings, may be seen in his garden trimming the heads of the Love Green labourers with a pair of sheep-shears. Yet Mr Pagan's influence is still discernible in those who grew up under his regiment. They preserve a certain good humour and natural self-respect which not even the acrimony, vanity, and squalor of village life has quite obliterated. They themselves are well aware that things have changed for the worse. Love Green was different in old Pagan's time, they say, in the days when it had a parson of its own. Actually, Mr Pagan had a successor before the parish was amalgamated with its neighbour, and so lost a resident cleric. But he, being a poorer man, giving away less and keeping no retinue of dogs, counts for nothing in the village memory; not even the fact that he went mad at his wife's funeral has endeared him to posterity.

Now, once a Sunday, the three church bells jangle their ditty for a formal minute or two, and the churchgoers walk up the road. It is a slender congregation. The old guard, Mr Pagan's remnant, attend pretty regularly, still holding to the belief that to put on their best clothes and join in the hymns is in some way a right and proper proceeding. The remainder attend only when they feel some special call to do so. Their reasons are various: a new pair of boots, a well-combed child to exhibit, a recent death in the family, or a smoky chimney. It is only for harvest festival that the whole village turns out to admire the decorations, the pulpit with straws in its hair, the font wearing moss gaiters, the phenomenal cabbage before the altar, the vegetable roasts of apples, marrows, and potatoes balanced along the hot water pipes, and to listen to the anthem – a yearly hazard, like the Derby. Deeply and contentedly excited they throng creaking in, and crowd the pews and sing, whatever the season, 'Now thank we all our God' with enthusiasm. The offerings go to the local hospital; and on the morrow everyone agrees that they are wasted there, thrown away or eaten by the nurses, with chapter and verse of how, when our Sheila was in, she never so much as set eyes on an egg or a good plateful of greens. But that is no bar, when harvest festival comes round again next year, to giving the crispest savoy or the finest beetroot, for the offerings are made to nothing so immaterial as a God or so concrete as an institution. Love Green is incapable of worship; but somewhere in their world, perhaps under the green hill, lurks a deity or demiurge, and it is this being, curiously compounded of manure and the weather, that they propitiate.

If the religion of Love Green is a trifle behind the times, its politics are up to date. Those who bestir themselves to think at all are Communists, and the rest, who know at any rate that something must be wrong with a world where wages are so low and summers so rainy (though the wireless is the likeliest cause of that), follow their lead. Every village has its Robespierre, and the Robespierre of Love Green is Mr Taddy, who understands everything. Mr Taddy is a small man, reddish and diligent, like an ant. So deep is his scorn for a capitalist society that it is his boast that he will beat his children within an inch of their lives if ever he hears them use a servile 'sir' or 'ma'am'. Meanwhile, by exemplary industry, enterprise and thrift, he has become the richest man in the village, and will shortly buy a car.

Mrs Taddy[6] is a Communist also, noticeably whenever her rival, young

Mrs Trey[6] appears in a new dress or buys new household gear. For the discontent of Love Green, that might seem so well justified by what people lack, is in truth aroused by what other people have. In the years since the war a new standard of living has been imposed upon the old, but imposed as paraffin upon water; it is the upper layer only that is kindled by discontent and flares up in anger and threatenings. In Love Green there are only outdoor privies; water has to be caught from the roof gutters or drawn from wells liable to contamination; the cottages are small and inconvenient, some barely weatherproof, and infested with vermin. These conditions are accepted without a murmur. No one minds the prospect of living for ever without a vestige of plumbing, or packing three into a bed, but not to be able to afford a wireless fills them with fury and resentment. When young Lucy Mendicott[6] came back from the sanatorium to die of tuberculosis, the fact that the one place where she could sleep apart from her family was the larder-cum-pantry was taken for granted, calling for no comment unless it were the remark that now she could get at the sugar whenever she pleased; but even down-draggled Mrs Mendicott, the poorest woman in the village, so poor that her children are fed upon biscuits and bottled lemonade, has spirit left enough to rail at a social scheme which denies her a string of imitation pearls and a fur coat.

This deep feeling for superfluities is not a new thing in village life or in human nature. But it is now of such rampant dimensions that it must be counted as a new social factor. At the level of life in Love Green materialism is inevitable, for in the pinch of not having the lust for possession is biologically quickened as a compensation. Winter sets squirrels hoarding, and the cottage living-room, unwieldy with belongings, is as sure a sign of poverty as the room poverty has swept bare. But now the Love Green appetite for possessions is fed upon biscuits and bottled lemonade, and is fast losing the taste for anything more solid. If proof be needed as to how this passion for rubbish is sweeping the countryside, the reader has only to visit a London Woolworth's and one in a country town and compare the wares sold in one and the other. The very cheapness and accessibility of these toys inflame the breasts that pant after them. When the Mrs Taddy of a previous generation outpaced her Mrs Trey it was by something solid – a marble-topped wash-stand or a set of grand fire-irons; and, however sternly Mrs Trey resolved to get even with Mrs Taddy, a certain time must elapse before enough money could be saved up for the riposte. But in this warfare of trumpery there is no time for desire to settle down into intention, or envy grow tired of watching the rival.

Meanwhile Mrs Taddy and Mrs Trey continue to fetch water from the same dubious well. The open quarrels and clapper-clawing that might have eased their ancestresses are not possible to them. Love Green has long known that it is low to quarrel – such doings may be left to the gipsies. So Mrs Taddy and Mrs Trey commend, with distant civility, each other's wall-flowers, or inquire, with pale, set faces, after each other's cats. Not even the intimacy of open hate is allowed them by their code of respectability. Their husbands stand apart from these dissensions – such things are women's work. But in such a community as Love Green any social relationship is women's work. The labourer, a-field for eight hours, walking perhaps two or three miles to his work, only knows his village as the place where he sleeps, breakfasts, sups, keeps his wife and children, and visits the inn. At the inn he meets other such tired animals as himself, and treats with them with an animal gregariousness, the comradeship of a team of cart-horses.

The fate of Love Green as a village – that is to say, as a compacted unit in English country life – is in the hands of its women. If they fritter away that feeling of community which has bonded village life since first men built their mud huts neighbourly together for the mutual society, help and comfort that they looked for and were even, in the necessarily slighter degree, prepared to give, there is nothing to save it from disintegration, from falling away, like an old lavender bush, from its dead centre. The church is powerless; the inn, under the attacks of respectability and refinement, is fast losing what power it had. Even badger's blood gave but a temporary fillip; and now the badger's earth is forsaken. Of the three sizeable houses in the village, whence one might expect some show of leadership, two belong to farmers who cannot manage even their own affairs; the third is let to a lady who is so busy organising county uplift that she scarcely knows the names of her neighbours. And even if one rose from the dead, from the extinct class of the squirearchy that produced Mr Pagan, it is doubtful if it would be of any avail. The atavistic feudalism of Love Green is worn very thin now, cadging old Mrs Tibbs with her curtseys, and a general aptitude to toady, its last manifestations. Yet the feeling of a common lot is still in existence among the Love Green women, however it may be smothered under a desire to seem superior to one's neighbour – so superior that one would prefer to having nothing to do with her. Women, by nature so much more susceptible to change than men, are by circumstance much more deeply tethered to permanence; and, confronted with a really rousing scandal or a saliently unfortunate childbed, Mrs Taddy and Mrs Trey will cast off their touch-me-not civility, gossip heart to heart at the well, or hurry up the road together to offer their services.

Such puffs of accident will rouse up and flame from the core of the old fire. But it seems doubtful how much longer it will last under the steady drench of new influence. Indeed Love Green is now so little a true community, so increasingly a fortuitous collection of dwelling-houses, that perhaps it is idle and epimythean to look for saving virtue in anything out of the past. With the decay of farming the labouring class is becoming migratory – people come to the village, stay for a year or two, and then are dismissed or move off in search of something better; motor transport brings town commodities and town novelties to the cottage door, education and the newspaper direct attention away from the village to the advantages of genteel professions or what is being worn on the Lido; and if any commendation of rusticity reaches Love Green it is of the folk-dancing, rustic pottery, sun-bonnet-rural kind – so many hand-made nails in the coffin of rural life. An adjunct to its tall barns and rickyards, Love Green waits upon tillage, and from the very decline of the old order draws a certain outward permanence – the little-changing aspect of something too weak to register change; but if there should ever come a revival of agriculture the facade which yet screens the change of heart must crumble, and Love Green be a village no longer, but instead, what even now it harkens to be, a small west of England Middletown.

BATH

(from *Somerset*, Vision of England, 1949)

Some towns are indifferent to the quarters of the compass. Approach them as you please they will turn you much the same face – usually rather a dull one. Others, like Edwardian beauties, have a right or a left profile. One of the pleasures of becoming on intimate terms with such towns (as perhaps with Edwardian beauties) is the discovery of the charms of an uncelebrated aspect. But this is all geography and masonry. History has a word to say also. A wind out of the past rustles the pages of the guide-book, and if one is to arrive properly one must have that wind behind one. Bath lies at the end of a westward journey, and is attained by the London-Bath road.

'If you leave me to suggest our destination, I say Bath.' It was Mr. Pickwick who said it, adding, as a reason in keeping with the aims of the Pickwick Club, 'I think none of us have been there.'

This seems a shocking admission for a reputable grown-up English gentleman with a taste for travelling. But when Mr. Pickwick spoke Bath was falling into its nineteenth century sleep. Cheltenham was more fashionable, foreign 'cures' were beginning to supersede English spas, and the healing Art was moving away from anything so mild as 'taking the waters' in favour of Lady Southdown's Black Draught and Mr Carlyle's Blue Pills. Deeply as one must compassionate the victims of Victorian medicine, those who endured the penitential nastiness of its tonics, the awful fervour of its pills and purges, one has to be thankful that during the Victorian age Bath was out of fashion. It would not look as it does, otherwise. The Pump Room, for instance, would have been re-modelled to resemble the waiting-room of a gothic railway-station (so much more in keeping with the Abbey opposite); a large and Lombardic hospital in yellow and blue brick would have broken the monotony of Royal Crescent; the Assembly Rooms would have been pulled down (thus sharing the fate of nineteen of Wren's City churches) long before Goering sent out German bombing-planes by Baedecker; and as the century ripened a dismal flounce of something like Bournemouth would have draped the environs. Thanks to calomel, and later, ozone, these improving touches fell elsewhere. Bath remained an eighteenth century town, and

310

towards the close of the century became more of a Roman one; for it was in 1878 that the City Corporation set their architect, Major Davis, to excavate Aquae Sulis systematically.

The Romans travelled to Aquae Sulis by Pontes (which is the river crossing at Staines) and Calleva Atrebatum (which is Silchester) if they came from the southern half of Britain; or through Corinium Dubonorum (which is Cirencester) if they came from the north. Either way, at the close of their journey they passed beneath the hill and British stronghold of Solsbury. Sul of the hill and the hot springs in the valley below was a British deity before she became the goddess Sul-Minerva. The Roman was kindly disposed towards deities; he accepted them wherever he found them and (almost as though he were a Scotsman) traced cousinships with deities of his own. Minerva, an armoured goddess, was a patron of medicine too: she could be comfortably cousined to a British goddess presiding over a healing spring and a fortressed hill-top.

Sul, a British Goddess, is the hostess of Bath. The first recorded bathers are, of course, Prince Bladud's pigs. Seeing them look so much the better for their wallow Bladud wallowed too, and was cured of his leprosy. Then, being a proper prince of Britain once more, he built a city and a temple, and finally fastened winged shoes to his feet and jumped off the temple roof in an endeavour to fly by Art-Magic. Bladud is a very fine early specimen of the English eccentric, and I daresay he closely resembled Walter Savage Landor.

The pigs bathed. In all probability the Britons bathed. They were heathen, and the heathen are usually given to bathing. Then came the Romans, and made a Roman city. Aquae Sulis was in essentials very much like a later Bath: there were the Thermae, and Sul-Minerva's temple, and a forum, and a few houses, some of which I suppose let lodgings. The Roman habit of inscribing on stone, which makes them so comfortable to antiquarians, allows us to know some of the people who visited Bath, or died there: a town councillor, a sculptor, soldiers of the Sixth and the Twentieth Legions. Other visitors came from Northern Gaul, and no doubt the overseers of the lead mines in the Mendips came to Aquae Sulis for a little relaxation and to do some shopping. The great bath, by the way, is floored with Mendip lead of Roman making.

It is melancholy to think of the last days of Aquae Sulis, and of the backward glances which must have been cast at the kind, safe city, and of the valetudinarian regrets of those who knew they had bathed for the last time in those 'three hot springs, of a blewish & sea-colour, which exhales a thin sort of mist, and something of an ill-savour'.[7] As for Sul, she went back to her dower house hill, for a Christian country had no use for her. Good stone blocks, however, are always useful. Though the Saxons made havoc of Bath, a monastic foundation settled in the ruins, and was a well-established Benedictine house by Domesday Book. In 1090 John de Villula, Bishop of Wells, moved his see to Bath, 'which occasioned some hot disputes between the Monks of Bath and the canons of Well'[8] – disputes now peacefully interred in the double title of the see. Six centuries of grass must have laid a good stout wadding over the Roman baths by this time, though the memory of the healing spring still persisted; in the 12th century Bishop Reginald founded a hospital (we should call it a hostel: the hospital of the Middle Ages succoured the sick but did not undertake to cure them) for poor people who came to use the waters.

It is unlikely that Bath had more than a hole-and-corner sort of reputation during the Middle Ages. Its hot springs were never baptised into Christianity, no saint took charge of them. Possibly Sul on her hill was too near a neighbour. The western church was chary of poking up old local deities[9]. I said that travellers along the Bath road travel westward. There is one notable exception. I cannot see the Wife of Bath travelling any way but eastward. The morning sun shines on her broad face under her flapping broadbrimmed hat, and brightens her scarlet hose and her business-like spurs as she sets out on one of her jaunts.

> *Thries hadde she been at Ierusalem,*
> *She hadde passed many a straunge strem,*
> *At Rome she hadde been, and at Boloigne,*
> *At Galice at Seint Jame, and at Coloigne.*
> *She koude muchel of wandrynge by the weye.*

And no doubt she was well acquainted with The George at Norton St. Philip, which is a very agreeable reflection.

The Wife of Bath represents Bath during those centuries when it was a place where people lived, rather than where people visited. Looms clacked, church bells rang, the Guild of Weavers held its feasts and its acrimonious committee meetings. An error on the part of time which I bitterly deplore is that the Wife of Bath was dead before Bishop King enriched the front of Bath Abbey with the sculptures of Jacob's Ladder. I am sure she would particularly have enjoyed the angels head-downwards.

Trade was not so brisk in the seventeenth century, and Bath had grown 'a verrie little poore cittie' when antiquarianism became fashionable and Bath a place to visit. Evelyn came here during that tour when he showed his young wife the beauties of England. He bathed, though Mrs Evelyn did not. Thirty-four years later Pepys was: 'up at four o' clock, being by appointment called to the Cross Bath, where we were carried one after another. And by and by much company came; very fine ladies; and the manner pretty enough, only methinks it cannot be clean to go so many bodies together in the same water. Strange to see how hot the water is; and in some places, though this is the most temperate bath, the springs so hot as the feet not able to endure. But strange to see, when men and women herein, that live all the season in these waters, that cannot but be par-boiled, and look like creatures of the bath! I staying above two hours in the water, home to bed, sweating for an hour; and by and by comes musick to play to me, extraordinarily good as ever I heard in London almost, or anywhere. 5s' [10]

A Fellow of the Royal Society and a buyer of new books, Pepys no doubt had read the *Account of the Bath Waters* in the *History of the Worthies of England: endeavoured by Thomas Fuller. D.D.*

Having explained that the waters contained *Bitumen, Niter*, and *Sulphur*, Fuller continues:

'But how these waters come by their great heat, is rather controverted than concluded among the Learned. Some impute it to Wind, or Airy Exhalations, included in the Bowels of the Earth, which by their agitation and attrition (upon Rocks and narrow passages) gather Heat, and impart it to the waters.

'Others ascribe it to the heat of the sun, whose Beams, piercing through the pores of the Earth, warm the Waters, and therefore anciently were called Aquae Sol is, because both dedicated to, and made by the Sun.

'Others attribute it to Quicklime, which we see doth readily heat any water cast upon it, and kindleth any combustible substance put therein.

Others referre it to a Subterreanean Fire, kindled in the Bowels of the Earth, and actually burning upon *Sulphur* and *Bitumen*.

'Others impute the heat (which is not *destructive*, but *generative*, joyned with moisture) to the fermentation of several Minerals.'

After all this, the wary Fuller contents himself by remarking: 'The worst I wish these Waters is, that they were handsomely roof'd over.'

Gentlemen have never been more handsomely roofed than at this period, and it is pleasant to imagine the chestnut, the black, and the golden periwigs shining against the grey stone, parties of elegant visitors strolling through the narrow streets, climbing the green hillsides, eating chicken and kissing girls. But there was a boorish and raffish element too, which hung about Bath to pick up what it could at cock-fights and card-tables. 'Splenetic, rustic, and vulgar' – so Goldsmith described the company at pre-Augustan Bath. It took a genius in manners, a genius in architecture, and a philanthropist, to make Bath beautiful, distinguished, and respectable (though even then Wesley must needs call it 'the head-quarters of Satan'). The genius in manners was Beau Nash. Nash had come to Bath to make his living as a gambler, but with a gambler's daring staked his career on the turn of the wheel which had brought politeness and urbanity uppermost. Himself neither polite nor urbane, he became Bath's Arbiter of Elegance. He abolished boots from the Pump Room. He put down the wearing of swords and spurs. He chastised the Englishwoman's assumption that anything will do to wear in the country. He enforced cleanliness, early hours, orderly behaviour. He got the streets paved and lighted. He combated rowdy *sederunts* in taverns by building Assembly Rooms where people could game on light refreshments. At the same time he kept every one well amused, and attracted more and more persons of distinction. When the Abbey bells rang for the arrival of some notable visitor the company left card-tables, medicinal sipping, conversation, and divine service (Nash, however, had made going to church part of the fashionable routine) to run out and see who had come now. Never had Satan's headquarters been more civilly organised, and a proof of this is the fact that Selina, Countess of Huntingdon, that evangelical Semiramis, and one of Satan's most ardent adversaries, lived in Bath herself.

So much for the genius in manners. The philanthropist was Ralph Allen, who did good by stealth and gave two hundred guineas to Fielding.

He came to Bath as a post office clerk, devised and carried out his own postal system, grew rich, bought the Combe Down Quarries, and set himself to convert Bath into a city which in politeness and urbanity of building should match the politeness and urbanity of Beau Nash's society. The project was practical – but I really cannot think it was less philanthropic for that.

'The ashlar back-yards of Bath' – so Thomas Hardy asserted – 'have more dignity than any brick front in Europe.' I suppose this is partly an expression of the architect's feeling about stone; and certainly Bath's backyards are very dignified, and some streets and squares of fallen fortunes near the railway had a sombre majesty beyond even Dublin's Belisarius slums.[11] But the stone-built dignity of Bath is compounded with many of the qualities one associates with the best style of brick: qualities of moderation and sobriety and – one might almost say – prudence. When you recover from the excitement aroused by the longitudinal magnificence of Wood junior's Royal Crescent or the sweep of Wood senior's Circus you realise that the unit on which the whole is built up is a dwelling-house, a dwelling-house whose dimensions are stately, but still human. Bath is a conversational city: when the situation justifies it, as in the two great Crescents, the conversation rises to eloquence – but never to rhetoric. The contribution of a third architect, Robert Adam's Pulteney Bridge, is like a summary of Bath's grand-mannered conversational style. The arches, making their nobly proportioned sentence about the River Avon, carry a street of small shops across it.

It is Allen and the first Wood we have to thank for the design of Bath, from the Parades which border the river to the streets and terraces which make the hillside as positive as a facade. Uniformity of building material, conformity of style, have much to do with this effect. But there is a quality in the layout of Georgian Bath which is more often found in the elevation of one great building than in the arrangement of a town.

As one looks at this architectural hillside it becomes peopled with names in the Dictionary of National Biography just as the west front of Wells Cathedral is peopled with names from holy writ. There is Queen Square, where Miss Austen liked the lodgings 'with dirty quilts and everything comfortable' (I pause to disagree with editors who suggest *dimity* as an alternative reading to *dirty*) and hoped that the Duchess of

315

York's removal would make the price of salmon more reasonable. There is New King Street, where William Herschel discovered the planet Uranus (in his spare time, for he was a professional musician). There is the Circus, where Gainsborough set up his easel. There is Gay Street, with Fanny Burney on one side of it and Mrs Piozzi on the other, there is Rivers Street where Prince Bladud Savage Landor expressed his individualism by liking Bath in mid-nineteenth century, and up there in Lansdown Crescent the old Beckford, a smoky beacon, ended his days. That is one way of looking at this view. In another mood it resembles an interior wall of Bath Abbey, a mosaic of moderately distinguished, unselfquestioning good society. When I have been inside Bath Abbey for a minute or two I become aware of a sort of well-bred English mumble going on all round me. Heavens, what quantities of people are here! It is ridiculous to look about for celebrities, no doubt they abound, but then there are so many others, who to themselves are just as well worth celebrating: for here is an Admiral, and here is a Divine, and there a Member of the Privy Council, and there a Gentleman eminent for Unaffected Piety, and there the Daughter of an Earl. And here, almost under my right foot, is *Evan Lloyd, of Pengwerne, Esq.*; and in that compact assertion what a mountain of Welsh pedigrees!

When one has admired the facade of Bath from below one should climb those steep streets and consider Bath from above. Trees emerge like fountains, roofs coalesce and slide downhill, the river crooks itself round the peninsula. There is the Abbey, and the pavement in front of it where the pigeons strut with so much deportment, and the Pump Room, the Roman Baths, the hot springs. There, rimmed by the solemn Roman masonry, in the water that reflects the sky and one's contemporary face as one leans over, is the eye of Bath . . . a green eye; for the 'blewish and sea-coloured' water leaves an orange stain, and these tints between them make up a smouldering lime-green. The three springs pour out half a million gallons a day. Their volume has never been known to alter, their temperatures never vary. They are radio-active. It is probable that they rise from a depth in the earth's crust not less than 5,000 feet. It is a queer experience to look into the well-shaft of the Hot Spring. As the heavy metal doors swing open one sees a pit in the rock, and a rising steam moistens one's face and fills one's nostrils with the odour that was old and mysterious long before a Roman nose snuffed it. This steam, rising with such gentle drowsy force, makes the stone-built city seem ephemeral. The Roman masonry, the old city walls, the Georgian town, the stone terraces rising one above another, are no more than the concentric petals of a rose. The sculptor from Cirencester, the ravaging Saxon King, the long line of Abbots and Bishops, the Georgian notabilities, the innumerable people who have come here in search of health, of entertainment, of history, of husbands ('I had a small property, and I went to Bath. Several of my friends had found charming husbands at Bath. However, time slipped away, madam, and by some strange fatality or other, I exhausted my little resources, and did not manage to get settled in life: that is the truth of it')[12] . . . the steam obliterates our outlines, we all look pretty much the same, and none much anterior to another.

SEDGEMOOR
(from *Somerset*, Vision of England, 1949)

From the Quantocks and the Mendips, and the hills along the southern boundary, one is always looking down on some part of Sedgemoor, Sedgemoor so open to inspection and yet so mysterious and remote. Perhaps it is this quality of engagement with high ground, of washing the bases of peninsulas and promontories and lying in land-locked pools, which gives Sedgemoor its particular air of secrecy and import. It is like a green flood, whose very slow tide waxes to the greenest day in the year and then recedes to winter.

And even now I have not finished with the hills of Somerset. There are still the Poldens: a narrow range, running roughly parallel with the Mendips. They are small hills, but they do a great deal with their moderate resources, partly because of their characteristic bandings of exposed reddish stones; this, and being wooded, gives them a romantic Italianate look. I cast no slur on the Poldens when I say that they always strike me as a painted landscape, and that the Hood Column on the right-hand side of the road from Somerton to Street is placed just where it should be, with all the assurance of good scene-painting. But nature's hand added the smoky wreaths of Travellers' Joy, looping from the top of one hedgerow tree to another, which make this road so lovely through the flowerless months of January and February.

Somerton, the old capital of Somerset, lies at the southern end of the Poldens. It is a small, silvery town, with that very civilising feature, a town square, and a post-office whose wood-work is painted an unusual and becoming shade of petunia – the inn along-side is also trimmed with petunia, and between them they make a very agreeable group. The church has fine brass chandeliers, of a branching pattern common in Somerset churches, but these are further distinguished by their dedication 'To God's glory and the honour of the Church of England 1782.' West of Somerton a spur of the Poldens runs to Langport, and on this spur is High Ham – a hilltop village with a certain Priddy-ish exclusiveness, and Low Ham, where the church stands in a bare field looking as mellow as a rick, and where the recent excavations of a Roman villa have uncovered a mosaic pavement illustrating the story of Dido and Aeneas. There are remains of several Roman villas on the Poldens. Standing high, but not too high, these fertile slopes have just that golden mediocrity which a sensible Latin would appreciate.

These Polden Hills form a Sedgemoor watershed. To the east is the territory of the River Brue; to the west the territory of the River Parrett.

The Brue rises in the Wiltshire border, and begins to be a river in Parson Woodforde's country, flowing under large oak trees and short thick bridges. The Cary accompanies the Brue in a sisterly way, keeping a course more to the south-west. A feminine river, shy, sly and gentle, the Cary imposes its ladylike character on a pastoral landscape of poplar screens dividing peculiarly slender fields, and wears like a family jewel the manor-house of Lytes Cary, with a garden full of clipped yew compartments, and a pair of very handsome gateposts rising from the scrambling margin of a country lane. The Cary's career as a river is not long. It has hardly slid through the Somerton Gap and begun to enjoy the pleasures of Somerton Moor before it is seized on – like any young woman seized on by matrimony – and disciplined into being the King's Sedgemoor Drain.

318

Keeping to the east of the Poldens, the Brue, embanked, and floored with water-lilies, traverses an expanse of very green flats, criss-crossed by lines of pollard-willows and draining ditches, towards Glastonbury. Here, I think, is the best on-the-level view of Glastonbury Tor; and I suppose it is the least seen, except by gipsies, who use these unfrequented roadsides for hanging out washing, whittling and bunching clothes-pegs, and boiling tea-kettles. But this is only a forecast of the flatness and greenness of the Brue Level 'that fenny spacious tract', as Camden called it. Spacious is still the word. Measured in miles it is not much, but its character is essentially spacious, and time seems to get oddly tangled into space, an hour here is much longer than an hour elsewhere. All the gestures of the landscape are slow; grazing cattle move through the pastures as majestically as barges; the man mending the ditch lifts another spadeful of black mud and deposits it on the bank as carefully as though it were a poultice; the water-rat gives an infinity of attention to his toilet; the tinman's van, with its bowls and saucepan lids reflecting the sun with a steady glare, has been drawn up for half-an-hour at the cottage gate. Even the policeman bicycling between the willow-banks is riding at a moderate speed.

Though draining and enclosure began here as far back as the 17th century, the pattern of the population is still pretty close to the pattern recorded in Domesday Book. The villages and hamlets stand warily dry-shod on small rises of ground. Both Meare and Pamborough are described by Domesday as islands: Pamborough a very Robinson Crusoe sort of island, for it consisted of six acres of ground, three arpents of vineyards, and one bordar; and was valued at four shillings. Wedmore is a handsome stone-built village with a pedigree. The treaty which Alfred made with the Danes after the victory of Ethandune was called the Peace of Wedmore. and in his will he bequeathed Wedmore to his son Edward. At Wedmore and in the neighbouring villages which string out along a small rise of ground there are such fine lilacs tossing over stone walls, such bright-coloured stocks and such flourishing ceanothuses, that it becomes possible to believe that a tolerable wine might have been made from the Pamborough vineyard. But they are only incidents in the spacious fenny tract, and winter puts them back in their place, with the sea-mist rolling in and the smell of earthy water blown over garden walls.

Even on the hottest and dryest day a sense of water washes round the fish-house at Meare. The Abbot of Glastonbury had a great fish-pond in the Brue Marshes, and the fish-keepers (as one says game-keepers) lived in this small stone house, with all their gear of nets and poles and osier baskets. Domesday records ten fisherman and three fisheries at Meare. This heron-grey Fish House, so sober and purposeful, is one of the most expressive mediaeval buildings in England. It now belongs to the best of owners, the National Trust. But I am not sure whether they ought to call it The Abbot's Fish House, which sounds misleadingly as though Abbots of Glastonbury came here for a little fishing. Abbots went hunting, but I very much doubt if they went fishing, for it was not until later that fishing as a sport developed from fishing as a labour.

Beyond Mark, where the church has a finely-panelled roof, Brue Level merges into Burnham Level, out of which Brent Knoll stands up as dominatingly as Glastonbury Tor, and even more astonishingly, since it rises from an unbroken flatness. Like Glastonbury, it is an outlier. Seen across the level it looks like a child's drawing, being so steep and so fortuitous: and even when you are close to it, it remains steep and surprising, the more so for being wooded in this sparse landscape of functional willow-banks. The spire of East Brent church is a seamark, and used to be kept white-washed to guide the ships in the Bristol Channel.

Along this stretch of the coast there is an odd territory of sand-dunes, spotted with bungalows and caravans, little huts and booths, all looking extremely uncomfortable and all expressing that steadfast British resolve to be happy and carefree at the seaside. It seems to have nothing to do with Somerset; and I would not be writing of it except for the accident that it was from the Brean and Berrow road, one rainy evening, that I looked inland and saw the Burnham Level, so undeniably green and yet one cannot forever be saying how green it is, washed with silver under a shining wet sky; and it looked so remote, so mysteriously sequestered, that I could not believe it would stay to be looked at longer than the time it takes to snap a soap-bubble.

The Brue and the Parrett run into the Bristol Channel not many miles apart, and share the Huntspill Level between them. They are both quiet, slow-running streams, and look as though their banks would not melt in their mouths. But the Parrett is the major river, richer in tributaries and, I think, richer in colour. Llewelyn Powys, writing with a native's affection and intimacy in his *Somerset Essays*, speaks of its 'modest cider-coloured reaches.' Some of that cider colour must be due to the same tincture of iron which colours Ham Hill stone, for the Parrett rises on the Somerset-Dorset border, and slides past the western shoulder of Hamdon Hill. Its first tributary is the Isle, and a little further on it is joined by the Yeo, another cider-coloured stream – and a full-bodied cider at that, having shuffled through much of the richest pasture land in Somerset.

It was in the valley of the Isle that a rather unusual country parson (he used to bless his parishioners' medicine bottles, which was believed to add considerably to the efficacy of what the doctor had put into them) heard his gardener break into a rambling ditty about sowing the seeds of love. The gardener was called John England. The parson was called Charles Marson. When Marson's friend, who was called Cecil Sharp, came to Hambridge to visit him, they began to collect old songs in the locality, and published the first volume of *Folk Songs from Somerset*. The songs were plentiful enough, but gone under ground, for their singers were ashamed of such old-fashioned wares, while musicologists were remarking (often in German accents) that England, as distinct from Ireland, Scotland and Wales, had no music in its soul.[13] Like the battle of Waterloo, it was a damned near-run thing. If Marson had not been such an unusual parson that his parishioners did not mind what they sang to him, if he had not such a voluminous acquaintance among tramps, gipsies, and doddering old paupers, if the loosest woman in the neighbourhood had not carolled to him with as much confidence as if she had been a choir-boy in F, the incentive to other collectors of folk-songs might never have been given.

Folk-picture, alas, is a different story. No doubt we had it: but only very occasionally does an inn-sign or a rood-screen offer an English equivalent of those votive pictures which Samuel Butler so properly praised in Alps and Sanctuaries. The 17th century Apostles in Martock church are hard to assess because of their elevation and their concavity – they are painted into a series of niches high on the nave wall; but the King David who hangs about the north door is majestically vernacular, and so heartfelt, so tipsy with sweet psalmody, that to see him is to love his maker.

King David was the centre panel of a gallery, since pulled down, so in all probability paintings by the same hand flanked him. We must be grateful that somebody had the sense to preserve him, and hopeful that, since he was in the middle, he was the best of the bunch, like the rose in the middle of a country nosegay.

Martock church resembles an allegory of sacred and profane love. Its chancel is lean, even by 13th century standards. Its nave, for which the parish was responsible two centuries later, is so happy and glorious that it warms the heart to look at it. Its decorations flow over it, and the nobly brawny tower is finished off with a weather-cock which must be a friend to every child in the parish. The nave interior is as good. The timbered roof is superlative, even in this county of fine wood-work, and the stone screen which fills the western arch completes an effect of comfortable grandiosity. Cornet Richard Symonds who was here in 1644 noted that: 'The houses are built of a brave free stone, colour of umber, here growing. No gentleman lives in this parish, a low deepe rich grownde.' Martock is still a Ham Hill stone town, and there must be many houses which Richard Symonds saw, still in use; notably the old manor-house and the Court House; for the inscription on it, 'Martock, neglect not thy opportunities' and the date of 1661, refer to its conversion to a grammar-school.

The Yeo comes into the county by cheese-making, glove-making Yeovil, and half-hoops a stretch of rather glum hedgerow country (famous for dairy farming, however, and memorably sweet in summer dusks during hay-harvest). Ilchester, on the Fosse Way, midway in the course of the Yeo, is a queer squat town which looks as though it were matching itself to its horizons. It was a Roman town, and Roger Bacon was born here. In the 19th century it became infamous because of its jail. The outer walls of Ilchester Jail were so high that no sunlight reached the prisoners. The inner walls were 'wet as dung' – the simile of a country prisoner there. The governor, William Bridle, had been appointed on the strength of an apprenticeship to brutality in the hulks. He was dismissed, however, and the jail pulled down because of an account of the conditions, published by Henry Hunt while he was a prisoner there. That is something which could not happen nowadays.

Beyond Ilchester the Yeo comes into one of those land-locked, fiordlike stretches of Sedgemoor, called King's Moor on the east of the Martock-Somerton road, Wet Moor (where the Yeo joins the Parrett) on the west. I remember seeing it from this road one winter's morning, when long rains had swollen it. Its lumbering speed and angry red-ochre colour made it a menacing sight. Already it was beginning to lap over its banks, and the water-logged moors were badged with pools and widening rivulets. When I came back later in the day the sky had cleared and was reflected in a brilliant expanse of floods, in which the Yeo was only perceptible as a thrust of water through water, like the movement of some furious shouldering fish.

The *ey* of Muchelney means *island.* Muchelney, Thorney, Middleney, are all names in this trident of Isle, Parrett and Yeo; and one sees the force of them when the floods are out. Muchelney has a beautiful old Priest's House, and the remains of a butter-coloured Abbey. The Abbey is now merged in a group of barns and ricks, a church tower looks over its shoulder, and smoke rises comfortably from the chimneys of the village. The technique of island life was different when the few serfs and bordars of Thorney and Middleney heard the Muchelney bells ringing across the swamp. A bishop who inspected Muchelney Abbey in the 14th century reported that the monks were infringing their rule by making themselves beds like tabernacles. An endless shiver of winter nights harps through the words.

It is strange to see the winter aspect of this landscape, which is dusky and rather severe, changed in a matter of hours to the vivacity of water. Floods, like snowfalls, by reversing the relative values of ground and sky convey a sense of levity. When one comes over the brow of a hill and finds trees standing up from a sky-blue surface instead of a sad-coloured one, it is impossible not to feel as if some delightful revolution had taken place during the night. This, of course, is followed by thoughts of all the people whose back-kitchens are flooded, whose cattle are endangered, whose autumn-sown onions may be washed out of the ground, who can't go shopping, etc. But except in very bad years, or where density of population has cramped the choice of building sites, floods are out-witted by management. Indeed, one might say that one has not seen Sedgemoor until the greater part of it is under water, for only then does one begin to appreciate its delicate economy of feet and inches above sea-level. Minute swells of ground never noticed before start up as islands and causeways, and the placing of houses and farm-buildings is seen to be as strategic as though they were demi-lunes and horn-works.

A good place from which to survey the floods is Langport churchyard. It lies on a neck of high ground, and one can look out as from the prow of

323

a ship over sheets of water, speckled with island homesteads and trimmed with lines of willows and telegraph posts. Langport is a pleasant small town with steep streets and bridges and what is called a hanging Chapel over the Huish Episcopi road – an enigmatical construction but very embellishing. Huish Episcopi has the loveliest of all the doctrinal Somerset church-towers, and a porch which matches it in spaciousness and serenity of design. The narrowed valley of the Parrett between the rise of ground by Curry Rivel and the steep wooded slopes by Aller is called the Langport Gap. There is a very fine view of the Gap from the Langport-Bridgewater road – a view which is a triumph of composition, for it has a little of everything in it, including a railway viaduct.

From Burton Pynsent near Curry Rivel (where the effigied Jennings tomb in the church includes some infant Jenningses done up in crimson sachets with only their faces showing) the elder Pitt,[14] walking among his plantations and hearing the masons at work on his column, must often have looked across West Sedgemoor, and the scalloping course of the river Tone, to Athelney – and as statesmen of his date were less officially modest than they are now, it may be that he sometimes made his own Plutarchian comparisons. It was to Athelney that Alfred the Great fled in that dire winter when England seemed lost. 'He forsook all his warriors and all his people, and crept by hedge and lane, through the wood and field, till he came to Athelney.' Afterwards he founded an Abbey in the place where he had found safety amid the floods and the reeds and the wet alder woods; and it was near Athelney that the Alfred Jewel was dug up: 'being plainly made.' says Camden, 'on purpose to hang on a string, it is very probable that he himself constantly wore it.' Later authorities prefer to think that he gave it to his Abbey.

Athelney is now merely the name of a little railway halt. The ruins on the sky-line admired by railway travellers are those of a church begun and left unfinished in the early nineteenth century. But when the floods are out, and the osier plantations smoulder under water like an inlay of copper, and moisture lies on every undrowned object like a close grey fur, it becomes easy to imagine back to the winter of 878, to an Athelney which was England and to Alfred in his small kingdom biding his time as patiently as a heron.

Aelfred the Kinge, Engleonde's deorlinge, wrote the Saxon poet.

Another England's darling haunts these watery lands, which were ruin to him as they were safety to Alfred. It is a story that when Monmouth was in Holland a fortune-teller said to him: *Beware of the Rhine*: which struck those who heard it as a rather unenterprising piece of prophecy. But rhine or rhyne is the name given to the great draining ditches which cut through Sedgemoor and hold it together. The Bussex Rhine, which halted Monmouth's men in their surprise attack on the royal forces, has been filled up. But one does not need to go far on Sedgemoor before finding oneself on the brink of one of these brimming ditches. Ten to one, like Monmouth's people, you do not know it is there until you are within a few yards of it. There it lies – muddy, nonchalant, unimpressive, and horribly disconcerting.

There is a vivacity of contradiction about a river which encourages the idea of getting across it. Rhines interpose themselves, which is a different thing altogether. Since the rhine is not to be crossed you walk along it first. The landscape is as flat as a board, and you feel yourself pinned in your own square of it. Reason assures you that the fields could not be in use, that there could not be cows in one square and a haystack in another unless it were possible to move over the chess-board. But if you do not know the moves, and especially if it is foggy or dusky, the voice of reason can sound thinnish.

That is one mood of Sedgemoor. In another – equally unreasonable – the chess-board takes on an Alice Through the Looking-Glass quality of indefinite extensibility. 'Look,' says Reason patiently. 'There are the Quantocks. Now turn your head and there are the Poldens. There is the tower of Othery, there is Middlezoy, there is Weston Zoyland. It is unusual to find three such fine churches lying so close to each other.' Meanwhile the part of you that doesn't listen to the voice of Reason persists in its belief that Sedgemoor is a limitless territory, and that Weston Zoyland tower only seems to be close because it is so tall. So you turn a deaf ear to Reason, and if you want to be further persuaded you lend yourself to the persuasion of the air. For of all things on Sedgemoor the most persuasive, the most personal to the place, is the air. It seems to have traversed a world-without-end of solitude, and all the smells it carries, the smell of the wild peppermint that grows along the ditches, the smell of a hay-stack, the bitter willow-scent, are qualified by water, just as the tone of stringed instruments is qualified by putting on a mute.

Other times, other smells. The road from Weston Zoyland to Bridgwater seems short enough to motorists. It seemed longer to those who rode or walked it in 1685, for gallows were set up all along it, where the rebels were left hanging and rotting in the harvest sun. The beautiful calm church of Weston Zoyland housed a sad congregation that July. An entry in the church register tells of 'about 500 prisoners brought into our Church, of which there was 79 wounded and: 5 : of them died of thire wounds in our Church.' In the revolting story of the Suppression[15] it is reviving to find one upright man. Bishop Ken, accused of sedition, was asked if he had favoured the rebels and helped them when they were prisoners. He replied: 'It is well known in the diocese that I visited them night and day, and I thank God I supplied them with necessaries myself as far as I could, and encouraged others to do the same.'

Sturdy and plain-headed, Bridgwater is exactly the right town to stand in this mysterious and haunted territory. It clinches it by contradiction, as a bridge clinches a river. Bridgwater, the birthplace of Admiral Blake, has a most Protestant and most English air, and yet it could not conceivably be called prosaic, for the tide rushes through it, hammering the mud-banks of the Parrett estuary, and its sky is full of gulls, and its quays and riverside taverns have that indescribable maritime cosiness which no English person can behold without spiritual pride and sensual affection. Once a year this plain-headed town enjoys a glorious frenzy. Bridgwater Fair is one of the great Fairs of the West, especially in the matter of fireworks (a particularly unbridled form of squib is known as the Bridgwater Bullet). Beyond Bridgwater the estuary flows broadening on, past the Pawlett Hams where the grass is so rich that cattle can be fattened on this feed alone. Here the Parrett has been joined by the last of its tributaries, the Cary, alias the King's Sedgemoor Drain. With its full tale of tributaries, Isle, Yeo, Tone and Cary, and heavy with its compound of pastures and orchards and Sedgemoor flats and distant woodlands, it takes a last bend, and then flows due north into Bridgwater Bay.

I wrote at the beginning that I am unfitted by nature to compose a guidebook, and by now I must have made that clear. The things I have left out, Cheddar cheese and Exmoor ponies, towns, towers, mansions, and more British Earthworks than you would believe possible, are too numerous to be bunched up together in an apology. But one omission must be set right. I have said nothing of the melodious oddity of Somerset's place-names. Let them speak for themselves:

Cricket St Thomas, Cricket Malherbie, Binegar, Wanstrow, Norton Malreward, White Lackington, Chedzoy, Chilthorne Domer, Chilton Cantelo, Stogumber, Stogurzey, Babcary, Temple Cloud, Orchard Portman, Bason Bridge, Cradle Bridge, Queen's Camel, and Compton Dando.

A BALEFUL INFLUENCE
(*Housewife,* July, 1945)

The greatest difficulty in going abroad is the problem of finding somewhere to go. Suspended over Europe, the harassed traveller jerks and plunges this way and that, alternately attracted and repelled, his wits forsaking him in this vertigo of indecision. Every place has so much to be said for it. How delightful it must be in Dalmatia . . . or in Dalecarlia! Trout-fishing in the Pyrenees; I believe the Danish tram system well repays study; see Naples and die! That is one mood. Another is; If only every country hadn't some impossible drawback! Mountains all over Switzerland, midges in the Crimea; Spain used to be all right, but now one might as well go to Italy. The Faroe Islands? Charming, no doubt, but what on earth are we to do when we've got there?

In such quandaries guide-books are worse than useless, flattering to deceive you –

With their vain mysterious art.

An oracle is the only hope, a succinct and impartial oracle. Travellers could be saved all this painful fuss, and fall to packing with a quiet mind, if they would but order it from their bookseller. For the oracle exists: it is called *Near Home; or Europe Described*[16], and has been a boon to thousands.

327

Open its pages – anywhere will do: instantly all is order and clarity:

> In Madrid there is a great deal of dust.
> In Amsterdam there is a great deal of water.
> In London there is a great deal of smoke.
> In Constantinople there are many troops of
>   very troublesome dogs.

It is admirable how promptly the oracle gets to work. Madrid, Amsterdam, and Constantinople are shown up in three lines; we will not go there, that's certain. Equally certain, though, that we are not basely to abandon our project of foreign travel, we cannot remain in London, because of the smoke.

What of other cities?

> Berne. Here some famous bears are kept.
> Geneva. Here there is a manufactory for watches.
> Madrid. There are many fountains in the streets.

(To lay the dust, no doubt; a thoughtful provision, but we have ruled out Madrid.)

> Warsaw. A great many coaches are made here, and sold to the great
> lords.
> Lisbon. The ladies of Lisbon dress very smart.

Besides making statements, the author of *Near Home; or Europe Described* can draw comparisons.

> Hungary is not so beautiful as Greece, though there are many
> sweet spots in it.
> Lyons is on the river Rhone, which is a finer river than the Seine,
> and which sometimes overflows and drowns many people.
> Copenhagen stands by the seaside. There is not so regular and
> handsome a town in all Europe; but as the ground is flat, it can
> not be as beautiful as Edinburgh.

Sicily. This country is an island. It is not at all like Iceland.

Every sentence strengthens the conviction that this is a book that may be relied on. Although written in 1849 it is not out of date, for it deals with essentials of national life and character, and such things do not change.

The Scotch observe the Sabbath better than any other people
The English send out more missionaries.
The Icelanders commit fewer crimes.

Though *Near Home; or Europe Described* was revised in 1902 there was no need to tinker such truths as these. I have compared both editions of the oracle with attention, and though it is only just to the reviser to say that her additions are so perfectly in keeping with the spirit of the original as to be almost undistinguishable, yet I can see no reason why any revision should have been made. What is an adjusted frontier, or a volcano brought up to date, set over against the searching discriminations, the marrowy conclusions which are the true glory of this short, stout volume bound in maroon cloth and richly gilt?

Undoubtedly, and very properly, the prime consideration of the author is with character. Cataracts, orange-groves, mountains and public monuments are all very well, but he who travels for these alone travels through a wilderness. How innutritious seem the purple passages of the ordinary travel-book when we turn the pages of *Near Home; or Europe Described*.

What sort of people are the Sicilians? They are very polite, but they are very superstitious. Their religion is the Roman Catholic.

The Laplanders are very short. They are often called Lapps, and that is a good name for such little people.

Greece is a charming country; but who would like to live so near the Turks?

The nations are judged; and no one could challenge the aptness of these summing-up. Yet for all her unflinching female gaze into the secrets of the

329

human heart (for I am proud to say that *Near Home; or Europe Described* was Written by a Lady), and command of the epigrammatic style, our author is no mere de La Rochefoucauld. There is no easy rancour in her condemnations, and she is always ready to make allowances and mention whatever is in people's favour. For instance, having stated that it is dangerous to provoke Italians (as it undoubtedly is – think of Fascismo!) she hastens to add that even their poor people love painted ceilings, and that in some places the Italians have a very good way of bringing water upstairs. Indeed, she sometimes displays singular ingenuity in finding grounds for mercy. She is hard put to it with the Russians, for what could such a refined and strenuous spirit find to praise in a nation which she must admit to be sly, lazy, and accustomed to sleeping in their clothes. Yet she is not content to dismiss them until she has expressed some redeeming trait.

Russians are very uneasy if they cannot bathe.

Perhaps the finest example of her talent for combining objective realism with sympathy is her description of Poland:

It is near Prussia, and it is like Prussia; but it is flatter and uglier. There are forests with wolves, and foxes and bears in them; but there are no mountains.

The people are not happy, and many of the lords are now wandering far from home, without money or lands.

Studiously low-toned in style and dry in statement, this is yet penetrated with true pathos. We remember Garnett.

One of the most searching obligations of foreign travel is the business of buying souvenirs. Even if we are not rich enough to purchase a coach at Warsaw, we should bring back some slight local objects to present to friends and relations; for a needle-case bought at Nijni Novgorod or the Maison du Blanc has a romantic value denied to a precisely similar article come straight from Sheffield. A section of *Near Home; or Europe Described* is specially devoted to this subject. Alfred, a young man of good family, is represented as having just returned from a tour on the

330

Continent and through the British Isles. We may imagine the company grouped round the shining mahogany, for the cloth has been removed and the wine has made its first circuit (the ladies, however, are still present, as it is a family occasion). A number of cases have been brought into the room. Alfred opens them. Says he:-

Dear Grandfather, will you kindly accept this cushion stuffed with eiderdown from Iceland? On this you may like to rest your leg, that often pains you so much.

Turning to his father – 'Will you, dear Father, accept this marble jar? I found it in Greece, and I thought you might like to place it in the grove.'

The family is large, its tastes are eclectic; but for everyone has this admirable young man found some suitable memento and some apt compliment. (He must have taken a great deal of trouble). I give a list of the mementoes, suppressing the compliments with reluctance, but there is not space for them.

His mother and grandmother: gown-pieces of silk and merino respectively (France and Spain).
Sister Helen, aged seventeen: a picture from Italy.
Brother George, aged sixteen: for his cabinet of minerals – specimen nuggets of gold from Hungary, silver from Norway, iron from Sweden, and tin ore from our own dear England.
Sophia, aged fourteen: a vase of china flowers from Prussia.
Henry, aged twelve: a watch from Switzerland, with hopes that it may go well.
Edward, aged ten: a writing-case of Russia leather.
Frederick, aged eight: a knife bought in England, where the best knives are made.
Walter, aged seven: reindeer's horns from Iceland.
Charles, aged five; a plaid dress from Scotland.
Emma, aged three: toys, made in Germany.
Sweet little Willie (age not stated, but by deduction from average, one): lace edging from Belgium.

'And for my dear old nurse,' says the generous youth (for this is one of those splendid families who call in their faithful servants to drink a glass of wine at dessert, and send them when they are dead, to the *Times*), 'and for my dear old nurse I have brought this flannel, which comes from the sheep of Wales.'

I like to think of this good young man, traversing Europe with a hundred kindly thoughts of those at home. With a great many parcels, too – what a time he must have had with the Customs! We are not told in what order the countries were inspected. Did the flannel go to Greece? Did the Prussian china flowers bloom imperturbably under the skies of Sweden or of Spain? And in how many languages did he say: 'Pray take care of the jar! I design it for my father's grove'?

The thirst for knowledge is never quenched, and the author of *Near Home; or Europe Described* mentions with regret that we do not know the name of a single place in the moon. (Still, it must have been a great consolation to her to know so much about Europe.) What drew her attention to the moon? Perhaps some exalted notion of a better world, of a lunar continent that might support her scrutiny without a blush; perhaps its chilly appearance. For, despite her impartiality, our author cannot quite conceal her preference for Northern climes; and if she has a favourite, it would seem that it is Iceland. But even so, her unfailing good sense prompts the admission that

Thule, the period of cosmography, may not be everybody's fancy.

The most northern town in Europe is Hammerfest. A French lady visited it on her way to Spitzbergen, and she saw a grey parrot there which felt so terribly cold that it never spoke.

LOVE OF FRANCE
(*New York Herald Tribune*, August, 1945)

During the fighting that freed Paris in August, 1944, a barricade in the Rue de Rivoli, constructed in the best architectural canon of local materials, was topped off with a metal shop sign displaying the word *Modes.*

This with its assertion that in Paris in August, 1944 a barricade was the correct wear for the Rue de Rivoli, was of course fortuitous . . . but one of those fortuities that express a situation, as the colouring of a wild flower will express a geological condition.

Respect for local materials is one of the elements in French culture. It underlies their art as it does their cookery whether they build a chateau or a barricade they will employ the means of the neighbourhood with appreciation

> *Plus me plaist le sejour qu'ont basty mes ayeux*
> *Que des palais Romains le front audacieux,*
> *Plus que le marbre dur me plaist l'ardoise fine.*

To be homesick is common to all mankind; but du Bellay's sonnet (it seems to me) is characteristically of France in its exact statement of what home is made of. I cannot imagine an Elizabethan poet, however much he longed to return to his small manor, particularising that it was roofed with thin slates: his love of home would have persuaded him that it was roofed with something quite as grand as any Roman marble. Because of this digested regionalism, French culture has been little troubled by the folk-art movements which other nations have had to undergo as a penance for not appreciating their natural resources. There is as much folk song, folk design, folk lore in France as anywhere else; but it has passed naturally into the idiom of the country, it does not appear with that anxious resurrected stare of what has been revived.

But how does it come about, this peculiar compactness and homogeneity of French life and culture? Certainly not from seclusion. France has always been receptive to ideas from elsewhere, it has exemplified the including aspect of Roman Imperialism as this country has exemplified Roman Imperialism's other aspect of extension. Our colonies are abroad; but the French colonial empire includes colonies within her borders, settlements from all over the world, the kind of colony inaugurated with the Latin Quarter, a district where scholarship, love of learning, love of thinking, drawn from all Europe met and settled around the University of Paris.

No seclusion: and not – in our sense of the word – patriotism. 'I love my country as I might love a beautiful woman. I love her, and I see her faults.' So, long ago, I heard a French student trying to explain to English hearers how he felt about France. The words were rivetted into my memory by the clamour of reprobation which broke out after he had gone. Who'd admit, and among foreigners, that one's country might have faults? Shocking, unnatural, cried those English voices.

But in the sense of loving one's country as a beautiful mistress rather than loving her as an irreproachable grandmother, the patriotism of France may explain the homogeneity of France. It is the glory of France that her nationals have watched her with the critical and jealous glances of a lover, exclaiming: 'I'm not sure of that shade of blue. I prefer you with pearls. Take care! There's a midge going to bite you. You have a smut on your nose. You must leave that tailor, he's not worthy of you.'

For it is impossible to be in France[17] without becoming aware of this critical solicitude, whether it is the man tying up lettuces in his allotment, the girl leading the cow along to stake her in a fresh bit of pasture, the artist and the house-painter alike standing back to consider their brush-work, the woman in the kitchen who tastes and muses, the man in the café who is talking politics, who leans forward, his cheek on his hand and says, *Pourtant.*
. . . And it is out of this habit of criticism and solicitude that France has become, not merely a territory, a nation, a manner of living, a collection of habits and turns of thought, but something approximating to a work of art.

Art is never a gentle process. From the violent stillness of conception to the violent restraint of execution, art is something in which mind and body are exerted to the limits of capacity. Above all, art demands the most violent candour. If France has this quality of approximating to a work of art, it is because her nationals have not failed in violence. Mother of arts, and arms, and laws, she is also the daughter of revolutions. The Rue de Rivoli, amiably purveying its pretty nonsenses for foreign buyers, can also supply its barricades. A barricade is also *Modes*, and fighting for liberty a characteristic elegance of France.

I say elegance, because I mean elegance. Whoever saw the film of the Liberation of Paris must have been struck by the predominant expression on those thin and fighting faces, by the peculiar air of lucidity in all those rapid movements. Through all the violence, the desperation, the danger, there was the dexterity and composure of people who, as in the execution of a work of art, are exerting mind and body to the limit of capacity, to the limits of life itself, and who know what they are doing and why. It was almost like watching sword-play or watching the flight of swallows. Yet it was not because the combatants were young, though many of them were young; nor because they were physically skilful, for some of them were old and clumsy. It was because they were mentally skilful, technicians of liberty. What one watched was an exhibition of civilised behaviour in that pre-eminently civilised act of rooting out fascism. It was another master-piece of France, prepared with critical solicitude, with the discipline of patience, endurance, cunning, audacity, and martyrdom, and executed in local materials, the men and women of the French Resistance.

ICES BY MOONLIGHT
(*Over the Alps*, Patrick Anderson, the *Spectator*, May 16th, 1969)

'Beckford may not enhance Florence or Lisbon; Boswell may not bring an additional smile to a morning walk in Siena, or Gray momentarily illumine an evening in Rome' – the Landorian cadence evokes and dismisses the travellers. Patrick Anderson's sensibility to aspects of the English language gives *Over the Alps* the flexibility and fascination of the impromptu. In fact, *Over the Alps* is a work of serious philosophic intention, an inquiry into the adjustment of the traveller's mind.

For those who regard their holidays abroad as in some sense an assault upon time, a reaching out towards the timelessness of a continuous present, the matter may be different; an intermediary from a different period, who looks both forward and back, is better known to us than the ancients and yet frees us from contemporary preoccupations, may help us in the process of dissolving barriers. What might be an absolute distinction (then and now) or what might, in a different mood, collapse into a sun-induced sentimental dream of a complete union, is given gradation and perspective.

This is the argument. The intermediaries chosen are Boswell, Beckford and Byron. It is imaginable that Boswell and Byron, for all their unlikeness and the barrier of 'then and now,' might discuss their travels with a degree of compatibility. They both set out with the impetus of escape. They both proposed to get something by it, they both pursued self-improvement (a not unworthy aim provided the self is positive enough to be improved). Boswell saw mountains as a background to men. Byron would have derided Boswell's presentation at seven German courts, his elation at a distant prospect of Frederick the Great, 'dressed in a suit of plain blue, with a star and a plain hat with a white feather, he stood before his palace with an air of iron confidence.' They would have been as one about Paoli. But whatever they sought, they sought it in its reality, and for what it was worth.

Beckford, a chronological link between them, travelled without a thought of gaining anything by it. He did not seek; he complied; and though he set out on his Grand Tour with some orthodox preconceptions, 'all impatience to reach that delightful classic region which already possesses the better half of my spirit,' his sensibility and brilliant attentiveness did not disturb his detachment. This gives a vivid freshness to his comments, whether lyrical or waspish: 'a level green where people walk and eat ices by moonlight,' 'a jumble over the Appenines.' He could not and would not submit to boring himself. 'I ran childishly by the ample ranks of sculpture like a butterfly in a parterre.' In Venice, after a day of rapturous first impressions, 'the dusk prevented my remarking the various sculptures with which the Loggietta is crowded'; and further dusks fell as conveniently, releasing him into the unimpeded, unguidebooked territory of his own imagination.

Four years later the ultimate scandal had broken. Society, long exasperated by the thorn in its flesh and a trifle anxious for its own reputation, had gathered for the social kill. Beckford was 'dropped'.

Moral romanticism would like to find the traveller in Portugal a changed man. He was not. This time he had not even complied. Setting out with a practical wish to investigate his estates in Jamaica, he was deflected to Lisbon by a storm. From this fortuitous beginning he proceeded to travel about Portugal and to find it deliciously entertaining. As he had no preconceptions, nothing impeded his reactions. Admiring, disdaining, enjoying, being satirical, feeling poetical, dawdling and guzzling with ecclesiastics, dancing minuets with young gentlemen, wandering in dusky, scented gardens and on the outskirts of palace politics, listening to nightingales, fountains, *modinhas* – 'the most bewitching melodies that ever existed since the days of the Sybarites' – whispering breezes and the screams of the mad Queen Maria I, he is Beckford at full gallop, Beckford to the top of his bent.

And as an intermediary, a solvent of barriers, a perspective-glass? There is much to be said for following a Jack o' Lantern. One is not distracted by milestones. Beckford represents his period by being so markedly askew from it that the actuality of his 'now' stings one into a realisation of the 'then' of his contemporaries, the 'now' of today. They do not fuse, but they almost co-exist. This pattern of time is what the traveller seeks, though a world where music amid moonlight and ices are one may be what the holidaymaker on a chartered flight to the Costa Brava hopes for.

Patrick Anderson, following Beckford's travels in Portugal, writes in his travel-diary, 'This morning I find myself actually trembling, not so much with excitement as anxiety, as I think of the number of things I must see during the coming day. Why this rage of sightseeing? I decide I am an auto-didact . . . Each new church or cloister gives me a bit more confidence, a slight increase in worthiness . . .' Beckford would have looked down his ineffable long nose at this. Confidence? Worthiness? Why limp on such crutches? Why not go by air? – for he would certainly be for a solo flight, and for the music-moonlight-ices destination.

Yet Patrick Anderson did well to choose him as chief intermediary. Beckford led him to the Gardens of Queluz, benignly stately, sleeping to the sound of water: 'I felt that I was face to face with a confirmation of some of my deepest longings'; and sent him home with a book which should also confirm a deep longing – for it is an uncommonly mature and perceptive one.

ELIZA FAY
(unpublished ms, Warner/Ackland Archive, Dorset County Museum)

During the 18th century the Pyramids had been rising in European esteem. In 1779 Mrs Eliza Fay[18], *en route* for India, wrote home about them: 'It has been supposed by many that the Israelites built the Pyramids during their bondage in Egypt, and I rather incline to that opinion, for though it has been proved that they were intended to serve as repositories for the dead yet each, being said to contain only one sarcophagus, this circumstance, and their very form, rendered them of so little comparative use, that most probably they were raised to furnish employment for multitudes of unfortunate slaves, and who could more aptly agree with this description, than the wretched posterity of Jacob?'

Mrs Fay was a mantua-maker: she viewed the Pyramids professionally as something too costly to be cut to waste. But at the time when she realised the use of the Pyramids she had exchanged mantua-making for the *metier* of being a married woman, and was accompanying Mr Fay, a young barrister, to Calcutta, where he intended to make his fortune as an advocate.

There was nothing inordinately sanguine in such an intention. India was where fortunes could be made. The impecunious, the unrelated, the superfluous, had gone there in scores and done well for themselves. The vast, calm sub-Continent was unaffected, but its ruling class, already irked by the power of the East India Company, was growing resentful.

Hyder Ali, who possessed the port of Calicut, was already meditating an extirpatory war against the English when the *Natalia* docked with her cargo of aliens, the Fays among them. The ship was stormed by his Sepoys, the newcomers made captives, their belongings searched and plundered. It is characteristic that Captain Ayres who commanded the Sepoys had also come to make his fortune in India. A Londoner convicted for robbery, his death-sentence had been commuted to transportation; making his way to Calicut, he had ensconced himself under Hyder Ali's

338

wing, and become his agent.

The path to fortune was not so immediately open to the Fays. 'Expecting a strict search and desirous of rescuing something from the general wreck, Mr Fay contrived to conceal our watches in my hair, having first stopped their going by sticking pins in their wheels. Having laid out a silk gown the day before, to put on in case I went ashore, I begged hard for that, and obtained it.'

It was the monsoon season. Drenched with rain and seawater, the Fays spent their first hour on Indian soil 'detained in an open Square, till the Governor's pleasure should be known. He sat all the while smoking his hookah, when having sufficiently feasted his eyes, he ordered us to be taken to the English Factory.' Factories were the residencies of the trading nations at Calicut. The English Factory had been abandoned under threat of hostilities some weeks before, since then it had been stripped of every article of furniture. A meal had been sent in by Mr Passavant of the Danish Factory. 'After Mr Fay had dined (for my anxiety continued so great that I could not touch a morsel of what was brought) I besought him to look round for some place in to which I might crawl, and lie down unseen by the Seapoys that guarded us.' He found a lumber-room where, in her wet silk gown and with her bundle for pillow 'I stretched myself on the floor, amidst dirt and rubbish, and enjoyed a fine sleep of more than three hours, when I woke completely refreshed.'

Exhaustion may have accounted for the fine sleep, but not for its measurement. To remember that watches must be wound, to take them out of one's hair and remove the pins from their wheels, and at such a bedtime, is heroine-like.

'Surprised and thankful for the change, I joyfully went down to Mr Fay, declaring that I would continue to make use of the lumber-room to sleep in, and as Mr Passavant had sent me a rattan couch, I was just going to have it conveyed there, when the place was found to be swarming with venomous reptiles; perhaps a hundred scorpions and centipedes. Had I moved hand or foot, what might have been the consequence!'

These venomous reptiles do not reappear in Mrs Fay's account of their imprisonment, which lasted from November 5th 1779 till February 27th 1780. Perhaps they went into hiding, daunted by a

339

clamour of conversations. The Fay's fellow-passengers visited them daily, some to recount their losses, or remedy them (Mrs Tulloh seized on a tea-kettle, part of a tea-equipment sent to Mrs Fay by a benevolent Jew), some to recount the latest rumours of war, duels, and hurricanes. Among them was the villainous Ayres who, hearing that Eliza's breast had been bruised by a Sepoy shutting a prison-house door on her, sent milk to be used as an embrocation. 'On Christmas Day all the Europeans and some of the natives attended our Levee.' This affable assembly of captors and captives continued into the New Year, when Mr Fay's account of their misfortunes had brought a sympathetic two hundred rupees from the Governor of Tillicherri. Having some money to bribe with, the Fays now planned to escape. 'A friar belonging to a Portuguese convent usually manages these affairs when properly instructed.' The proper instructions having been handed to him, Father Ricardo told them to meet him on the beach at dusk, when he would arrange with a local smuggler to meet them. 'When it grew dark, Mr Fay put on a sailor's dress, and I equipped myself in a nankeen jacket - a pair of long striped trousers – a man's night cap, Mr Fay's shoes tied on my feet, and a stick in my hand. In this dress Mr Fay declared that I was the very image of my dear father, which highly gratified me. I had tied the clothes we had taken off in a handkerchief; with that in one hand and brandishing my stick in the other, I boldly sallied forth. Father Ricardo met us at the smugglers, and we paid him twenty rupees and gave him security for the other twenty; nothing remained, we supposed, but to step into the boat, when behold news was brought that the sailors had made their escape no one knew whither; after waiting two hours in that dangerous situation, to see if they would return, and raving in all the folly of angry disappointment against those who had misled me, we made a virtue of necessity, and trudged back to our prison, whence we effected an entrance without exciting suspicion.'

While as much as a rupee of bribe-money remained to them, the Fays would have gone on being the laughing-stock of Calicut if it had not been for the benevolent Jew who gave Eliza her tea-equipage – 'a fine venerable old man, with a long white beard, his complexion by no means dark, his countenance benign yet majestic.'

Isaac was one of the many who visited the English captives. He had seen that his hostess was in poor health, and determined to free her. To Mr Fay's lamentations about ill-usage and a sickly wife, he replied that a three mile walk to an authority called Sudder Khan would bring an order of release. Two such walks were undertaken. The second did the trick. 'On Friday 18th February at 5 a.m. we joyfully quitted our prison and repaired to the house of our steady friend, and benefactor, Isaac, when we found one of his own sloops prepared to convey us to Cochin, with every necessary refreshment on board.'

At the house of the friend and benefactor they were welcomed by the two wives of Isaac 'who were most splendidly dressed to receive us, rather overloaded with ornaments yet not inelegant. Though religious prejudices banished us from *their* table, ours was loaded with every delicacy – all served on massive plate,' and included silver spittoons. 'You will judge what a change these apartments were to me, the house in which I had so long lived, without any furniture at all, save my unmattressed couch, an old table and three broken chairs. My own face I never saw during the whole period, there not being so much as a fragment of a looking-glass to be obtained.'

The only record of that face is the portrait of Mrs Fay by Devis. Entitled *The Authoress in Egyptian Costume*, it shows a short plump young woman, whose arched eyebrows and small tight mouth accord with her style of writing – observant, amused. But her erect carriage and complacent bearing are intimidating; she advances over the sands of Egypt as though she would tread them down. One's residual impression is compassion for Mr Fay.

THE STEAM WHISTLE
(The Deer Cry Pavilion, Pat Barr; the *Spectator*, January 10th, 1969)*

It is one of the pleasures of age to realise that at the Battle of the Nile one was there all the while. Reading Pat Barr's admirable study of the Meiji era, *The Deer Cry Pavilion*, I remembered how a travelling uncle had enriched my nursery with a picture-book from Japan. The pictures showed the various games of Japanese children. Some of the games, like flying kites and blind-man's-buff, I recognised. Others were baffling: even as a game for girls, fanning a bowl of goldfish struck me as an unrewarding pastime. But most baffling of all were the occurrences among the robed, sashed, high-sandalled children of boys wearing Norfolk jackets and short trousers of quite remarkably ugly shepherd's plaid, cloth caps and boots. To my eyes they looked pauperised. In fact, they were at the height of fashion and elegance, for they were dressed in the western style.

The westernisation of Japan is the theme of *The Deer Cry Pavilion*. The story begins in 1853 with the arrival in Tokyo Bay of Commodore Perry. He came not to conquer but to trade. He came to a formalised ritualistic civilisation where century after century had enforced the jealously guarded tradition of keeping itself to itself. He showed it a small-sized model railway. Like children at a fair the inspecting officials leaped on to it, bestrode its miniature coaches as children ride merry-go-round horses and 'went whirling round, their robes flapping in the breeze, "grinning with intense interest" and crying out with enthusiasm every time the steam whistle sounded.' Fifty-two years after Commodore Perry's arrival, Admiral Togo out-fought, out-gunned, made drowned hay of the Russian fleet at the Battle of Tsuschina.

It is an astonishing story, creditable or saddening according to the way one looks at it. Pat Barr achieves the remarkable feat of not taking sides. Her narrative is substantial, vivid, without sentiment, without partiality. It is as though she wrote with the detachment of someone observing a process of history through a telescope of impartial magnification. Extraordinary figures cross the scene. Mr Holtham, who laid railways over mountains, marshes, headstrong torrents, through virgin forests, who foresaw how after emerging from a tunnel 'the rail would ride "high on the shoulders of transverse spurs, winding round or piercing them and spring across gullies and ravines of a very precipitous character"'; Miss Isabella Bird, an Edinburgh spinster with a spinal complaint, who endured bugs, mosquitoes, blow-flies, stinking wayside inns, agonising horseback-riding, extremes of cold and heat in her search for 'the real Japan,' the Yesu territory of the Ainus, so real that few Japanese ever penetrated to it; Professor John Milne, whose insatiable passion for earthquakes hurried him from one stricken area to another, to measure fissures, interrogate survivors and give very sensible advice against building in the western style. He could even find a sort of usefulness in earthquakes: 'Those who live in remote localities might use them by subsequently comparing their observations with newspaper reports as a means of obtaining a very close approximation to Tokyo mean time and thus furnishing themselves with the means of giving their clocks and watches a new starting point.'

But no comers from the outer world – engineers, English teachers, missionaries of science or commerce, traders, promoters, exploiters – could have westernised Japan without Japan's will to be westernised. It was a national movement which stripped the Samurai of his sword, forced supple waists into stiffly-boned corsets and modal musicians into the rigid European scale, imposed an expensive inappropriate architecture, the Gregorian Calendar, an alien social code, a second language. These upsetting changes were welcomed as symbols of escape from the dead hand of the past: a *toga virilis*, even if it didn't fit; and Tory elements in society, if not welcoming, complied, because of their traditional loyalty to the Emperor.

The sweep and speed of the westernisation was implemented by the industry and adaptability of the workers. Holtham commented that his coolies 'were "uncommon quick" at interpreting orders. They sat and watched quietly as E.G. and Tom made their calculations and then, at a sign, jumped up and mimed the driving-in of a pole, the cutting-down of a tree, the rattling-out of a length of chain, and so learned by a process of elimination what was required of them.' Dr Henry Faulds, a few days after his arrival in Tokyo, 'was awakened at daybreak by some young doctors' apprentices tapping gently at his window and greeting him with a deferential "good morning" and a plea for lessons in anatomy.'

By the time travellers for pleasure began to visit Japan, beguiled by the beauty of its artefacts, the charm of its legend, that Japan was

343

disappearing. A brisk trade in fakes had sprung up. There were tours to shrines and brothels, There were agents for Butterfly marriages. Nagasaki specialised in these; 'its girls were supposed to be the prettiest, arrangements were cheap and made with the minimum of fuss. Nagasaki had always been an easy-come-easy-go sort of place.' For easy comers and goers, this Japan was a pleasant interlude. Not so for Lafcadio Hearn, who had come to love and to stay and to outstay. 'What is there to love in Japan except what is passing away?' he lamented.

Only in remote villages and crannies of aristocracy did the legend survive. It is like coming on a page of Murasaki to read in *The Deer Cry Pavilion* of the yearly emergence of the Empress Dowager when she and her court went mushroom-hunting. Special dress was worn for this excursion into a particular woodland; bright green leggings for the men, white silk gaiters and a white kerchief for the women. Bamboo baskets were carried. 'When the bamboo baskets were piled high, the hunters returned to the clearing and those who have gathered much are congratulated, while those who have made a poor harvest traditionally apologise in mock humility for their stupidity and awkwardness, which render them unworthy to be members of such a distinguished party.'

NOTES

1   Invented for the purpose of describing the Middlesex countryside c.1800 before places like Harrow, where Warner grew up, had become engulfed by Greater London
2   Warner's unsentimental portrait of Chaldon Herring, Dorset
3   The Sailor's Return. See also p.54-55
4   Billy Lucas. See also p.54
5   Rev'd. Cope. See also p.57-59
6   Characters based loosely, if at all, on Chaldon Herring residents

Notes 7-15 are those provided by Warner in *Somerset*

7   Camden: *Britannia*
8   Fuller: *Worthies of England*
9   It seems likely that Sul does a little back-door magic to this day. On the eastern side of Solsbury Hill there is a long valley (with an Elizabethan house in it, called St. Catherine's

Court). A friend of mine, walking in this valley, stopped to talk with a woman, and commented on the spring beside her cottage. 'It is good for the eyes' she was told. 'My mother always kept a bottle by her, and they say it is because the spring faces sunrise on Midsummer Day.' Another venerable character, the ithyphallic Giant of Cerne Abbas, was, within living memory, resorted to by childless couples, who took him gifts of eggs. How can our bishops say that England is no longer a religious country?

10 Celia Fiennes gives a very full account of the ceremonial of bathing (c.1687) including the 'garments made of a fine yellow canvas, which is stiff and made large with great sleeves like a parsons gown, the water fills up so that its borne off that your shape is not seen', and the 'broad brim'd hatt with the crown cut out' worn by those being 'pumpt on their heads for palsyes.'

11 The Baedecker air-raid on Bath puts this sentence into the past tense

12 Memoirs of Harriett Wilson

13 Marson himself had lived for eight years in Somerset without suspecting the existence of a Somerset folk-song

14 If so many little Jenningses had not been laid away in sachets Pitt would not have been there. William Pynsent, who left him the property, got it through marrying a Jennings heiress

15 Jeffreys was only more showly vile than the rest of the King's party. Mary of Modena, that virtuous queen-consort, complained furiously at being allotted only 98 Somerset prisoners to make her profit on by selling them as slaves to the Virginia plantations and demanded 100 more

16 One of several amusing reviews of instructive Victorian compendiums. See p.348 & 381

17 Warner and Ackland took a holiday in Paris in 1932

18 The original 1908 edition of Fay's letters from India was discovered by E. M. Forster who arranged for its reissue by the Hogarth Press in 1925

ARE PARENTS REALLY NECESSARY?

ON THE PASSING OF MONARCHS
(*Our Time*, June, 1946)

I shall never forget the death of Queen Victoria.

Perhaps it would be more accurate to say that the death of Queen Victoria remains in my memory because it coincided with my first strong aesthetic experience. For whenever I hear a mention of the death of Queen Victoria I feel an instant thrill of extraordinary pleasure and surprise, a distant but unmistakable *Pop!* which no passage of years can mute; but which cannot really refer to the passing of the great Queen.

I am sure that my mother must have told me at breakfast that Queen Victoria was dead; and I feel equally sure that she told me the news with solemn emotion, and that she was in tears. I would wager a fair sum that she was, moreover, in black. For my mother was notably quick off the mark, though we lived in the provinces she was always dressed in the fashion of the moment. I take it then, that my mother, with tears, and wearing black, told me at breakfast that the Queen was dead – or perhaps she put it more suitably, and told me that the Queen had gone to the sky.

But I have to reconstruct all this because I cannot remember a vestige of it. The fact of Queen Victoria's death did not register with me till the afternoon, when my nurse took me for a walk and we passed the post-office. History tells me that it was a cold and foggy day, that the air was full of the tolling of bells, that people stood about the streets, blowing their noses, incredulously, that all flags were at half-mast, shop-windows shuttered in token of mourning, and that the humblest of Queen Victoria's subjects was wearing some little tag of crape or black arm-band.

I do seem to remember that it was a nasty cold afternoon, but again my memory gives out on every other item, even the bells. And that is the more odd because there were three bells in our town, the church-bell, the school-bell, and the bell at the fire-station; and to have them all tolling simultaneously must have been a very unusual state of things. We walked up the High Street[1], my nurse and I, amid the tolling of bells, the sighs of a stricken nation; and we came to the post-office. There, suddenly, like a light turned on, Queen Victoria begins to live, or rather begins to die. For displayed in the post-office window was a picture.

It was a coloured picture, I believe it was a chromo-lithograph. Afterwards I sometimes wondered how they had got it done, and sent to our post-office, in the time; for it represented Queen Victoria lying dead. But at the moment I was above such speculations. In one bound I had soared to the realms of art. The Queen lay on her back, wearing a nightgown and the Order of the Garter. Her hands were folded on her bosom, a few lilies lay across her feet. Her head, circled with a light, dishabille sort of crown, rested on a pillow, and an angel, or perhaps a brace of angels, hovered in waiting by the bed's head.

There she lay, the Queen, and dead, lit up with the double majesty of the Queen of England and the King of Terrors. Never before or since have I seen any portrayed person looking so dead as Queen Victoria looked in our post-office window. One contributory factor to this aweful impression of deadness was the extent of the change which had taken place in the well-known features. There was not a wrinkle on the august countenance, she was as smooth, and as white, and as peaceful as my mother's pot of cold cream. There she lay, far handsomer than the angel or angels, and only a degree or two more mature. Yet it was unmistakably Queen Victoria, the Queen of the pennies, and the photographs, Jubilee ones mostly, on the walls of my loyal nursery. It may have been the dignity, it may have been the Garter; but there could be no doubt who was lying dead in the post-office window.

In that moment, in the twinkling of an eye, I was snatched up into heaven. Fortunately my nurse, too, was much pleased with the picture, so I was able to stay in heaven for quite a while, rejoicing in the magic workings of art, taking in every detail for my own future private use.

That night, and for many nights after, I fell asleep on my back, with my hands folded on my chest and my features composed into an expresston of deathly serenity. Time wore on. The nation's grief tilted towards a national rejoicing. A picture of Queen Alexandra was added to the nursery mantelpiece, and my nurse often pointed out the beauty of her features, the sweetness of her smile, the size of her pearls. But Queen Alexandra never got a glance from me. She was not dead.

The death of King Edward VII brought me no such enlightening catharsis. Indeed, what I chiefly remember about his death is that he died at a very inconvenient time of year for my mother. She had just fixed her clothes for the summer, they were all coloured and had to be dyed and were never the same again. Afterwards, eating lobster and drinking hock, we watched his funeral procession from the window of an office in Whitehall. Or maybe this was not the funeral of Edward VII but the coronation of George V. This is more likely, because I recollect that the hock was drunk out of mugs, and mugs are a phenomenon of royal accessions rather than of royal demises.

Perhaps the British monarchic system runs a shade too smoothly. It is too much like those slot machines into which one puts a penny and instantly a drawer, containing a piece of toffee neatly wrapped in silver paper, is shot forth. One takes the toffee, swallows it, slams back the drawer, drops in another penny. Out shoots the drawer, containing an identical silvered packet. Just as veteran motorists complain that pre-selected gears take all the fun out of gear-changing, so a truly loyal heart might look back regretfully to the days when the succession to the throne was not quite so glib, to the days when an axe, or a revolution, diversified the series of exemplary lives and universal mournings. This unfailing flow of monarchs defeats the very purpose of Kingship. Here, for instance, am I, having lived in five different reigns. And what is my reaction? I look forward with a tranquil, and I hope not too sanguine, assurance to increasing my average.

This of course, is partly the spirit of acquisition, latent in all human hearts, and increasing with age. I have no reason to suppose that the death of his present Majesty will afford me the same profound and soul-enlivening rapture as was afforded me by the death of his great-grandmother. On the contrary, I can presume that it won't; unless it should happen to coincide with another searching aesthetic experience. *Vita brevis, ars longa*. It was the picture in the post-office window that glorified the occasion.

DOMESTIC PETRONIUS
(*Time and Tide*, 1927)

'Whether you wish to model a flower in wax; to serve up a relish for breakfast or supper; to supply a delicious *entrée* for the dinner table; to cure a headache; to get married; to bury a relative; to establish acquaintances according to the rules of etiquette . . .'

These are all very natural aspirations, particularly the last but one. Information on the following subjects, too, would be welcomed by any proper-minded person, for knowledge is always agreeable, even, or even more so, if there is no need to make use of it.

> Adulterations, Practical Hints upon
> Body in Flames, what to do.
> Broccoli, to Pickle.
> Brogues, to Correct.
> Earthenware teapots, why preferred by Aged Cottagers.
> Gloves, Dyeing Purple.
> Hair, Dyeing Green.
> Hair, Restored by Onions.
> Marine Glue.
> Poisonous Wine.
> Potichomanie.
> Skylights, ornamental.
> Women, Immoral, as Lodgers.
> Wow-Wow Sauce.

This is but a random nosegay culled from an index of forty-two close-printed columns.

What a work! As erudite as the *Anatomy of Melancholy*, but more practical; as comprehensive as the *Encyclopaedia Britannica*, but far more genial. It is called (but some readers, happy are they that love thee! will know already what I am writing about) *Enquire within upon Everything*; and the title, so superb as a boast, so obliging as an invitation, exactly fits it.

No! On second thoughts, not exactly. It is one of the hardest things in the world to find a representative title, and that of *Enquire Within upon Everything*, vast and snug though it be, is on one important count inadequate. For it suggests only a work of reference. It does not hint of the refined spiritual aroma wafted from these pages. At first sight such subjects as Marine Glue do not seem very likely vehicles for moral uplift. But they can be made to subserve it, and do. For the scheme of this book includes page-headings, short breathings of higher things; and the reader has only to raise his eyes from learning How to Make British Anchovies to be reminded that *Music is Soul embodied in Sound*, while a recipe for Bug Poison is ennobled by its position immediately under the statement that *Knowledge is the Wing whereby we Fly to Heaven*.

It should be needless to point out that *Enquire Within* is a compilation. No one mind could claim to be an authority on subjects so various as Portable Soup, How to address the Privy Council, Restoring Leeches, Walking Gracefully, and Marbled Goose. And it is to be hoped that no single life-span could include personal experience of Bites of Mad Animals, Poisoning by Gamboge, Shoes (Tight) to get on, Scorpions, Drowning, Breach of Promise of Marriage, Loss by Boiling, Cries of Infants, Relaxed Uvula and Religious Doubts. In any case, such an existence would lack leisure, and I should think inclination, for such lighter pursuits as the Cellarius Waltz, the Management of Guinea Pigs, Writing for the Press, Making Artificial Seawater, Dyeing Feathers Pink, and Kite-flying while Swimming.

Enquire Within first appeared in the late eighteen-fifties, a period generally considered rather grovelling in regard to the taste displayed in interior decoration and applied art. Yet see how the subject of Carpets is approached.

The most truly chaste, rich, and elegant carpets are those where the pattern is formed by one colour only but arranged in every variety of shade. For instance, we have seen a Brussels carpet entirely red; the pattern formed by shades or tints, varying from the deepest crimson (almost a black), to the palest pink (almost a white). Also one of green only, shaded from the darkest bottle green, in some parts of the figure, to the lightest pea-green in others.

The Curtains, Sofas, etc., of course, were of corresponding colours, and the effect of the whole was noble and elegant.

The implication that carpets must be noble and chaste before they can be truly elegant reminds me so strongly of parallel reasonings in *Sesame and Lilies* that I am inclined to believe that this section was contributed by Ruskin himself. If this possibility be granted I should also attribute to Ruskin one, at least, of the short breathings, which runs thus: 'A bird's nest is a natural egg-cup.' Sometimes I dream that I have found some missing pages of *Modern Painters*[2] where it is argued from this premise that egg-cups should be framed to resemble a natural bird's nest.

From the applied let us turn to the Fine Arts.

To construct caves of Cinders – Arrange the cinders in such a manner as to resemble the intended design; then cover in such parts as require it with brown paper soaked in thin glue until quite pulpy. When nearly dry dust over with sand, powdered brick, slate, and chopped lichen and moss, from a pepper-box; touch up the various parts with either oil, water or varnish colours; and if necessary form your trees of wire covered with brown paper, and moss glued on.

When a cave is constructed in the way we have pointed out, on a large scale, and the interior sprinkled with powdered fluor spar or glass, the effect is very good by candle light.

Monuments, ancient or modern, are better constructed of cork. We once constructed a model of the Acropolis of Athens in Cork, which was completed in one fifth the time occupied by other materials, and looked much better.

(Perhaps the last assertion is a little trenchant. But as I have not seen either the marble Acropolis or the cork one, I am not in a position to judge.)

To model from Living Objects. We will imagine that the reader desires to model the features of some friend, and as there is some difficulty on the matter of the person operated upon having a natural tendency to distort the features when the liquid plaster is poured upon the face, and some danger of suffocation if the matter is not well managed, we will proceed at once to describe the various stages of operating.

Lay the friend upon his back.

– No I cannot go on. It is too painful. Instead I shall proceed at once to Suffocation, Treatment of:

Rub the surface of the body with the hands enclosed in warm dry worsted socks. To restore breathing, put the pipe of a common bellows into one nostril, carefully closing the other and the mouth. Blow the bellows gently.

Cautions. 1. – Never rub the body with salt or spirits. 2. Never roll the body on casks. 3.Continue the remedies for twelve hours without ceasing.

There is also a certain degree of etiquette to be observed in cases of fire.

Should the staircase be burning so as to cut off all communications, endeavour to escape by means of a trap-door in the roof, a ladder leading to which should always be at hand.

Avoid all hurry and confusion.

How peculiarly sensible that is; and how much pleasanter conflagrations would be if people would only follow these directions!

I hope I may have said enough to show some of the merits of this work. But I cannot quit it without touching on the subject of economy. As everyone knows, economy is an essential part of a wise conduct of life; yet there is no subject so commonly made repulsive to us by those who would inculcate it. For instance, there is the story of the lady who overnight would fill her hot water bottle with tea for early morning drinking. Ugh! There are no such squalid recommendations in *Enquire Within*. There, even economy is made to wear a modest, decent, temperate look; and what is more, it is kept within reasonable bounds. Thus:-

There is not any real economy in purchasing cheap calico for gentlemen's night-shirts.

It is equally true that there is no real economy in employing a poor bare calico style of writing, ungraced and meagre. The reader, I hope, has already noted several niceties of English in my quotations other than those in that fine passage from Ruskin. Those quotations were chosen, however, for their matter. The paragraph which follows has been chosen for its literary value; although, of course, it is very sensible, too.

No article in dress tarnishes so readily as black crape trimmings, and few things injure it more than damp; therefore to preserve its beauty on bonnets, a lady in nice mourning should in her evening walks, at all seasons of the year, take as her companion an old parasol to shade her crape.

I cannot easily express my admiration of this passage. The first thought perhaps is: 'What smooth, harmonious prose! But its still waters run deep; for observe the depth and complexity of the implications. Poor bereaved lady, she walks out at evening, under the willows maybe, or along the banks of the canal; the places that pale passion loves are usually damp. She walks alone, her sole companion an old parasol, for the dejected creature has not the spirits to buy a new one. Yet amidst her distress she is still refined, still an ornament to society and an example, still 'a lady in nice mourning.' I do not see how one could better it.

ON CHOOSING A COUNTRY RESIDENCE
(*Time and Tide*, June 17th, 1927)

I suppose that a considerable number of my readers are Londoners; and having supposed that, it is reasonable to suppose that they have followed the Londoner's custom of spending some part of the Whitsun holiday in the country; and these suppositions being granted me, I think I may go on to a third: that they have been playing the same pleasant game that I have been playing, the game of fitting themselves with a country house.

Children play the game of Houses too; but their's is an earlier and more ancestral version of it, for which little more is necessary than a table with a drooping table-cloth, a corner behind the window curtains, or a weeping ash. The elements of Taste and Personality scarcely enter into this pure and primitive state of the House game. Shelter, privacy, and a certain degree of darkness are the desiderata. A few stones for bread may be thrown in, and a doll's tea-pot gives a fine sense of stability, but they are not essential, for however much children may think that they are imitating their parents, the motto of their play is *Antiquam exquirite matrem*, and the parents they set themselves to reproduce are exceedingly grand ones – so grand that they might eat with their fingers without rebuke; so grand that though their pies were not made of mud, their pie-dishes were.

Grown-ups add to these primitive instincts – Dens and Domesticity – many more complicated considerations; but I do not think that they play the game with any less ardour. And like children too, their longings are of an immortal kind and have nothing whatever to do with a personal Housing Problem. Baucis may be perfectly contented with her cot beside a rill, but that is no reason why she should not spend the afternoon rambling round a shooting-box in the Midlands, or poking her nose and her imagination through the barred slot-windows of an extensive cellarage; and I have seen Horatia, whose villa at Tivoli is the envy of all hearers, stand for ten minutes in the rain and the raining dead leaves, with her mouth watering over a damp Victorian-Gothic Vicarage that had happened to strike her fancy.

So great a passion goes to the playing of this game of Houses, and so surprising and inexplicable are the elections of those who play it, that I have sometimes wondered if we grown-ups have not added a moral and metaphysical tincture to the original brewage, which, working and fermenting, results in the draughts of strange rapture tasted by its players. Perhaps the soul of man is always in revolt against that ordinance which declares that though it may change its sky itself it may not change. Perhaps we all believe that where the change of sky is unavailing a change of ceiling will do the trick. Or it may be that a simpler explanation can be found in the old saying that every personality is but a bundle of personalities, so divers, so ill-assorted, so numerous that, whatever house we may live in, that house is bound to be overcrowded. In either of these hypothetical cases the true devotees of the House game submit themselves humbly enough to the rigour of the game and the laws of their being; for they are not mentally ambitious, they have none of the spiritual pride which says 'I shall never be removed,' they do not flatter themselves that their choice is a permanent one, never to be sapped or superseded. I myself have chosen as many as five ideal homes in one day's walk, and if the day be spent in a car or a train my chosen may be numbered in two figures.

Yet for one's own pleasure solely, it is best not to be too profuse. A seemly facade, an agreeable grotto, a sagging thatch that caresses a

357

squinting window, a garden trim or neglected according to taste . . . one may fall in love with these if one pleases; but to love for these alone is to love like a libertine, and the true player of the Home game will always play it with a view to honourable matrimony, examining into the state of the roof, taking note of the soil and the prevailing winds, and being properly exigent about the aspect of the larder window and the nursery. At least, if he is a her, he will. I do not know what men look for in their House game; but if they have any sense they will look to the larder and the nursery as the chief points.

One further consideration must be noted, and that a serious one. In choosing one's habitation one must look beyond it to another, remembering that day when one will pass out from one's gate to a new and final resting-place . . . the grave. And whoever plays the House game with a single heart and honest observance will go and take a stroll round the churchyard. There too he will note the soil, and the moss upon the stones will tell him from which quarter he may expect the wind to bring the rain. He will discover how the sun falls slanting through the sycamore, and at what hour the sword of Orion pierces the great grave heart of the yew tree; and if he is wise he will make what acquaintance he can with the names and qualities of those who will one day be his neighbours, that when he comes among them he may not come as a stranger and unadvised.

ZIZANIAS
(*Time and Tide*, 1927)

It was the first day that the sun had really warmed my back, and I was mooning in at the gate in an ecstasy when I beheld my neighbour . . . if neighbours can be vertical as well as horizontal, standing on the doorstep and surveying the front garden with a very splenetic expression.

'Just look at it!' she exclaimed, waving a kid hand contemptuously. 'Isn't it disgraceful? The landlord ought to be ashamed of himself, letting it get into such a state.'

'He doesn't appear to take much interest in it, certainly,' said I, inwardly much relieved to discover that the upkeep of the front garden was the landlord's affair, and not that of the tenant of the ground floor flat.

'It's an eyesore, that's what it is. Those weeds! If he doesn't send a proper man about it soon, I shall do something with my own hands.'

With this awful threat she went indoors. I remained standing in the sun; but now the virtue had gone out of it, it did not warm me any more, and at the thought of a proper man arriving, a man with a rake, a pair of shears, and a bottle of weedkiller, a cold shudder ran down my back.

The said front garden is an area of about six square yards, gravelled and containing one spotted laurel and a tree which looks much like an ash, but which knowing friends inform me is an ailanthus. I daresay that when it was first laid out this pleasaunce looked a trifle bleak; but neglect has softened its asperities, and added to the indigenous flora a sprinkling of grass, several dandelions, some groundsel, and a colony of superb thistles. These thistles are my especial pride. I admire them daily, I mark their growth with complacency, reflecting that nobody else in the terrace has reared such noble thistles as I. I watch over them with the solicitude of a mother; or perhaps I should say, since the solicitude of a mother is usually expressed in action, that I watch over them with the solicitude of a father. Anyhow, I like them very much.

And now they are threatened, and another of London's amenities is in the balance. First the Foundling Hospital, and now my thistles . . . and of the two I think I shall regret the thistles most; they are so uniquely rural, it is almost as good as a day in the country to walk through them. What's more, if I am to lose them, I shall lose with them a most valuable subject of conversation. I shall no longer be able to hold up my head in the society of horticulturalists.

Heretofore it has been an easy matter. When the horticulturalists paused for breath I remarked with modest assurance:

'Of course one can't hope to do much in a London garden. But last summer I had a splendid show of zizanias.'

Zizania is the Latin for tare; but that is no real obstacle, at least, it has never proved so. I have yet to meet the amateur gardener who will admit to ignorance of any herb mentioned as consenting to grow for another amateur gardener.

'Ah yes. Zizanias. One sees them in quite a lot of gardens nowadays. Do you find them difficult to manage?'

'No, I am rather lucky with mine. I have heard people complain that they are so weedy, but I shouldn't say that.'

'Of course there is a tendency to weediness. Still, once they are properly established . . .'

'Exactly. Do you grow them too?'

'Oh yes! They simply used to ramp in my old garden. In fact a time came when I had to take them up because they were smothering everything else in the border. But I had an idea that they didn't like clay.'

'Well, as it happens, mine are in gravel. But I don't think zizanias have any special crochets about soil. I believe the secret with them is a little wholesome neglect. All mine are self-sown.'

'Yes, so were mine.'

And so on. But now, perhaps, these pleasant conversations are numbered; for I can hardly pretend that I look on my zizanias as a matter of conscience, yet I do not think that I shall be able to exploit them with such conviction when I know that they have shared the common fate of tares, and have been cast into the burning. What shall I talk about then? Good God, I may have to make my boast of crazy paving! . . . for now that my vertical neighbour has taken the matter to heart I feel that almost anything may happen. I try to comfort myself with the thought that crazy paving is said to be very expensive (though if that be true, a visit to any suburb should convince the most confirmed pessimists that there is still a deal of money left in the country), but that is a doubtful comfort, a bruised reed that may snap at any moment . . . for have I not seen among the home-from-home splendours of the Mayfair Hotel that vast expanse of crazy paving carpet, with the craziness and the little green smudges repeated at intervals in what one might call recurrent mania? And if crazy paving can be procured in Wilton Pile, will it not soon be procurable in linoleum also? . . . an out-door species of linoleum, especially suitable for urban pleasure-grounds because it can be speedily cleansed with our patent mop, Madam? Alas, my poor thistles! *Heu tibi, O Zizania!*

But under this shadow of impending catastrophe two sources of consolation are left to me. One is my own firm unbending mind; if the front garden be put down under linoleum I shall not sit weakly and womanishly smiting my breast, but going to some stone-mason's yard I shall buy a garden statue. A garden statue always makes a garden look so distinctive. Mine will, at any rate. None of your storks or cupids for me, I am for a statesman, a larger than life-sized statesman. And in the summer dusks, I shall steal out and have an assignation with Gladstone, twine about his marble limbs like a clematis, twirl my fingers through his sculptural curls, and toy with the buttons above his stony heart. That is one source of consolation. The other is that there is a back-garden also, and I do not think that anybody will tidy up that haunt of ancient peace. It grows thistles too, the groundsel flaunts its domesticity unbridled, the dandelions were a perfect sight this April, and I see no reason why I should not rear some nettles, *urtica repellens*. And there among the dustbins I shall find a refuge.

ARE PARENTS REALLY NECESSARY?
(*Good Housekeeping*, January, 1949)

When people use the word 'necessary' they seldom mean more than half what they say. If they wish the word to carry its whole force, they qualify it with an 'absolutely' or a 'vitally,' or they use some other word like 'indispensable.'

So when I received an editorial request to write on the question *Are Parents Really Necessary?* I could be sure that I was not being asked to give my opinion as a biologist on the desirability of babies being grown in hygienic containers, like sweet-peas. From the presence of that qualifying 'really' I knew that I was expected to express my views on whether or no parents can be conveniently dispensed with.

I must say at once that I have a mild prejudice in favour of retaining them. I admit that, like other survivals from a pre-mechanical age, they have their drawbacks: they are unwieldy, they tend to last too long, they cannot be fitted with standardised spare parts, and they are too large to look well in prefabricated houses. Yet many people like having them about, and others positively rejoice in them. No one who has heard a private schoolmaster privately exclaim to the wife (or matron) of his bosom, 'I have just caught another parent,' could doubt the gladdening import of such a blessed event.

Indeed, there is a large and worthy section of the community to whom parents are so necessary that it is doubtful if they could continue to exist without them. Besides schoolmasters, makers of toy yachts, and ladies wishing to go to South Africa who will take charge of a child or children in return for travelling expenses, there are those numerous persons who support themselves by giving advice and guidance on parenthood – especially to mothers.

I suppose there is no one, not even a Home Secretary, to whom so much advice is directed as the present-day mother of a young family. If she opens a newspaper, her eye will be met by the picture of some compellingly matronly body directing her to a baby food. If she turns on the wireless, she will shortly hear a voice telling about juvenile delinquency, the best way to sew on buttons, or the number of children killed on the road. If she goes to the pictures, there will be a documentary on the whooping-cough. If she opens a novel, she will find some frustrated character whose misfortunes spring from a maltreated infantile suppression. If she rushes into the open to get away from it all, her path will be crossed by someone who knows how interested she is in child welfare, or a kindly old gentleman who asks her if she is sure the elastic is not too tight under the child's chin.

All these persons supplying advice, information, guidance, constructive criticism, helpful analysis, home hints, etc., agree in assuring her that whatever she does or doesn't do will determine the health and happiness of her children. This, unfortunately, is about the one thing they do agree in. She staggers on through a tempest of guidance. Some are guiding her to look on her children as so many pots and pans, to be cleaned, and filled, and cleaned again, and hung up at night in airy surroundings. Others are guiding her to look on them as so many potential neurotics and criminals. Her children must develop freely, they must learn the meaning of discipline, they must eat a balanced diet, they must not be compelled to eat what they don't want to, they must not be afraid of the dark, they may be given a nightlight, they must be encouraged to co-operate, their individualities must be respected, their tongues must not be coated, their extremities must be kept warm, their heads must remain cool, they must not be coddled. As for herself – she must do as the experts advise, she must rely on her maternal instinct, she must make full use of State provisions, she must always put home first, and she must never allow domesticity to become an obsession.

The directions to fathers, if less profuse, are quite as peremptory. In addition to paying the bills and being legally responsible for any torts or malfeasances committed by his children, he must take an interest in his home, preserve a sense of proportion, and always be ready to lend a hand. If he tends to let domesticity become an obsession, there will be no real harm in it.

At this point it would appear that the question as to whether parents are really necessary has answered itself. Not only do they afford a *raison d'être* for all these valuable professional advisers; but if they don't carry out the advice, who will?

But there is more advice to come – there usually is; and this time it is a stern warning to parents to know their place. Fathers must not be Roman Fathers. Mothers must not be broody hens. Children must never, never be encouraged to feel dependent. Parents must not be puffed up into fancying themselves really necessary. As cooks, nurses, laundresses, dressmakers, charwomen, gardeners, psychologists, bootboys, dietitians and hairdressers parents can play their useful humble part; if need be, and as the occasion demands, they can be medical orderlies, stokers and electricians; later on they can make themselves obliging as bankers, bowlers, and *dames de compagnie*; but there is no call for them to behave as though they were parents.

Perhaps the warning is needed. Anyone who has seen certain matriarchs in full maturity (say, about sixty, dressed in ice-blue, and sucking the juices of ashen-haired sons and wan daughters) will agree that there should be a limit to parental claims. But the fact that some tigers become man-eating tigers is really no reason for refusing to keep a cat. Cats are a great embellishment to the home. Children like playing with them, and find them comfortable to hug. Why should we not allow the same to be true of parents?

It is worth noting that the question whether parents are really necessary agitates the grown-up only. Children just know their own minds. Their judgments may sometimes seem harsh, but they are clear. Children are known to be materialists, so one might expect to find them sloughing their parents when those parents are of no further use to them.

Oddly enough, this is not so. We see some little materialists, whose parents are still in perfect running order, discarding them like so much junk. Others cling to parents who have demonstrably become superfluous. Then there is the perplexing phenomenon of those children whose parents are no credit to them, parents who are lazy, or dirty, who drink, who never get up in time for breakfast, who cannot thread a needle, whose investments always fail – and yet the offspring of these shocking persons love, and even honour them, turn to them in emergencies, remember their birthdays, and carry up their breakfasts on trays.

In fact, it would almost seem that the worse you are as a cook, nurse, laundress, etc (I cannot go through the whole catalogue again; readers will find it four paragraphs back), the more likelihood there is that your children will find you necessary – not merely 'really necessary,' but plain, flat, outright necessary. By challenging them to admit your inadequacy you are on the way to become the child's most valued possession. You will be friendlier than the cat, more alluring than the garbage-man. You will be a responsibility.

It is the misfortune of children that we fail to recognise their immense untapped capacities to take charge of us. They are more washed against than washing. How many children are allowed to shampoo a mother? 'Even quite small children may be encouraged to fold up their own clothes,' say the advisers. They would need no encouragement at all to get to work with a father's trouser-press. The hair, perhaps, might look tangled, but the parents would look much better in their children's eyes. They would look as if they belonged to the family.

For the possessiveness of parents, which leads to ice-blue matriarchs, protracted infantilism, and all the other dreadful things which impel us to cry out, 'Are Parents Really Necessary?,' is biologically compensated for by the possessiveness of children. To a child a parent is not merely a synthesis of parental functions, a hand that feeds and washes, a lap to sit on, a voice that answers questions; a parent is the child's immediate portion of the wide world to come, a territory to explore, a dominion to map and take possession of, a problem to master, a responsibility to assume. Or should be. But the child can only enter that world and begin its exploring by finding a weak place in the fence; parents who show no weaknesses deny that entrance to their children. They refuse to be possessed. They are not humble enough to be necessary.

IMPERFECT GUESTS
(*Good Housekeeping*, 1949)

'Well, my dear,' said thc honoured guest, who had just partaken very heartily of roast pheasant – '*Well*, my dear – I have never eaten a more delicious chicken.'

He was a man of genius, and may have preferred his chicken decomposed, for men of genius are notoriously perverse of palate; or he may have been misled by the bread sauce. The very few critics who praised him, praised him for his exalted mind (the others referred to him as grovelling in the lowest aspects of human nature), and an exalted mind, soaring about among eagles and angels, might not be able to spare attention for the details of the lesser-winged creation. But as he had obviously enjoyed this roasted specimen of the winged creation, whatever he may have taken it for, my feelings as a hostess were unruffled. Besides, he had only come to dine. I daresay that if I had had him for a week-end his inattentive praises might have become rather wounding. 'I have never seen a finer fox-terrier,' for instance, would have seared me as an estimate of my honoured chow-dog.

In those distant days of pheasants abounding, the distinction between guests who come to dine and guests who come to stay did not need to be made. Anything that went to bed was called a visitor, and the beds they went to were in spare rooms. Personally, I am attached to the word 'visitor,' whose affinity to that more sorrowful word, visitation (a Visitation of the Plague), expresses so well the melancholy and mistrust that distend an Englishman's bosom when an Englishman's home

365

becomes a place of entertainment. The term 'spare room,' too, carries an interesting national implication that such a room only has visitors sleeping in it because one can find nothing better to put there.

But whether they come as Old English visitors or Americanised guests, people who come to stay come to be judged, too. Even on the doorstep the process of judgment lies in wait for them – like a door-scraper. There is, for instance, their luggage. Personally, I mistrust persons who arrive with very neat luggage. It looks so hardened. Such persons, I opine, make a habit of being guests. They will have a wide field of experience, they will be in a position to draw comparisons; and ten to one comparisons drawn from me and my house will be invidious ones. Such persons will arrive with cut-and-dried notions of what a hostess should do. They will expect the crusts to be cut off their sandwiches, and a fire in the bed-room will be no novelty to them – unless it smokes.

On the other hand, one must admit that people with very neat luggage are usually good at going away. They are packed and ready just when they should be, and they don't leave things behind. Yet leaving things behind – again I speak for myself – is not such a vile trait as it is made out to be. There is even a kind of pensive pleasure to be got from gathering up the fragments that remain – the packet of razor-blades, the solitary stocking, the book from the lending library, the mysterious framed snapshot of an old gentleman leaning against a cow. These vestiges make the departed guest seem more real to one. They make the departure seem more real, too; one can dwell on it more maturely than when actively engaged in crying out, 'Such a delightful visit! Isn't this your umbrella? I think this must be your return ticket. Enjoyed every moment of – here are your gloves.'

A more crucial degree of judgment begins after the first meal, for it is then that a guest discloses itself as helpful or unhelpful. If, while the words 'May I help with the washing-up?' are spoken, the willing hands remain folded in the lap, there is nothing to fear. If these words are accompanied by a purposeful fidgeting, they are ominous. A moment later the balance of the tray one is carrying is imperilled by the swift rape of two spoons and the butter-dish, which the guest conveys in an unhesitating swoop to the ground-floor toilet. 'The kitchen is this way,' one says. Fatal words! But what else can one say?

There may be some women so angelic that they do not object to the presence of helpful guests in the kitchen. I am not one of these. However noisily I run the hot water, however suicidally I sink myself in the sink, I remain aware of that hovering helper behind me. 'What shall I do with the butter-dish?' 'Put it down,' I reply, trying not to let the remark sound as though addressed to an imperfectly-trained retriever. Clatter-clatter. 'Here are the spoons!' Jammy end forward, the spoons glide along my sleeve. 'And now where shall I find a cloth?' Rolling my maddened eyes towards the dish-cloths, I see that they are all too workaday to be offered to a guest. I go to fetch a clean one. On my return the guest turns round from the sink, saying archly, 'I've got my way, you see. *I'm* washing up now!' – and with a liberal gesture, soap-flakes are sprinkled inside the teapot. I often wonder why more sinks do not flow with blood.

I also wonder why it is that helpful guests, if they are in the plural, always clot; and why they invariably choose to clot in the gangway, making it impossible to get to the larder unless one lies down on the floor and worms out between their conversational legs.

The helpful guest, unless purely a dotter, is generally a she-guest. Reforming guests can be of either sex, and for devastation there is little or nothing between them. Reforming guests see their mission at a glance. As the Psalmist says, they are swift as vultures, and before they have wiped the How-d'ye-do off their lips they are clamouring for putty and gimlets and step-ladders. They borrow all the pudding-basins to mix paint in; in the midst of a *sauce Béarnaise* they only want to warm a little glue; they are determined to make one a dew-pond (all that is needed is some wet clay and a few loads of straw); they can knock up bookshelves, fell trees, varnish floors, enamel baths, re-proof raincoats and mend the clock. They take off all the door-knobs, in order to see how to put them on again. And when they quit the scene of half-baked ruin, they administer the *coup de grâce* by saying lightly, 'I'll finish it off when I come again.' Not – I say it from tested experience – that when they come again they do. New plumage has sprouted on the vultures, new missions summon the reformers. They do something to the electricity, and all the fuses are blown.

By comparison with a reforming guest, how tranquil, how almost benign, is the guest who is taken ill! And when recovery sets in, how gladly one prolongs the little attentions of convalescence, pinning down any tendencies to helpfulness under a tray, observing the beautiful phenomenon of a guest clotted in a *cul de sac* instead of in a gangway. Sometimes they will even become so obligingly bored that they offer to do a little mending. I always keep a few worthy hand-towels in store, or half a dozen tarnished spoons, in order to fall in with such offers. For I have nothing against industry so long as it is undertaken in a submissive spirit.

Submission, liking to breakfast in bed, lack of enterprise, a moderate punctuality, peccable, as opposed to impeccable, luggage, hypocrisy and mendacity – enough, at any rate, to keep up an appearance of enjoying the visit – a flow of conversation and an unhelpful nature: these are my requirements (and surely they are simple enough!) from the good guest.

But goodness and perfection grow on different trees; and when I come to think of my perfect guest – for I have such a one, a rose among onions – I realise that she contravenes almost all my requirements. She is totally lacking in submissiveness, she grasps the pruning saw and demands the step-ladder, she says what she thinks, she does as she pleases, and in the course of doing what she pleases she mislays all sense of time. In fact, the only canon she regularly observes is that little matter of peccable luggage. Her luggage, indeed, is so far from being neat that I hesitate to call it luggage at all. It is more accurately described as the things she brings with her. On her last visit one of the things she brought with her was a large copper tea-urn filled with quinces. The quinces were for me – she had remembered how much I like quinces, and gathered them just as she was about to start, which was why she came by the later train. The urn was for her next hostess, a person given to parish convivialities. But it did not go empty away. It went away filled with leaf-mould and with a faggot of willow-slips tied on to it, like an osprey. Arrivals and departures such as these broaden the mind of the local railway station, demonstrate the freedom of the human spirit, and warm the cockles of my heart.

Still, it may be that knowing a perfect guest tends to make one rather censorious about all the other poor wretches.

SOMETHING ABOUT AUNTS
(*Modern Woman*, 1950)

I was once told by an historian that Dido, Queen of Carthage, was Jezebel's aunt. Or perhaps he told me that Jezebel was aunt to Dido. I cannot positively remember which was which, and I have forgotten how he found it out. But what I shall always remember is the tone of ruminating emotion in his voice as he spoke the word 'aunt,' and the thrill I felt at finding Jezebel! – or Dido – embellished with a new meaning for me.

At the mention of an aunt, the English bosom resounds with a deep rich chord. We are as a nation extremely sensitive to the music of words, and the word 'aunt' certainly falls on the ear with a sombre harmony.

But the mention of an aunt does more than strike a black velvet paw on one's hearing. Even when pronounced *ant*, as in Northern Ireland, or rhymed with *gaunt*, as by Sydney Dobell[3], the word aunt affects us to the depths of our being. And if I were a psychiatrist, just as old-fashioned medical men when sounding their patients' breathing said, 'Say ninety-nine,' I would say to my patients, 'Say aunt.' And I have no doubt but that the results would be most illuminating.

The word aunt, as Sydney Dobell probably realised, has very few rhymes, and of these few, two are *can't* and *shan't*. It would be tempting to suggest that, being such a poetical nation, we are all intuitively aware of the difficulty of rhyming about our aunts without becoming involved with these forbidding monosyllables, hence the hallucinated state into which we fall when aunts are mentioned. Tempting, but fallacious. There is no rhyme to window, but you can shout 'window' at an Englishman without arousing any thought in his mind beyond the thought that you may want it opened, or shut, coupled with an instantaneous decision to keep it shut, or opened.

What is an aunt? She is the sister of a mother or a father, and a man may not marry his aunt (*vide* the Table of Affinity in the *Book of Common Prayer*). But I am sure that it was no thwarted passion to marry his aunt that made the historian's voice thrill as he spoke of the relationship between Dido and Jezebel. Women have aunts, too, quite as often as men, cannot under any circumstances marry them, would not (except most hypothetically – '*If I were Mr. Jackson . . .*') wish to; and are just as much

369

subject to the aunt-spell as men.

Legend clusters round aunts as ivy clusters on ruined castles. Every one has a story about an aunt: if not an aunt legitimately owned, then borrowed from another. Hostesses know this, and avail themselves of it. Many a dumbfoundered party has been got going again by a well-placed story about an aunt. Even the words, 'Talking of aunts,' will do it. They are scarcely spoken before all those tongue-tied guests are clamouring of aunts, shouting each other down to relate how an Aunt Jezebel of theirs over-balanced while varnishing her toe-nails at the window, fell out, and was eaten by her Pekingese, or to tell the very sad story of poor Aunt Dido.

If one longs for fame, enduring fame and widespread notoriety, one has only to be an aunt. And it is a saddening reflection, if one is an only child, that one's oddest or most revolting traits, one's most remarkable adventures, one's most blood-curdling eccentricities, will never be given their due.

Of course one could make oneself into an aunt by marriage. But aunts by marriage are not the same as Blood Aunts. There is not that certain something about them, they don't ring true. Envious listeners to a really superb aunt story will sometimes ask, 'But was she *really* your aunt?' And if the answer comes, 'Well, an aunt by marriage,' much of the effect is lost.

Legend clusters round aunts, authors find them invaluable. For years now I have been pursuing aunts through English Letters. It is disappointing that Milton and Shakespeare yield such poor results. There is not the breath of an aunt in *Paradise Lost* and the Lady in *Comus* is only an aunt *in petto*.

Shakespeare has not a single full-length aunt, only a few sketches and kit-cats, and though Autolycus sang that the lark that tirra-lirra chants made summer songs for him and his aunts while they lay tumbling in the hay, I think no one maintains that Autolycus meant that kind of aunt.

But by the eighteenth century that Aunt appears in majesty, usually a maiden aunt and living in a disagreeable rural seclusion. The worst threat to a Miss Hoyden is to be packed off to an aunt. With the rise of morality and Queen Victoria, aunts become even more numerous, but tend to grow benign, though in a tyrannical busy-body way. They bring up quantities of orphans, and abound in useful information, as in *Aunt Louisa's Alphabet* and *Aunt Judy's Magazine*.

During the present century aunts have shed their benignity and become increasingly macabre. Under the appearance of living quietly in the country with some marjoram, they frighten little boys, or know more than they should about the head which is missing from the bank manager, and very strange things happen at their funerals. Yet I do not think one need be seriously alarmed by the current vogue for sinister aunts. Times change, and aunts change with them. What is significant is the fact that for two and a half centuries of our literature aunts have held their own, and that during that time, while changing from the severe to the benign, from the benign to the macabre, they have never lost the attributes of being both powerful and knowing.

There is – I suppose I may mention it – an organisation called Universal Aunts; and whether or not one has availed oneself of its services, one knows it by repute and reposes on the thought of it. If there is no one to meet the pet, though rather excitable, hyæna at the railway terminus, if there is no time to sew all the name-tags on the children's under-clothing before they start for school, if one doesn't feel strong enough to look for a suitable wedding-present for a K.C. – in short, at a pinch, one can turn to those Universal Aunts. But if the organisation were called Universal Nieces, would it seem so balsamic? Nieces, in point of fact, can be quite as efficient as aunts, and statistically likely to be younger and more active. But the thought of a Universal Niece cannot carry the same assurance. There is something about an aunt. . . .

But what is there about an Aunt?

A very early aunt, so remote that she makes Dido and Jezebel seem mere chits, has been preserved to us in the Polynesian version of the story of Joseph and his brethren. The Polynesian Joseph is a close resemblance to the Joseph of the Old Testament, except that he has no father. It is his mother and her sister who bewail his loss and go in search of him. For the Polynesian Joseph represents the earliest forms of human society, when mating was so haphazard that the relationship between father and child was not recognised at all.

The family of this matriarchal society knew of no kinship except kinship through the female line: a mother, a mother's mother, aunts and uncles in the maternal line, sisters, brothers, and sister's children. So it was natural that when the Polynesian Joseph was carried off in a canoe,

371

his grieving mother should turn to her sister as the person most likely to take an interest in the boy, and be active on his behalf. She was his aunt.

Of course, all this is extremely ancient history. But it is the history of the human race, and all societies have passed through the stage of a matriarchate. And then the English are so devoted to their traditions, long, long after they have ceased to understand them. Vestigial loops linger on the hats of our bishops. Rents of red roses or peppercorns are still valid. Many of us feel uneasy when we spill the salt. Perhaps the afterglow of the matriarchal system still glorifies the Aunt.

AN EDINBURGH CHILDHOOD

(unpublished ms, Warner/Ackland Archive, Dorset County Museum, written at Frankfort Manor, Norfolk, 1933 or '34)

In the old days, when servants' legs, if not longer and stronger, were certainly more enduring than they are now, nurseries were established as a matter of course at the top of the house. Some parents, with a feather of enlightenment in their caps, might talk of the superior purity of the air at these high altitudes; others were content to admit that children were noisy beings, best insulated with a layer or two of bedrooms from the polite part of the house. There, from the windows of their lofty world, the children of the last century looked down on the comings and goings of their elders with an interest, and I think, a critical faculty, sharpened by the barrier then set between the old and the young. That other world was to them something like a stage; and Papa, and Mamma, and their grave friends, and the doctor, and the clergyman, a great deal more like players than it would have suited their dignity to know.

In one of those lofty nurseries, ninety years ago, there was a little girl called Flora[4], whose mother, a Flora also, was the god-daughter of the god-daughter of Flora Macdonald. With this profoundly Scots genealogy it is proper that her nursery crowned one of those tall stone houses which now, even in that city of grave and decorous Georgian, make Charlotte

Square one of the architectural glories of Edinburgh. But to the child whose memoir of her childhood admits me to that nursery and to the vanished world it surveyed, Charlotte Square had other beauties, other glories, than those of wood and stone. There, a daily spectacle, glittering in a downward perspective, were the flunkeys, 'Sir John Sinclair's in light blue, and Sir John Dick Lauder's in crimson plush.' There passed the postman, with 'a scarlet tail-coat with gilt buttons and a shiny top-hat with a cockade' – a resplendent object at all times, most firework-like of all on the morning of the Queen's Birthday, when this gaudy plumage and crest were put on new. And there – less colourful, but with the circus-like possibilities of anything to do with animals – was the man with the goats; who appeared each morning, driving his small flock, and milking them before any door where goats-milk, that much-prescribed fluid, might be required.

Goats-milk was strengthening. It was also natural. And then, an echoing wave from the explosion of *Emile*[5] upon a sophisticated Europe, natural, and frequently nasty, remedies were in vogue. The child's first recollection was of one of these. Salt-water baths had been prescribed as bracing 'and I remember sitting crying in a great wooden washtub full of sea-water up to my chin.' Another of these natural remedies the child saw practised upon a younger brother, whose lingering whooping-cough was exorcised by holding him over a lime-kiln so that he might, willy-nilly, breathe up the fumes. These were holiday diversions, and took place at Dalmeny. But though the Firth of Forth was salutary in a wash tub, its unrestricted billows were not to be made free with, and when Flora's playmate recklessly launched his basket upon that ocean, he did a perilous thing. 'It was carried out by the waves to what seemed to us an immense distance. Our nurse put down the baby on the shore and valiantly took off her shoes and stockings, and kilted her coats, and waded in after it. I have the distinctest recollection of the breathless interest with which we saw her hook out the basket with a long stick, and the relief of Edward who would no doubt have had a whipping had he returned without it. Afterwards we had a cherry tart at dinner.'

To Edward, aged about six, the thought of that whipping 'scaped must have given a rare sweetness to the cherry tart. Whippings were part of the established regimen – a natural and nasty remedy; cherry tarts occurred less frequently. Parents, as well as children, submitted to a great deal of plain living. 'Our Sunday dinner was invariably the same, and a very nice one: roast beef and an arrow-root shape with damson jam and cream.' Even allowing for a slight seasonal variation of the jam (and could even a Scots cook of that exemplary epoch have made sufficient damson jam for fifty-three Sundays?) we should scarcely consider this recurring bill of fare *a very nice one*.

The outer man was adorned as austerely as the inner. Save the light blue and crimson flunkeys there was little to satisfy a child's craving for colour and display. Clothes were 'plain and sensible'; not from any economical motives, since there was a grim insistence upon good quality, velvets of everlasting solidity and blackness, silks which had been searched like consciences, but because plainness and sense were the fashion of the day. 'Bright colours were considered very unladylike; drabs and lilacs for summer and browns and maroons for winter were the only wear. Black beaver bonnets, worn with a bonnet-cap inside, and some very funereal-looking black feathers outside were the general winter fashion. In summer we had straw bonnets trimmed with white ribbon, or with maize when the straw began to get burnt' (admirable example of Scots economy, so decorous and so sly). 'Large bonnets of Leghorn straw with straw trimmings were very fashionable, and it was considered an immense advantage that they could never wear out but might be reproduced for a dozen successive summers.'

Brighter skies had brighter manners. In August 1846 Flora's uncle returned with his wife and family from the West Indies, where he had estates. 'The three girls were so unlike us and our contemporaries that on the first meeting I could do nothing but stare at them. They were dressed in very short flounced frocks, frilled drawers down to the ankles, tight-fitting black silk casaques, drawn silk bonnets and their hair in long plaited pig-tails' (cf. the appearance of the Misses Kenwigs in *Nicholas Nickleby*). 'I daresay they thought us in our print frocks (scanty and rather long in the skirt) tippets and straw poke bonnets and our hair all about our ears at least as queer-looking.'

Uncle Alexander's party included also two negro servants, 'Clarke and Dan, without whom Aunt Eliza found it impossible to move. Clarke was an enormous fat woman, more yellow than black. I remember seeing her

374

at supper in the nursery, in a loose white dressing-gown and a yellow silk handkerchief like a turban on her head – an extraordinary vision.' What Clarke and Dan thought of the Edinburgh winter and the easterly haar, that icy sea-breath which seems able to chill even granite, is not recorded. Aunt Eliza with her romantic grand airs, her lackadaisical graces, escaped its worst rigours; for before Christmas she died in childbirth, and her three daughters exchanged their flounced frocks and frilled drawers for deep mourning, made after the plain and sensible style smiled on (if smiled be not too florid a term) by northern skies.

Clarke and Dan were not the only hapless West Indians to shiver as a result of this family bond between Edinburgh and Santa Cruz. 'One day when I went to Grandmamma's Aunt Jane introduced me to a little black boy called Abraham.' Abraham's father was a Spaniard, married (so at any rate Flora was told) to a coloured woman, and a Santa Cruz acquaintance of Uncle Alexander's. For some reason he had set his desire upon 'a good but not expensive education in Great Britain' for the boy, and Uncle Alexander, invoked, and sure of that reliable article, Scots *esprit de la famille*, had written 'begging Grandmamma to receive him and look out a good school for him. He was only considered *rather dark* in the West Indies but to us he appeared a complete Negro; however I felt no antipathy to him on that account. He taught me to play marbles and I remember quite well the look of his black hand beside mine. He used to talk a great deal about his slaves and his authority over them, and I compared his happy lot with mine: he could have his slaves flogged, while my nurse could slipper me. How I envied and admired him!'

The required education, 'good but not expensive,' was found at an Academy at Dollar. Here no doubt the poor child had good reason to recall with tenderness those fair distant days of slave owning, and to long for the time when he might return to a warmer climate and the pleasures of authority. But if those pleasures were ever regained it can only have been for a short while, for the slaves in question were freed not long after this.

While Abraham was at Dollar another liberation took place: Flora was freed from her tyrant, and passed from the nursery to the school-room. There was a daily governess – 'a lady with sausage curls, not a highly educated woman (she taught me that this was the eighteenth century)'; but the main

375

part of her education was carried out by visiting masters, the sausage curls were not expected to do much more than sit by while those lessons were given, and escort their pupil to classes. No young woman of those days could be considered educated without a good knowledge of foreign languages, and Flora had masters for French, Italian, and German. The Italian master was a patriot, and so, an exile. 'Once I was wearing some yellow and black ribbon (the Austrian colours). "Ah, Miss," he said; "no young lady should wear those colours."' There was also a writing master. This gentleman did not only teach an elegant script; his instructions included the conventions and niceties of letter-writing, the proper phraseology in which to be delighted or dignified, condoling or congratulative.

A lighter study (though still to be approached with becoming seriousness) was dancing. Madame d'Egville, dressed in black velvet, was much admired by Flora. 'She used to *swim* into the room.' Besides quadrilles, reels and waltzes Madame d'Egville taught the mysteries of deportment to the northern barbarians. 'To this day the March in *Norma* recalls the whole scene of our dancing lessons to me; it was the tune Monsieur invariably played (Monsieur provided the music for his stately spouse's teaching, playing on a 'kit' or small fiddle) for our final walk round, at the end of which each girl had to advance alone from the door to Madame, take her hand and wish her an elegant farewell, and if it was not elegant enough the ordeal was repeated three or four times, always to this imposing air.'

Deportment, however, was only for girls. Boys might be as manly and tormenting as they pleased, and Flora was very much of the opinion that the pleasantest parties were those at which only girls were present. One of the queerest features of the society depicted in these memoirs is the matter of fact assumption by the Edinburgh ladies, so sincerely prim, so severely refined, that their menkind should abide by an entirely different standard of behaviour. Flora describes how, when her parents gave a dinner-party – an occasion for solemn preparations, when 'the great plate-chest with its three locks was opened, the cut-glass dishes, cut in such sharp diamonds that it was quite painful to hold them, displayed on the sideboard, the table laid with eighteen bishop's mitres', she descended from the nursery regions to sit in the drawing-room with Mamma and the ladies after they had quitted the dessert. There they sat, the Mammas, civilly conversing, decently draped in their 'silk or embroidered or lace shawls, or, what was very much admired, very long boas of ermine or swansdown; something at any rate over the shoulders, although low dresses in those days were seldom much below the collar bones;' and there sat Flora, civilly seen and not heard, unless she were called upon to 'play her piece.' *Lang, lang, might the leddies sit Wi' the kames in their hair* – but long as it was, Flora had been discreetly dismissed ere the gentlemen quitted their wine and joined their ladies. 'Even till I left Edinburgh (which was to be married) the gentlemen's after-dinner sittings used to be prolonged sometimes till after ten o'clock (dinner would not have begun later than six), and many of them used to come to the drawing-room very hazy and stupid or else unnaturally funny and confidential.' Indeed, some of them did not climb to the drawing-room at all, but were assisted from the mahogany to their carriages, where on a discreet hint from the host, their ladies joined them.

However, all this was made up for on Sunday. Sunday behaviour allowed for no respect of persons, male and female alike bowed to a universal law. 'Sometimes we had colds and did not go to church, and then it was quite a sight to sit at the window and see the people passing. For about ten minutes the pavements would be crowded with a continuous stream of people and several sedan chairs (cabs were thought wrong, because they prevented the drivers from getting to church; but the sedan chairs could stand in the vestibule, and *Donal* and *Sandy* could come in). There would be the same stream coming back, and then between and after the services the streets absolutely deserted. A few frivolous people went to the occasional evening sermons that were announced in the papers, but the stricter sort never stirred out after five o'clock.'

Did I say that there was no respect of persons? Perhaps that is not quite correct. 'Papa spent Sunday evening in his business room, where I fancy he read a little secular literature, which it would not have been considered correct to do in the family circle.' But Papa, cultured, adventurously-minded and hedonistic enough to have the walls of his business room hung round with line engravings after Rubens and Le Brun, would sometimes break away like this – a trait very endearing to a daughter. 'This summer (1852) I first tasted the insidious joys of "Puseyism" in a little chapel at Dalmahoy[6]. The minister of Currie[7], our parish, was ill, and the succession of Candidates and Stickit Ministers who filled his place proved too much for Papa's patience, though he generally went very submissively to the Presbyterian church when in the country. So he and I used to start immediately after breakfast (not without some tacit disapproval from Mamma) for a long delightful walk to the chapel at Dalmahoy, where there was a surpliced choir and an organ in blue and gold, and the chapel roof in blue and gold stars like the vault of heaven and a cross and flowers on the altar, and a very meek priest in a green stole . . . and when I heard the boys chant the Nicene Creed for the first time not all the glories of a mass in S. Peter's could seem to me more sublime.'

Flora was growing older. The world was opening out round about her, and she could speak quite naturally of S. Peter's. She had already been to London, had seen the Great Exhibition, the fireworks in the Surrey Gardens, 'the Polytechnic with the Diver and Professor Pepper's lectures,' and other delights. They travelled to London by night, 'and it was considered *de rigueur* that we should all wear nightcaps on the journey; everyone at this time slept in a nightcap and it was not thought safe to leave them off. I suppose we slept at first, but I can remember the interest – almost the awe – with which in the grey morning I looked out at the unfamiliar landscape, the close hedgerows and tall trees like feathered poles, and felt that I was in a new country.'

A new country indeed – irrevocably distant from the boundless Firth of Forth, the Queen's Birthday, the blue and the crimson footmen, the awful, solitary advance to the March in *Norma*. Step by step, not tumbling now, but moving with the disciplined paces of well-learned deportment, the child had come to the frontier of childhood, and crossed it, and was in the new country, the other world which she had scanned from the nursery windows, and whence, afterwards, with her own children about her, looking back, she was to write the memoir of her childhood, a guidebook to the lost land.

WEEDS
(The Countryman, Summer, 1942)

Once I knew a garden – quite a large garden, too – whose owner requested me, out of my abundance, to spare her a little groundsel for her canary. I thought the request lacking in delicacy; but it started a train of thought. When we consider how much of the gardener's time is taken up with weeds – whether, like a professional gardener, he hoes them and turns them in, or whether, being an amateur, he tries to root them out – the sparing mention of weeds by those who write about their gardens seems hypocritical.

The tiresome aphorist who said that dirt was matter in the wrong place might have had something equally sage to say about weeds – though it is difficult to think, off-hand, of a right place for such a plant as goose-grass – or perhaps you call it cleavers.

Locality, undoubtedly, has something to do with it. The dandelion in the hedge is a praiseworthy creature enough, and it is a delight to children, who enjoy the way its sticky white juice turns black on the hands and face. But let the dandelion settle down to 'praise a lawn for growing green', and country gentlemen, during the months when they cannot carry a gun, will walk out with a dandelion spud.

Mare's-tail is another of these weeds by circumstance. A survival of the flora of the coal age, it is sufficiently aristocratic not to grow in every soil, and, when found by botanists and fossil-lovers, it is often greeted with scholarly enthusiasm. But interesting and queerly handsome as it is, with its stiff green bottle-brush, gardeners with whom it condescends to thrive greet it with ill words. Its roots, earth-coloured and ramifying, are almost invisible and break at a touch; and every fragment left in the ground will send up a shoot. There is no hope but in patient persecution, snapping off every head as it appears, and so gradually bleeding the roots to death. The same method will get rid of bracken (a plant of the same lineage) but it is a slow process and may take several years.

No amount of surface discouragement will abolish ground elder, bind-weed, or that grass which is called couch, twitch, or squitch – and what a wealth of exasperated loathing must have exploded in the naming of any plant *squitch*! Every dog knows the virtue of couch-grass, and every gardener its vices: its strangling growth, its banyan-like power of being able to root anew from the joints of its long tendrils, its ramping, spear-tipped roots which can burrow through the thickest clay. Ground elder is not so universal a pest; visitors from a happier world have even asked me the name of that 'pretty little plant'. I can see nothing pretty about it. Its green is insultingly bright and perky, and its pointed leaves recall the most fidgety ornaments of Revival Gothic.

Bind-weed, on the other hand, observes every canon of beauty and elegance, and to beauty and elegance the lesser bind-weed adds the most exquisite almond scent. Contemplating it I feel, I suppose, something almost identical with the mourning morality with which our great-great-grandparents contemplated the young ladies of the *demimonde*, sighing that anything so lovely should be so lost, and mixing with those sighs a brisk intention to keep it out of the ground. When George Eliot wished to convey the sharpest insinuations of depravity she made a gentleman, in a fit of *delirium tremens*, cry out upon a siren whose arms were like 'grand white serpents'. The roots of the greater bind-weed are like grand white serpents also, with the additional immorality of being branching serpents. As the tendrils twist and twine themselves about other plants, so do the roots twist and twine, till the victim is strangled above and below ground alike. During the summer the harbourers of bind-weed may as well resign themselves to admiring those candid angel-faced blossoms, those tresses of heart-shaped leaves, the grace of those murderous embraces; for to attack the assailant is to attack its victim also. In autumn there should be a thorough excavation, a disentangling of roots and a sifting of the soil to the depth of two foot or more. The resulting barrow-load of serpents will be, so to speak, a sight for sore backs. Even so, there will be some left for the next summer. The bind-weed's roots go down to the pit. A quarryman told me that he had found them as much as six foot below the surface.

NOT TO BE DONE IN MAY
(Good Housekeeping, May, 1949)

In May one must not eat oysters, cast a clout, marry – and May kittens grow into dirty cats who bring snakes and lizards indoors. On the other hand, in May one should drink mugwort and wash one's face in morning dew. Mugwort (I speak from experience) compares badly with oysters; and I suppose that few enamoured couples would look on an early morning excursion for dew – even with all their winter underclothes clouted about them – as an efficient alternative to a honeymoon. The prohibition of oysters is canonical. Whether or no you comply with the remaining injunctions will be determined by your respect for superstitions and your tolerance of uncomfortable. Superstitions are not for the comfort-loving: what they recommend is never as agreeable as what they forbid. But presumably that is how we like them, so we have only ourselves to blame.

Clouts, kittens, marriages and mugwort are established pieces of May-lore, and can be found in any Dictionary of Superstitions, Pseudodoxia, or Guide to Making Yourself Uncomfortable. Most people have, as well as the superstitions that everyone knows, one or two private fiddle-faddles of their own, to which they cling, even when they neglect the others. If I caught whooping-cough I should be slow to avail myself of roast mouse, or nine lice on a piece of bread and butter, infallible as these well-tried remedies may be, and I trim my nails on a Sunday in spite of that gloomy distich:

Who on the Sabbath pares the horn,
'Twere better for him he'd never been born;

but nothing can dislodge me from my private fiddle-faddle, that it is unlucky to tell fortunes in May – or, if you prefer it,

Who on a May day reads the palm
Will have a future far from calm.

Like so many human misadventures, it all began through being too obliging. A friend of mine had madly consented to organise a village fête (I've forgotten what for; some worthy purpose, no doubt – ridding the old Rector of death-watch beetle, or re-roofing the village bank), and a

381

fortune-teller was to be one of the attractions. When at the last moment the fortune-teller could not come, I as madly undertook to replace her.

Considering how exhausting it is to sit in a small booth made of blankets inventing futures for perfect strangers, and considering the very moderate degree of silver that crossed palms – 1s. for futures, 1s 6d. for spells, individually blended, like tea or face-powder – I went back to town that evening feeling that I had done nobly by whatever the worthy purpose was. I had made £3 0s. 6d. (most of my clients took a spell), and brightened, I hoped, many workaday lives with a dash of fancy.

That was in May. A month later, when it was raining as it can only rain in an English June, my doorbell rang, and I opened my door to a very wet woman, who immediately exclaimed: 'Thank Heavens you are in!' I was thankful, too, for it was no day to be out. But I couldn't believe she had come just to say that. She hadn't. Looking ready to eat me, she continued: 'I had to see you again, so I tracked you down through the Rector. Everything you told me is coming true O Madame Python, how on earth did you know?'

This was not a question I could answer. Besides, other questions were thundering in my ears, and the loudest of them was, What had I told this trustful, grateful, rain-sodden creature? Was it she I had warned against buying violets from a cross-eyed man? Or foreseen riding on an elephant? Or promised a legacy from an uncle struck by lightning near a canal? Was she a simple shilling's-worth, or complicated by a spell?

Meanwhile I had got her sitting down and quietly dripping.

'I did exactly as you told me,' she said.

This was awful; because towards the end of the afternoon I had begun to let myself go over the individual blendings. But, keeping up a Madame Python demeanour, I said that this was wise of her; it never does to tamper with a spell.

'Yes, I remember everything you said. I bought the dried haddock and went out of the shop backwards; and at midnight I stuck in the 49 black pins, and wrapped it up in silver paper and tied it with a white ribbon. But I had to carry it about with me for over a week before I saw a strange man with a rose in his buttonhole. It was nerve-racking, really. I got so nervous, I thought I should never get rid of it. Even then I had a job with it, for he was getting on to the bus. But I ran as fast as I could, and shoved it into his left hand just as the bus started. And when I got home, they had gone!'

I wondered what had gone. Warts, mice, visitors . . . there are so many things one might wish to go.

'How nice of you to come and tell me,' I said.

Looking rather taken aback, she continued: 'I hunted everywhere for them. Because, you see, if they weren't there, how could I tell them my wish? I had just taken off my shoes, feeling so disappointed, when my neighbour came in, and said, "Mabel," she said, "your bees have swarmed at Pett's Garage, and he'll be bringing them round this evening in a fish-kettle." Fish-kettle! That struck me at once as having a meaning, after the haddock. Well, it *had*! But the trouble is, he's not a widower.'

Startled from my sibylline repose, I said: "Did you particularly want a widower?"

'I understood you to say he would be a widower. I haven't known whether to encourage him or not, not without consulting you again. You're so wonderful, you're certain to know best. And there's another thing. I'd like a lucky date for the wedding.'

I said that the first day of September would be very suitable. Again my wet admirer remarked on how wonderful I was. I was thinking so myself, when she dashed my confidence by observing: 'That's why I feel Mrs Ruddock and that Miss Lark are both behaving so ungratefully. They ought to have more faith. Besides, I know for a fact that Mrs Ruddock didn't soak the hair-net in rum before she buried it. I sat behind her in church, and it smelled of linctus, unmistakable! What sort of dark stranger could she expect after that? It served her right when the sweep fell off his bicycle on top of her just when she was taking in the milk. But Mr Marple's the worst of the lot. He says you gave him a bad sixpence in his change.'

Here was something I could hope to put right. I offered to send Mr Marple a good sixpence.

'Ah, there's more to it than that. He passed on the bad one, you see, buying a ferret. When he got the ferret home it bit him, and ever since then, he says, he feels as if a cold hand were running up and down his right leg, and he's positive you're at the bottom of it. Of course that's not for me to say, is it? – but he's intending to come and see you, and I believe Miss Lark and Mrs Ruddock may come along too.'

Too timid to enquire just how I had been a disappointment to Miss

Lark, I remarked that it seemed to be clearing, and advised my visitor to take advantage of this. When she had gone I sat listening to the rain and reflecting on my errors. As for the rain, that did not matter so much: I had never professed to be a weather prophet; but the thought that at any moment Mr Marple, Mrs Ruddock, and Miss Lark might cross my path, or, more prosaically and painfully, march up my doorsteps, filled me with gloomy apprehensions. They would be so cross with me for not giving satisfaction as a fortune-teller; and if I should explain to them that I was not a fortune-teller at all, merely an obliging stop-gap, they would probably be even crosser. Besides, if I finally succeeded in robbing Mr Marple of his faith in my powers to run up and down his right leg like a cold hand – and I suspected it would be less dangerous to rob a lioness of her cubs – he would return home and denounce me as a fraud to my wet admirer; and ten to one she would then break off her romance, and the man from Pett's Garage remain a bachelor still, shedding unavailing tears into the void of a fish-kettle which matrimony would have filled with boiled cod, or even a nice halibut.

This was a sorry speculation. But it was followed by another even sorrier. For suppose the man from Pett's Garage, not the widower that fancy painted him, was one of those bigamists or murderers of whom one reads so profusely on Sundays, and my wet admirer were to all intents and purposes tossed by my casual hand into a marriage which was no marriage at all, or into a blood-stained sack probed by the local constabulary? And then there was the man in the bus, pondering fruitlessly over the dried haddock with 49 black pins in it. He, too, I daresay, could track me down through the Rector.

Whichever way I looked I saw nothing but menace, calamity, disaster, and people saying it was my fault. After a night of insomnia and remorse, my nerves were in such a state that I dropped my favourite teapot. It had blue and brown sprigs on it, and the knob on the lid was shaped like an onion, and the loss of such a teapot brought home to me, once and for all, that it is unlucky to tell fortunes in May. Hoping that a change of scene might soothe my bereavement, I went off to stay in the country for some weeks, so whether or not Mr Marple, Mrs Ruddock or Miss Lark came wrathfully to visit me I cannot tell.

A RAILWAY ALPHABET
(Housewife, May, 1946)

'Not quite so fast next time, Mr Conductor, if you please.' It was at the close of a railway journey that Albert, Prince Consort, made this request (though one can imagine him saying the same thing at the close of a Mozart symphony). The words are typical of the very moderate enthusiasm with which the good and great of the Early Victorian age accepted a new and revolutionary means of transport.

Landowners (there were more of them then, and more conscious of ownership) stipulated that not a yard of railway track should be visible from their windows. Farmers were convinced that sparks would fire their ricks, smoke poison their cattle, whistles frighten their breeding stock. Headmasters of the great public schools foresaw with certainty that the vicinity of a railway station would corrupt the young gentlemen.

Town councillors of towns with any pretensions to gentility were equally certain that the noise and the dirt of a railway and the influx of the sort of people who travelled by train would drive away the better class of citizen. Railways would ruin the carriage makers and the horse breeder, aid the escape of criminals, encourage Sabbath-breaking, and frighten pheasants.

Travelling by train today, one can still see from the window that the English railway system began life under a cloud: country towns several miles away from their stations, joined to them now by a long straggle of mean street; the cuttings and plantations and embankments which interpose themselves between the railway and a view of stately homes; the reach-me-down architecture of most small railway stations – all speak a severe intention to keep an upstart thing in its place.

At first it is difficult to reconcile this grudging outlook on the locomotive with the enthusiasm felt sixty years earlier for the balloon and seventy years later for the automobile. But the reason is plain enough. It was not distinguished to use the new railway travelling; only eccentric, or hardy, or at best public-spirited. The rich had carriages, stables, and endless leisure, and found it more in keeping with their standards of living to travel by road in their own equipages, attended by their own servants, and to spend a few nights in hotels or staying with relations than to jolt more expeditiously behind an iron horse.

Though the railway companies began by trying to woo the upper classes by First Class trains ('to obviate the inconvenience occasioned by the frequent stoppages to take up and set down Passengers' First Class trains were non-stop), by glazing in the sides of the coaches (Second and Third Class trains were open), or by supplying trucks on which passengers could travel in their own carriages, it was the middle and working class who welcomed the railways and patronised them. Most inventions begin as luxuries and spread downwards through the social scale. The railway became almost immediately proletarian and worked its way up.

The Great Exhibition persuaded many people into long-distance journeys. Travellers came from all over Great Britain to see the wonderful palace made all of glass, to hear the organ and admire the fountains and the Koh-i-noor and the modern machinery and the replica of Her Majesty's boudoir (one such family, catching the Night Excursion train from Edinburgh, settled themselves in by putting on their nightcaps). Queen Victoria – never so aristocratic as her aristocracy – went by rail even for such short journeys as that from London to Windsor, and is not recorded as having commented adversely on her train arriving up to time. The railway, from being useful to some had become indispensable to all – and did not blow up half as often as expected. It had been received into the Church, too, and was often used as a metaphor in sermons.

> *A bright new railway, like the one*
> *That rushes up and down,*
> *And carries nearly every day*
> *Our dear Papa to town.*

This is the introduction to *Aunt Louisa's Railway Alphabet*, which was published in 1866. Each letter of the alphabet is supplied with a luridly coloured picture ('printed in colours by Kronheim') of something to do with the railway, and each picture is explained by a rather halting couplet.

I do not know who Aunt Louisa was; to me she could never be anything but Aunt Louisa, but, like all writers of her date, she takes a moral view wherever possible and is much more interested in the human side of travelling than in its mechanics, F, for instance.

> *Is for Fire, the best Slave we know*
> *But once our Master, the direst foe.*

and

> *R is for Rails which the wheels run on;*
> *I hope that we shan't find that one is gone.*

Aunt Louisa's young readers might have come to mistrust railway travelling if all the couplets expressed this fatalistic acceptance of its dangers – the more so as the violent tints of Kronheim, together with the fact that for some reason the sky in all the illustrations is printed a solid black, are, to say the least of it, upsetting. But Aunt Louisa, true to her age, knows that Man is more than matter, especially if the man is a respectable functionary in a position of authority.

> *K is the Key which the Guard retains*
> *Lest men should leap out of moving trains.*

And this is not all a guard does to reassure and control. The guard has a picture and a couplet all to himself. In the picture he is standing on a platform, holding his flags, together with a small crocodile handbag, and looking masterfully at his watch. Aunt Louisa's summary of his duties, if a trifle vague, is extremely devout and moving.

> *G is the Guard, taking care of all,*
> *And watching lest harm the train befall.*

(Perhaps Aunt Louisa was recalling the railway travel of her own youth, when a guard sat on the roof of the first coach facing backward, in order to observe if any rear coaches became uncoupled and left behind.) Nor was this all that her young friends could rely on to save them from perils of outbreaks of fire and missing rails under that terrible sable sky. As well as the guard, and the driver of the engine.

> *whose mighty pow'r*
> *can carry us forty miles an hour,*

there were the other benevolent beings classed under the letter O.

> *O the Officials who ready stand,*
> *A brave, efficient, kindly band.*

And there they are, in blue frock-coats and whiskers, in noble attitudes, dispassionately anticipating a few well-merited gratuities.

After P for platform

> *where on starting*
> *We suffer oft the pain of parting,*

we come to one of the finest pictures, and to a subject which enables Aunt Louisa to let down her hair in a big way. Under the usual canopy of inky darkness is a platform covered with crimson carpeting, and down it a lady in the profoundest of widow's weeds, holding a large white handkerchief in her gloved hands, is slowly advancing, followed by two heart-broken gentlemen who hold their top hats above their bowed heads, and watched by two equally commiserating footmen. The likeness is not striking, but there can be no doubt of this letter of the alphabet.

> *Q is our Queen, most dear in woe;*
> *May heavenly comfort with her go!*

Naturally Aunt Louisa could not always have such subjects to rise to, and at times she is trite, though always true.

> *L is for Lamp, of whose welcome light*
> *We are glad, when travelling by night.*

She does better with N,

the Newsboy, whose day's success
Shows England's love for the Daily Press.

Such a love in those days even the most scrupulous Aunt Louisa could approve of.

As I have said, Aunt Louisa's interest lay in the human side of railway travelling – though she cast a glance at the animal creation by including a Horse-box.

Which trav'llers need
Who carry by train a gallant steed.

Perhaps if she had been Uncle Louis she might have put in more about brakes, signals, boilers, and Bradshaw's Guide. But the letter J pins her to a technical consideration, though, typically, she glides off to a personal equation as fast as she can.

J is for Junction; fearful danger
These trains appear in to a stranger.

If the stranger studies the illustration the danger seems less fearful; for though there are two trains, running on lines that cross in the foreground, and though a man, one of the brave, efficient, kindly band, no doubt, is watching them and trailing a red flag on the ground, one train is approaching, the other going away, and so unless they happen to blow up or catch fire they should get on all right.

When I was a child (I suppose it must be clear to my readers that I could not know Aunt Louisa so intimately unless I had pored over her as a child) this discrepancy between the couplet and the illustration used to trouble me. Try earnestly and hopefully as I would, I could see no danger in this picture for anyone: no junction could be behaving in a more quiet and orderly manner. Sometimes I made the retreating train run backwards; but it was never convincing, because neither the crowd on the platform nor the official with the red flag showed the least discomposure. When one is young one has high ideals about book production. If anyone had told me that Aunt Louisa penned her couplets and the gentleman who was printed in colours by Kronheim painted his pictures without consulting each other over every detail I just wouldn't have believed it.

Readers with a systematic outlook on the alphabet may have noticed that the letters ABCD and VWX, etc., have not been touched on. My copy of the *Railway Alphabet* came to me via aunts and uncles, great-aunts and great-uncles. I do not know which generation tore out the first and last pages of Aunt Louisa's rhymes; but gone they are. A must be Arrival, for two ladies and a child are watching a train come in, and the child is already hurrying towards a porter with discriminating affection. B, as clearly, is Bell. Another of those officials, in a top hat, is ringing one with great perseverance on an empty platform. C might be anything. D is a Driver, V is a Viaduct, Y is a Yeoman, X must be an excursion for the scene is thronged with people dressed for every emergency of weather and adventure, but W is another puzzle. Yet another official is standing beside the track, and one might expect W to be Whistle, but there is no sign of a whistle about him. His expression, though, is attentive and gratified; possibly he is thinking that the engine is whistling rather well today. On the other hand, there is a background of factory chimneys, so perhaps a train is just leaving Wolverhampton.

As for Z, there is no sign that Aunt Louisa had such a letter in her railway alphabet. But if she had, I presume it would have been Zeal, another attribute of those officials.

> *Z is the Zeal, by all display'd*
> *Who give to travellers their aid.*

NOTES

1 Harrow-on-the-Hill
2 Ruskin's five volume work, 1834-60
3 Sydney Dobell (1824-74), poet
4 Based on the memoir of Warner's favourite grandmother, Flora Warner (née Moir), who was brought up in Charlotte Square, Edinburgh
5 Jean Jacques Rousseau, 1762
6 Six miles south west of Edinburgh on the Whitburn road (A71)
7 Five miles south west of Edinburgh on the Lanark road (A70)

THINKING ALOUD

WRITERS AT WORK
(from *Writers at Work*, 1931)

'I wish,' said Sylvia Townsend Warner, 'that I could tell you I wrote standing on one leg. Then you'd have something really entertaining and original to say about me!'

'You do it, if not standing on one leg, then in some other way quite as unorthodox, I'm sure,' I answered.

She settled down then, lighting a cigarette, 'to think how she did it.' The blue of her Chinese coat against the Spanish red of the cushions suddenly created a new harmony in a room that sang with colour. At first sight of her flat (which is in a quiet corner not far from Lancaster Gate) one would say it belonged to a painter—a painter who had lived a great deal in the South of Europe and loved the sun. The walls are in Egyptian yellow and red, and the curtains are of patchwork. The colours are all of a bright, glowing kind, yet at the same time of an infinite softness. To come into these rooms out of a London rain, as I did, was like stepping off the magic carpet into another country altogether.

She herself has that same quality of unexpectedness. It is part of her great personal charm that she keeps her listener constantly on the alert, and never by any chance gives him what he is prepared for. As a result, she sets one chuckling at once. She rarely laughs herself, however. All her expression is put into her voice, which is like a viola with harp accompaniment. In appearance she is tall and pale, and she moves her arms in a way that subtly suggests wings.

'I never work in the morning,' she began.

'Does that mean that you don't get up early?'

'If I did get up early, I shouldn't pride myself on it. This getting up early is entirely overrated. Most people get a wholly unjustifiable kick out of getting up at eight in the morning. They do it merely for the purpose of expressing their moral superiority over those who don't!'

'So you never work in the morning?'

'Never. I go to the greengrocer's instead. Or William takes me out for a walk.'

William was a contemplative black chow with impeccable manners who lay very decoratively on a rug during the whole course of our conversation.

'That's one of the advantages of a dog to a writer,' she went on. 'William *must* have his walk. And if I get absorbed in something and forget it, he comes and reminds me. He keeps me to regular hours, and exercises me. Every writer should own a dog.'

'When, then, do you work?' I persisted.

'After lunch sometimes. Generally in the evening.'

'Every evening?'

'I know I ought to, but I don't.'

'Do you write for long at a stretch?'

'Once I get started I could go on for ever. But I take a very long time boiling up!'

'And then you boil rapidly?'

'Quite fast. But on the whole I write slowly because it takes me so long to get down to it.'

'What is this process of "getting down to it"?'

'I think for a long time about a book before I begin writing it. I find that anything I've written has lain dormant for three or four years. The idea floats up in my mind from somewhere. But it must take its shape before I think out any of the details, or even the characters. I used to compose music, and I believe I write like a composer still. I must get the shape first, before the actions or words.'

'Do you depart from that shape later?'

'I may modify it in details, but I never change it.'

'Your ending remains the same?'

'Except for unimportant details.'

'When you do get down to writing, do you write straight off without stopping?'

'I get stuck occasionally. Then I leave off completely for the time being.'

'Do you revise very much?'

'I make dozens of revisions, but quite half of them are done before I

394

begin to write at all.'

'You like music, I take it.'

'Very much. Yes, I have played one or two instruments. Very badly. But I am chiefly interested in music on the constructional side. I have edited a good deal of sixteenth-century music, and I mean to edit some more.'

'Do you like the gramophone and the radio?'

'The radio I think is very bad for musical taste in general. It makes music seem to many people like water in a tap, to be turned on whenever needed, or just allowed to drip. I've been in houses where it dripped all day long.'

'And the gramophone?'

'I have never wanted one for an instant, but of the two I prefer it to wireless. It is more honest about its limitations. . . a useful little instrument like a potato-peeler. Wireless is so damned God-like, and cheats all the time.'

'What do you think of that other modern invention, the cinema?'

'I've seen very few films. I like the abstract ones.'

'Are you fond of the theatre?'

'I don't go very much.'

'What *do* you like, besides writing and music?'

'I like pictures, and architecture. And I'm interminably interested in people – quite ordinary people, the kind you meet in the street or see in buses. Not to talk to them. To watch them like rare wild animals. I love anything to do with cooking. I really enjoy cooking. I make jams and pickles too. I'm considered to be quite a successful cook!'

This interest of hers in cooking is not so odd as it might seem, for it goes with a feeling for the classic and the formal, which she has in exquisite degree. The eighteenth century, it will be remembered, when form reached its perfection, was a period when cooking was regarded as one of the arts, and ladies of high degree prided themselves on their triumphs in the kitchen.

'Have you any special secret in cooking that you don't mind giving away?' I asked.

'One should always use butter.'

'To go back to writing, what part of it do you like best?'

'I like best the beginning. I don't like it when it's all done and you feel you haven't brought off what you've wanted to. But I'm happy when it's shaping itself, and I'm thinking it out. It took me fourteen months to write *Mr. Fortune's Maggot*[1]. For six months I lived on that island. I had a delightful time there. That was before I began writing. During all that time I saw real people in a sort of dream. They were there, like people in a railway carriage on a night journey, but I was scarcely aware of them. I was living my real life on the island. I was haunted by it.'

'Are you haunted by your characters too?'

'I suppose I am. I take them about with me for a long time while I am getting to know them. They need understanding. It threw a light on Mr Fortune's character when I discovered his favourite composer was Haydn. I knew him fairly well before that, but not intimately.'

'Are you conscious of the process by which your characters become familiar to you?'

'By always preferring real life to them, not the other way round. I speculate as to what they would think of this or that; do in such circumstances. Sometimes they take one by surprise by striking out quite new lines for themselves.'

'Are they founded on real people?'

'I never put a real person into a book. There's no trace of actual people in my characters. I see someone at a street corner, and speculate about him.'

'You mean your characters are purely fantastic?'

'Oh no. You could look out all my characters in the ABC. Or rather in Bradshaw, where you find all the very slow country trains that stop at every junction. Ordinary people and the adventures of the everyday are much the most interesting. Wilamovitz-Moellendorff was a great archaeologist, but the best pages in his memoirs are those in which he tells how he ate ham in his childhood or fell off a mule in Greece.'

'Have you ever thought of writing the life of any special person?'

'John Thomas Smith's *Life of Nollekens* is almost the ideal biography. Smith disliked Nollekens, and his dislike gave the book vitality. But though he disliked him he did not despise him. There the book differs from much modern biography, which is sneering. It's usually men of action that are made the subject of biography. But they are poor material compared with ordinary people. Think, for instance, what a marvellous subject for biography Mrs Beeton would make. A life of Mrs Beeton would be enthralling!'

'Why not do it?'

'Nothing is vital unless you want to do it, and I don't particularly want to write a life of Mrs Beeton.'

'Whom do you like among the writers of today?'

'I'm very ordinary in my tastes. I like most of the seriously admired writers. I think T.F. Powys is the most important writer at the moment. I admired D.H. Lawrence immensely. And what exciting things the Americans are doing! I admire Elizabeth Madox Roberts[2] extremely. And Hemingway – I like his stream-line style.'

'Whom do you like among the writers of the past?'

'Richardson – Samuel. I don't know how many times I've read *Clarissa*. Of nineteenth-century writers to me the most thrilling is G.M. Hopkins. He's very hard to get nowadays. I believe he's the only modern poet who is learned by heart as Homer was. I know of two men who have many of his poems by heart. One learned from the other. The first man had seen the poems in manuscript. Neither had seen a printed book of the poems.'

Here the telephone rang again, for the fifth or sixth time.

'This accursed telephone!' she sighed, and proceeded very affectionately but firmly to tell the speaker at the other end that she was busy for the rest of the day. And then, as she had with all the others, she relented.

'If you really must,' she said. 'But it can't be for long. Just one minute. Come at seven, then. But only for one minute.'

'When did you begin to write?' I asked when she had put down the receiver.

'I began to write when I came to live alone in London. I wrote first quite by accident, to amuse myself, without thought of publication. David Garnett saw my poems and showed them to a publisher. I had a novel done, too, by that time. The poems were published in 1925[3], and the novel in 1926[4]. The publisher would do it, though I protested against the polygamy of bringing out poetry and prose by the same author.'

'Can you write them both at the same time?'

'No, they are written at different periods. They are two different things altogether, requiring a different approach and technique.'

'Could you define this difference?'

'Put it like this. In prose one tries how much one can get out of a subject; in poetry, how far one can get into it.'

'Do you use a typewriter?'

'Yes. If it's ordinary work, I use a typewriter. But if it's difficult I use ink. I don't like either. I hate having to scratch out mistakes. If one sees a mess before one, one's mind becomes messy. But in a tight place the familiar feeling of holding a pen in one's hand is reassuring.'

'Is it a fountain-pen?'

'I can't endure a fountain-pen.'

'Do you use a thesaurus of any sort?'

'I borrowed one for crossword puzzles. The only dictionary I possess is a French dictionary.'

'Where do you do most of your writing?'

'Here. I do all of my writing in London. In the country I'm like the dogs – I rush out rabbiting. But I suppose I'd write wherever I lived.'

'Does the weather affect you?'

'I like a long rainy afternoon with its sense of security and isolation. That always puts me in a writing mood.'

'Do you mind being interrupted?'

'Bitterly.'

'Does noise distract you?'

'I don't like noise. I came here mainly because it was quiet.'

"Do you find health affects your work?'

'I'm not abounding in health. But it doesn't affect me in the least. Some of the work I like best was written when I was very tired.'

'Are you very orderly about your writing?'

'I sympathise with Haydn, who always put on his best suit and his best wig to compose in. I like everything clean and tidy and in order before I begin writing.'

'Do you ever discuss work with others while it is in progress?'

'Never. I'm superstitious about that. If I should talk it over with any one else, I should lose the whole thing. I'd be bound to get that other person's point of view, and it would destroy my own.'

'Do you read your books once they appear in print?'

'I should only read a book of mine if it were so long after publication that I'd forgotten all about it, and could read it as a new book by a somebody called Warner. My work always seems dead when it comes from the typist's. It seems even deader in proof. And the book is its coffin.'

'Have you anything to say about the present arrangement between author and literary agent?'

'It seems satisfactory enough. The only exception I take to literary agents is that they beg one to write such strange things. If one excels in light verse, they want one to do treatises on theology.'

'In case you could be persuaded to give a word of advice to beginning writers, what would it be?'

'That's difficult, because each writer has his own special way of writing. It's like a natural parting – sometimes it comes in the middle and sometimes on one side. But if I said anything, I'd say, Don't write with a sense of duty and don't fuss. Flaubert is responsible for the bad tradition that one must write in misery. This has spoilt many a book that might otherwise have been a good one.'

William, divining the end of the inquisition, at this instant lifted his bulk from the rug and approached his mistress. Like her, he evidently has an infallible instinct for the right gesture.

IN CONVERSATION
with Val Warner and Michael Schmidt in 1975
(*Poetry Now Review* 23, 1981)

I am what is that odd thing, a musicologist. I've done a lot of work on church music. I was one of the editorial committee on Tudor Church Music, which was financed, much to our surprise, by the Carnegie U.K. Trust.

Have you written music as well?

I have composed music; it's not at all good. I play the piano, and I tried to play the viola because I liked the noise. But nobody liked the noise that I got out of the viola when I was learning and so I gave it up.

You were a music scholar, but not at a university.

No, I never went to a university. I never went to school . . . well, I went to kindergarten for about two terms, and then I was dismissed for being a bad influence. I was a natural mimic, and I mimicked the unfortunate people who were teaching me. I didn't mean any wickedness by it, but like Mary's lamb, I made the children laugh and play and was a very bad influence. They sent me back with a very dubious report; only one kind word in it and that was, 'Sylvia always sings in tune.' That sort of thing decides one's destiny, of course.

I left home when I was twenty-two and went to London. By that time I'd got my job on the Tudor Church Music Committee. I made a living from that – rather a penurious living to begin with. I got £130 a year from the United Kingdom Trust and it annoyed me very much because the money came from Scotland and was paid monthly and it seemed to me wasteful to have to pay sixpence on a Scotch cheque once a month. I could barely afford it, so I wrote to their treasurer and said that it was very inconvenient and could he change his arrangements and pay me once a quarter. After that, I think he felt I was serious.

And it was about that time you began writing poetry?

When did I begin to write? I was led away by paper. I'm always led away by blank paper. We had a great many photographs in our work, black and white photographs of manuscripts, and there were always some throw-aways. And the white was the most beautiful smooth white photographic paper and nobody wanted it, and I wanted it, and having collected it by degrees I thought, 'I must do something about all this handsome paper – I think I'll write a poem.' So I started writing poems on this handsome paper.

My first book was *The Espalier*, and that came out in, I think, 1925. After Chatto & Windus had seen my poems (they were sent there by David Garnett who liked them) and they said tentatively, 'You don't think you could write a novel, do you?' and I, with exasperating brightness, said, 'I've written a novel, but it isn't worth anything. I only did it to amuse myself in the evenings when I had nothing better to do.' And that was *Lolly Willowes.* And except that Charles Prentice[5] wanted me to rewrite the ending, I didn't get to alter it much. I could have altered it more.

I never thought of being a professional writer. I never thought of being a professional anything, to tell the truth. I just slopped along like Mrs Warcornisher's English Lady, you know, doing one thing at one time and another at another.

When did your political activities begin?

I'm trying to remember. I think it was in 1933. . . I know what influenced me and what influenced almost all the people of my generation more than anything was the Reichstag Fire trial. Extraordinary courage and enterprise and *poise* of Dimitrov[6]. And that was very well reported in *The Times* and made me interested in contemporary politics. And that of course made me immediately interested in the doings of the Black Shirts, and that's how I came to meet the people in *Left Review*[7] and eventually to do some writing. That's how I met Edgell [Rickword].

The *Left Review* I should say began about 1934. We went to Spain in 1936, to Barcelona. We had the greatest difficulty in getting across the frontier but everything went smoothly after that. And then the next year, with Valentine Ackland, I went to the Congress of anti-Fascist writers which had been scheduled to be held in Madrid before the war broke out, but in 1937 they still held the Congress; and a very fine Congress it was.

I wrote a few articles about life in wartime Spain and got them in where I could simply as propaganda[8]. And of course by that time it was getting rather hard to get in any propaganda because the English authorities and respectables were clamping down on freelance journalists who had anything to say in favour of the Republic. I had a great deal to say. . . . I've never seen people who I admired more. I never again saw a country I loved as much as I loved Spain. A most ungainly country to love, but it is extraordinarily beautiful. I've never been back – I said I wouldn't go back till Franco was dead and the old brute is still hanging on.

The experience affected my writing to the extent that I wrote *After the Death of Don Juan*, which is definitely a political novel – at least perhaps I should say it's a political fable. It's very rare to get now, but I think it's an extremely good story because I took the Mozart subject as my frame-work but continued it into the Spain of this day and age. The trouble was it was published in 1938 and in not a very large edition and was soon swamped in the circumstances of the time.

Would you describe yourself as a Communist or an anarchist?

I was a Communist, but I always find anarchists very easy to get on with. I think that's because, if the English turn to the left at all, they are natural anarchists. They are not orderly enough to be good Communists and they're too refractory to be good Communists. I became a Communist simply because I was agin the Government but that of course is not a suitable frame of mind for a Communist for very long. But you can go on being an anarchist for the rest of your life, as far as I can see, and doing very well. You've always got something to be anarchic about – your life is one long excitement. And anarchists are the most *charming* people!

Summer Will Show is very much a political novel too.

That *sounds* communist, but I think at that date for anybody of intelligence, that was the only way for them to go. When I wrote that book I had the most interesting time because I thought I ought to do a little research and so I poked up from the London Library books about that date written from the Orleanist point of view and then the Monarchist point of view, and the Socialist point of view and then casual memoirs, and *nothing* agreed with anything else.

Did your political commitments affect the reception of your work?

Oh, it affected it very badly. I usually had two or three amazingly good reviews, but I never had reviews from the sort of reviewers that *sell* books. I've never produced a best-seller. I sell very well to the *New Yorker*[9], that's my only claim to being a bestseller. They were providential. I began writing for them as the result of a dare because we had an American friend staying with us and I was telling her of some absurd thing which had happened in the village and she said, 'You really ought to write that for the *New Yorker*.' I said, 'Ba Pooh! I can't write for the *New Yorker*. People who write for the *New Yorker* are a special race – they are like nothing else. I couldn't write for the *New Yorker*!' And she said, 'Oh write it; I think they'd take it.' I said, 'Bet you they wouldn't!' She said, 'Well, try it!' I said, 'I bet you £5 that they won't take it.' And they did, so I had to forfeit the £5. But on the whole, it was a good bargain.

I'm now concentrating on an entirely different new kind of short story and have been for the last three years because I suddenly looked round on my career and thought, 'Good God, I've been understanding the human heart for all these decades. Bother the human heart, I'm tired of the human heart. I'm tired of the human race. I want to write about something entirely different.' And my first story in my new vein was called 'Something Entirely Different'[10]. It was a study of the problems of changelings. It was about a human child that was taken into Elfinland and what became of him, and also what became of the elfin child who was planted in the human child's cradle and had to grow up in a small Scotch village. I found that so engrossing and I kept on making the most delightful discoveries of great social importance. I discovered that no well-bred fairy would ever *dream* of flying; they leave that to the servants. When one has discovered some truth of that sort, it's *so* reviving, it's such fun. And I don't want to write a respectable, realistic story ever again!

But of course there was a great deal of fantasy in your novels too, in Lolly Willowes for example.

Yes, it put its ugly face out in *Lolly Willowes*, didn't it? I think that I've always been interested in the supernatural in its social aspects, partly reading Pitcairn's Law Trials of Scotland. It's by far the best record of the activities of witches and witch hunters in Scotland and written in the most beautiful Scotch and I enjoyed reading that. And I suppose I went on from there. Of course I was very much influenced by old Margaret Murray's[11] book, *The God of the Witches*. She was a surprising old lady – looked exactly like Queen Victoria.

Of your novels and poetry, which has taken precedence, and which would you say is most important?

By now, I suppose, my novels. *The Corner That Held Them* took a long time to write and that was an important book in my life. I wrote it all through the war at intervals of all the other horrible things I had to do and whenever I got a moment to myself I went on with that.

I think that it is my most personal book, probably, and I believe that *After the Death of Don Juan* was my next most personal, though it appears to be quite impersonal because it's written with an arid degree of satire.

Would you call yourself a Christian?

Oh no! I couldn't possibly do that. I couldn't do that to anyone! No, I've never had any temptations to be a Christian. I think partly because of the Christians I met as a child. There was a dreadful old woman who was the family nurse in a family I knew, and having studied her all through one joint holidays I said to my mother in confidence, 'Are all Christians cross?' She replied, with great justice, 'Not all of them.'

In *The Corner That Held Them* I had to include religion, but then I began that book on the purist Marxian principles because I was convinced that if you were going to give an accurate picture of the monastic life, you'd have to put in all their finances, how they made their money, how they dodged about from one thing to another and how very precarious it all was, how only the very rich orders had any sort of financial security. The small houses just dodged about on the edge of the abyss; they were nearly always bankrupt. That's why the monastic houses were dissolved in England – they were all bankrupt, except just three or four and they were so rich that everyone wanted their money. But it's a strictly capitalist story.

What about your poems? You published a volume of poems with Valentine Ackland, called Whether a Dove or Seagull, *in which none of the poems is attributed to either writer, saying in the foreword that too much importance was attached to the poet rather than to the poem. Was that a successful gesture?*

That was because I'd seen so many people snaffling through anthologies, picking out poems by the poet they liked without ever troubling to read the others. I think it was a vain gesture; I think people still read by the name of the author rather than by the contents of the work.

And you published a volume of poems to accompany engravings, too.

Yes, *Boxwood*. That was a ridiculous affair because Reynolds Stone[12] was a friend of mine and we'd gone to visit him one day and found him sitting on the floor in an attitude of despair, tossing over anthologies. It developed that Ruari Maclean wanted to do a collection of his woodcuts and thought it would be child's play for Reynolds to find suitable quotations to 'illustrate' the woodcuts. Poor Reynolds was going out of his mind looking for suitable quotations and I thought to myself that it was far more important for him to go on with his woodcuts than to be hunting out quotations and I said to him, 'Leave all this nonsense. I'll write you poems to illustrate your drawings; I can do it in half the time! And that's what they were.

What about form? In the poems especially, you keep to very strict forms, by and large. . . .

Well, that's a different strand. I keep to a formal mode. I'm extremely fidgety about form, but that was because of music. I really learned all my ideas of form from studying music. I think there's something to be said for the formal shape if you've learned how to manage it and if you've got something to say. Really I believe that the thing that forms the structure of any narrative and holds it together is the importance of the narrative, the interest one has in the narrative. That's why Defoe is such a master, because he's *really* interested in the story.

Isn't there some incompatibility between political anarchism and formalism in writing?

I dare say there is. I remember a passage in Walt Whitman where someone or other is accusing him of being inconsistent and he says, 'Am I inconsistent? Well, I *am* inconsistent. Within me I contain millions!'

I'm more at home with seventeenth-century poetry than with any other. I'm a very great admirer of Dryden, because Dryden can say anything. He makes the most ridiculous statements and he can always bring them off. The line in 'The Hind and the Panther' that I particularly like – it's the last line of a section: 'The Lady of the spotted-muff began'. Now that is a line which is purely nonsensical and yet Dryden is so stately in his control of the medium and so sublime that one hears it almost with awe. When that line comes, one is merely delighted: Here is a splendid line.

Dryden has much more meat to him than Pope. I'm always attached to Marvell. I'm devoted to Defoe, and I'm fairly well at home with the Russians. I was very lucky: my mother liked reading aloud and she only read aloud the books which she liked herself and so it was that I heard the whole of *War and Peace* read to me before I was fourteen. Thackeray doesn't stand up to time so well. My passion for Flaubert and Stendhal, particularly for Stendhal, has never wavered. Stendhal is a very interesting Romantic because he's satirical. He's being intensely Romantic with half of him and there's a small cold beady eye which is fixed on the Romantic Stendhal saying, 'My God! What antics will this man get up to next?' I like inconsistencies in authors; I think I like inconsistencies in any creative work.

At the moment, I think the novel is falling to pieces, but I don't know how it will pull itself together again. Of course, it may be a varying form. It's been around for a very long time. I'm quite sure that the biography is an up-and-coming form, that much more in the way of biography will happen, partly because there's such a demand for it. Think how people seized on Boswell when Boswell's *Diaries* were put out.

You've written a biography of T. H. White, a writer who admired your work.

That was a queer assignment, because I didn't know White, although I knew various friends of his and I think we had occasionally exchanged polite letters praising each other's books. And then White made a demented departure because he never made a will and he never appointed a literary executor. He left all his manuscripts of his unfinished books to the Bank of Alderney, which poor creature hadn't the least idea what to do with them. His literary agent, a good worthy man, but a fool, was very anxious to get a great deal of White published and wanted to have a biography of White and naturally wanted to write it himself. White's friends were appalled at the prospect because they didn't think he'd do it very well, and after a great deal of consultation and tossing to and fro, they asked me if I would like to take it on and I said I didn't think so. But I was led astray because Michael Howard[13] turned up in a very large car, most of which consisted of boot, and he opened up the boot and out came so many pages, hunks of typescript, hunks of unfinished books, and I was told that this would be *some* of the material, but of course there would be a great deal more. And when it had filled a whole room in my house I thought, well the only way to get rid of all this is to read it and do the book! By that time, I was beginning to find White rather interesting. He's an inconsistent character. He could never finish anything, that was the trouble about him.

What are you working on at the moment?

I'm working on those short stories. I'm not working on anything else. And I'm steadily refusing to write an autobiography.

Why's that?

Because I'm too imaginative.

Do you still write poems?

Oh yes, usually just when I'm about to pack or catch a train or have someone to stay. Always at inconvenient moments like that. And I revise them endlessly, endlessly. I revise everything that I do.

For a good forty years Sylvia Townsend Warner has been contributing stories to the *New Yorker*. Stories that have been praised and made her an established name for their cool, dispassionate handling of the human lot, so much so that a short while back she said to herself, 'Oh hang the human heart! I am going to do something to please myself.' The result is her new book *The Kingdoms of Elfin*, published tomorrow, which takes a satirical jab at mankind by transposing the customs and manners of the mortal world to the spirit kingdoms of Elfindom.

'I like the immaterial world. I like to live among thoughts and images of the past and the possible, and even of the impossible, now and then,' states Mr Falconer in Peacock's Gryll Grange which serves as Townsend Warner's epigraph to her new collection. But it is a remark that equally applies to Miss Townsend Warner's own writing instinct, for her novels and stories disclose no pattern being worked out; rather she has gone from subject to subject as they have happened upon her. She has trusted her imagination throughout and found it more rewarding than fiction loaded with a message. 'I'm sure I shouldn't know how to comment on society. It's a mystery to me,' she says with some irony.

Her house, standing fast by a river and set at the edge of a Dorset hamlet[14], could appear too idyllic for a writer's habitat but her workroom has an austerity that questions her comment, 'I've never felt very conscientious about it.' Certainly she has gone her own way, indifferent to the demands of any literary coterie, but behind her are seven novels, eight volumes of stories and a much acclaimed biography of T. H. White.

That she has returned to the supernatural in her latest book is no surprise for her first novel *Lolly Willowes* (1926) details a maiden aunt's encounter with the devil. The *Times Literary Supplement* called it 'a remarkable presentation of the devil,' which she says, 'delighted me because that was exactly what I had in mind. I thought it was high time

407

somebody treated him as an ordinary member of society; which if you believe in the devil obviously he is.'

Since *Lolly Willowes* a reputation for the supernatural has stuck to her and this she feels has been overplayed. 'People always want to fix a standard for everything. I do wish they would just let something happen and watch it without thinking they must look it up in Crockford's or somewhere,' for she has no more inclination for the devil than she has for God, and to humanise him was in fact no more than 'moving to a new place to get a new view.' She is interested not so much in the supernatural as in what characters can be, but wasn't Baudelaire's treatment of the devil as more entertainer than downright villain an influence on her? 'Yes, yes indeed. Baudelaire's a very good thing to have in mind, isn't he?'

At the success of *Lolly Willowes* Townsend Warner went on to write *Mr Fortune's Maggot* (1927), a fantasy on a missionary's attempt to convert the natives of a South Sea island. She wrote it as a mild tease on Christianity and also to experiment with a realistic description of a volcanic eruption and earthquake. Her research came from a book by a missionary's wife who had lived in the South Sea which contained a matter-of-fact description of one. 'She said that lava was like porridge and sensible remarks of that sort which I based it on, and I've twice been complimented on the accuracy of my earthquake by people who have actually been in them.'

Her curiosity is that of the novelist and although her father was a schoolmaster she is thankful that her education was neglected. 'I wasn't educated, I was very lucky,' she says and so she had to lose no time in freeing herself from the danger of fixed attitudes. Educating herself, she decided to avoid causes and careers so that her life should have the simplicity that her work has demanded. She has no doubts about her horror of the career: 'I'm always so sorry for people who have to drag a career about with them, like those enormous cabin trunks that Americans will have that won't go up any English stairs. A career is very much like that. You take a lot of things about with you that you don't want any longer.'

But Sylvia Townsend Warner has done her share of commitment. During the twenties and thirties, like others, she aired her political grievances and was a representative at the writers' delegation for the

Congress of Madrid in 1937, and as a result witnessed the war there. She wrote a novel set in Spain – *After the Death of Don Juan* modelled from the characters in Don Giovanni but she has no liking for using fiction as a vehicle for political commentary. 'I gave up grievances long ago. I thought they were very poor material' she says and her stories often draw their power from an ability to observe slight incidents that reveal the mood of the times. Working as she puts it from the particular to the background she catches the dramatic turn that reverses the trivial issue.

Looking out at her own immediate view across the river to rising pasture land beyond, she sees it as a question of lighting: 'Just a shift in a cloud will transform a landscape, however well you know it. There are details about it you never noticed before, and I think it's so with ordinary daily life. There's a shift of lighting and you see everything quite differently, and if you can catch that moment before the effect has gone then you can hope to write something that is convincing.'

Few of her stories miss that level, and her longer stories like A Love Match – a tale of incest between a brother and a sister – hold a depth that is rare in the short story. For A Love Match, published in her collection *A Stranger With A Bag* (1966), she was awarded the Katherine Mansfield Short Story Prize, but otherwise her work has of late suffered a neglect in this country. Through the *New Yorker*, in America, the opposite has been the case, but most of the hardback editions of her stories over here have 'dropped imperceptibly.'

The quirks of fashion have not been kind to her and she puts it down partly to the inconsistency of her subject matter. To veer from satirical and supernatural fantasy, to the disturbing realism of her stories, to a novel on convent life in the fourteenth century[15] is confusing to many. This confusion and a slightly false reputation as a scholar of the supernatural puzzles her: 'I was interested in what nuns were like and I wrote a novel on those lines. I was interested – and I still am – in what elfins could be like . . . it's nothing to do with the supernatural, it's varieties of different people. I think I could possibly be very interested in newts if it occurred to me to write a novel about them.'

For *The Kingdoms of Elfin* it might appear that she has researched into supernatural myth but no, it was much more inspired by Saint Simon. 'When I realised that it was common or ill-bred for elfins to fly I discovered what my elfin society was like, and I could go on from there.' It was the *New Yorker* which first braved the publication of most of the 16 stories that make up the book, feeling that they were 'on to something remarkable,' and if it is a book that will irritate those not prepared to indulge her fantasy this, she considers, could be to the good. 'I hope some of it will annoy people because that is the surest way of being attended to.'

But elfin habits have their parallels in our own society and although the stories are not intended as allegory she does see them as a social diagnosis. Giving a full rein to her imagination elfins inhabit Gothic estates and are known to move invisibly among mortals whom they plague, mock and defy while at the same time mirroring mortal customs in themselves. Beneath the light-hearted humour is a dryness of tone suitable for what she described as 'an essentially disparaging book on everyone.'

In writing *The Kingdoms of Elfin* to a general theme Sylvia Townsend Warner has written a collection of stories that uses the advantages she has found the novel to have over the short story. For a writer who has made her name in both mediums she is quick to observe the difference: 'You can get punch into a short story but I don't think you can get weight. It takes a certain number of pages before you can have that quality. In a short story the author seems to appear in public more and he has to be on his better behaviour. In a novel he's very often hiding behind a bush and you almost forget he's there, and so he can do much more.'

As I leave her house Sylvia Townsend Warner walks back along the passage to the room where she writes that looks down to the river. She is glad on the whole not to have been too much in the company of fellow writers for unlike painting, writing does not discuss well, there being no technical side to exchange. It is, she knows, a solitary pursuit, and one which you must make up as you go along. A Siamese cat keeps her company: she once had a black cat to whom she recited all the magic potions she could think of and then waited for something to happen. In the event nothing did, but she still enjoyed imagining it.

NOTES

1   Warner's second novel, 1927
2   Elizabeth Maddox Roberts (1881-1941), a Kentucky novelist and poet, primarily known for her stories about the Kentucky mountain people
3   *The Espalier*
4   *Lolly Willowes*
5   Charles Prentice of Chatto and Windus. He first published T. F. Powys and Warner
6   Bulgarian communist accused of organising the Reichstag fire in 1933
7   Established by Edgell Rickword in 1933
8   See DISPATCHES p.132-63
9   Over 150 of Warner's short stories appeared in the *New Yorker*
10 In Warner's last collection of stories, *Kingdoms of Elfin*, 1977
11 Margaret Murray (1863-1963), Egyptologist and anthropologist
12 Engraver who lived at Litton Cheney in Dorset a few miles from Warner
13 From Jonathan Cape, publisher of Warner's biography of T. H. White
14 Frome Vauchurch where Warner lived beside the river Frome from 1937 until her death in 1978
15 *The Corner That Held Them*, 1948